Witchcraft Works

vol.10

Ryu Mizunagi

CONTENTS

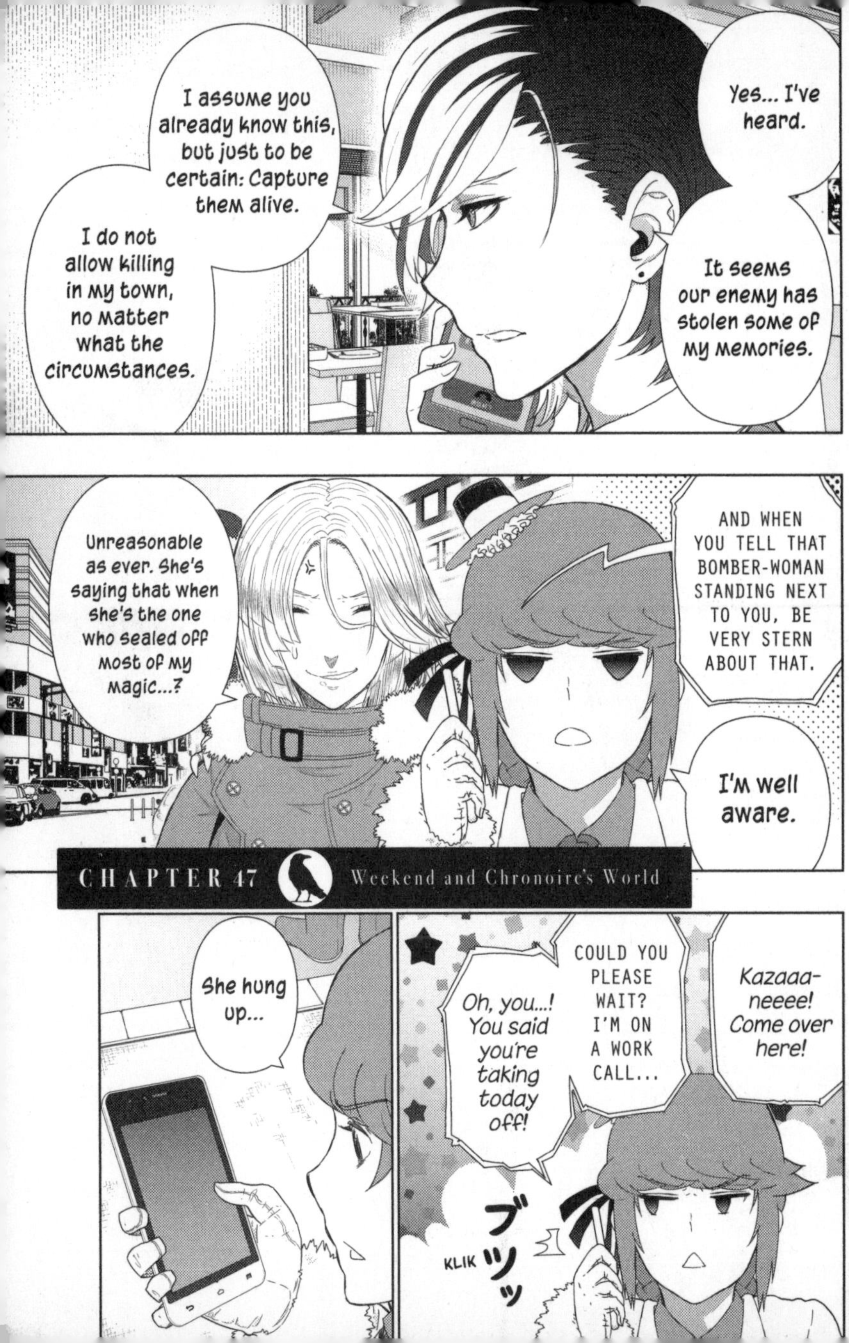
Yes... I've heard.
It seems our enemy has stolen some of my memories.
I assume you already know this, but just to be certain: Capture them alive.
I do not allow killing in my town, no matter what the circumstances.
AND WHEN YOU TELL THAT BOMBER-WOMAN STANDING NEXT TO YOU, BE VERY STERN ABOUT THAT.
I'm well aware.
Unreasonable as ever. She's saying that when she's the one who sealed off most of my magic...?
CHAPTER 47 Weekend and Chronoire's World
Kazaaa-neeee! Come over here!
COULD YOU PLEASE WAIT? I'M ON A WORK CALL...
Oh, you...! You said you're taking today off!
ブツッ
KLIK
She hung up...

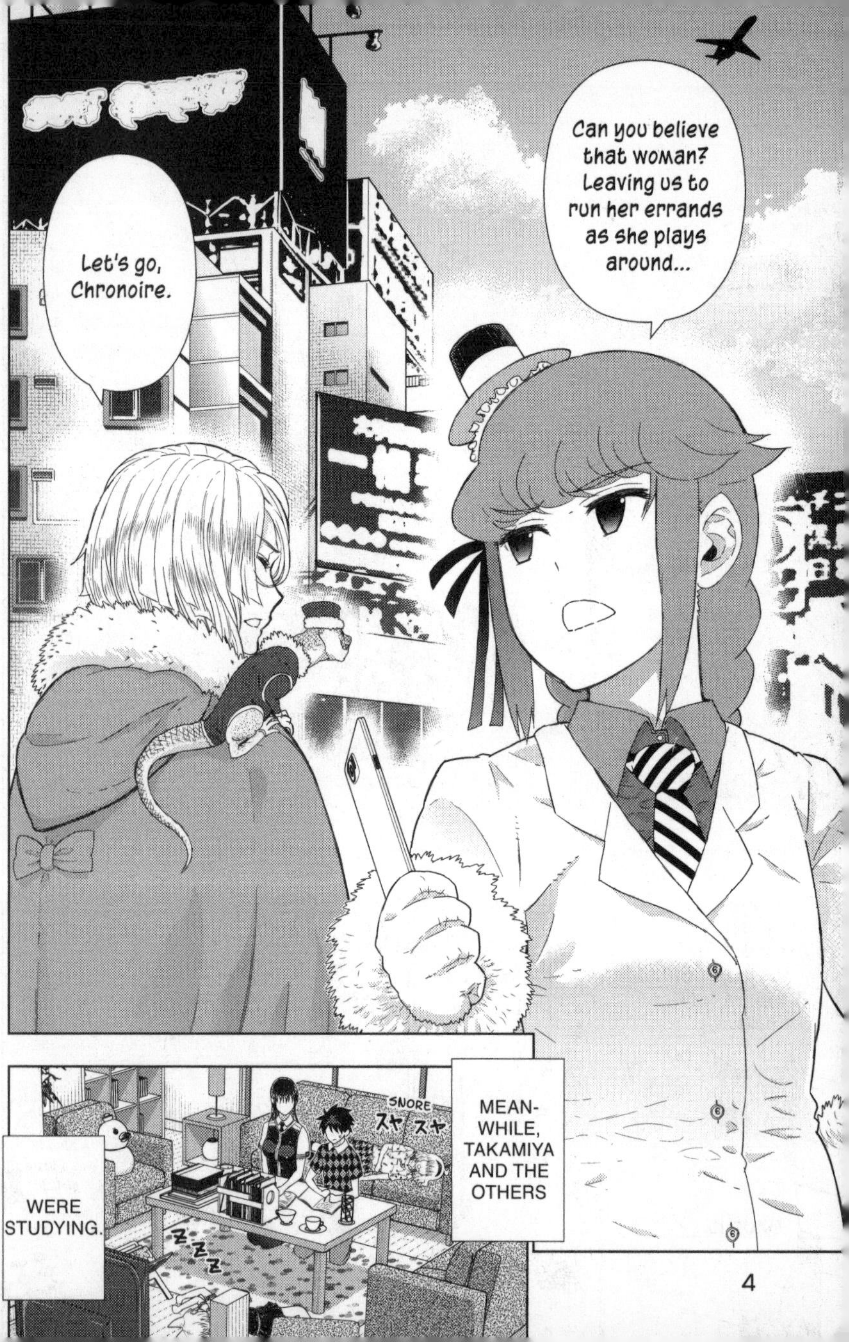
Can you believe that woman? Leaving us to run her errands as she plays around...
Let's go, Chronoire.
MEAN-WHILE, TAKAMIYA AND THE OTHERS
WERE STUDYING.
SNORE
スヤ スヤ
Z Z Z

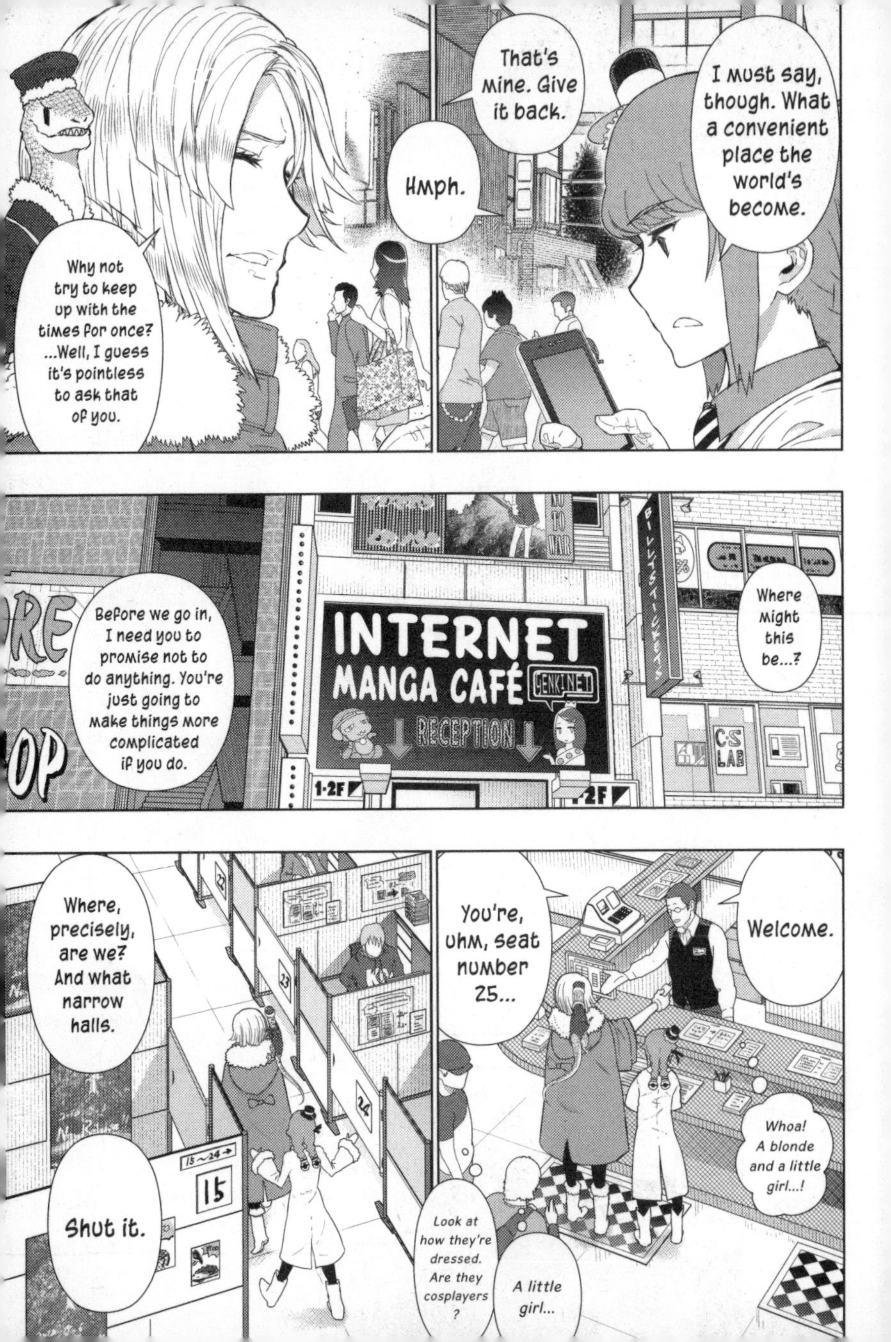
I must say, though. What a convenient place the world's become.
That's mine. Give it back.
Hmph.
Why not try to keep up with the times for once? ...Well, I guess it's pointless to ask that of you.
Where might this be...?
Before we go in, I need you to promise not to do anything. You're just going to make things more complicated if you do.
INTERNET MANGA CAFÉ
GENKINET
RECEPTION
1·2F
C·S LAB
Welcome.
You're, uhm, seat number 25...
Whoa! A blonde and a little girl...!
A little girl...
Look at how they're dressed. Are they cosplayers?
Where, precisely, are we? And what narrow halls.
15～24→
15
Shut it.

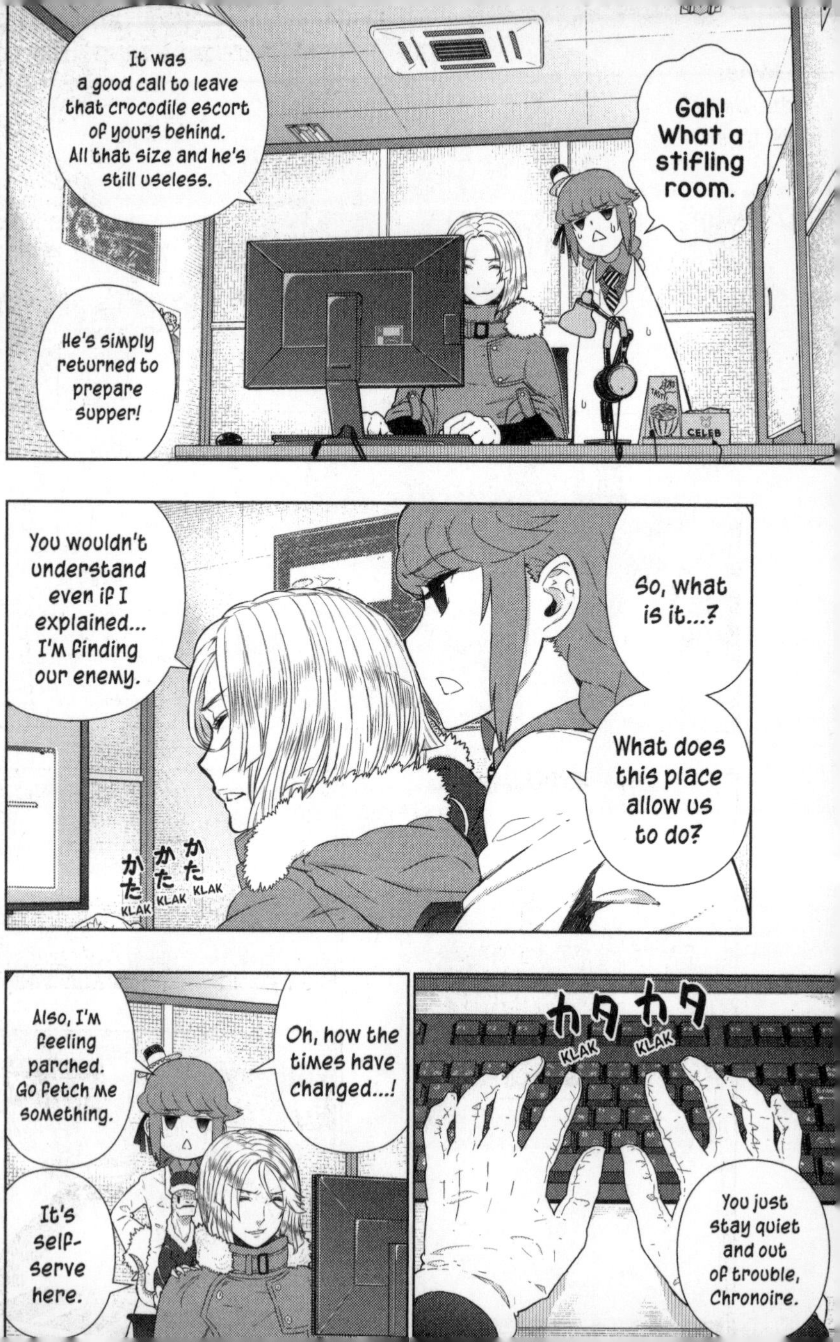
Gah! What a stifling room.
It was a good call to leave that crocodile escort of yours behind. All that size and he's still useless.
He's simply returned to prepare supper!
CELEB
So, what is it...?
You wouldn't understand even if I explained... I'm finding our enemy.
What does this place allow us to do?
かた KLAK かた KLAK かた KLAK
カタカタ KLAK KLAK
You just stay quiet and out of trouble, Chronoire.
Oh, how the times have changed...!
Also, I'm feeling parched. Go fetch me something.
It's self-serve here.

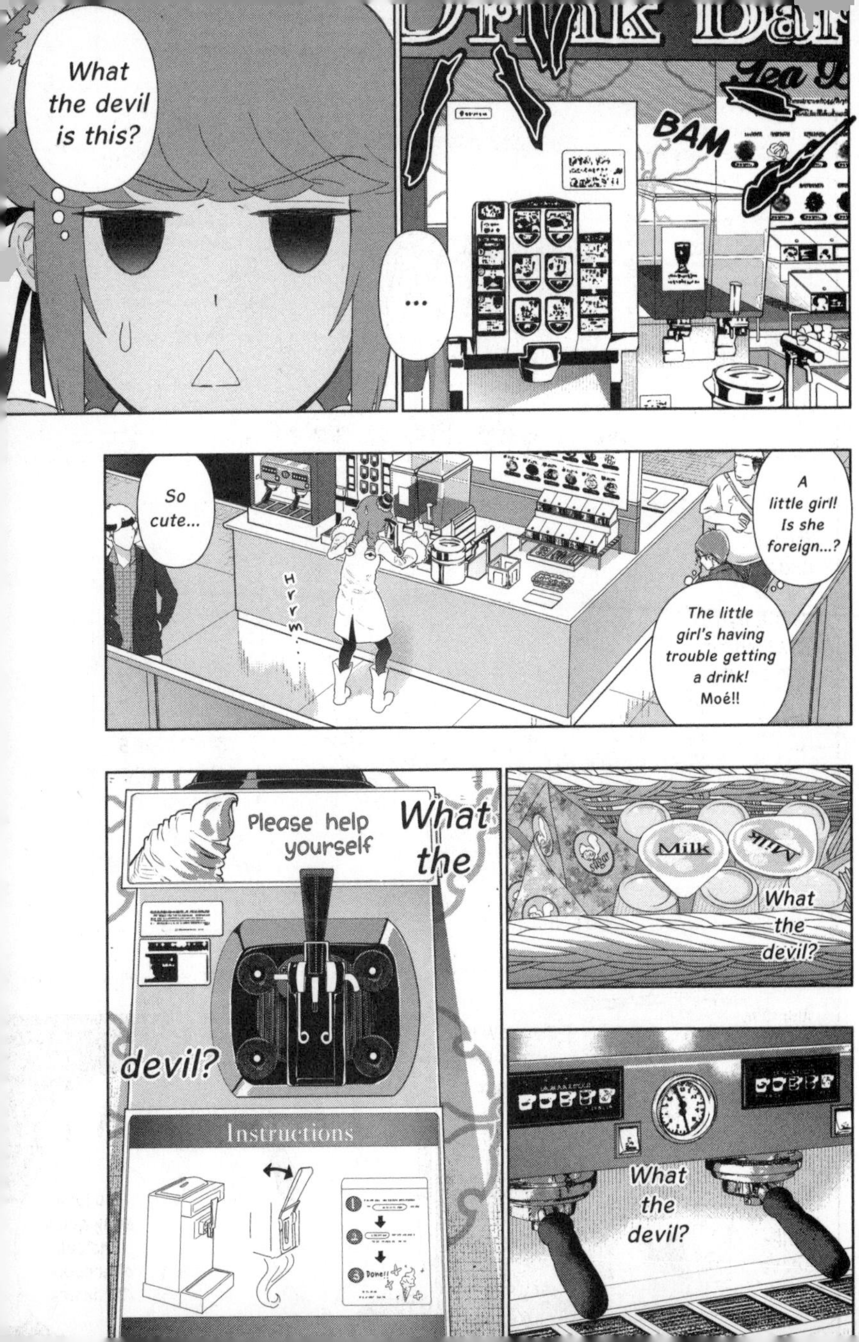

BAM
...
What the devil is this?
A little girl! Is she foreign...?
The little girl's having trouble getting a drink! Moé!!
Hrrm...
So cute...
Milk
What the devil?
What the devil?
Please help yourself
What the devil?
Instructions
Done!!

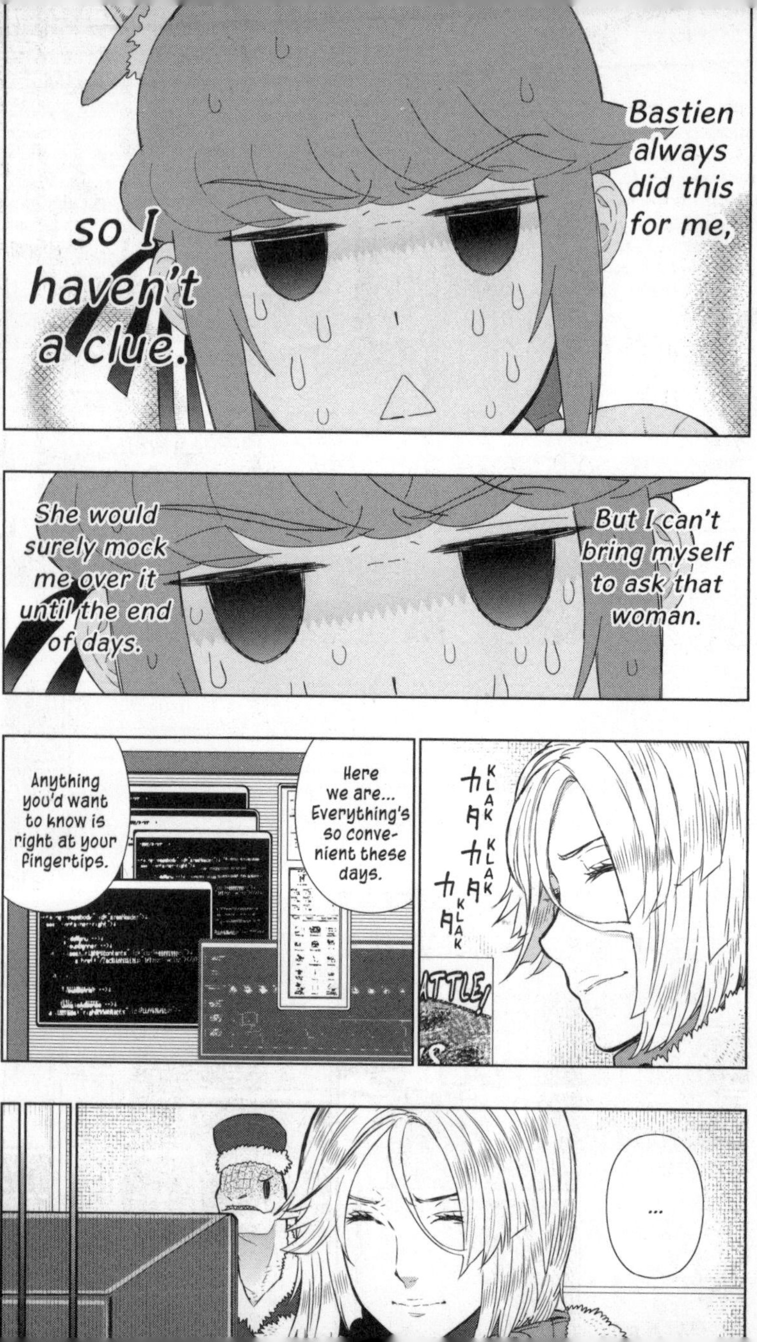
Bastien always did this for me,
so I haven't a clue.
But I can't bring myself to ask that woman.
She would surely mock me over it until the end of days.
KLAK KLAK KLAK
Here we are... Everything's so convenient these days.
Anything you'd want to know is right at your fingertips.
...

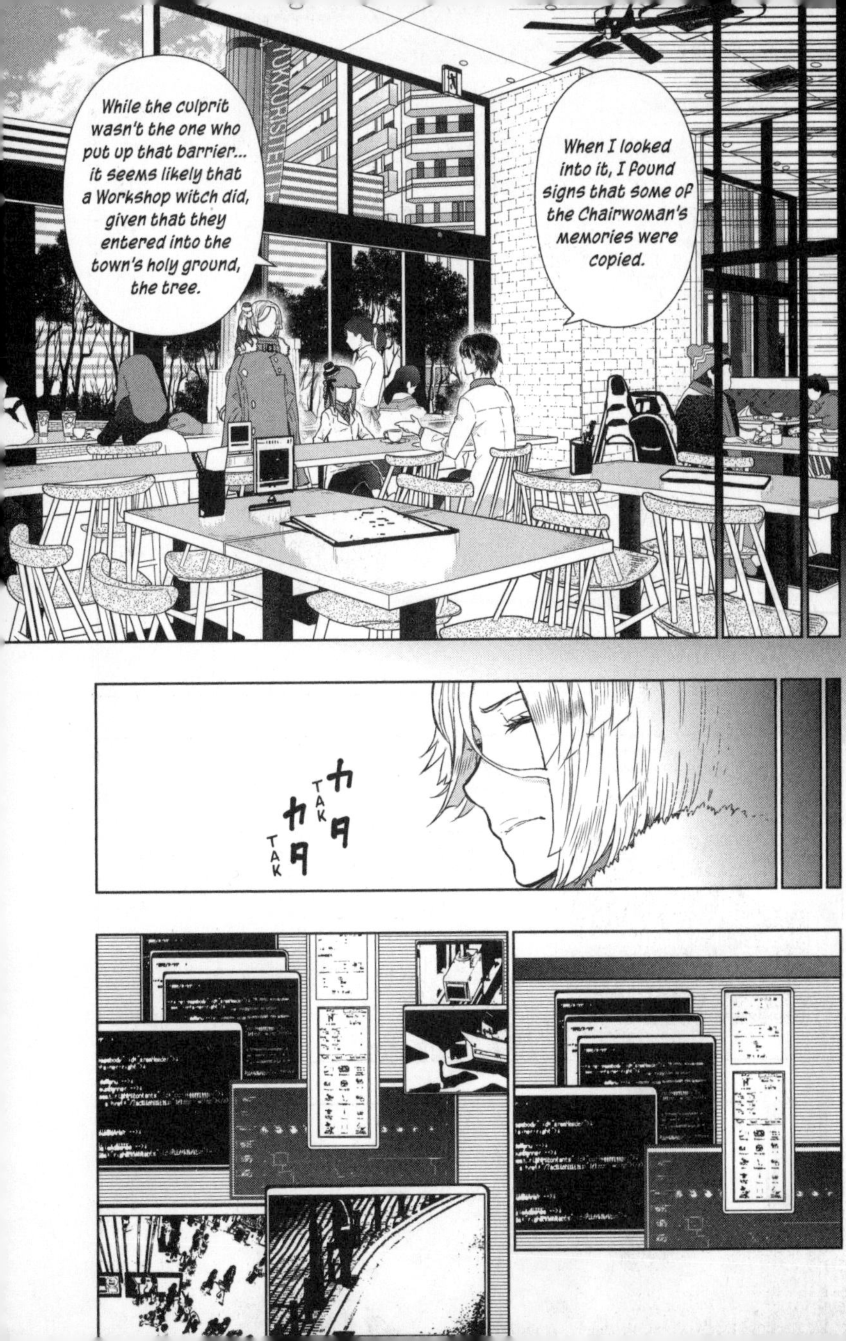
When I looked into it, I found signs that some of the Chairwoman's memories were copied.
While the culprit wasn't the one who put up that barrier... it seems likely that a Workshop witch did, given that they entered into the town's holy ground, the tree.
カタ TAK
カタ TAK

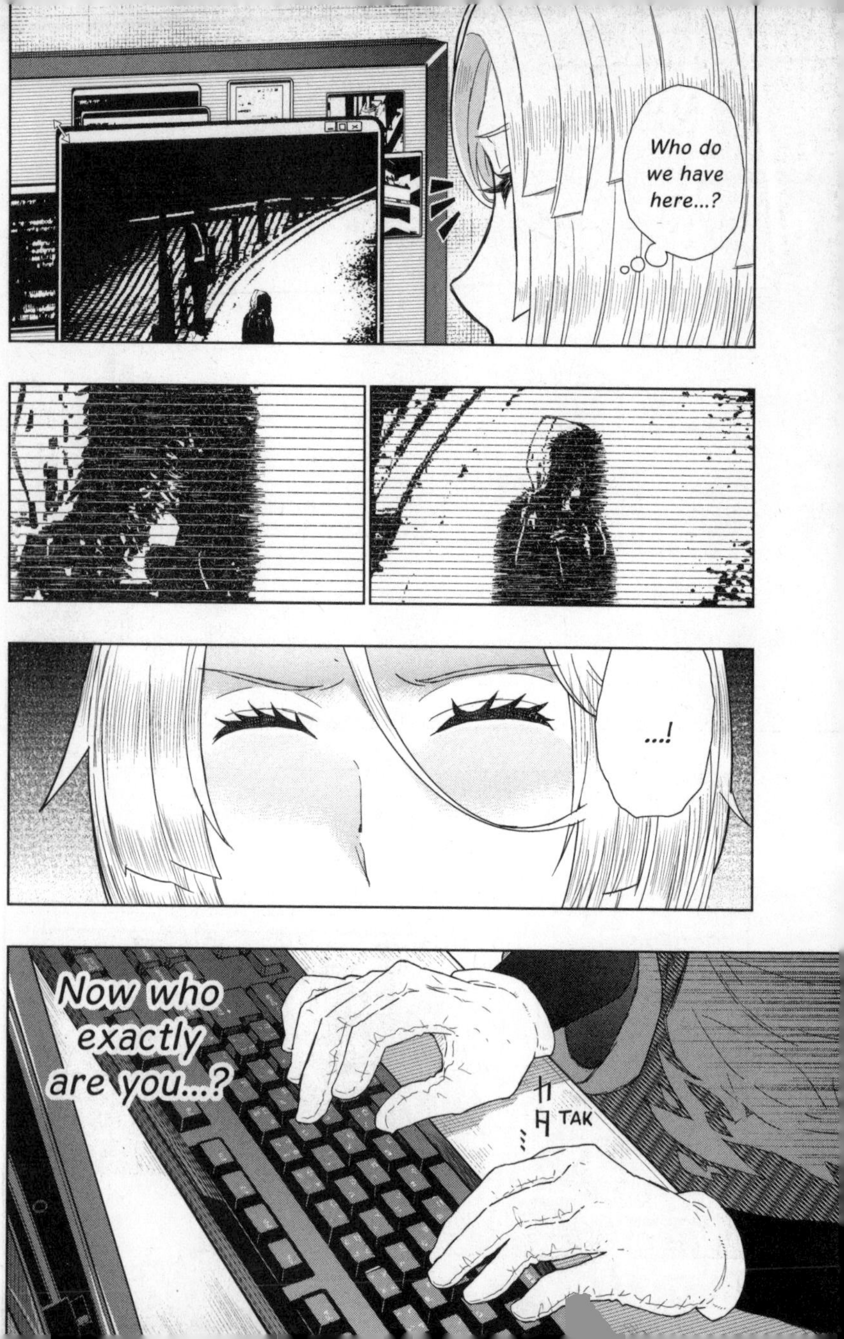
Who do we have here...?
...!
Now who exactly are you...?
TAK

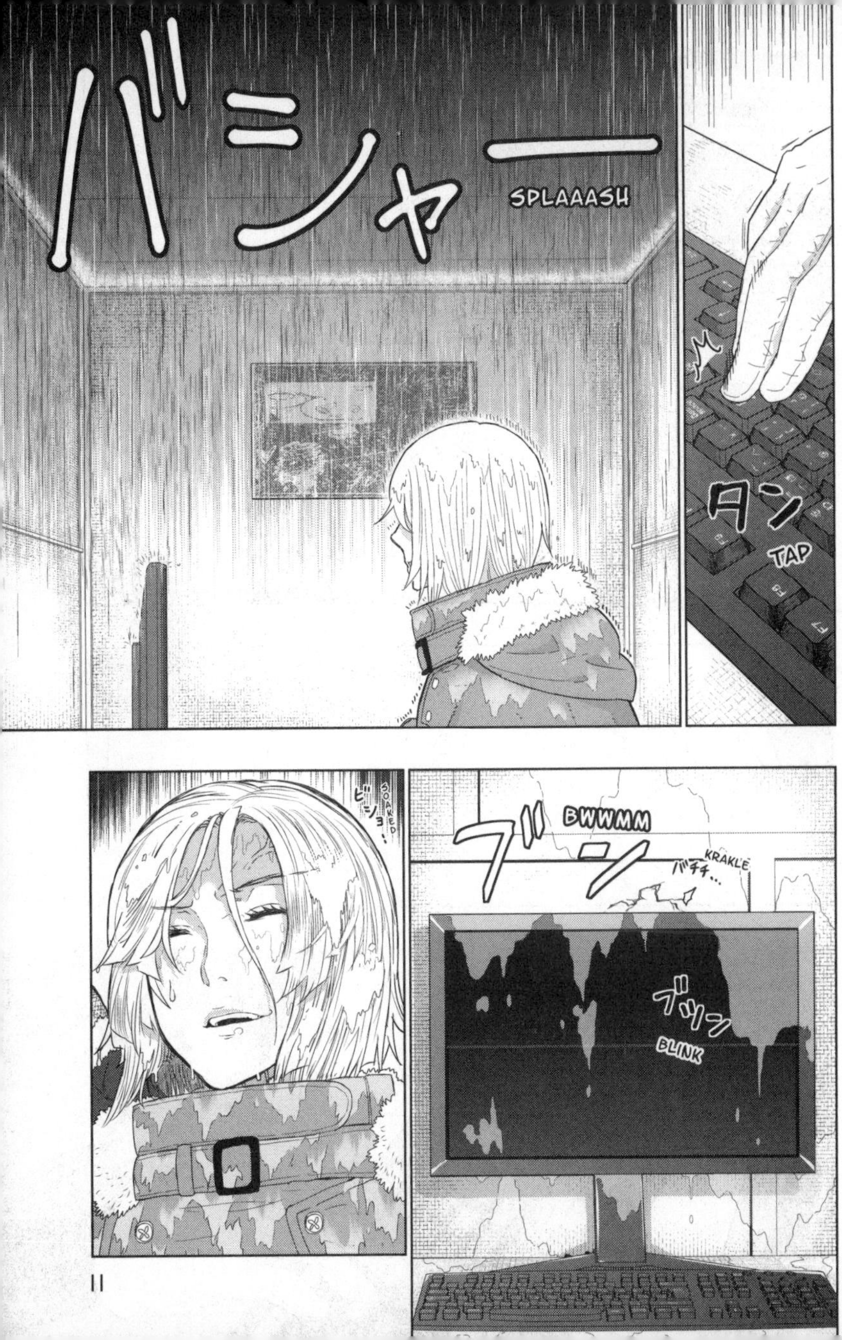
タン
TAP
バシャー
SPLAAASH
ブーン
BWWMM
バチチ…
KRAKLE
ブツン
BLINK
ビショ…
SOAKED

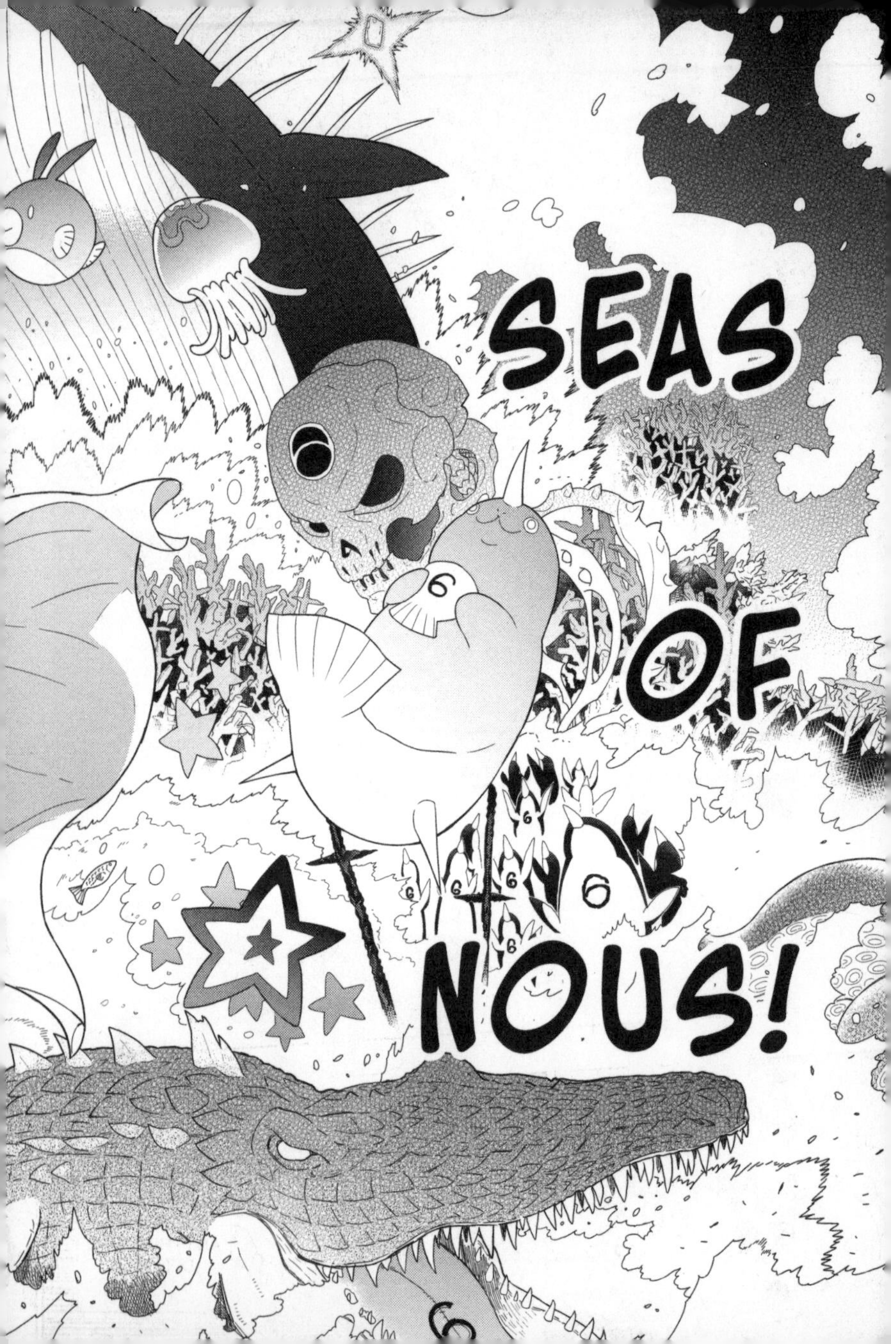
SEAS
OF
NOUS!

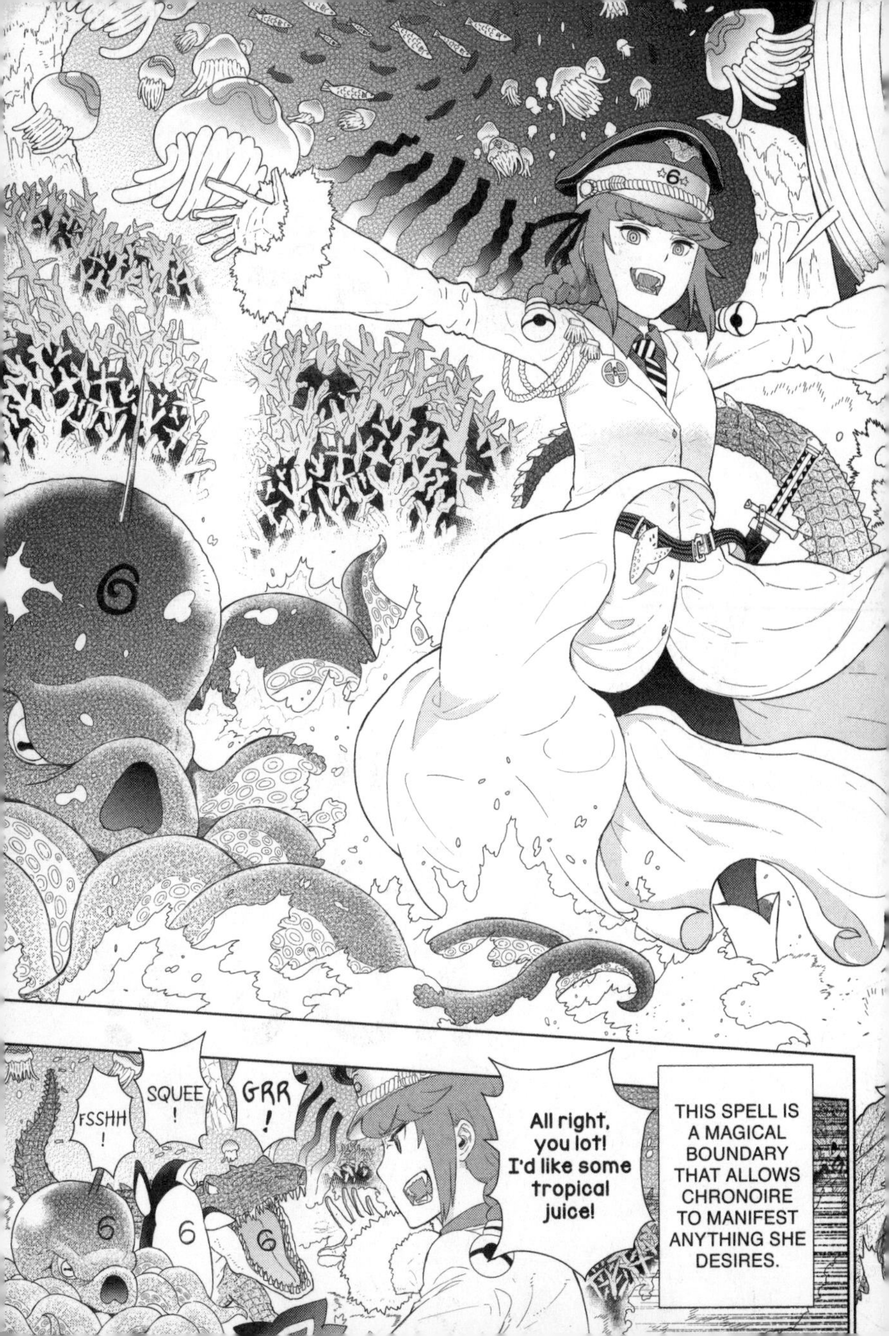
THIS SPELL IS A MAGICAL BOUNDARY THAT ALLOWS CHRONOIRE TO MANIFEST ANYTHING SHE DESIRES.
All right, you lot! I'd like some tropical juice!
GRR!
SQUEE!
FSSHH!

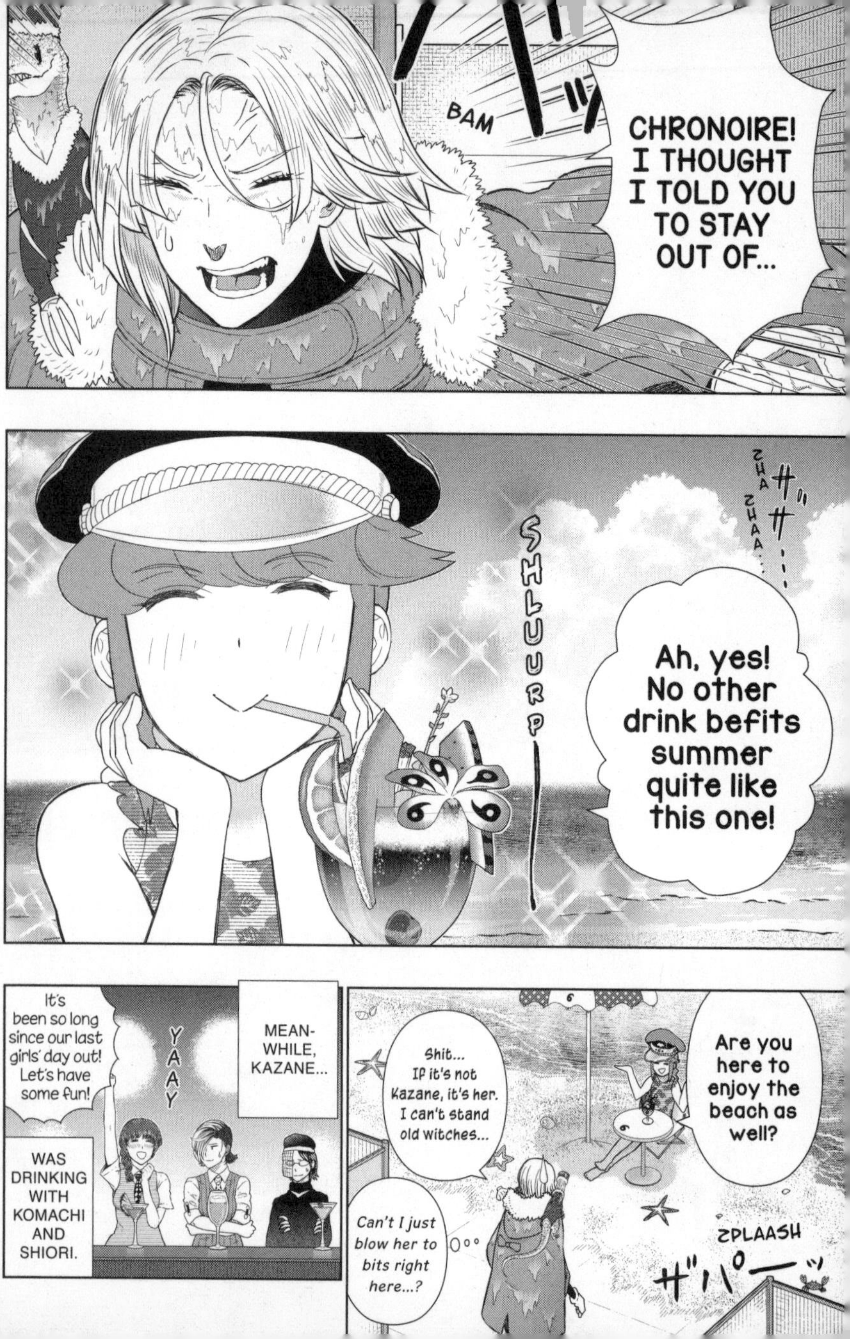
BAM
CHRONOIRE! I THOUGHT I TOLD YOU TO STAY OUT OF...
ZHA ZHAA...
SHLUURP
Ah, yes! No other drink befits summer quite like this one!
Are you here to enjoy the beach as well?
Shit... If it's not Kazane, it's her. I can't stand old witches...
Can't I just blow her to bits right here...?
ZPLAASH
MEAN-WHILE, KAZANE...
It's been so long since our last girls' day out! Let's have some fun!
YAAY
WAS DRINKING WITH KOMACHI AND SHIORI.

CHAPTER 47 END

Witchcraft Works

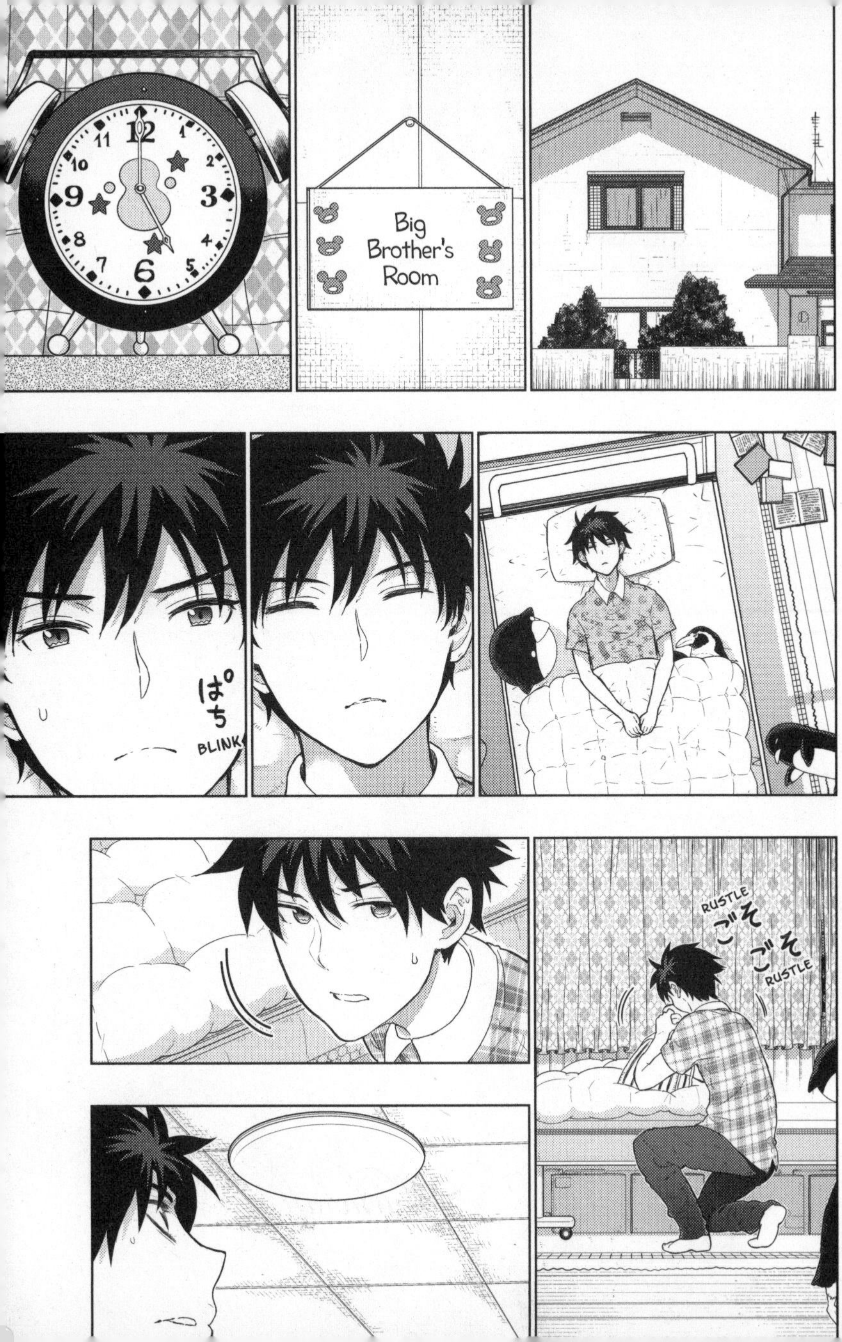
Big Brother's Room
ぱち
BLINK
RUSTLE
ごそ
ごそ
RUSTLE

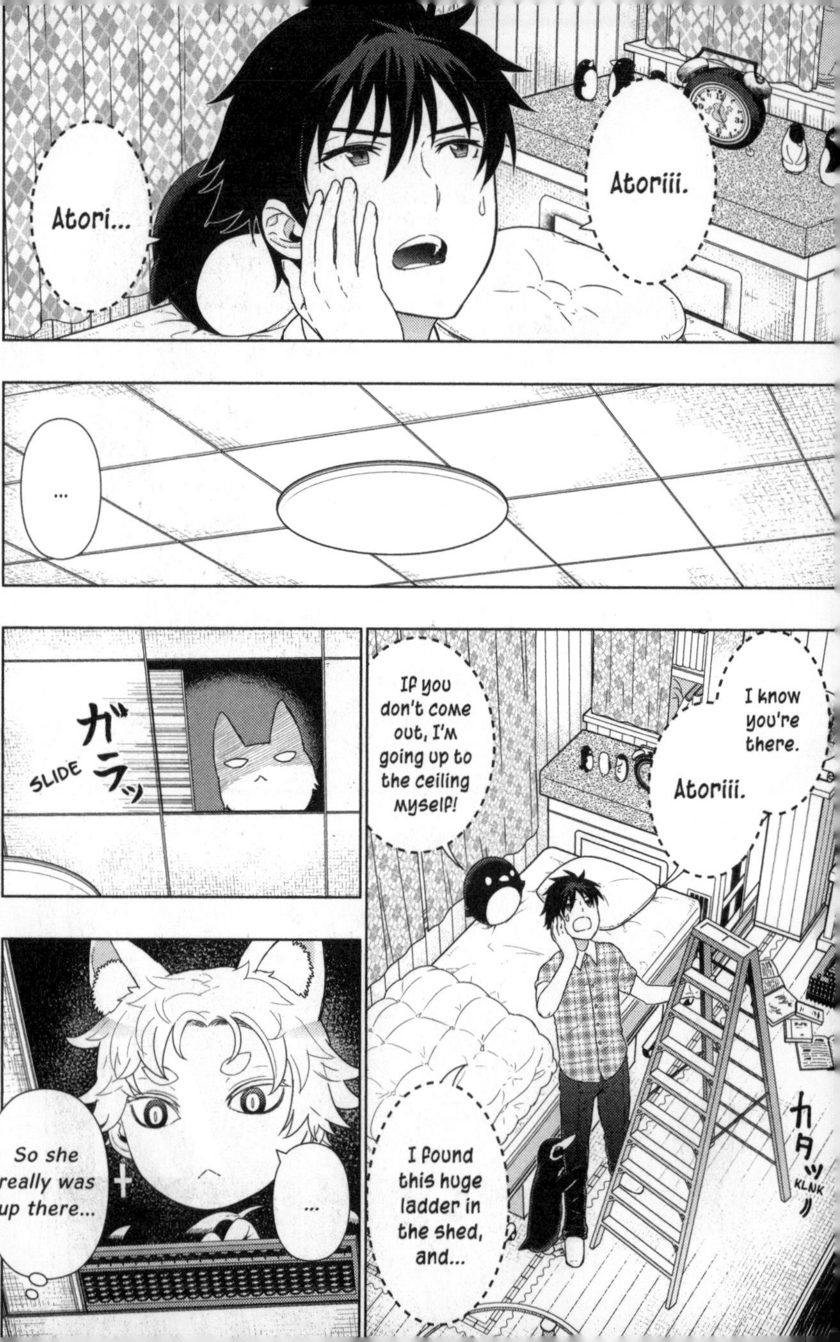

Atoriii.
Atori...
...
I know you're there.
Atoriii.
If you don't come out, I'm going up to the ceiling myself!
カタッ
KLNK
I found this huge ladder in the shed, and...
ガラッ
SLIDE
...
So she really was up there...

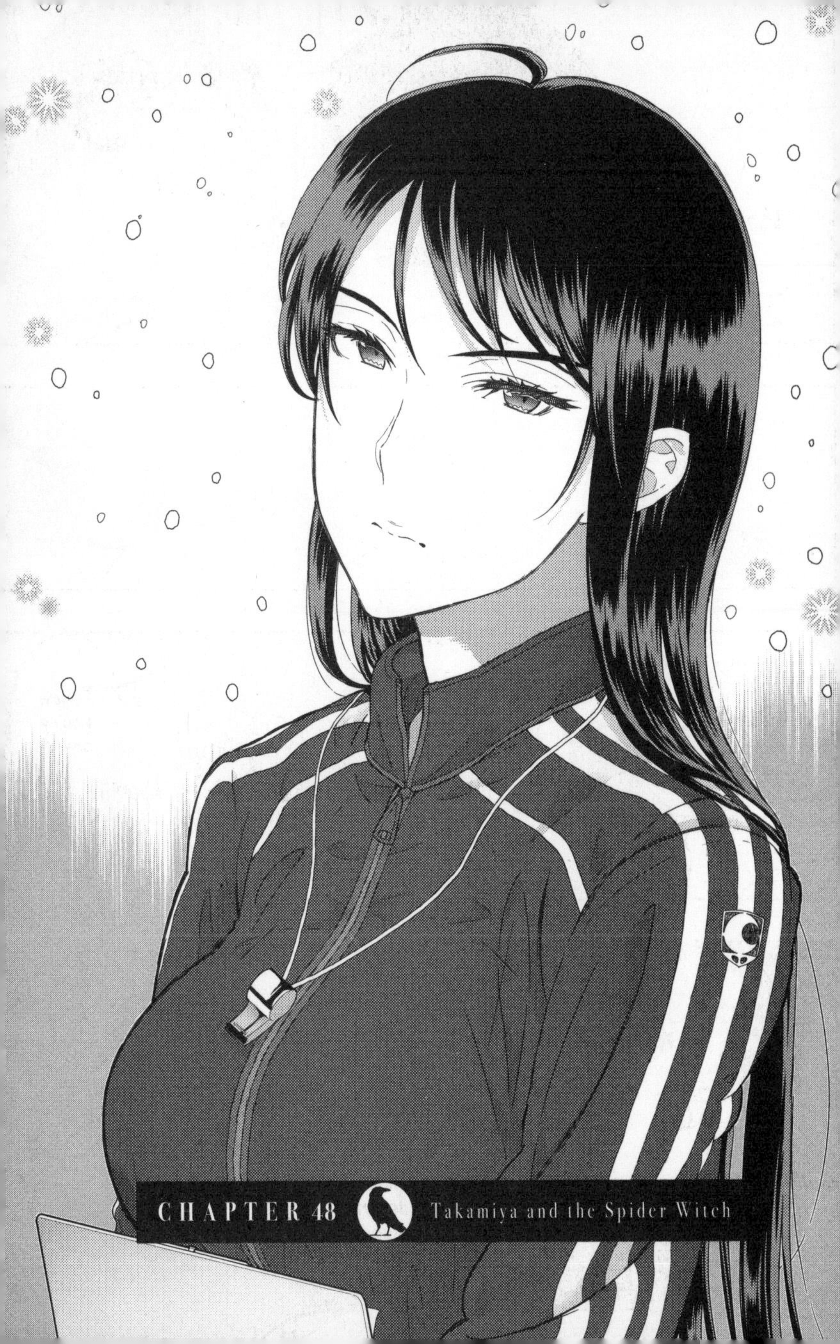
CHAPTER 48
Takamiya and the Spider Witch

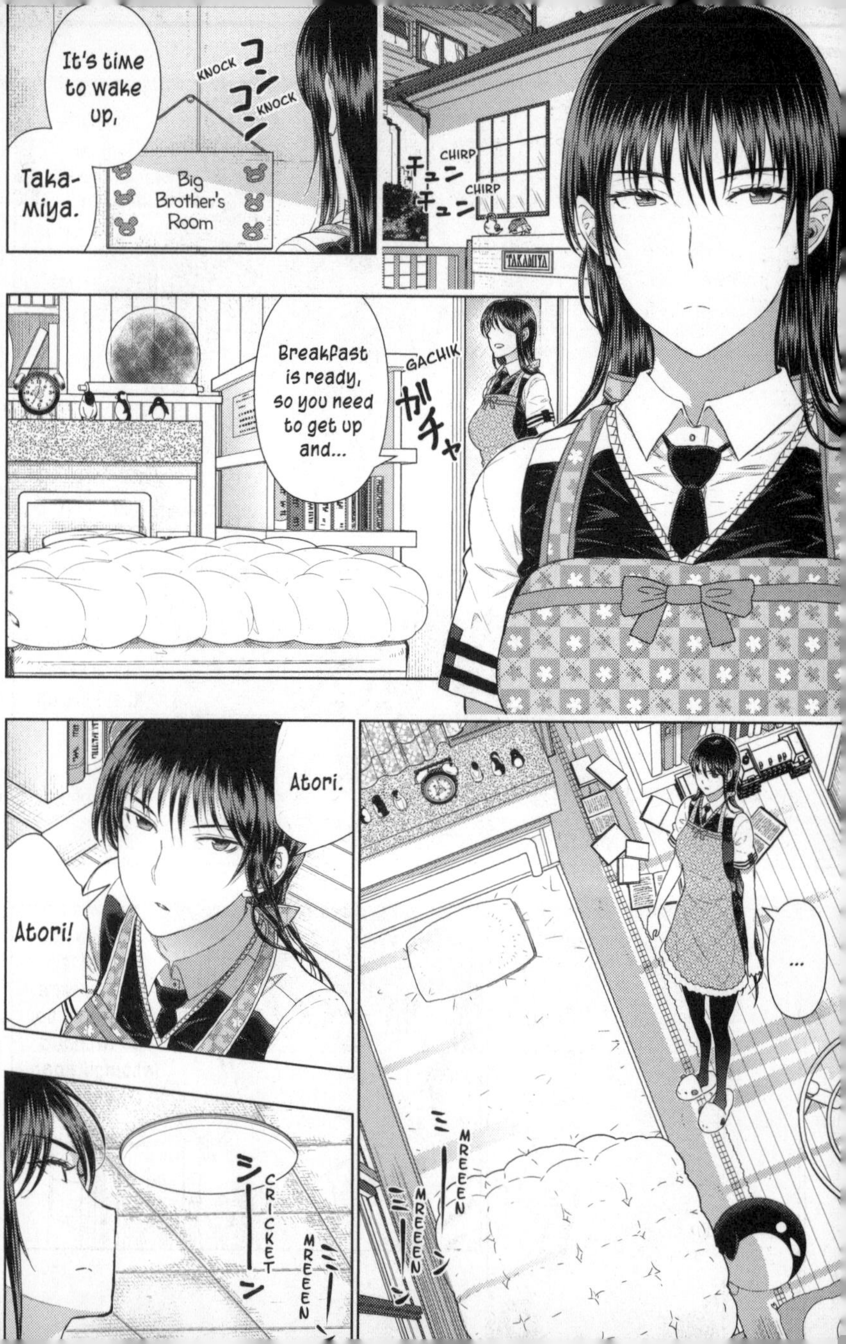
チュン
CHIRP
チュン
CHIRP
TAKAMIYA
It's time to wake up,
コン
KNOCK
コン
KNOCK
Big Brother's Room
Taka-miya.
Breakfast is ready, so you need to get up and...
ガチャ
GACHIK
...
ミーン
MREEEN
ミーン
MREEEN
Atori.
Atori!
ミーン
MREEEN
シーン
CRICKET

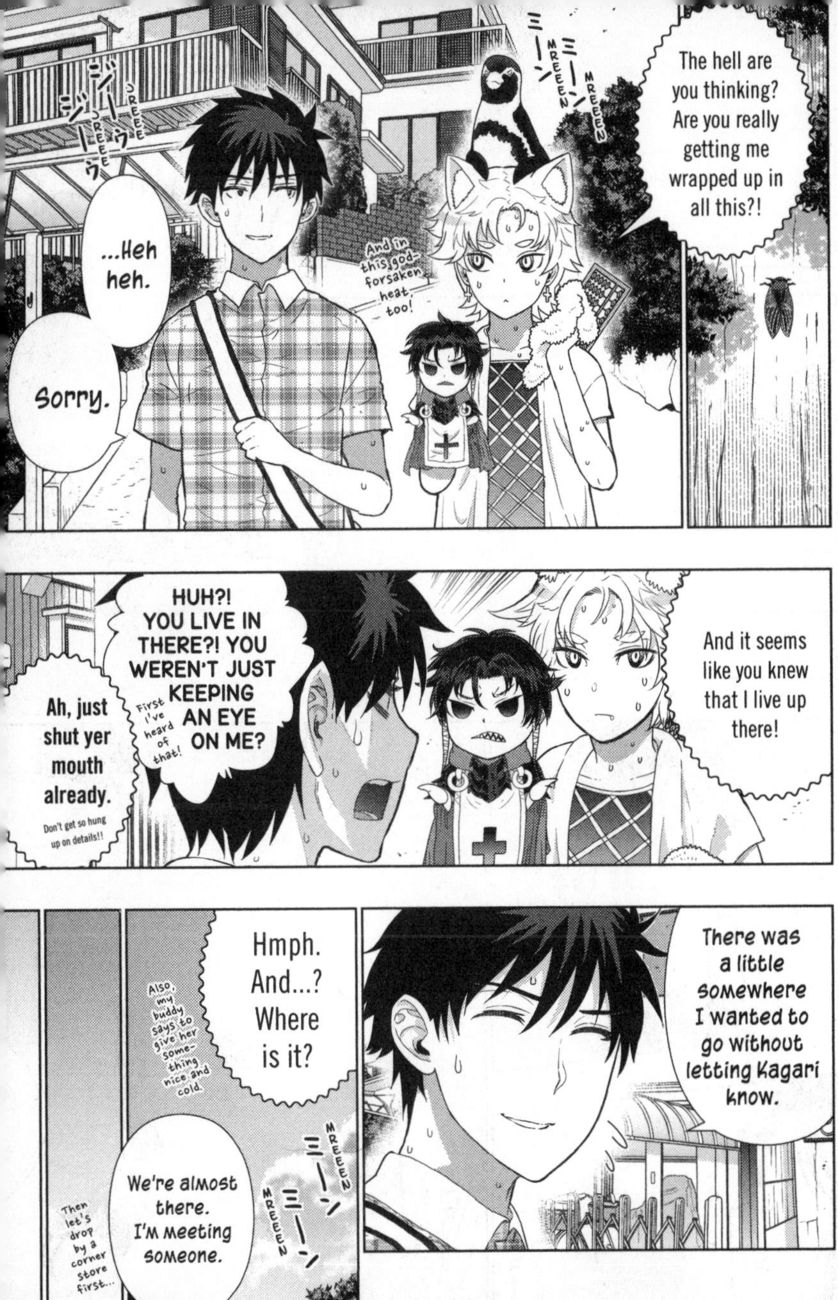
The hell are you thinking? Are you really getting me wrapped up in all this?!
MREEEN
MREEEN
And in this god-forsaken heat, too!
REEE
REEE
...Heh heh.
Sorry.
And it seems like you knew that I live up there!
HUH?! YOU LIVE IN THERE?! YOU WEREN'T JUST KEEPING AN EYE ON ME?
First I've heard of that!
Ah, just shut yer mouth already.
Don't get so hung up on details!!
There was a little somewhere I wanted to go without letting Kagari know.
Hmph. And...? Where is it?
Also, my buddy says to give her something nice and cold.
MREEEN
MREEEN
We're almost there. I'm meeting someone.
Then let's drop by a corner store first...

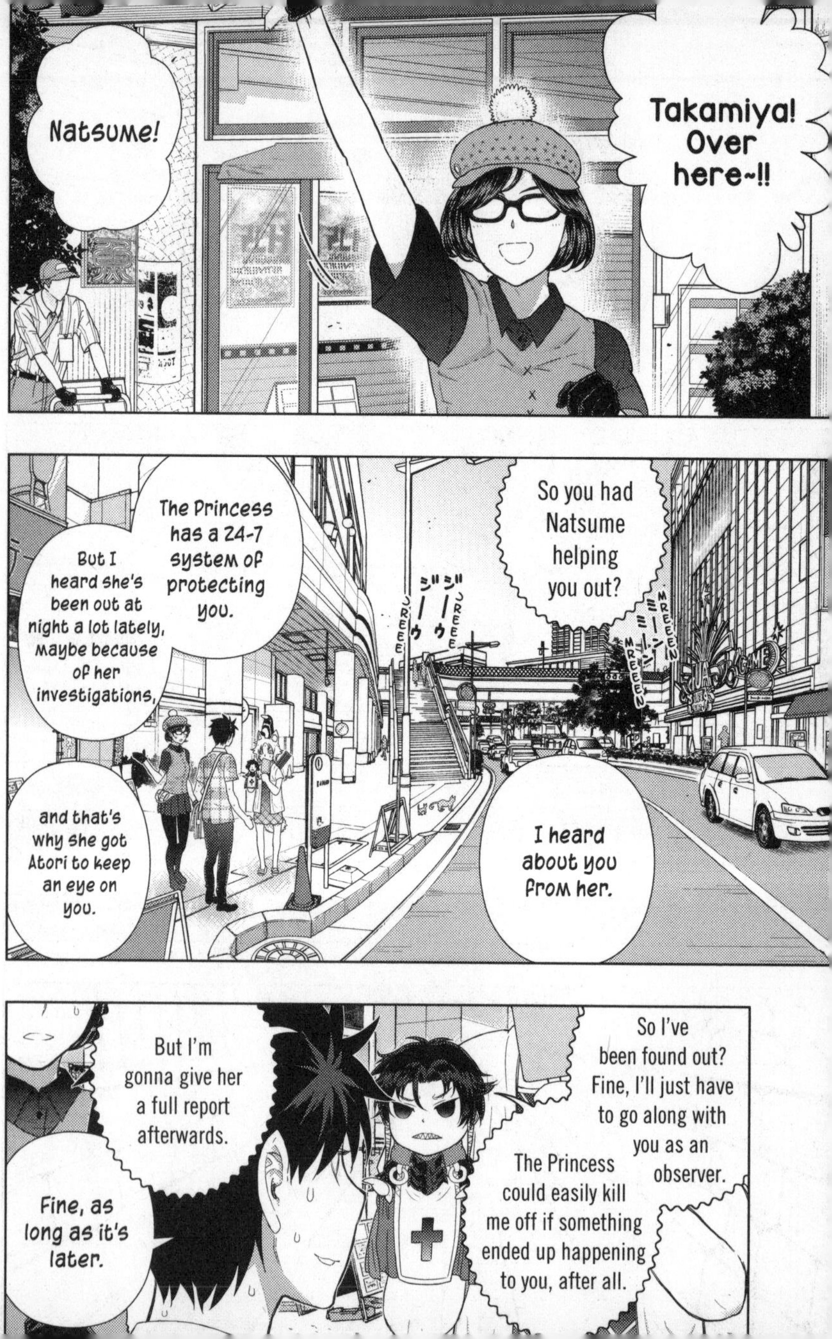
Takamiya! Over here~!!
Natsume!
So you had Natsume helping you out?
MREEEN
ミーン
ミーン
MREEEN
ジーウ
JREEE
ジーウ
JREEE
I heard about you from her.
The Princess has a 24-7 system of protecting you.
But I heard she's been out at night a lot lately, maybe because of her investigations,
and that's why she got Atori to keep an eye on you.
So I've been found out? Fine, I'll just have to go along with you as an observer.
The Princess could easily kill me off if something ended up happening to you, after all.
But I'm gonna give her a full report afterwards.
Fine, as long as it's later.

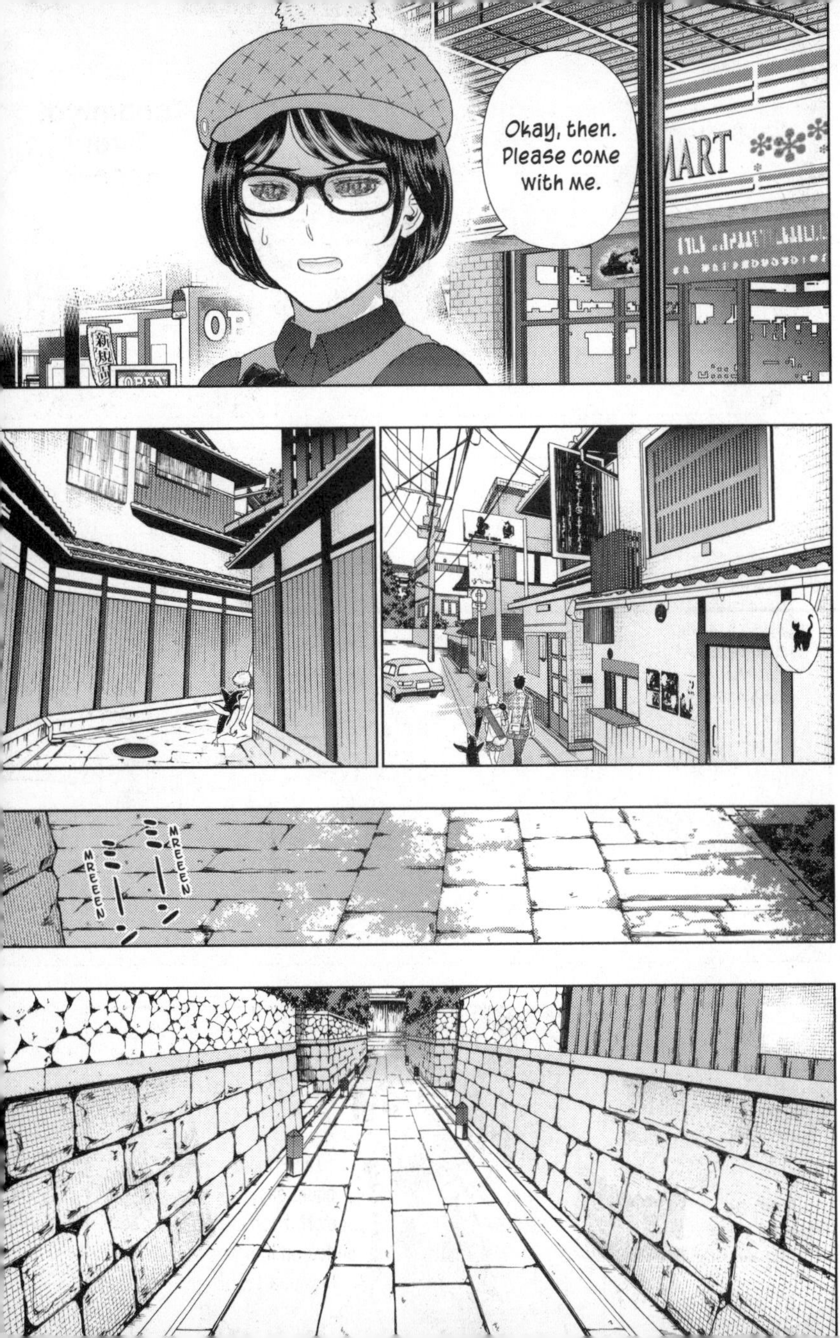
Okay, then. Please come with me.
MART
OPEN
MREEEN
MREEEN

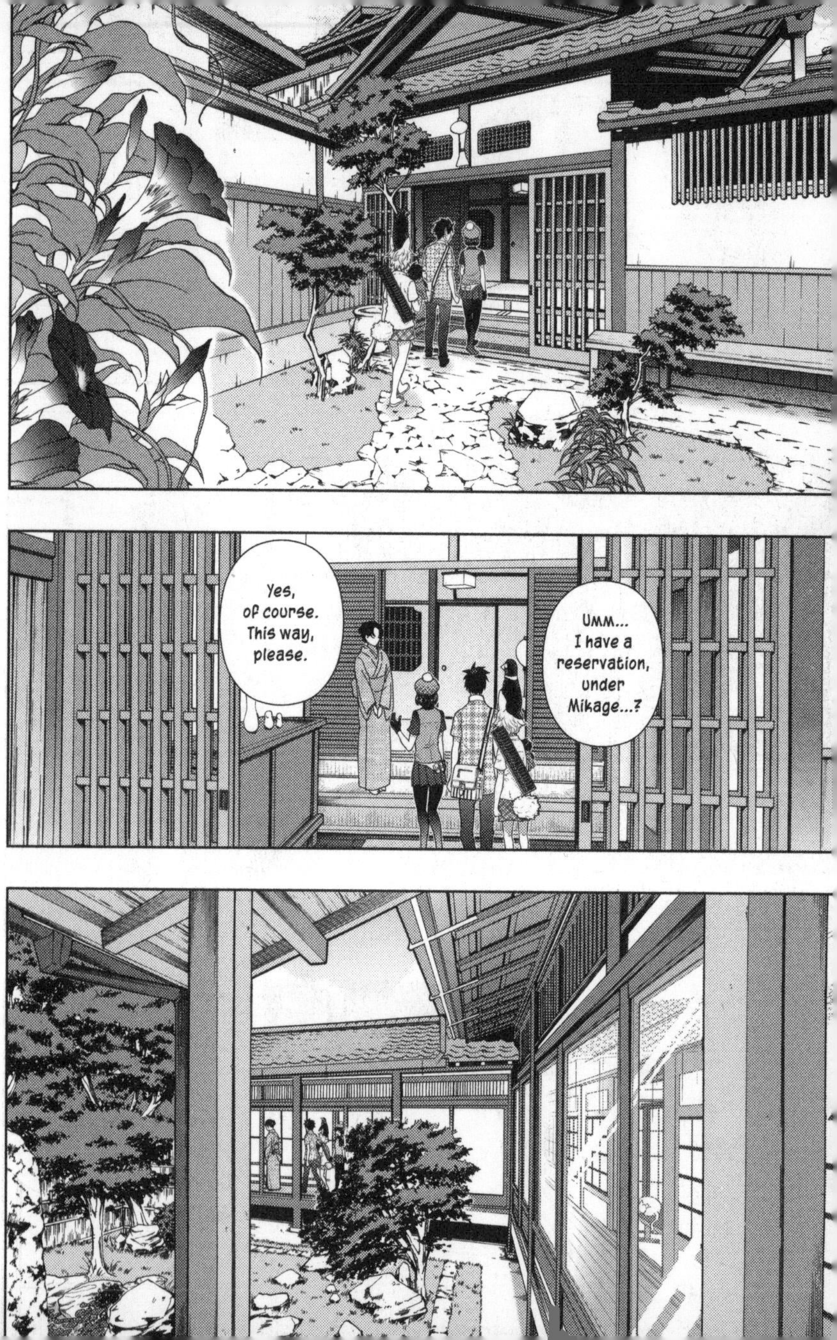
Umm... I have a reservation, under Mikage...?
Yes, of course. This way, please.

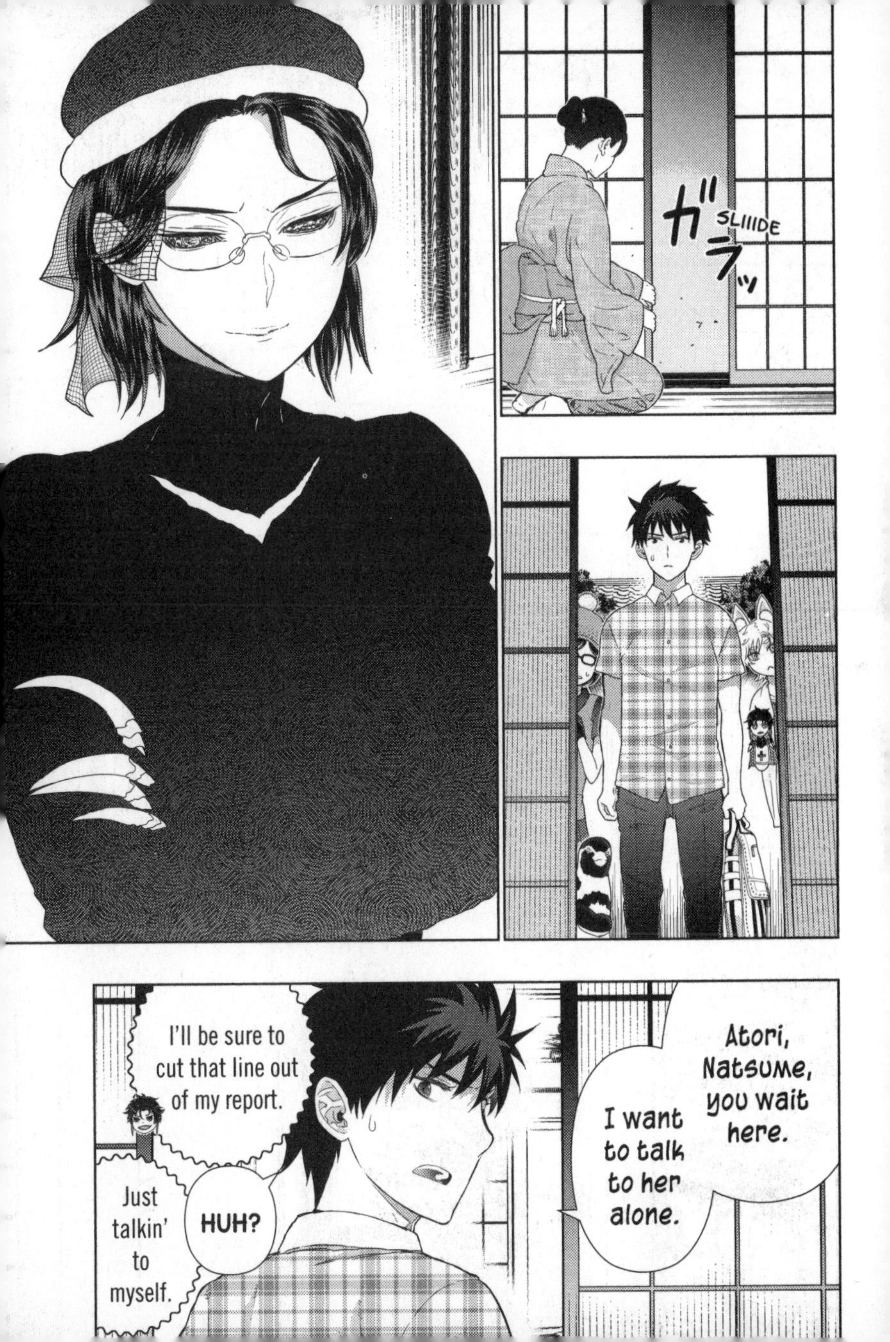
ガラッ
SLIIIDE
Atori, Natsume, you wait here.
I want to talk to her alone.
I'll be sure to cut that line out of my report.
HUH?
Just talkin' to myself.

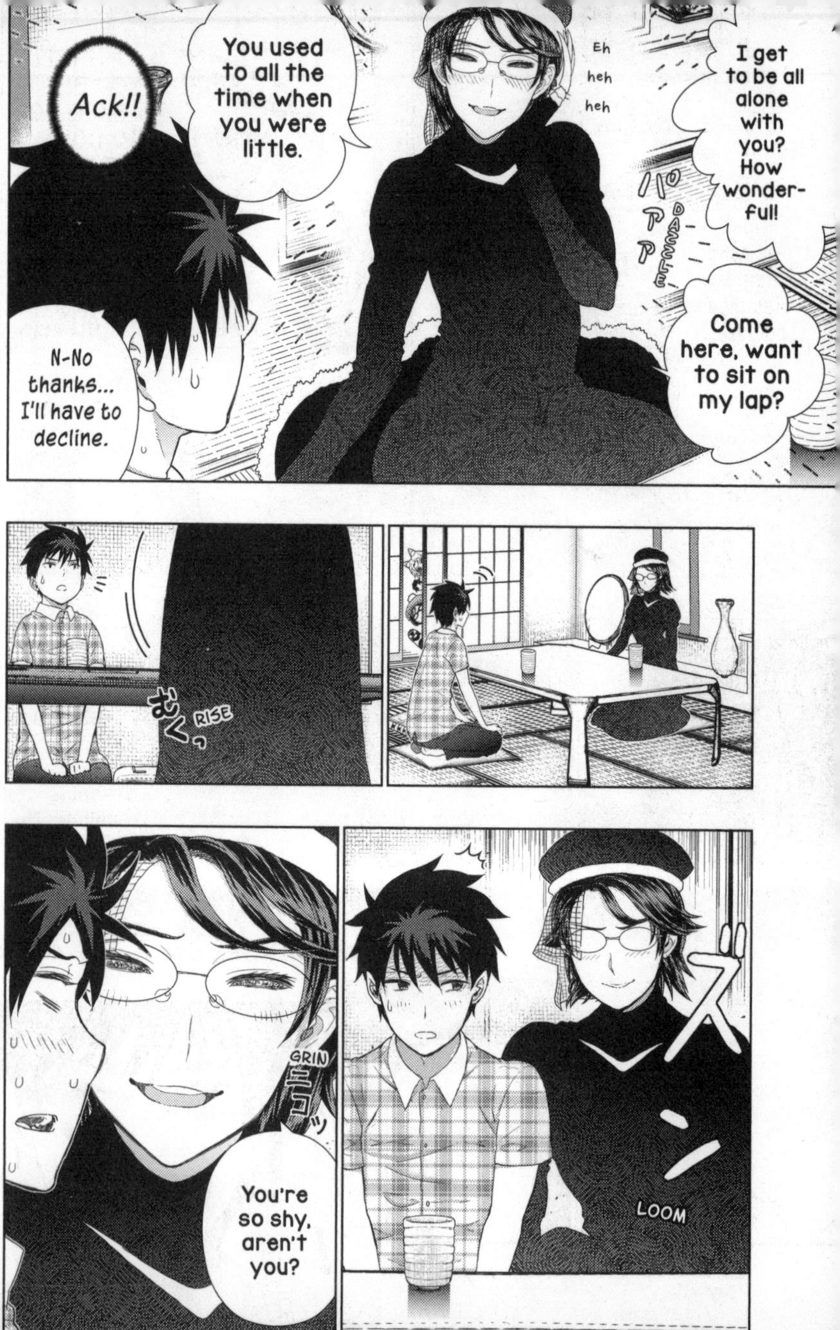

I get to be all alone with you? How wonderful!
Eh heh heh
パァア
DAZZLE
Come here, want to sit on my lap?
You used to all the time when you were little.
Ack!!
N-No thanks... I'll have to decline.
むく, RISE
ズ
LOOM
GRIN
ニコッ
You're so shy, aren't you?

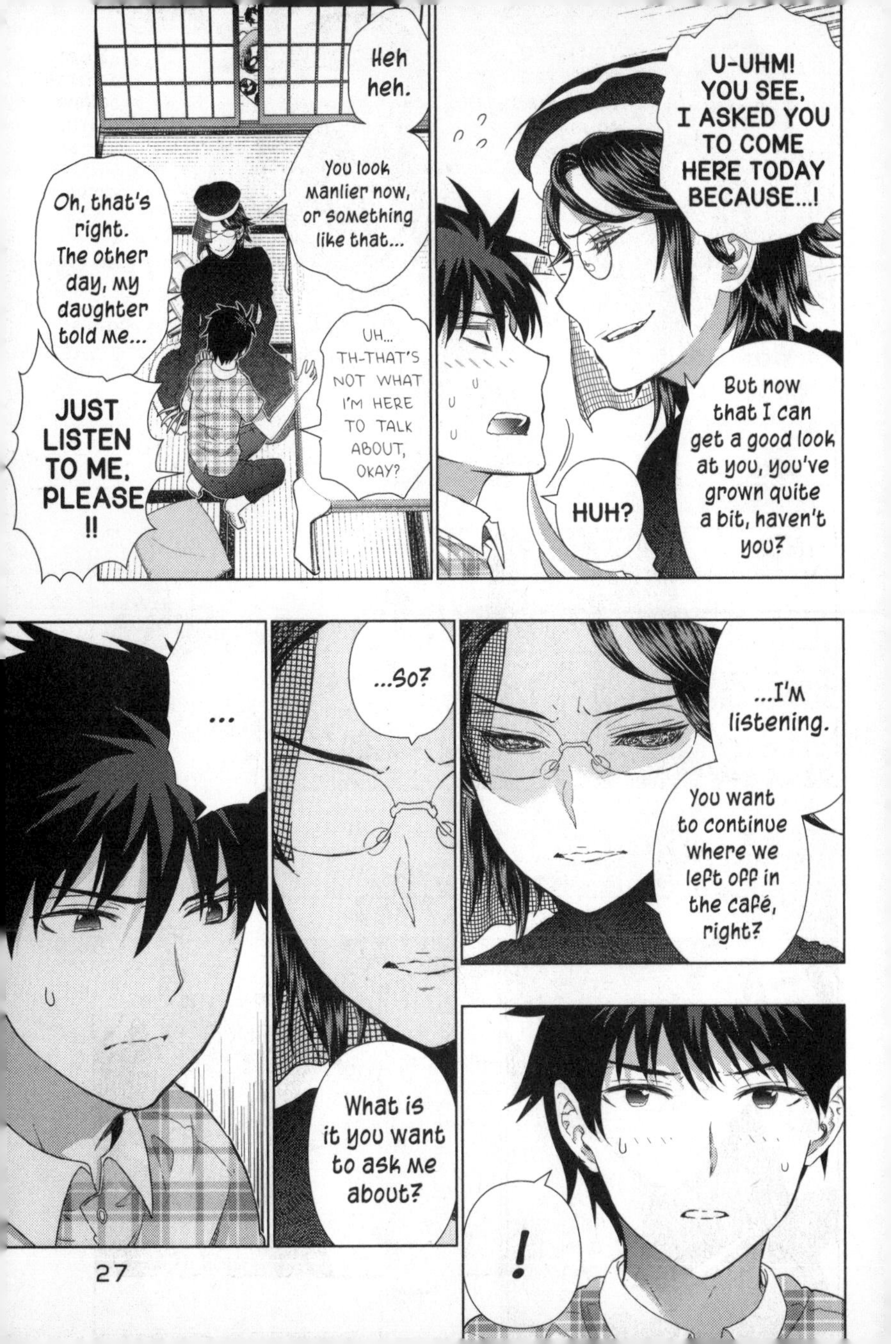
U-UHM! YOU SEE, I ASKED YOU TO COME HERE TODAY BECAUSE...!
But now that I can get a good look at you, you've grown quite a bit, haven't you?
HUH?
Heh heh.
You look manlier now, or something like that...
UH... TH-THAT'S NOT WHAT I'M HERE TO TALK ABOUT, OKAY?
Oh, that's right. The other day, my daughter told me...
JUST LISTEN TO ME, PLEASE !!
...I'M listening.
You want to continue where we left off in the café, right?
!
...So?
What is it you want to ask me about?
...

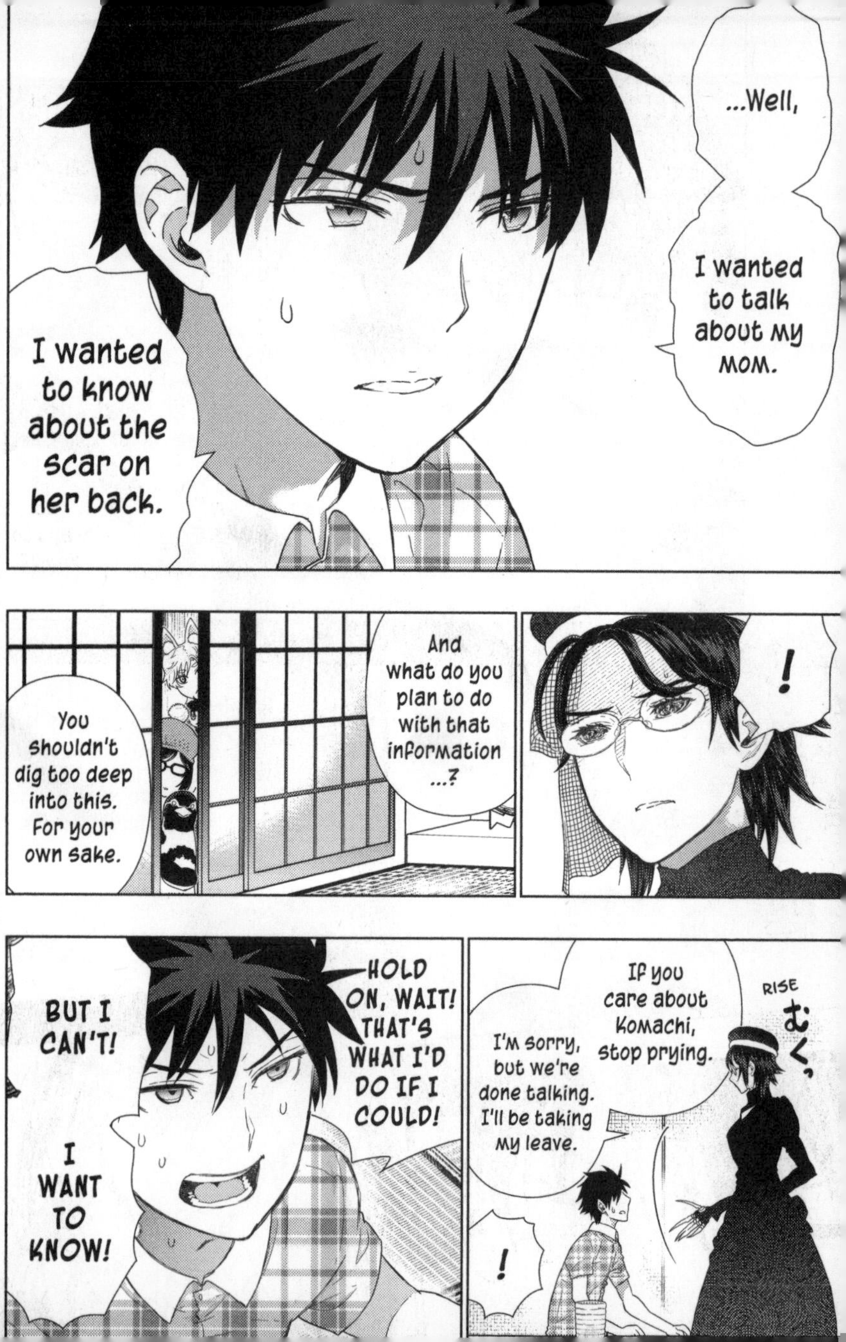
...Well,
I wanted to talk about my MOM.
I wanted to know about the scar on her back.
!
And what do you plan to do with that information...?
You shouldn't dig too deep into this. For your own sake.
RISE
むく,
If you care about Komachi, stop prying.
I'm sorry, but we're done talking. I'll be taking my leave.
!
HOLD ON, WAIT! THAT'S WHAT I'D DO IF I COULD!
BUT I CAN'T!
I WANT TO KNOW!

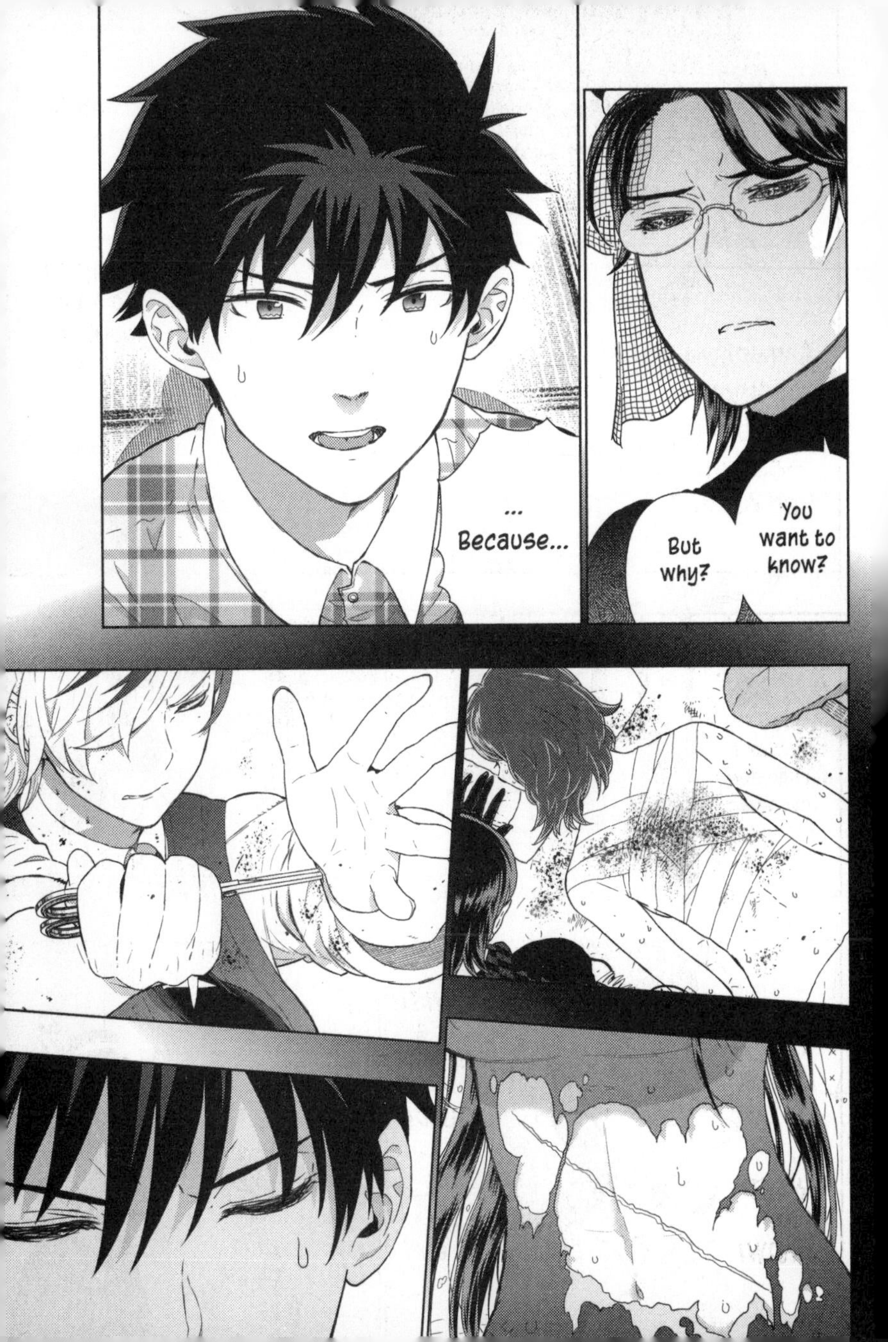
You want to know?
But why?
... Because...

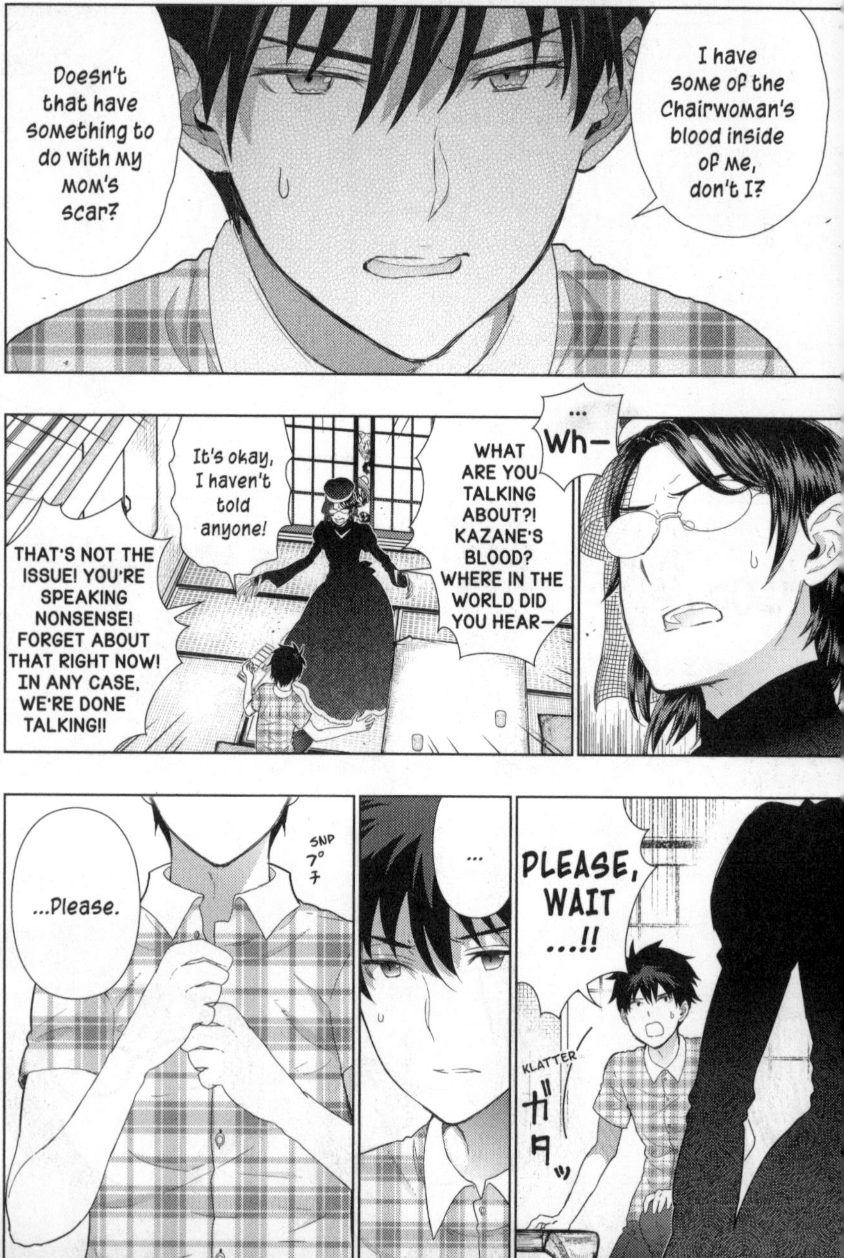

I have some of the Chairwoman's blood inside of me, don't I?
Doesn't that have something to do with my MOM's scar?
...Wh—
WHAT ARE YOU TALKING ABOUT?! KAZANE'S BLOOD? WHERE IN THE WORLD DID YOU HEAR—
It's okay, I haven't told anyone!
THAT'S NOT THE ISSUE! YOU'RE SPEAKING NONSENSE! FORGET ABOUT THAT RIGHT NOW! IN ANY CASE, WE'RE DONE TALKING!!
PLEASE, WAIT ...!!
KLATTER
ガタッ
...
SNP
プチ
...Please.

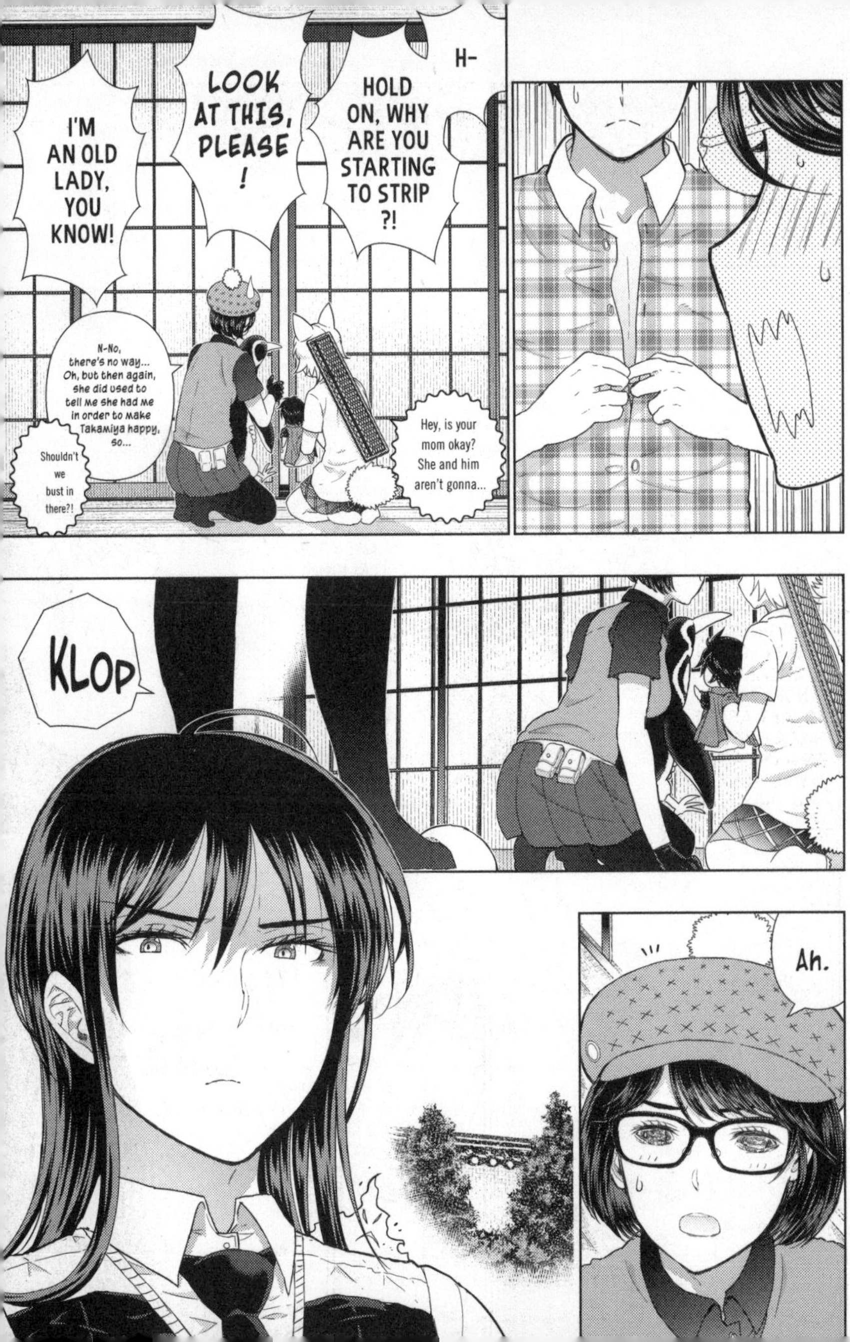
H-
HOLD ON, WHY ARE YOU STARTING TO STRIP?!
LOOK AT THIS, PLEASE!
I'M AN OLD LADY, YOU KNOW!
Hey, is your mom okay? She and him aren't gonna...
N-No, there's no way... Oh, but then again, she did used to tell me she had me in order to make Takamiya happy, so...
Shouldn't we bust in there?!
KLOP
Ah.

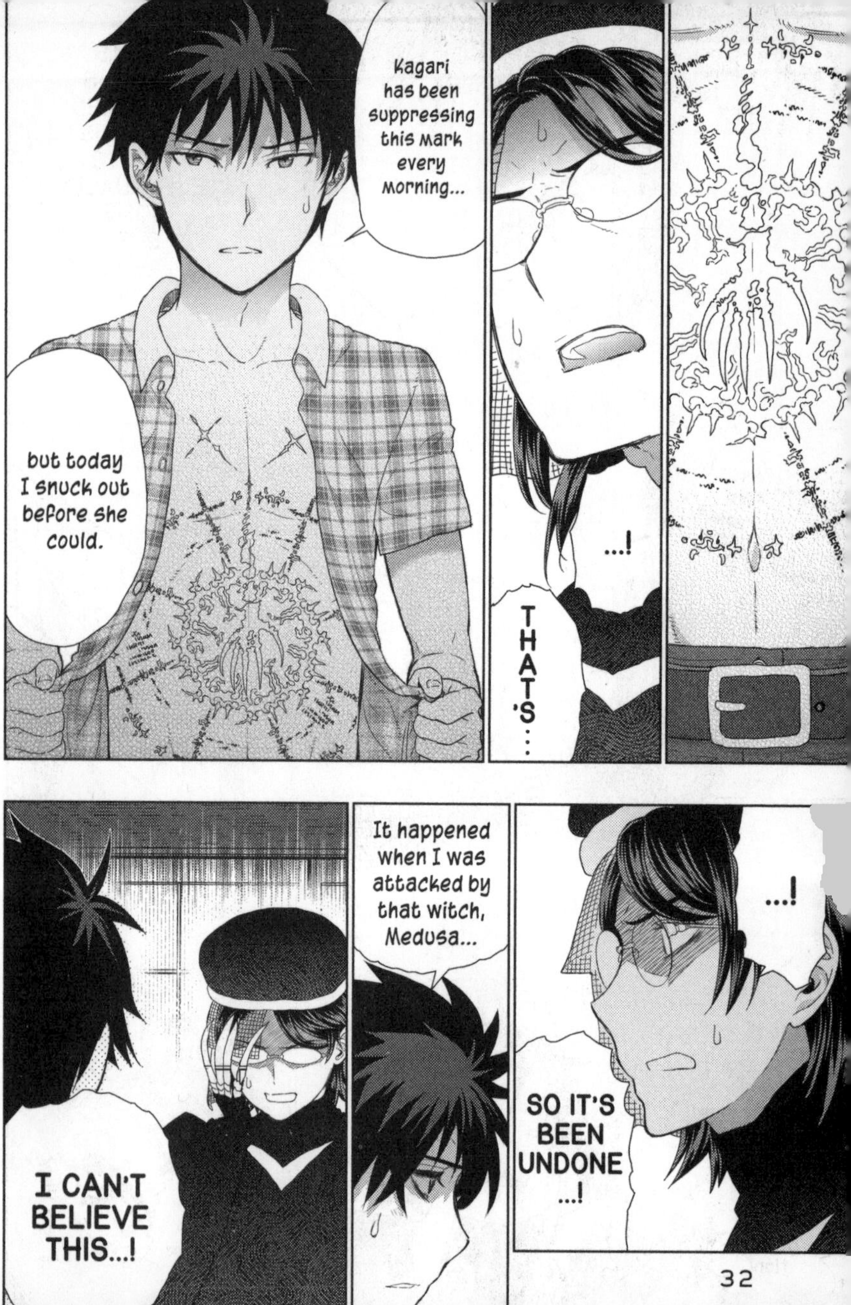
...!
THAT'S...
Kagari has been suppressing this mark every morning...
but today I snuck out before she could.
...!
SO IT'S BEEN UNDONE ...!
It happened when I was attacked by that witch, Medusa...
I CAN'T BELIEVE THIS...!

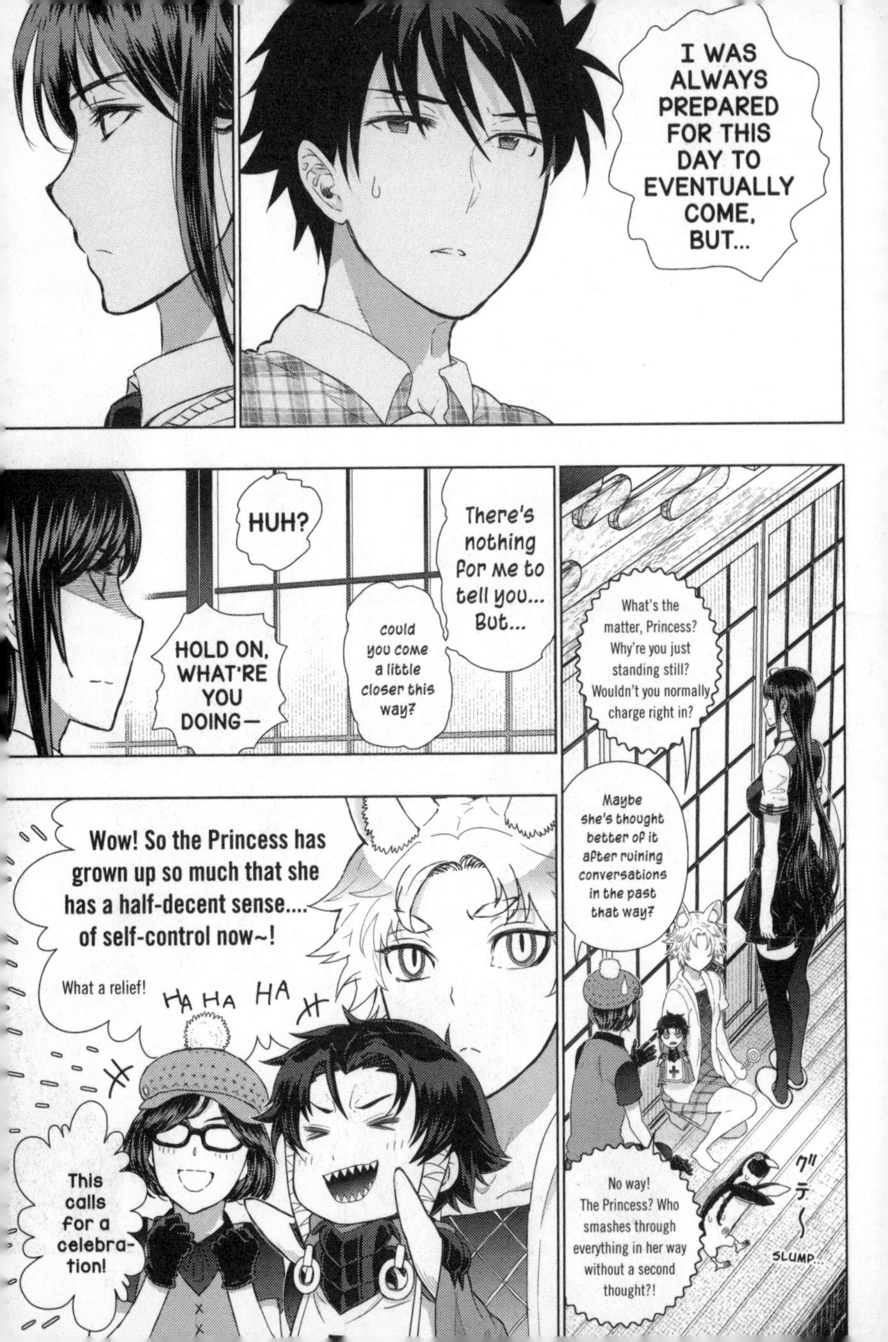

I WAS ALWAYS PREPARED FOR THIS DAY TO EVENTUALLY COME, BUT...
What's the matter, Princess? Why're you just standing still? Wouldn't you normally charge right in?
Maybe she's thought better of it after ruining conversations in the past that way?
No way! The Princess? Who smashes through everything in her way without a second thought?!
グデ～
SLUMP...
There's nothing for me to tell you... But...
HUH?
could you come a little closer this way?
HOLD ON, WHAT'RE YOU DOING—
Wow! So the Princess has grown up so much that she has a half-decent sense.... of self-control now~!
What a relief!
HA HA HA HA
This calls for a celebra-tion!

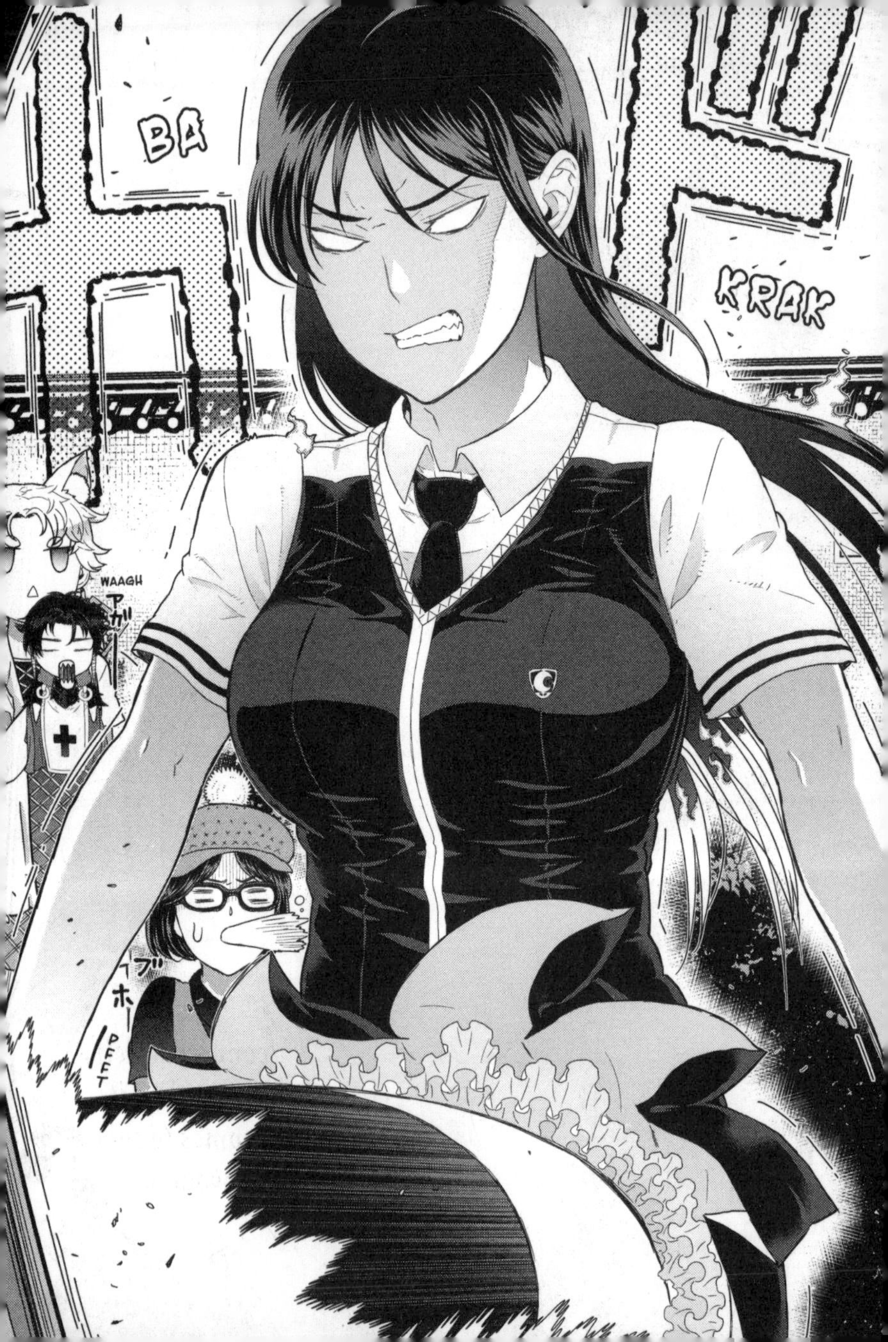
KRAK
BA
WAAGH
アガー
ブホー
PFFT

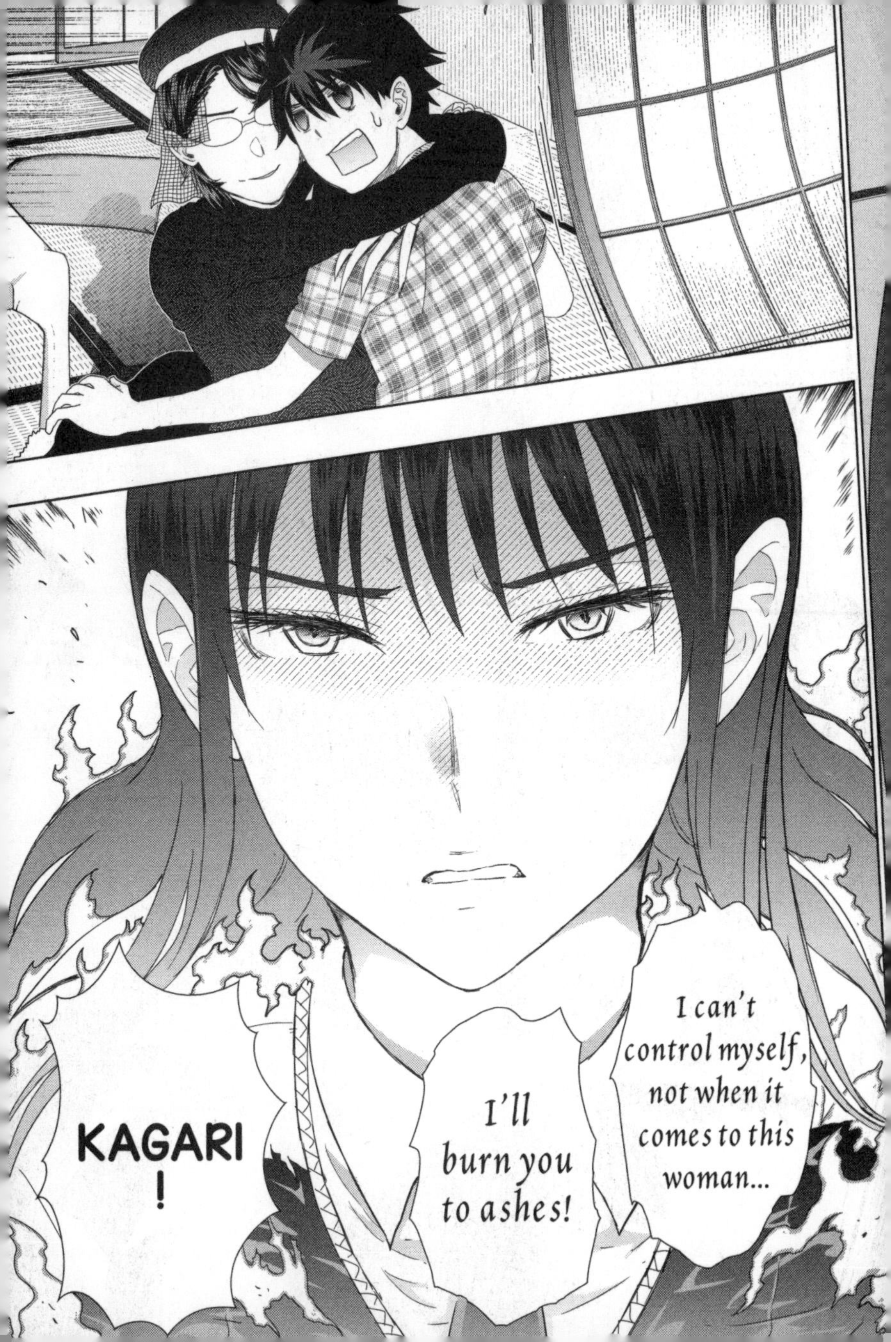
I can't control myself, not when it comes to this woman...
I'll burn you to ashes!
KAGARI!

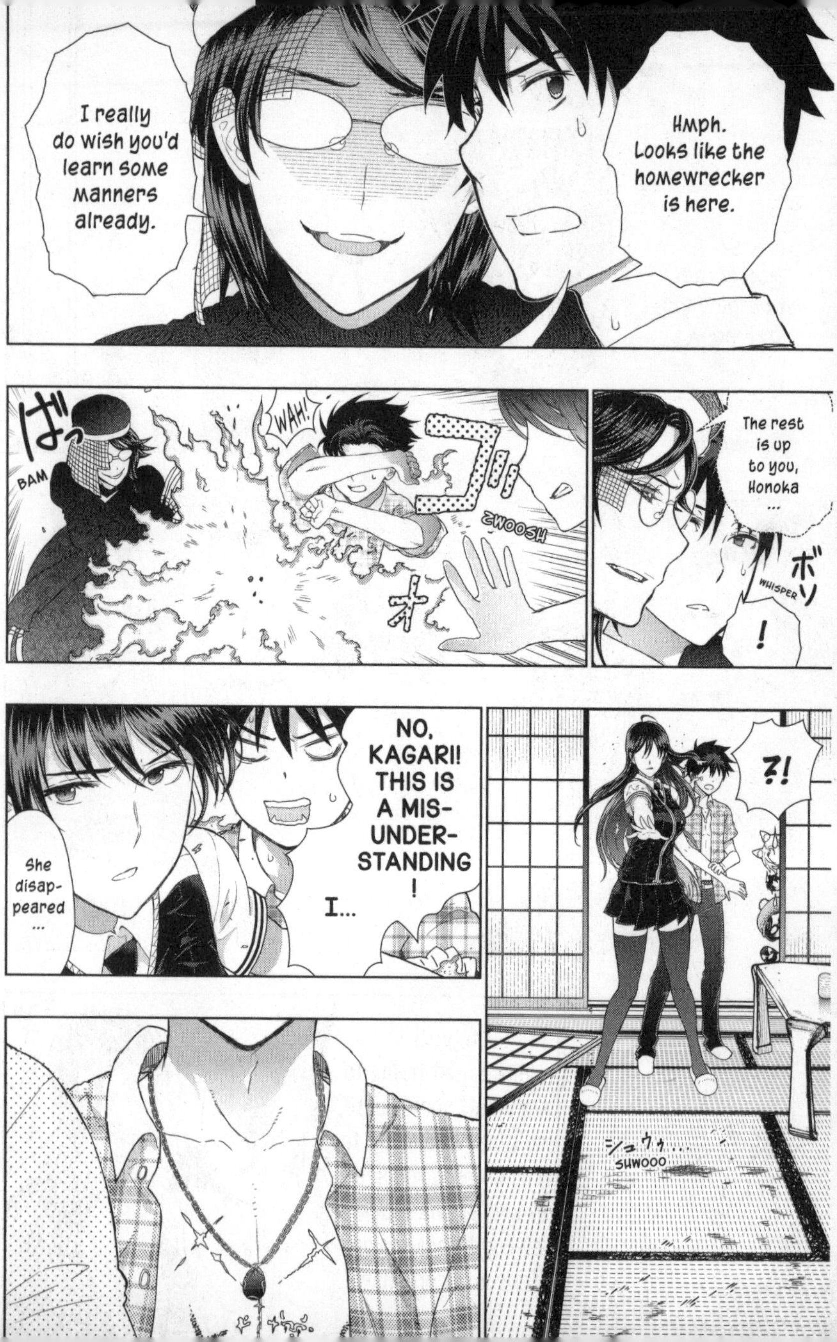
Hmph. Looks like the homewrecker is here.
I really do wish you'd learn some manners already.
The rest is up to you, Honoka ...
ボソ
WHISPER
!
ゴォ
ZWOOSH
オ
WAH!
ばっ
BAM
?!
シュウ...
SHWOOO
NO, KAGARI! THIS IS A MIS-UNDER-STANDING!
I...
She disap-peared ...

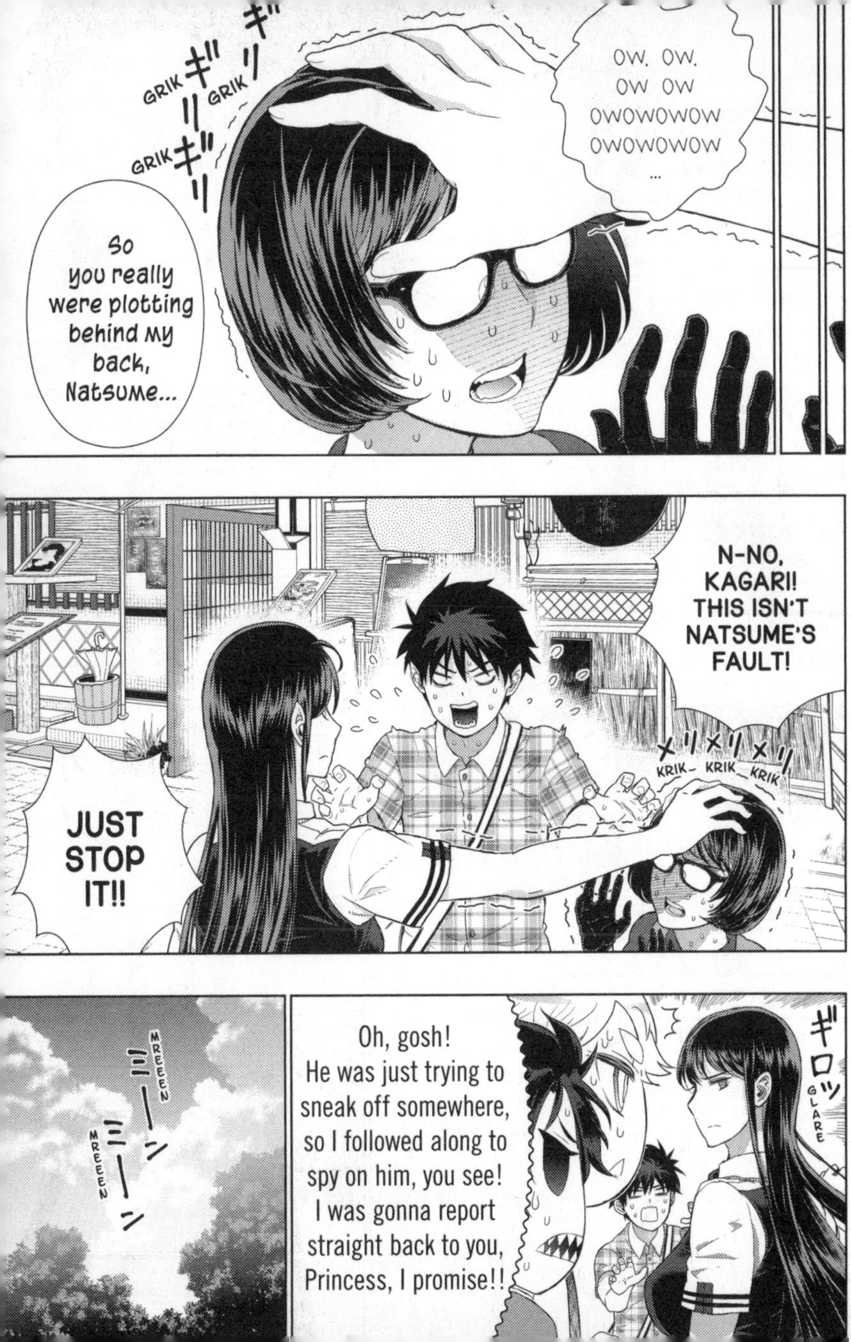
OW. OW.
OW OW
OWOWOWOW
OWOWOWOW
...
GRIK
GRIK
GRIK
So you really were plotting behind my back, Natsume...
N-NO, KAGARI! THIS ISN'T NATSUME'S FAULT!
KRIK KRIK KRIK
JUST STOP IT!!
GLARE
Oh, gosh! He was just trying to sneak off somewhere, so I followed along to spy on him, you see! I was gonna report straight back to you, Princess, I promise!!
MREEEN
MREEEN

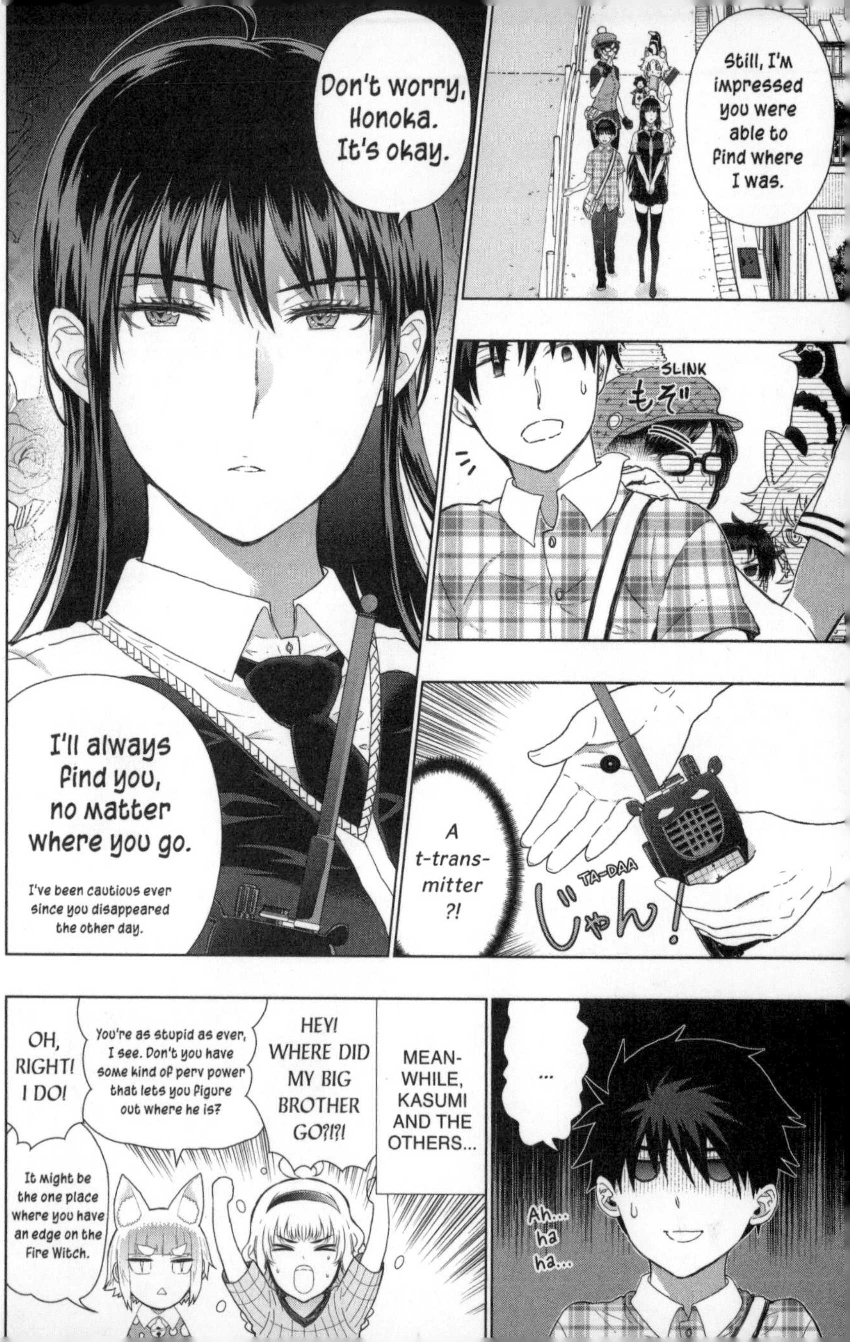
Still, I'm impressed you were able to find where I was.
SLINK
もぞ
A t-trans-mitter ?!
TA-DAA
じゃん!
Don't worry, Honoka. It's okay.
I'll always find you, no matter where you go.
I've been cautious ever since you disappeared the other day.
...
Ah... ha ha...
MEAN-WHILE, KASUMI AND THE OTHERS...
HEY! WHERE DID MY BIG BROTHER GO?!?!
You're as stupid as ever, I see. Don't you have some kind of perv power that lets you figure out where he is?
OH, RIGHT! I DO!
It might be the one place where you have an edge on the Fire Witch.

CHAPTER 48 END

Witchcraft Works

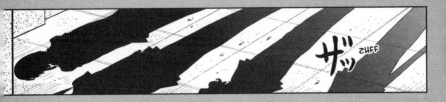

SHFF

The preparations are complete.

SHUMP

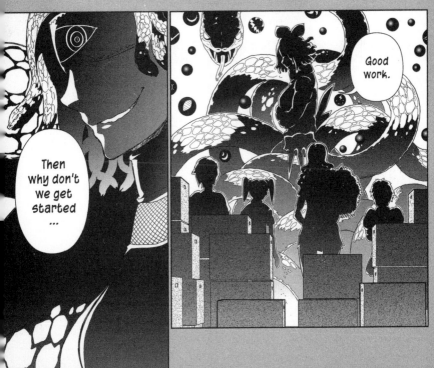

Good work.

Then why don't we get started ...

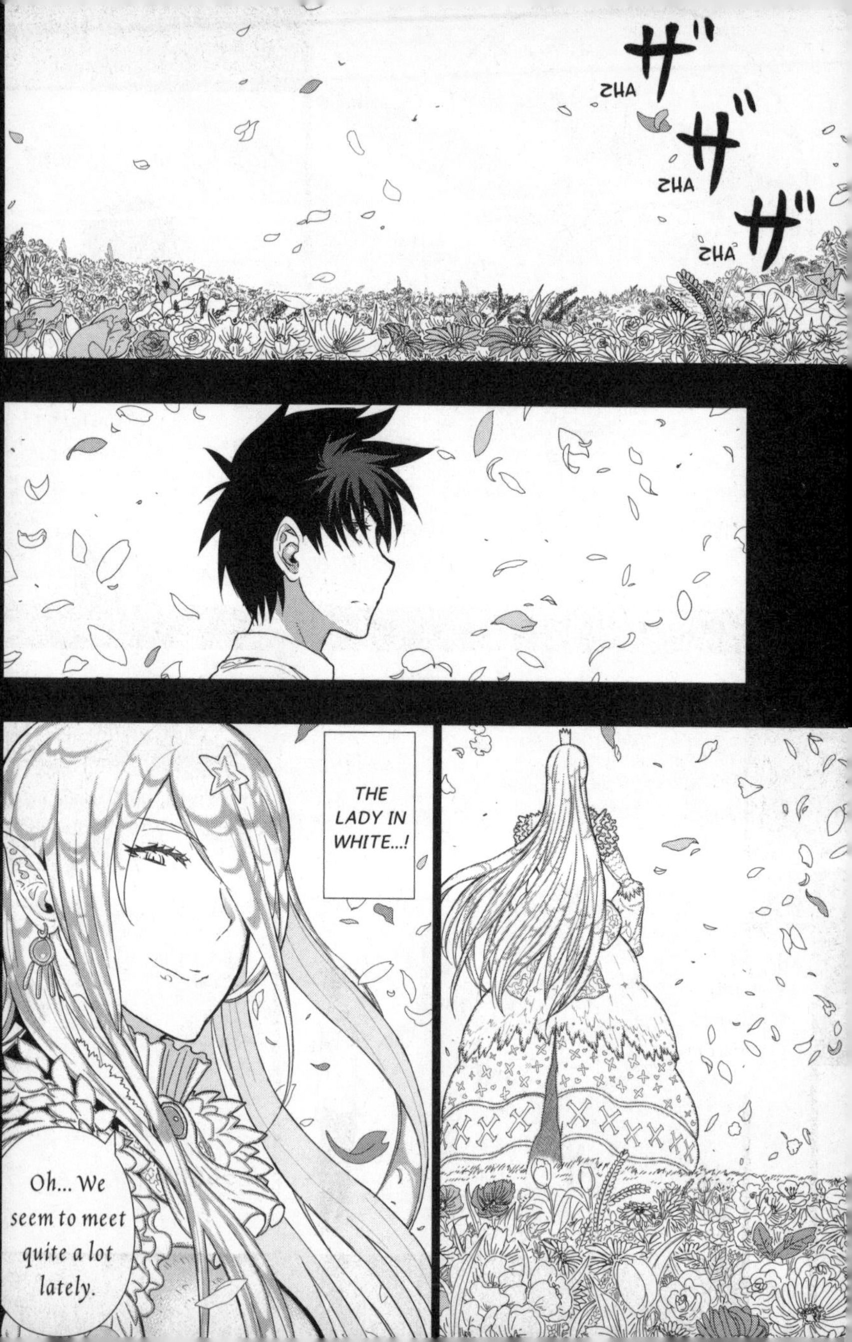
ZHA ザ
ZHA ザ
ZHA ザ
THE LADY IN WHITE...!
Oh... We seem to meet quite a lot lately.

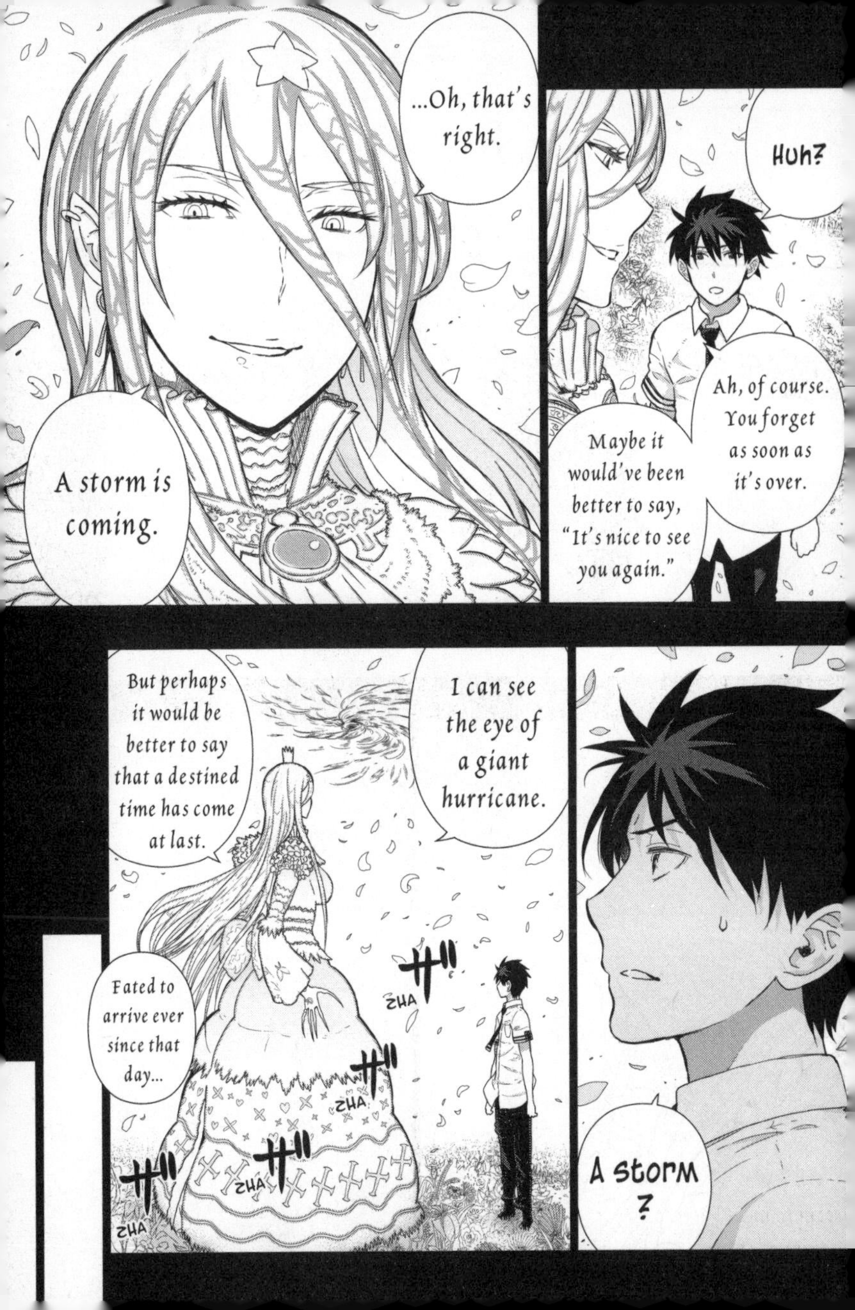
HUH?
Ah, of course. You forget as soon as it's over.
Maybe it would've been better to say, "It's nice to see you again."
...Oh, that's right.
A storm is coming.
A storm ?
I can see the eye of a giant hurricane.
But perhaps it would be better to say that a destined time has come at last.
Fated to arrive ever since that day...
ZHA
ZHA
ZHA
ZHA

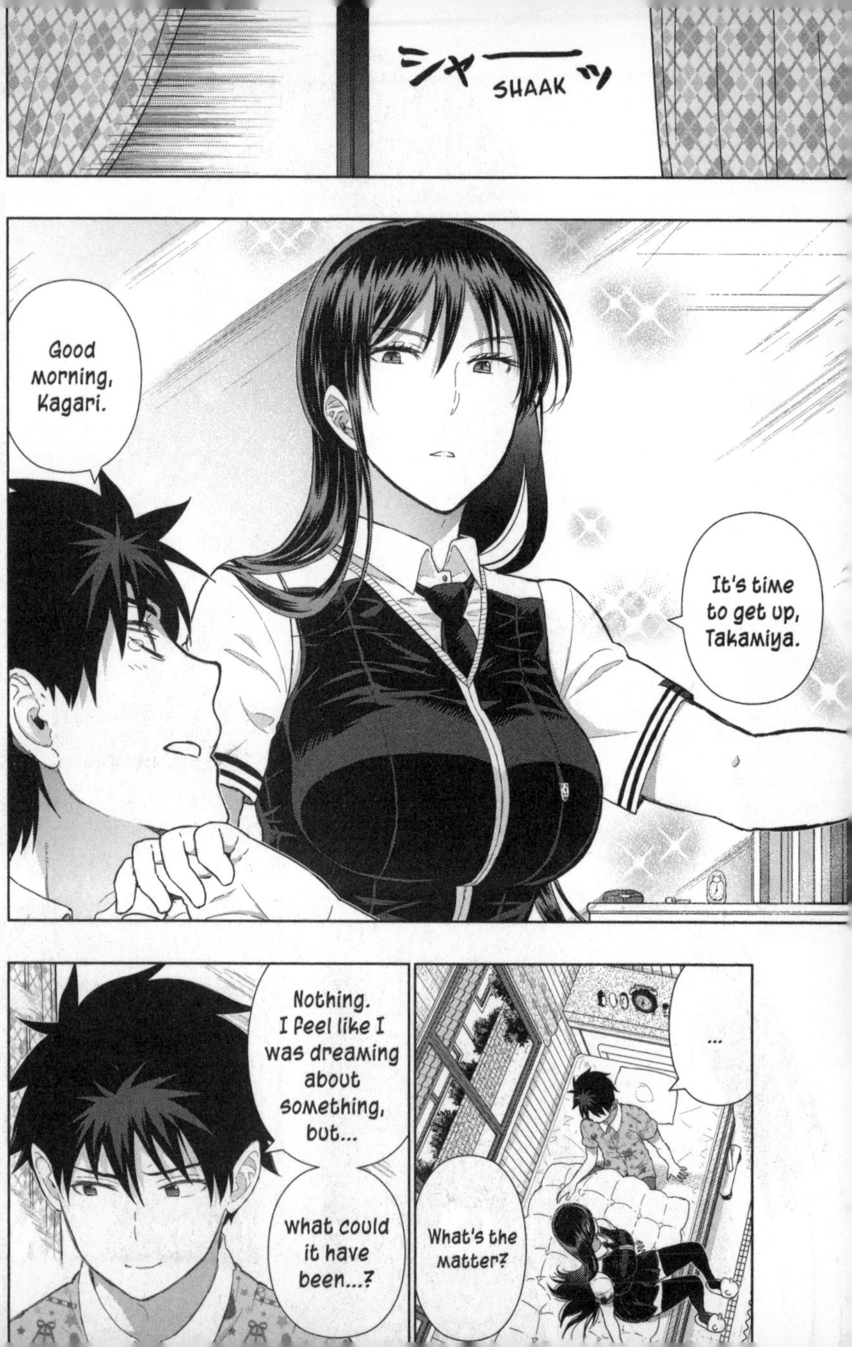
シャーーッ
SHAAK
It's time to get up, Takamiya.
Good morning, Kagari.
...
What's the matter?
Nothing. I feel like I was dreaming about something, but...
what could it have been...?

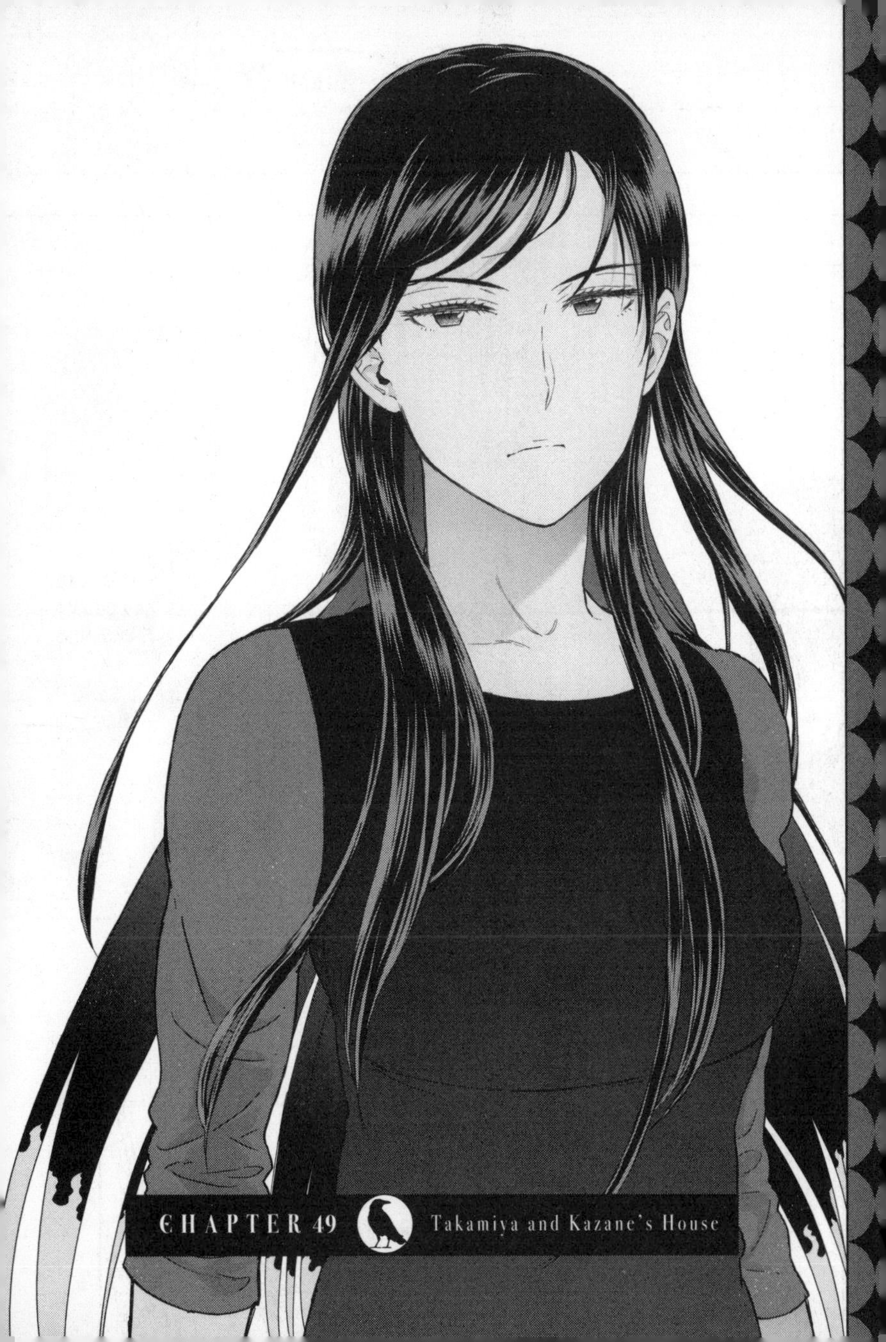

CHAPTER 49 Takamiya and Kazane's House

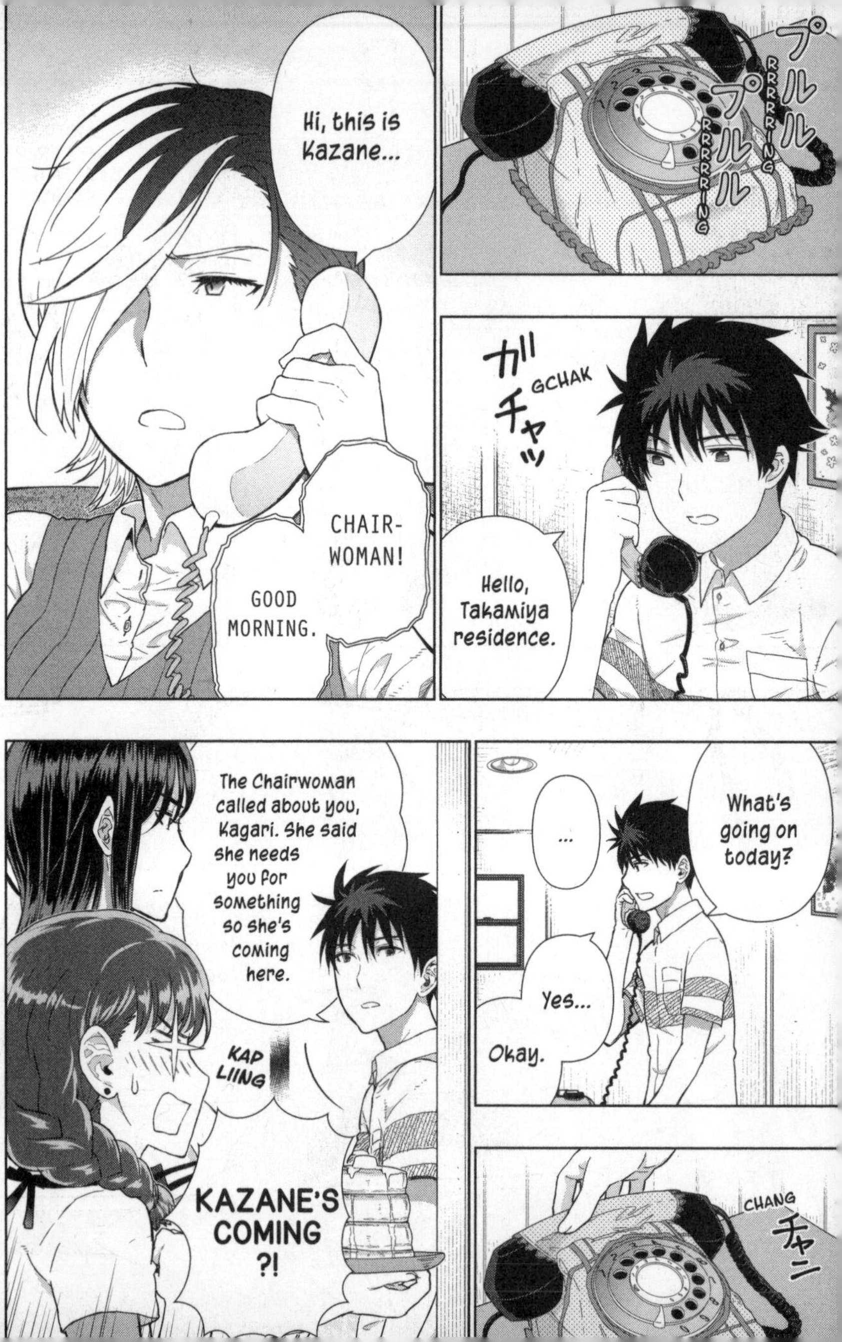
プルルプルル
RRRRRING RRRRRING
ガチャッ
GCHAK
Hello, Takamiya residence.
Hi, this is Kazane...
CHAIR-WOMAN! GOOD MORNING.
What's going on today?
...
Yes...
Okay.
チャン
CHANG
The Chairwoman called about you, Kagari. She said she needs you for something so she's coming here.
KAPLIING
KAZANE'S COMING ?!

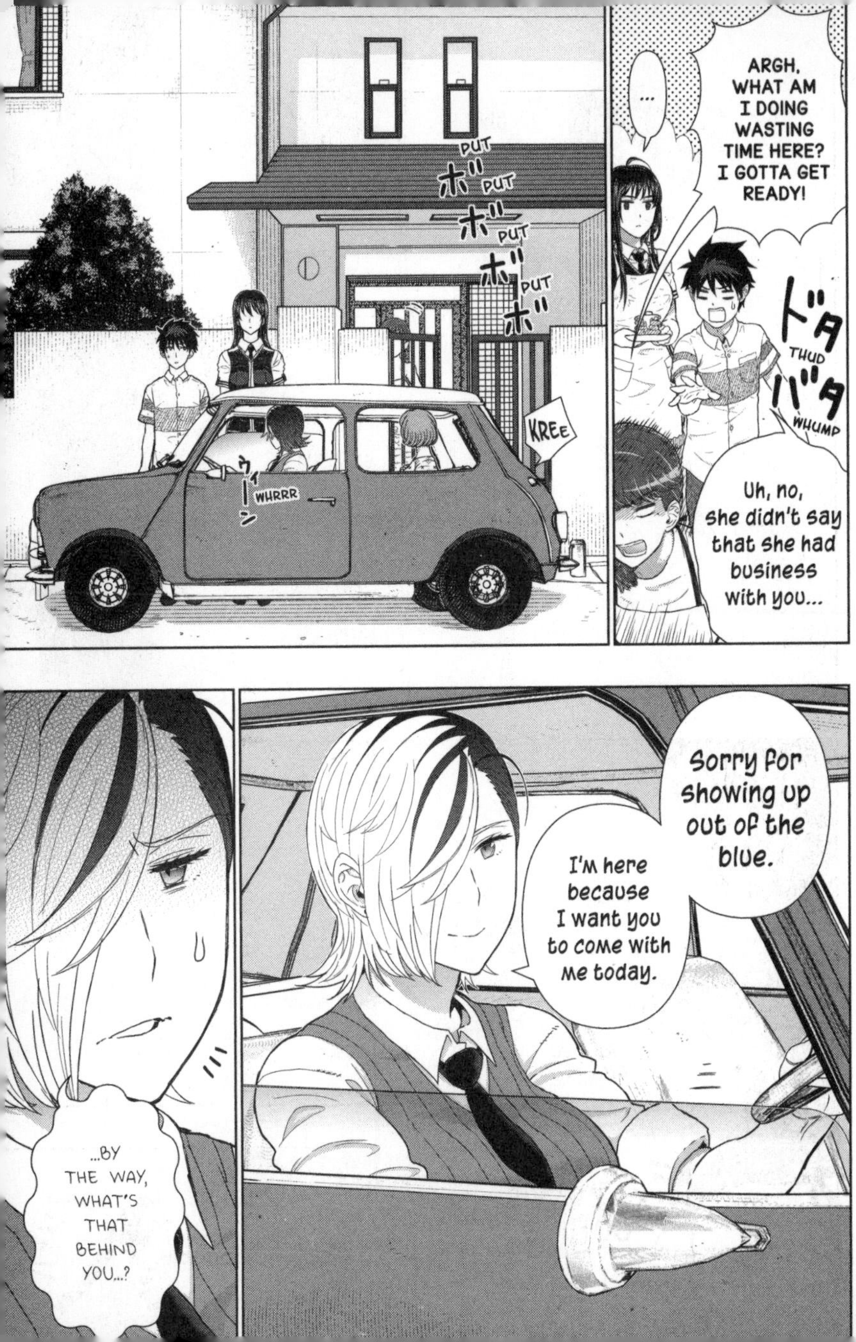
ARGH, WHAT AM I DOING WASTING TIME HERE? I GOTTA GET READY!
...
ドタ THUD
バタ WHUMP
Uh, no, she didn't say that she had business with you...
ボ PUT
ボ PUT
ボ PUT
ボ PUT
KREe
ウィーン WHURR
Sorry for showing up out of the blue.
I'm here because I want you to come with me today.
...BY THE WAY, WHAT'S THAT BEHIND YOU...?

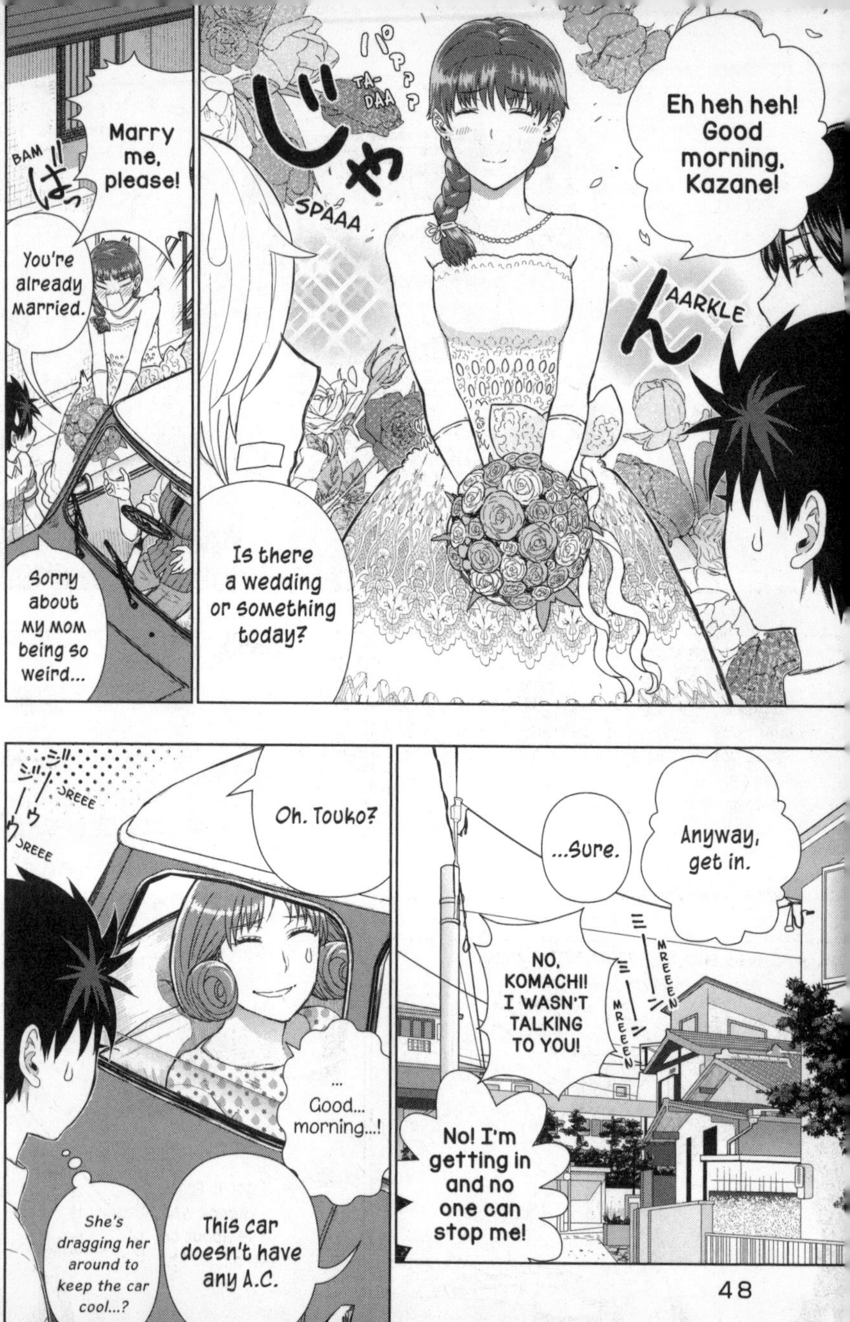

Eh heh heh! Good morning, Kazane!
TA-DAA
SPAAA
AARKLE
Is there a wedding or something today?
Marry me, please!
BAM
You're already married.
Sorry about my MOM being so weird...
Anyway, get in.
...Sure.
MREEEN
MREEEN
NO, KOMACHI! I WASN'T TALKING TO YOU!
No! I'm getting in and no one can stop me!
Oh. Touko?
JREEE
JREEE
... Good... morning...!
This car doesn't have any A.C.
She's dragging her around to keep the car cool...?

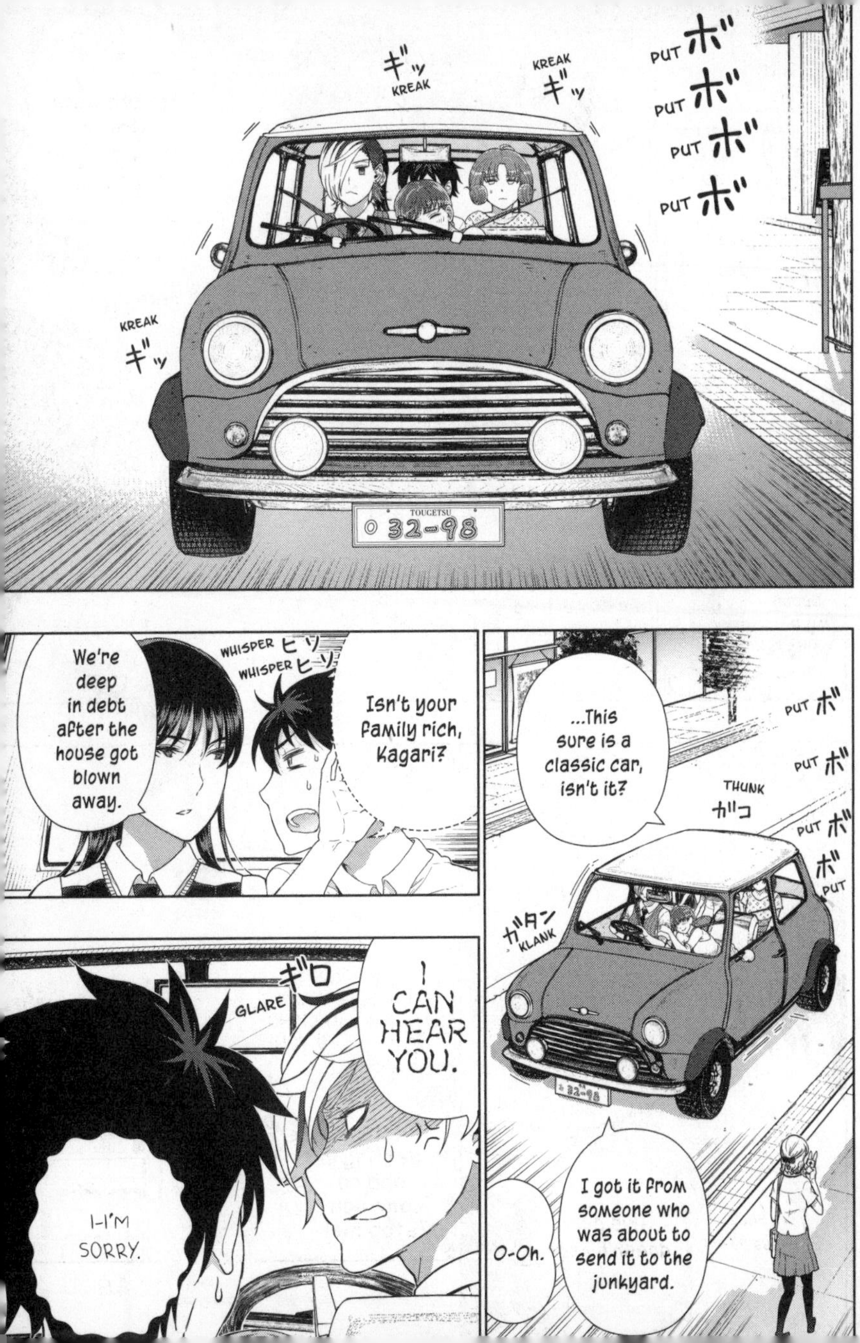
PUT ボ
PUT ボ
PUT ボ
PUT ボ
KREAK ギッ
ギッ KREAK
KREAK ギッ
PUT ボ
PUT ボ
PUT ボ
ボ PUT
...This sure is a classic car, isn't it?
THUNK ガコ
ガタン KLANK
I got it from someone who was about to send it to the junkyard.
O-Oh.
WHISPER ヒソ
WHISPER ヒソ
Isn't your family rich, Kagari?
We're deep in debt after the house got blown away.
ギロ GLARE
I CAN HEAR YOU.
I-I'M SORRY.

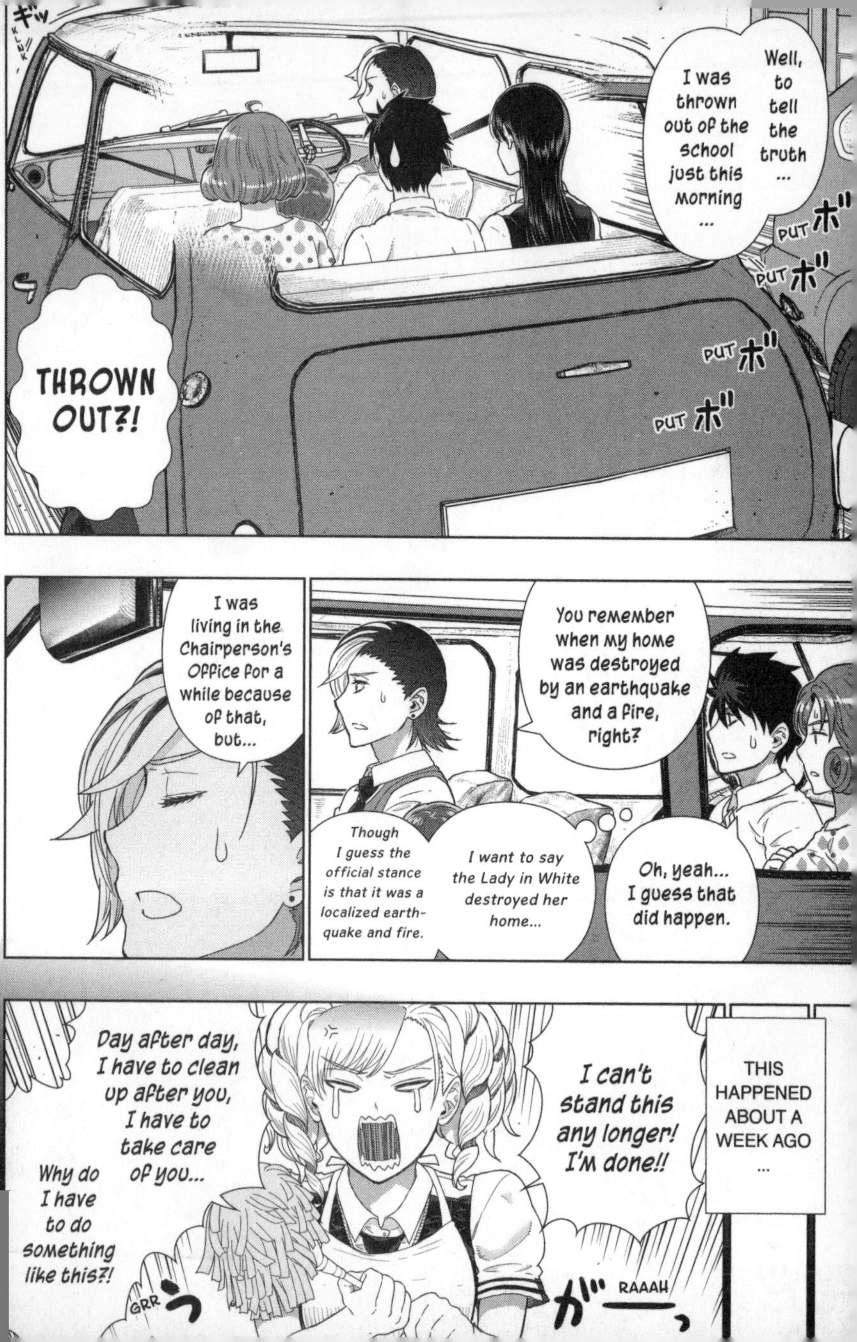
ギッ KLNK
Well, to tell the truth ...
I was thrown out of the school just this morning ...
PUT ボ
PUT ボ
PUT ボ
PUT ボ
THROWN OUT?!
You remember when my home was destroyed by an earthquake and a fire, right?
Oh, yeah... I guess that did happen.
I want to say the Lady in White destroyed her home...
Though I guess the official stance is that it was a localized earth-quake and fire.
I was living in the Chairperson's Office for a while because of that, but...
THIS HAPPENED ABOUT A WEEK AGO ...
I can't stand this any longer! I'm done!!
Day after day, I have to clean up after you, I have to take care of you...
Why do I have to do something like this?!
RAAAH が—
GRR う

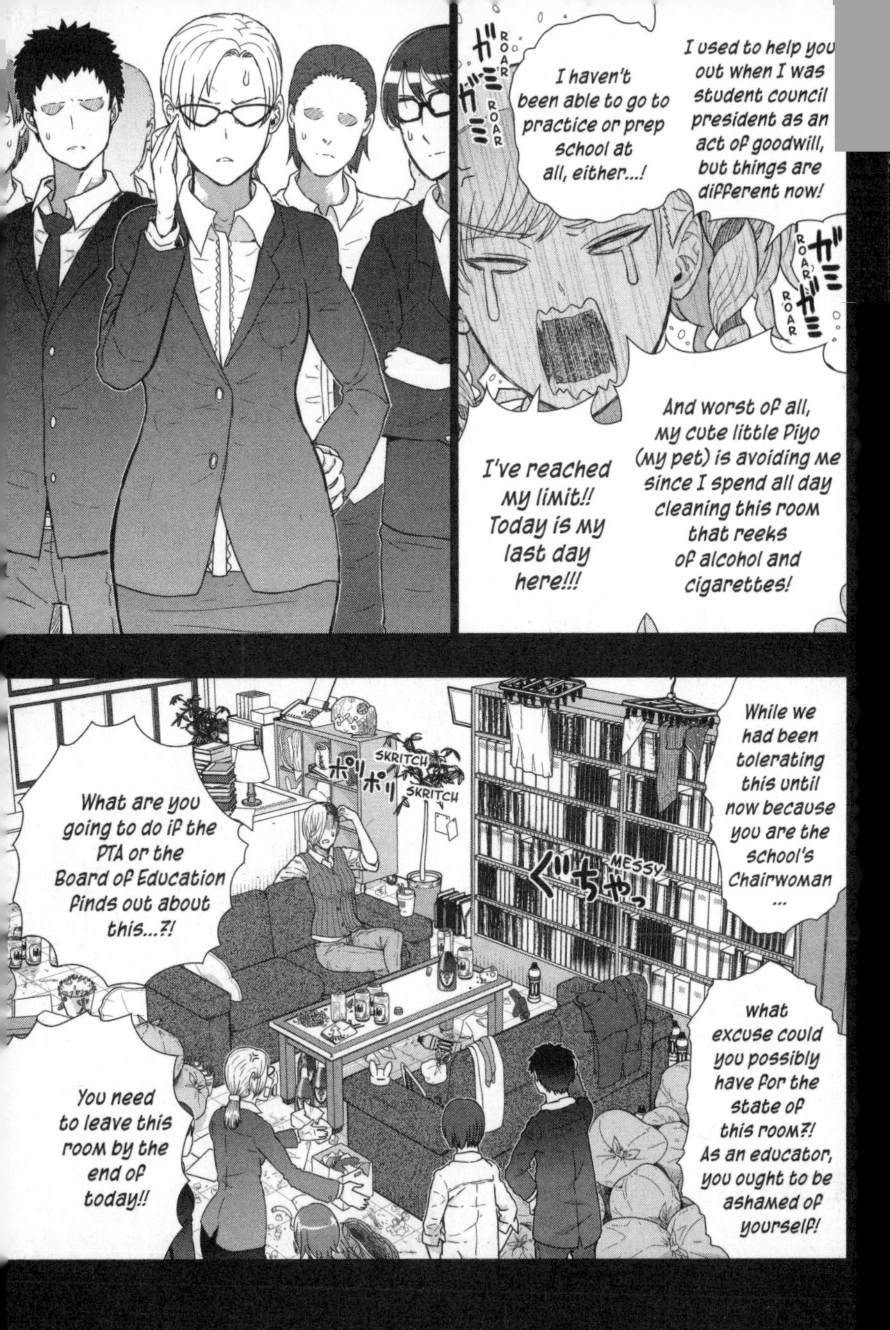
ROAR ガミ ROAR ガミ
I used to help you out when I was student council president as an act of goodwill, but things are different now!
ROAR ガミ ROAR ガミ ROAR
I haven't been able to go to practice or prep school at all, either...!
And worst of all, my cute little Piyo (my pet) is avoiding me since I spend all day cleaning this room that reeks of alcohol and cigarettes!
I've reached my limit!! Today is my last day here!!!
While we had been tolerating this until now because you are the school's Chairwoman ...
ポリポリ SKRITCH SKRITCH
ぐちゃっ MESSY
What are you going to do if the PTA or the Board of Education finds out about this...?!
what excuse could you possibly have for the state of this room?! As an educator, you ought to be ashamed of yourself!
You need to leave this room by the end of today!!

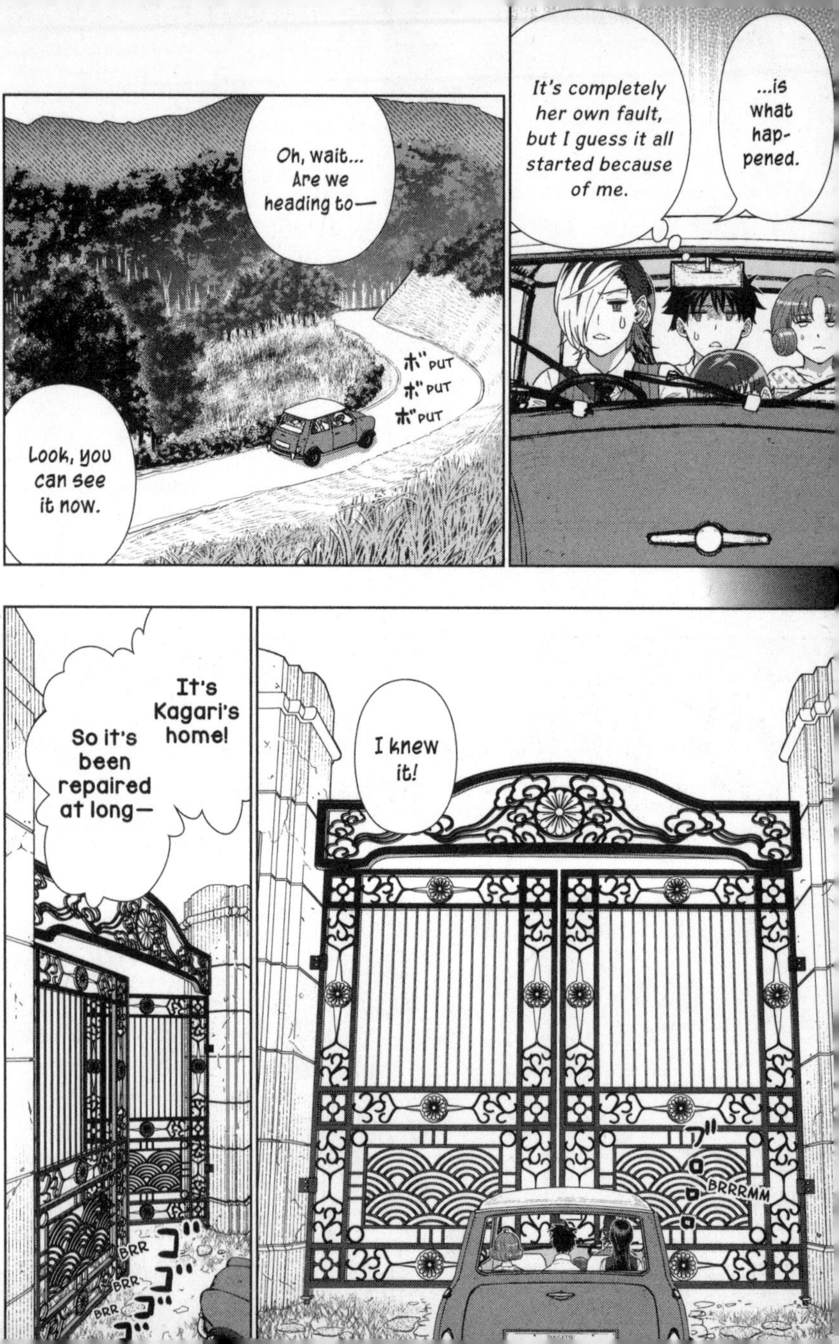
...is what hap-pened.
It's completely her own fault, but I guess it all started because of me.
Oh, wait... Are we heading to—
ボ PUT
ボ PUT
ボ PUT
Look, you can see it now.
I knew it!
ブロロロ BRRRMM
It's Kagari's home!
So it's been repaired at long—
ゴゴゴゴ BRR BRR BRR

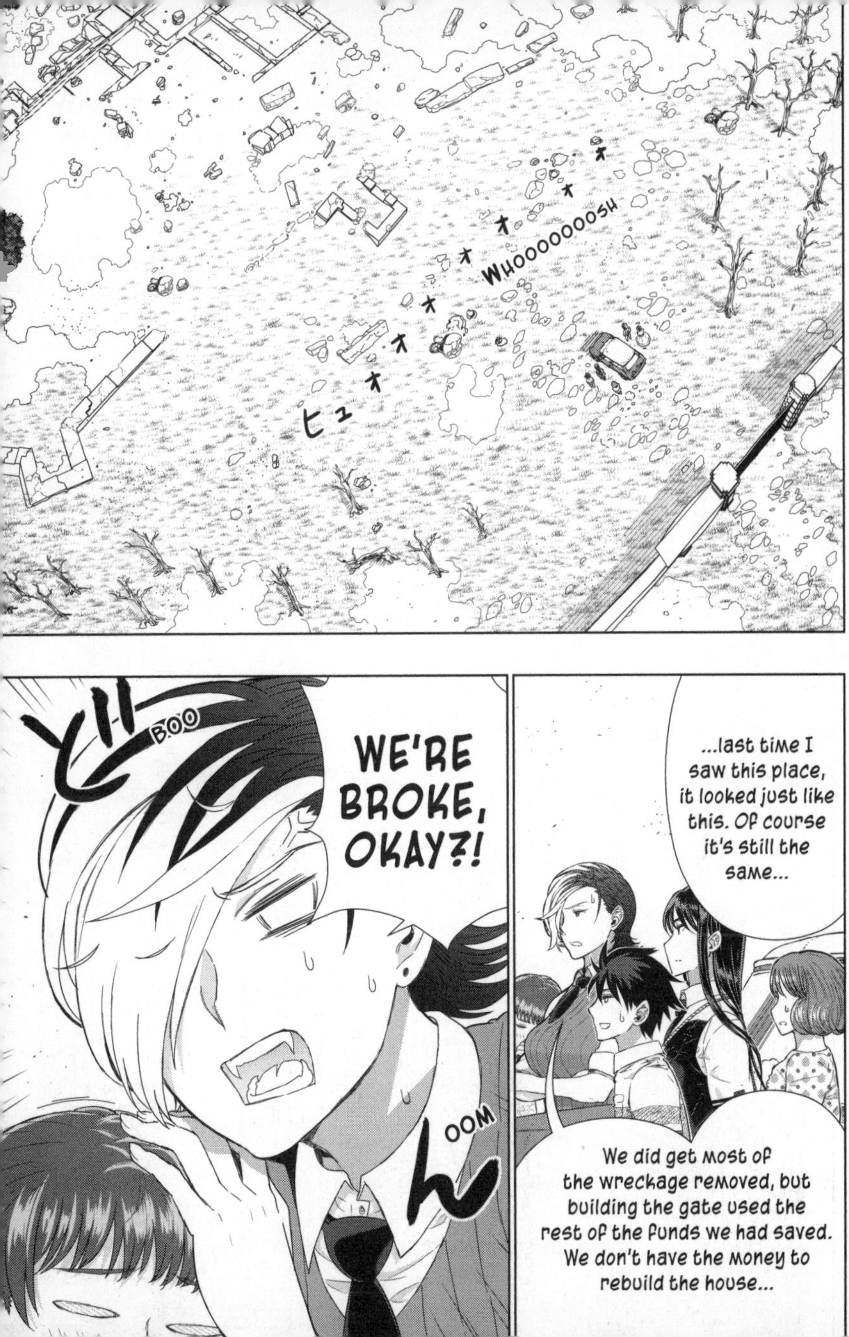
ヒュオオオオオオ
WHOOOOOOOOSH
...last time I saw this place, it looked just like this. Of course it's still the same...
We did get most of the wreckage removed, but building the gate used the rest of the funds we had saved. We don't have the money to rebuild the house...
ど!!
BOO
WE'RE BROKE, OKAY?!
ん
OOM

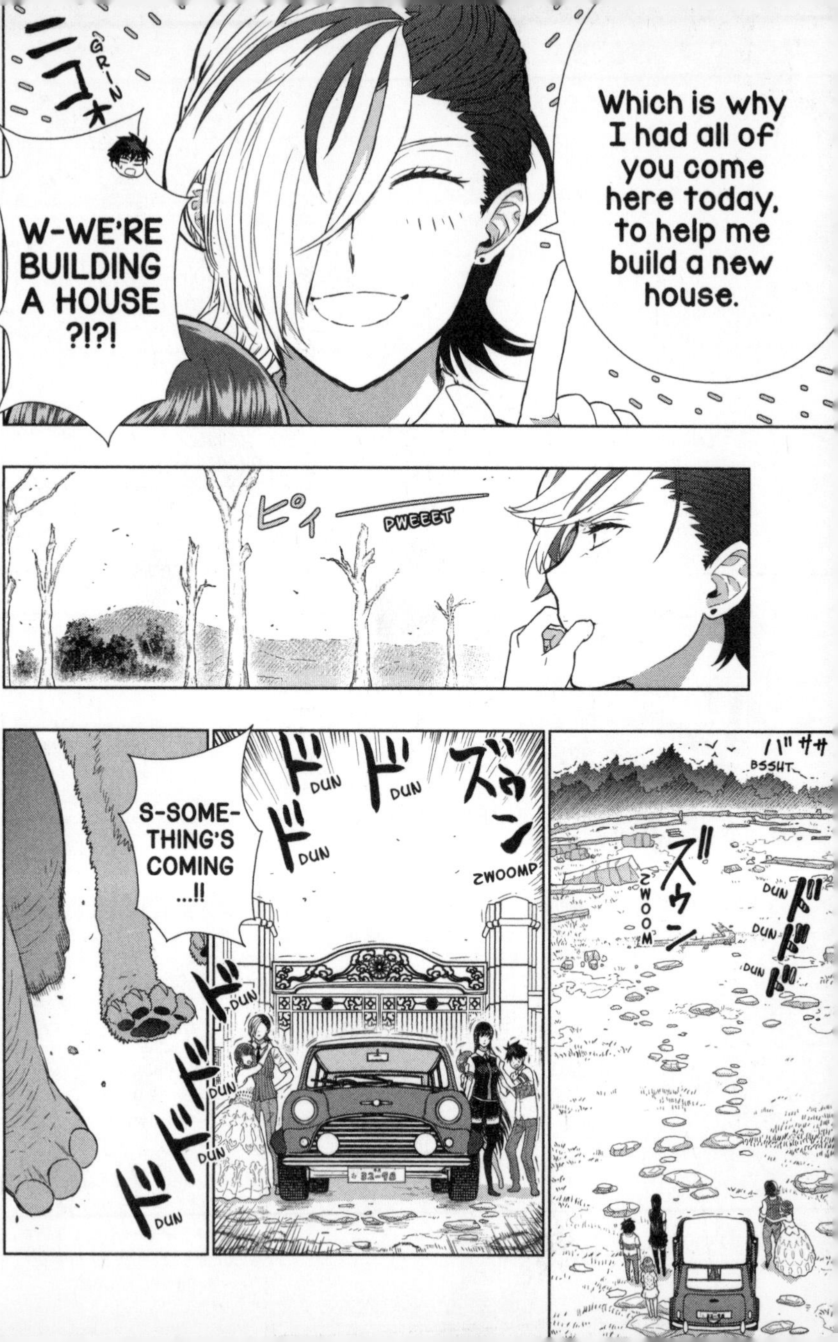
Which is why I had all of you come here today, to help me build a new house.
ニコ
GRIN
W-WE'RE BUILDING A HOUSE ?!?!
ピィ
PWEEET
バサ
BSSHT
ズゥン
ZWOOOM
ドドド
DUN
DUN
DUN
ドドドズゥン
DUN
DUN
DUN
ZWOOMP
S-SOME-THING'S COMING ...!!
ドドドド
DUN
DUN
DUN
DUN

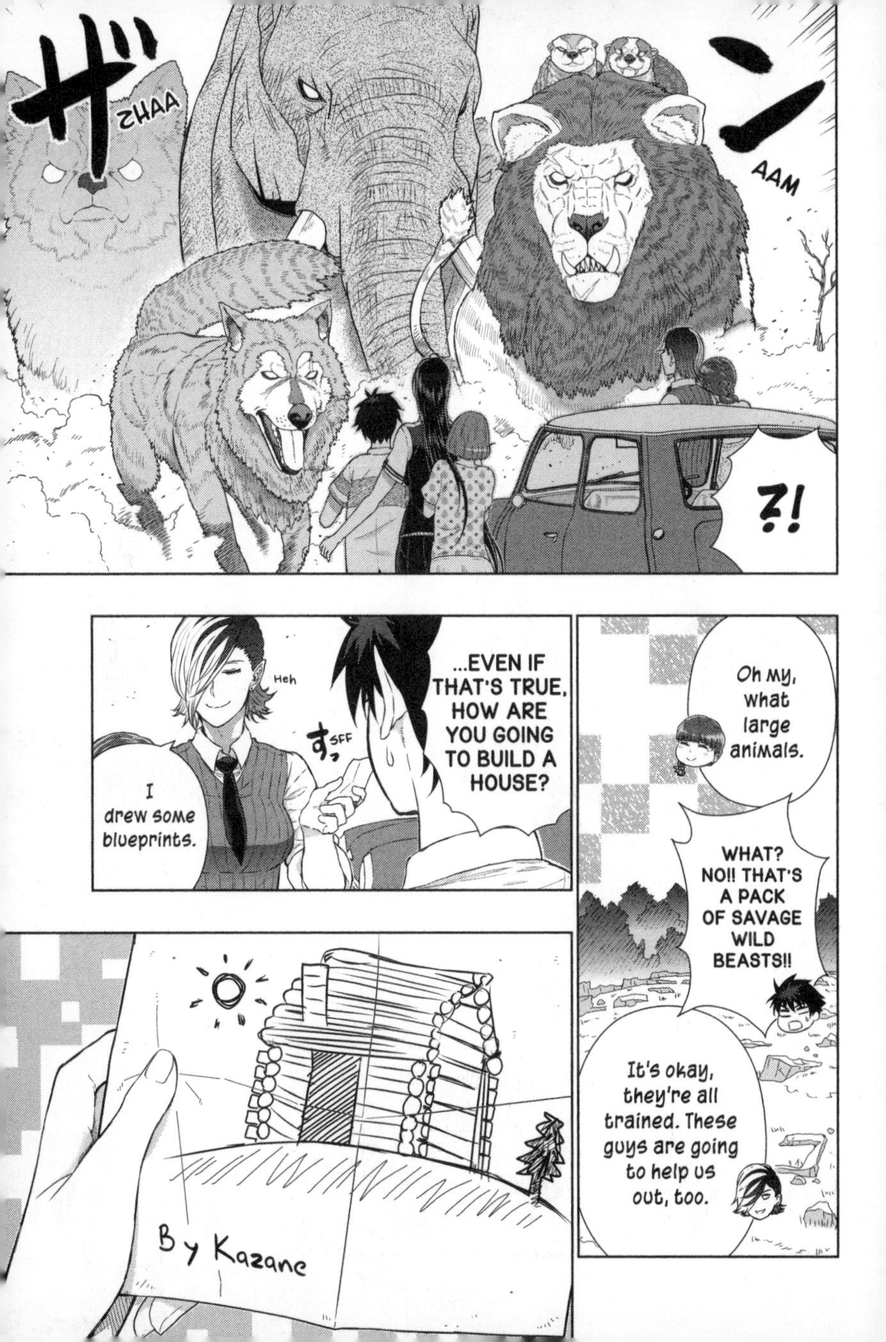
ザ ZHAA
ン AAM
?!
Oh my, what large animals.
WHAT? NO!! THAT'S A PACK OF SAVAGE WILD BEASTS!!
It's okay, they're all trained. These guys are going to help us out, too.
...EVEN IF THAT'S TRUE, HOW ARE YOU GOING TO BUILD A HOUSE?
Heh
すっ SFF
I drew some blueprints.
By Kazane

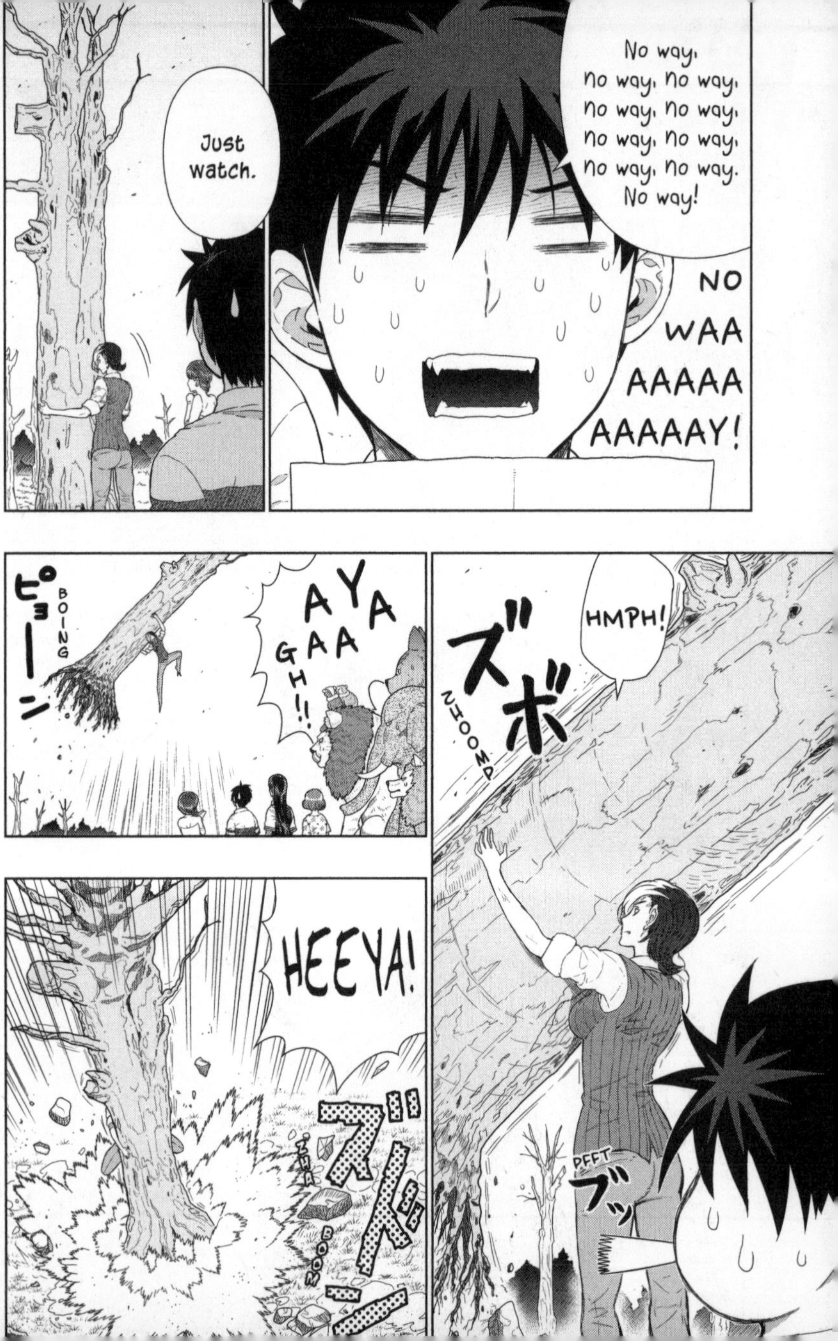
No way, no way, no way, no way, no way, no way, no way, no way, no way. No way!
NO WAAAAAAAAAAAY!
Just watch.
HMPH!
ズボ
ZHOOMP
ブッ
PFFT
AYAGAAAGH!!
ピョーン
BOING
HEEYA!
ズドーン
ZHA
BOOM

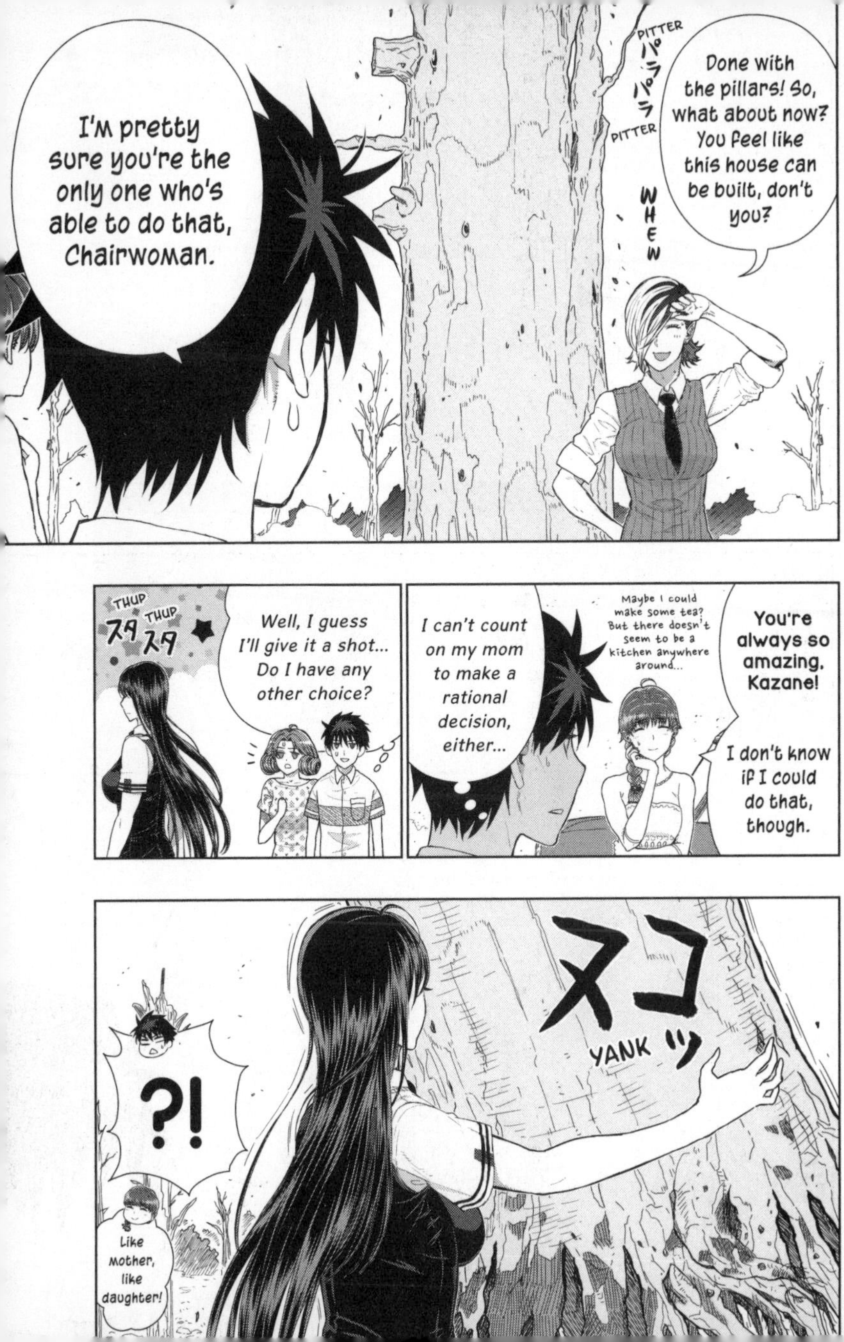

PITTER
パラパラ
PITTER
Done with the pillars! So, what about now? You feel like this house can be built, don't you?
WHEW
I'm pretty sure you're the only one who's able to do that, Chairwoman.
You're always so amazing. Kazane!
Maybe I could make some tea? But there doesn't seem to be a kitchen anywhere around...
I don't know if I could do that, though.
I can't count on my mom to make a rational decision, either...
Well, I guess I'll give it a shot... Do I have any other choice?
THUP
スタスタ
THUP
ヌコッ
YANK
?!
Like Mother, like daughter!

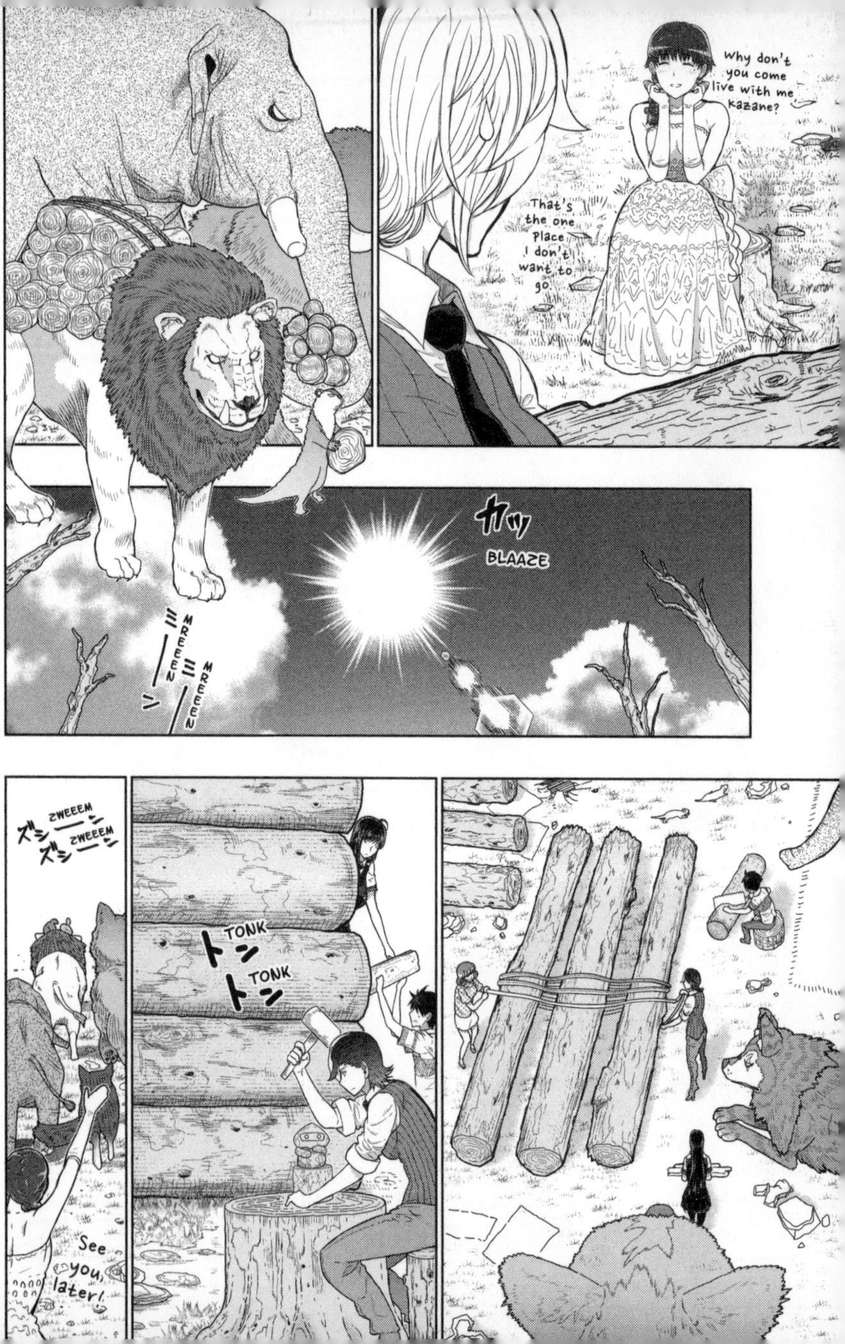
Why don't you come live with me, kazane?
That's the one place I don't want to go.
カッ
BLAAZE
ミーン
MREEEN
ミーン
MREEEN
トン
TONK
トン
TONK
ズシーン
ZWEEEM
ズシーン
ZWEEEM
See you, later!

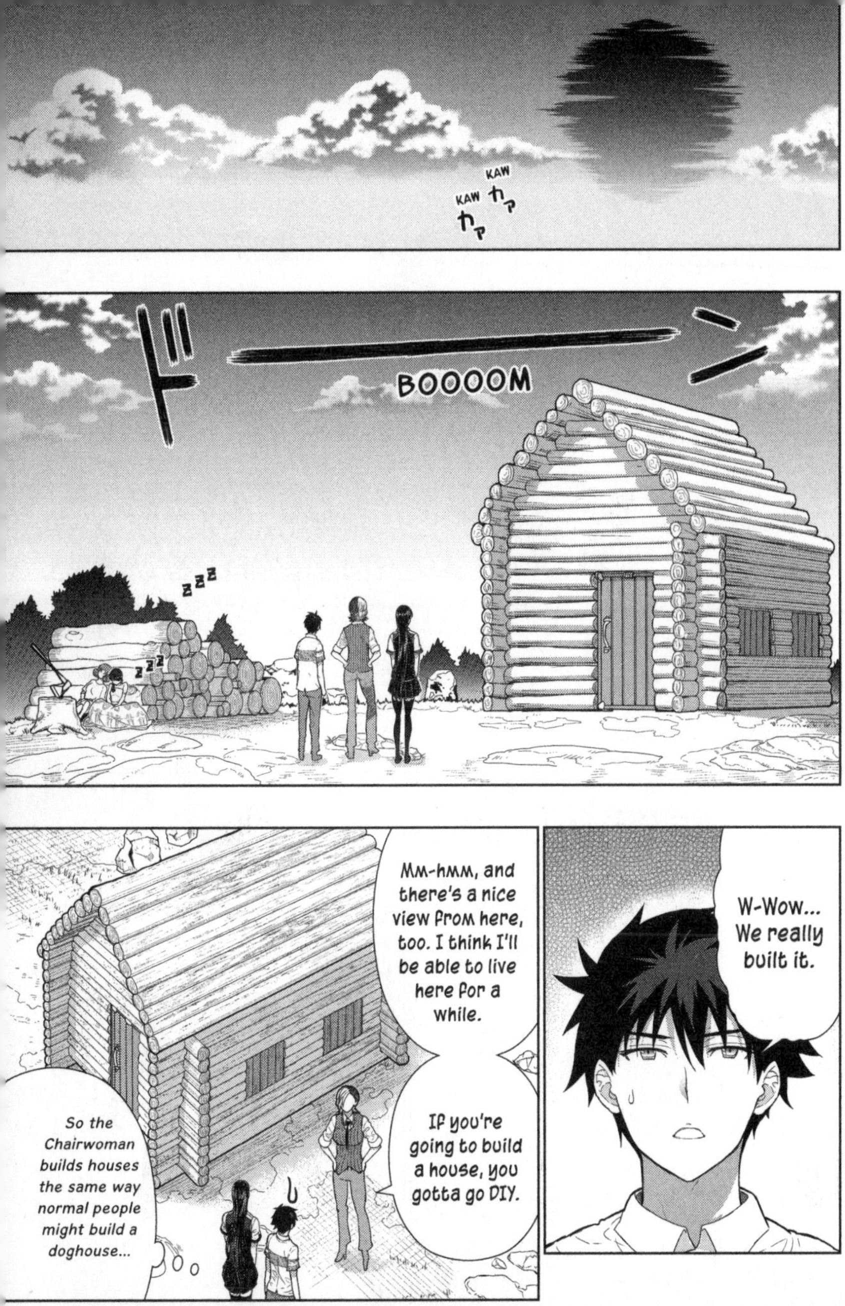
KAW
KAW
BOOOOM
W-Wow... We really built it.
Mm-hmm, and there's a nice view from here, too. I think I'll be able to live here for a while.
If you're going to build a house, you gotta go DIY.
So the Chairwoman builds houses the same way normal people might build a doghouse...

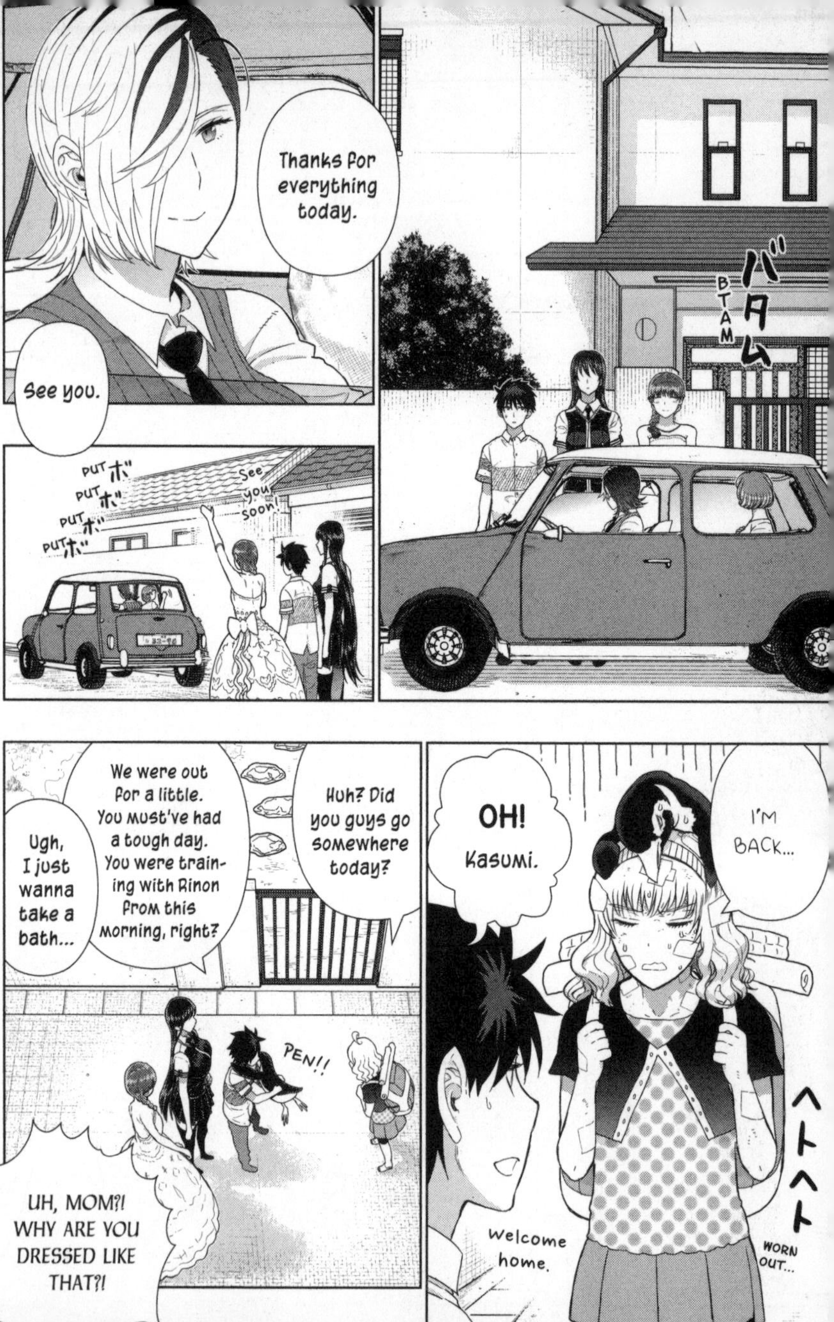
バタム
BTAM
Thanks for everything today.
See you.
See you soon!
PUT ボ
PUT ボ
PUT ボ
PUT ボ
I'M BACK...
OH! Kasumi.
ヘトヘト
WORN OUT...
Welcome home.
Huh? Did you guys go somewhere today?
We were out for a little. You must've had a tough day. You were training with Rinon from this morning, right?
Ugh, I just wanna take a bath...
PEN!!
UH, MOM?! WHY ARE YOU DRESSED LIKE THAT?!

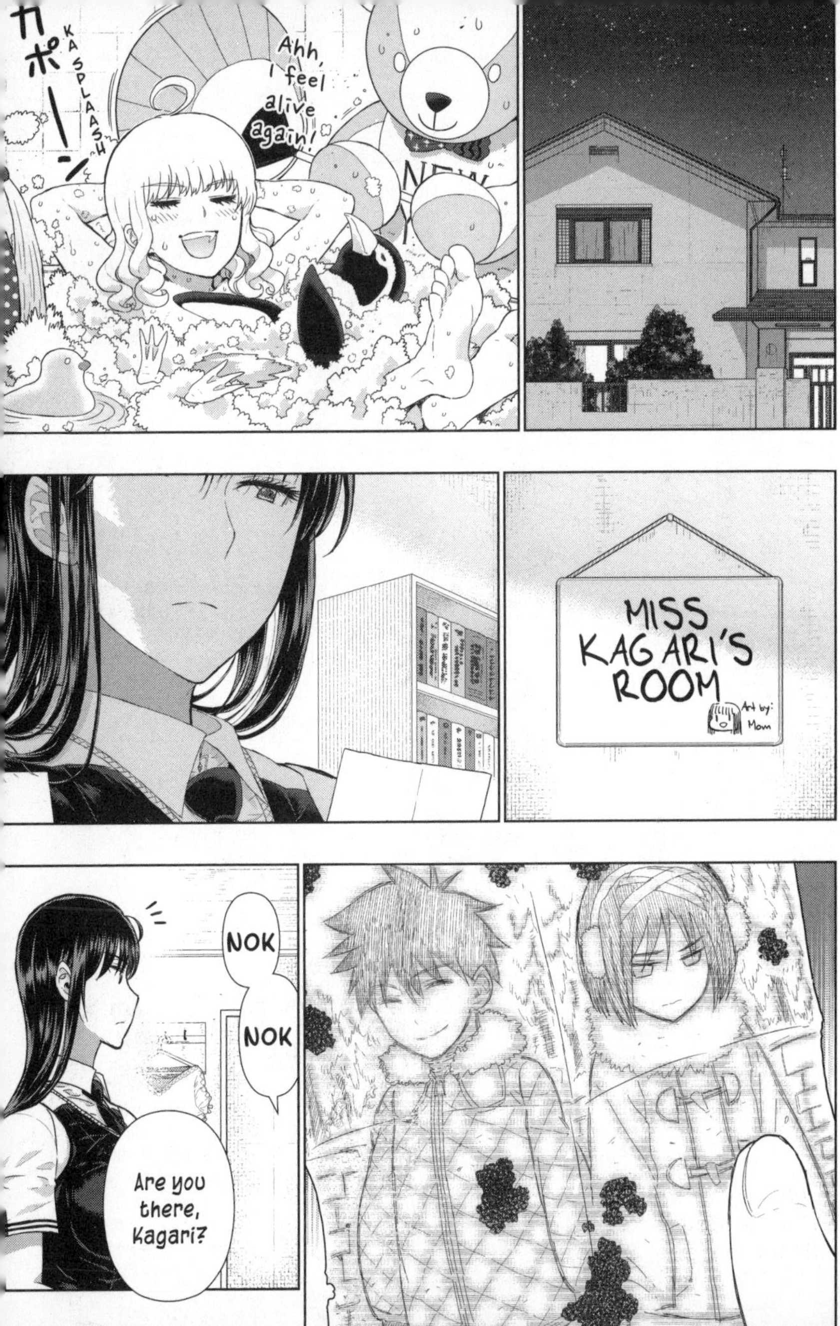
カポーン
KASPLAASH
Ahh, I feel alive again!
MISS KAGARI'S ROOM
Art by: Mom
NOK
NOK
Are you there, Kagari?

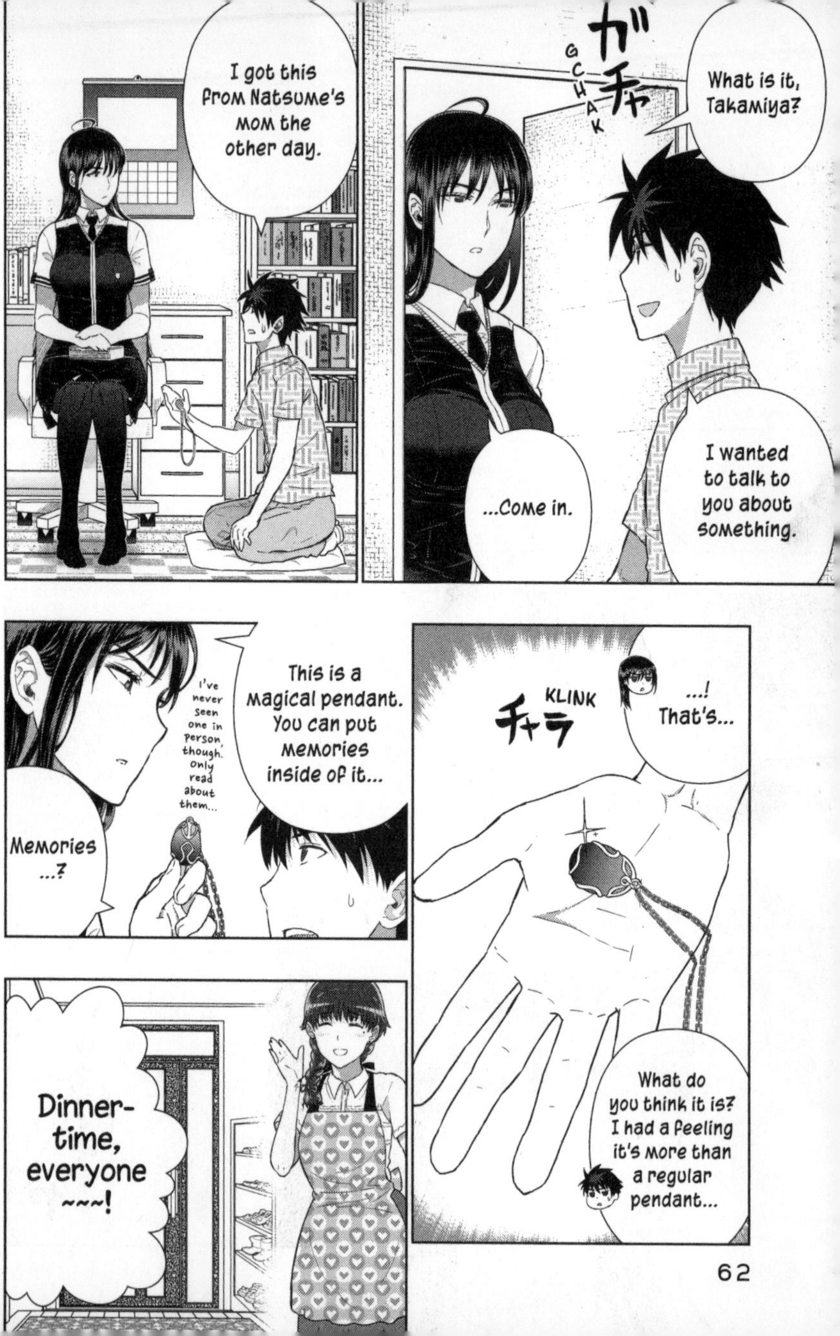
ガチャ
GCHAK
What is it, Takamiya?
I wanted to talk to you about something.
...Come in.
I got this from Natsume's mom the other day.
チャラ
KLINK
...! That's...
What do you think it is? I had a feeling it's more than a regular pendant...
This is a magical pendant. You can put memories inside of it...
I've never seen one in person, though. Only read about them...
Memories ...?
Dinner-time, everyone ~~~!

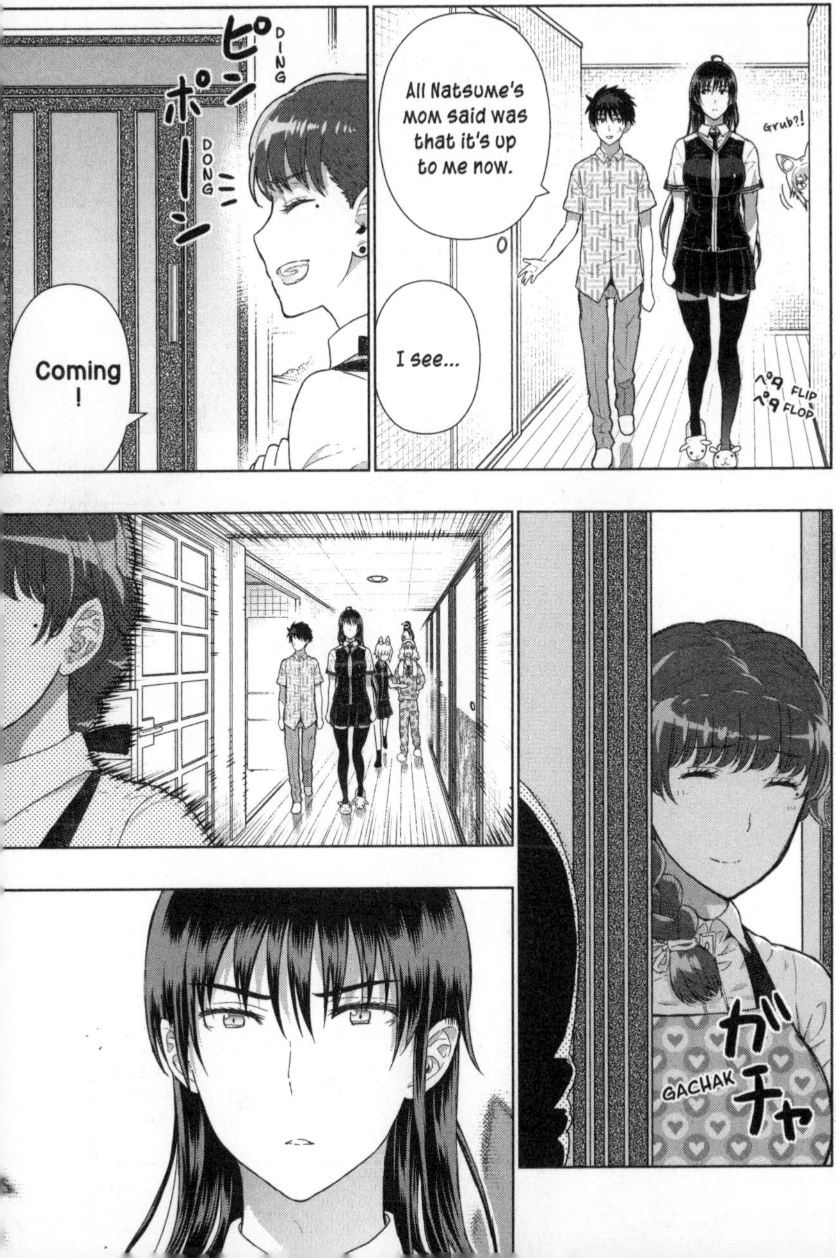
All Natsume's MOM said was that it's up to me now.
I see...
Grub?!
ペタ FLIP
ペタ FLOP
ピンポーン
DING DONG
Coming!
ガチャ
GACHAK

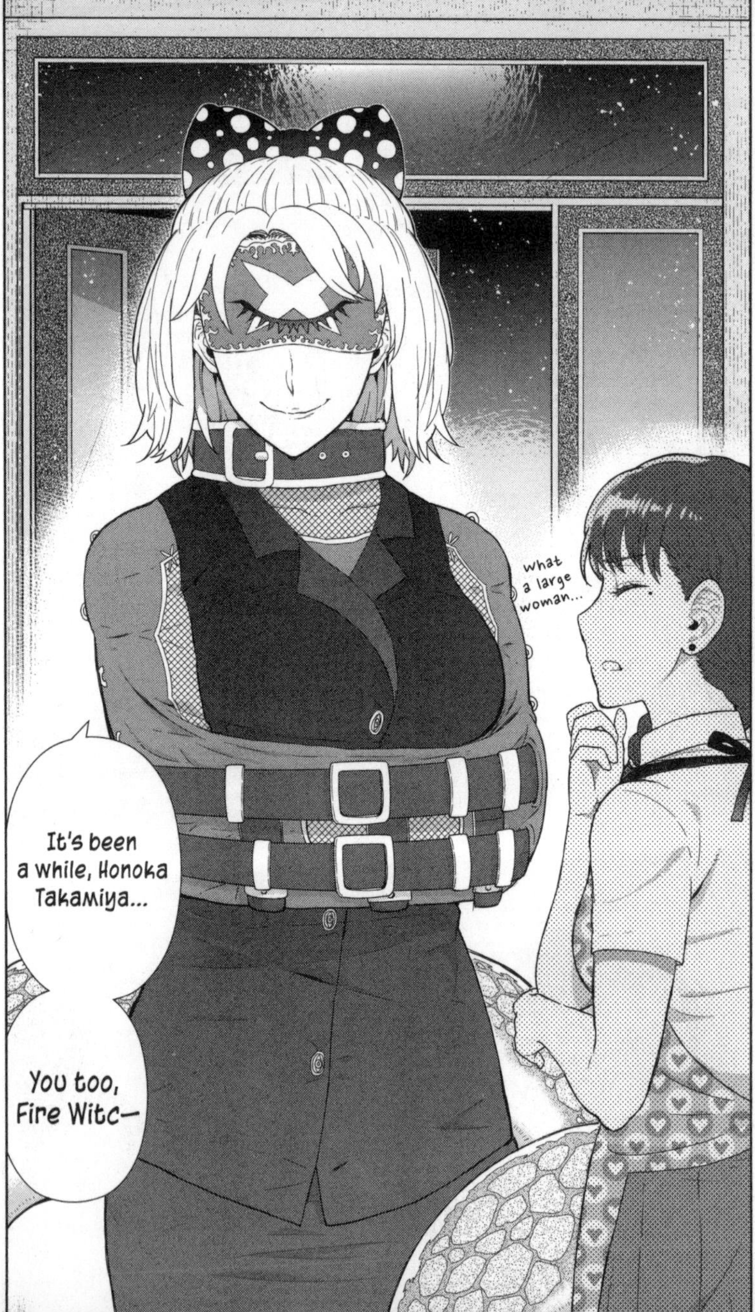
what a large woman...
It's been a while, Honoka Takamiya...
You too, Fire Witc—

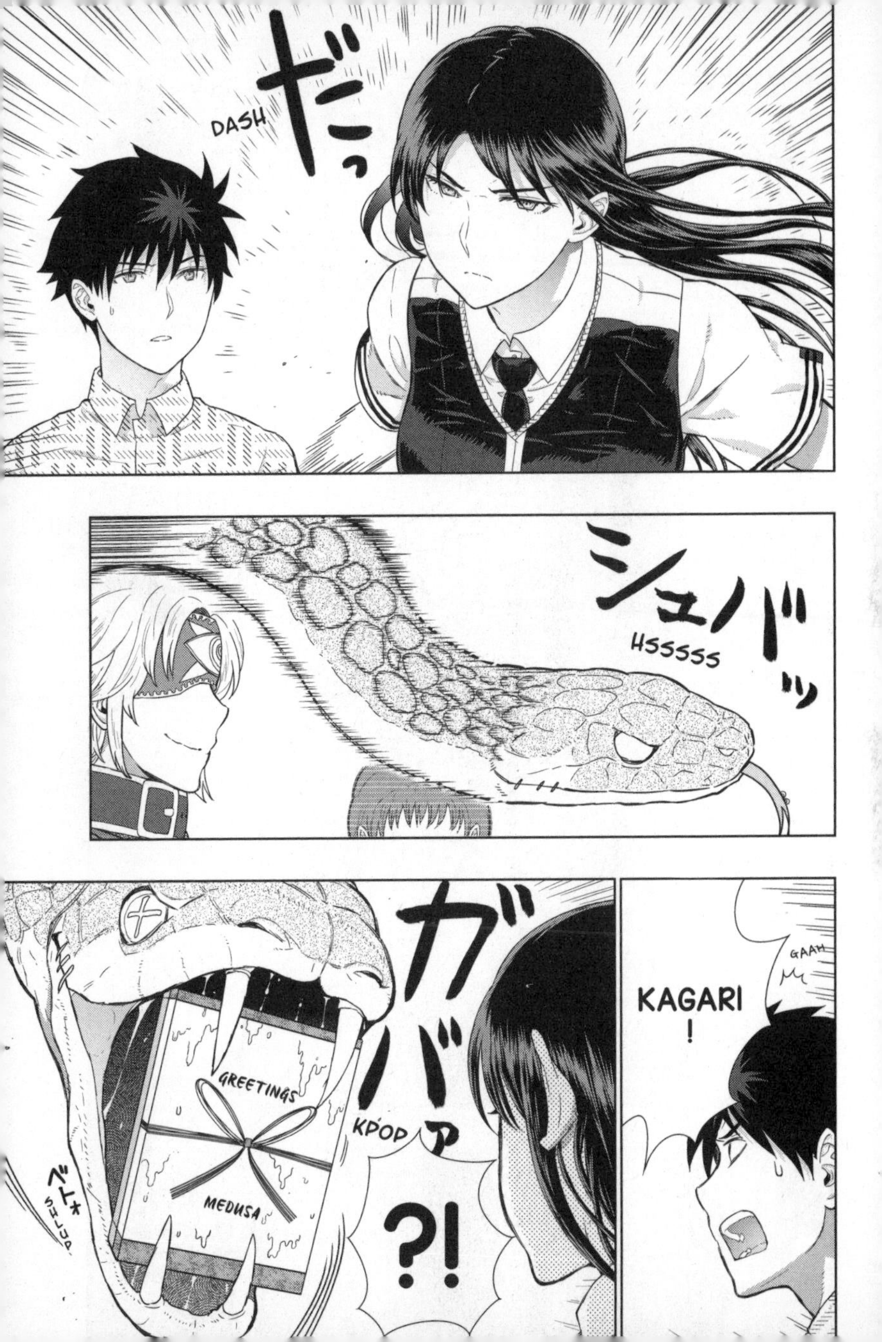
だっ
DASH
シュバッ
HSSSSS
GAAH
KAGARI!
ガバア
KPOP
?!
GREETINGS
MEDUSA
ベトォ
SHLUP

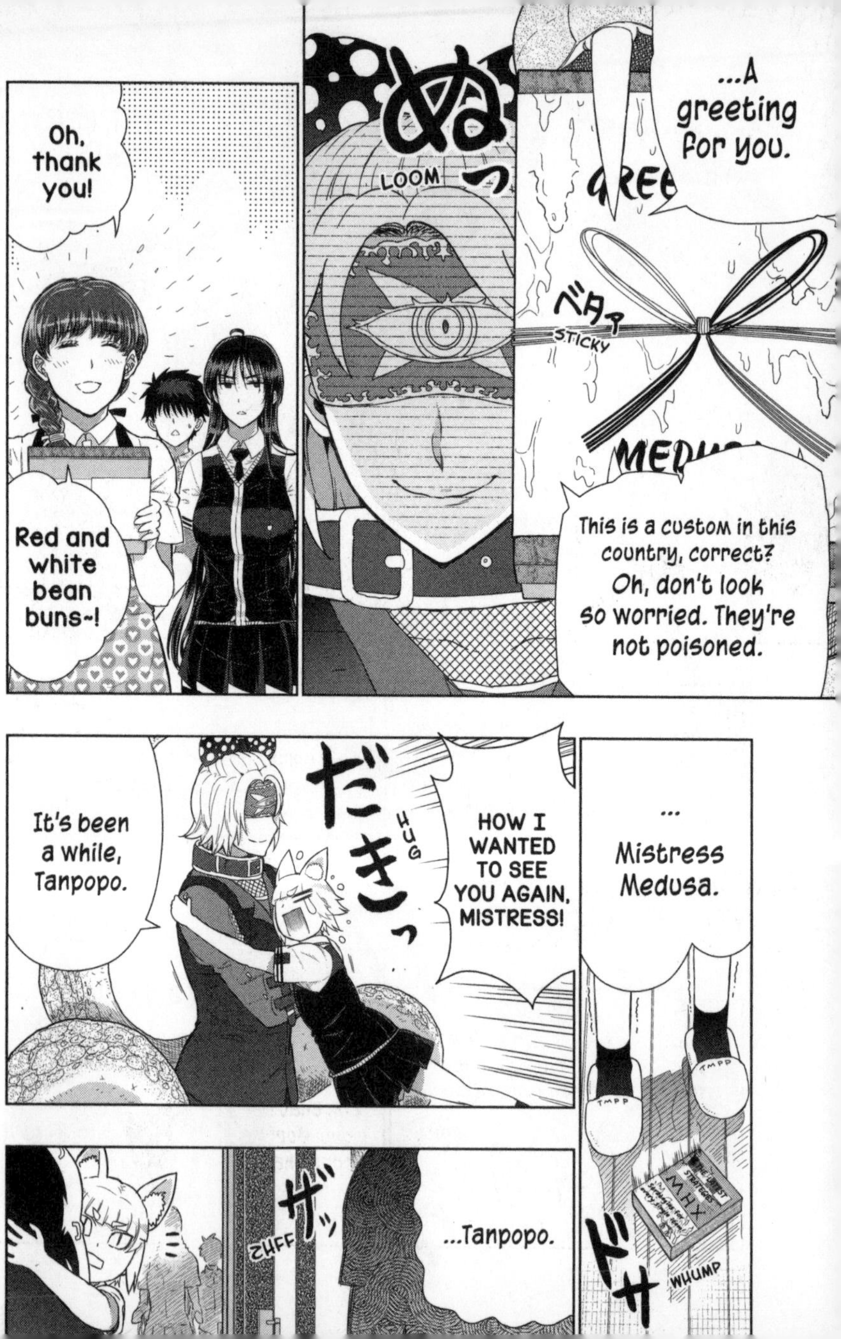
...A greeting for you.
GREE
ベタァ
STICKY
MEDU
This is a custom in this country, correct? Oh, don't look so worried. They're not poisoned.
ぬっ
LOOM
Oh, thank you!
Red and white bean buns~!
... Mistress Medusa.
TMPP
TMPP
HOW I WANTED TO SEE YOU AGAIN, MISTRESS!
だきっ
HUG
It's been a while, Tanpopo.
ドサ
WHUMP
...Tanpopo.
ザッ
ZHFF

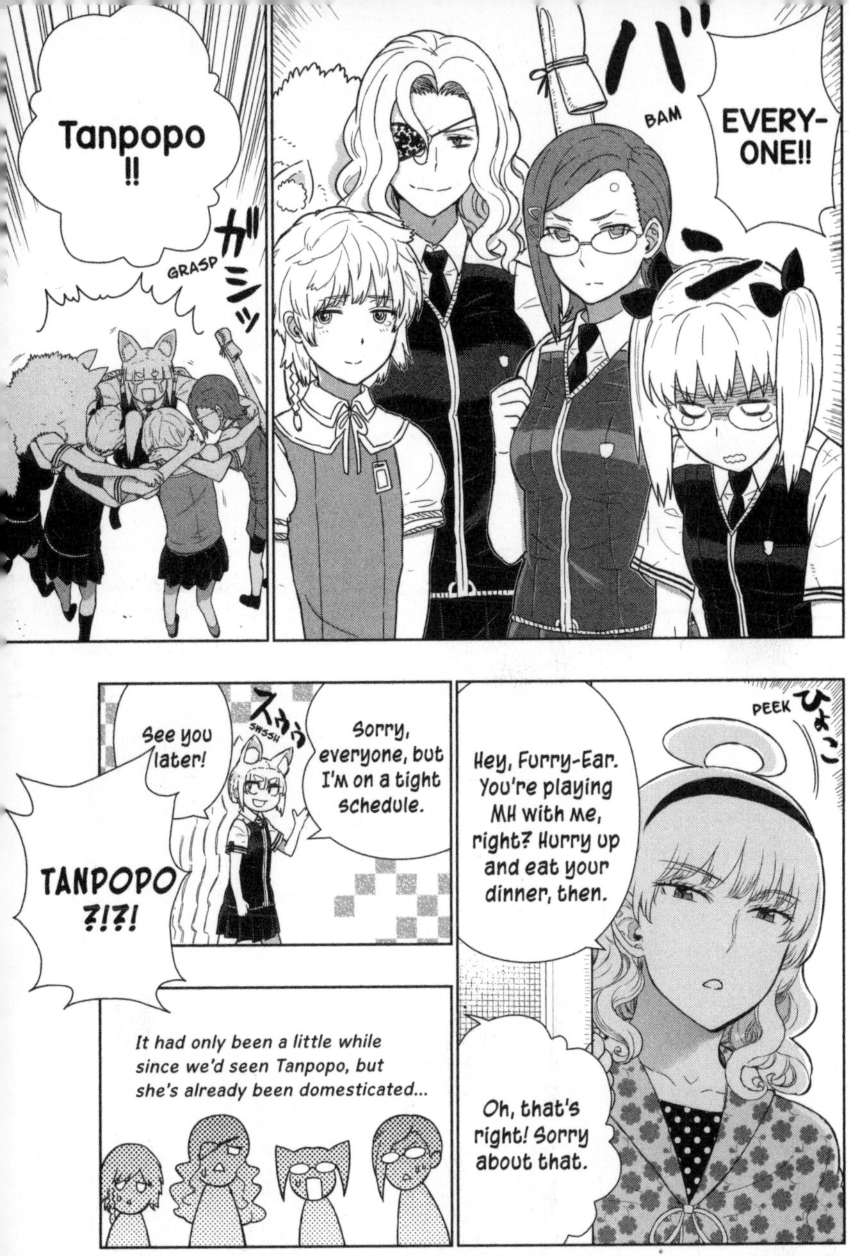
バ
BAM
EVERY-ONE!!
Tanpopo!!
ガシッ
GRASP
Hey, Furry-Ear. You're playing MH with me, right? Hurry up and eat your dinner, then.
ひょこ
PEEK
Oh, that's right! Sorry about that.
Sorry, everyone, but I'm on a tight schedule.
スゥゥ
SWSSH
See you later!
TANPOPO?!?!
It had only been a little while since we'd seen Tanpopo, but she's already been domesticated...

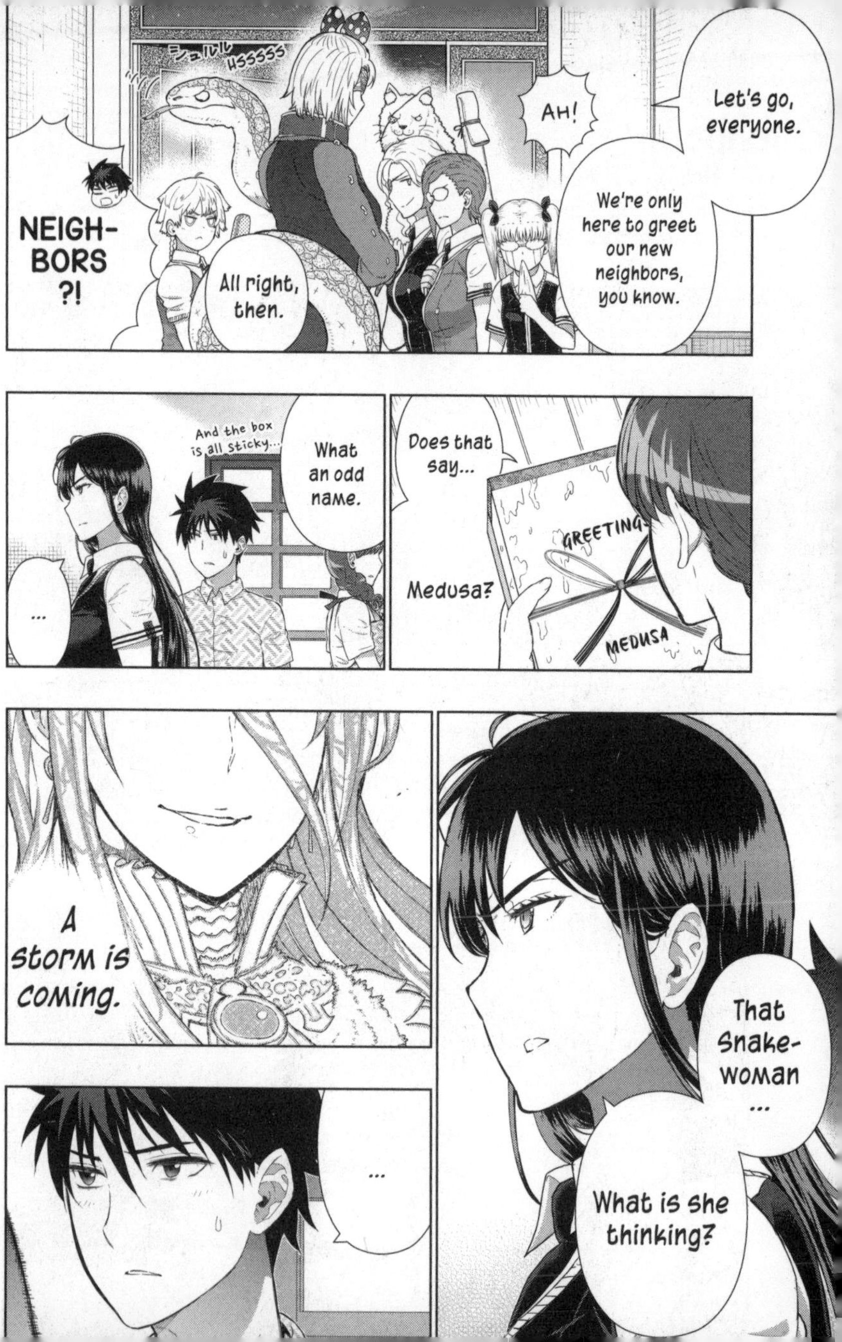
Let's go, everyone.
AH!
We're only here to greet our new neighbors, you know.
シュルル
HSSSSS
All right, then.
NEIGH-BORS?!
Does that say...
GREETING
MEDUSA
Medusa?
What an odd name.
And the box is all sticky...
...
That Snake-woman...
What is she thinking?
A storm is coming.
...

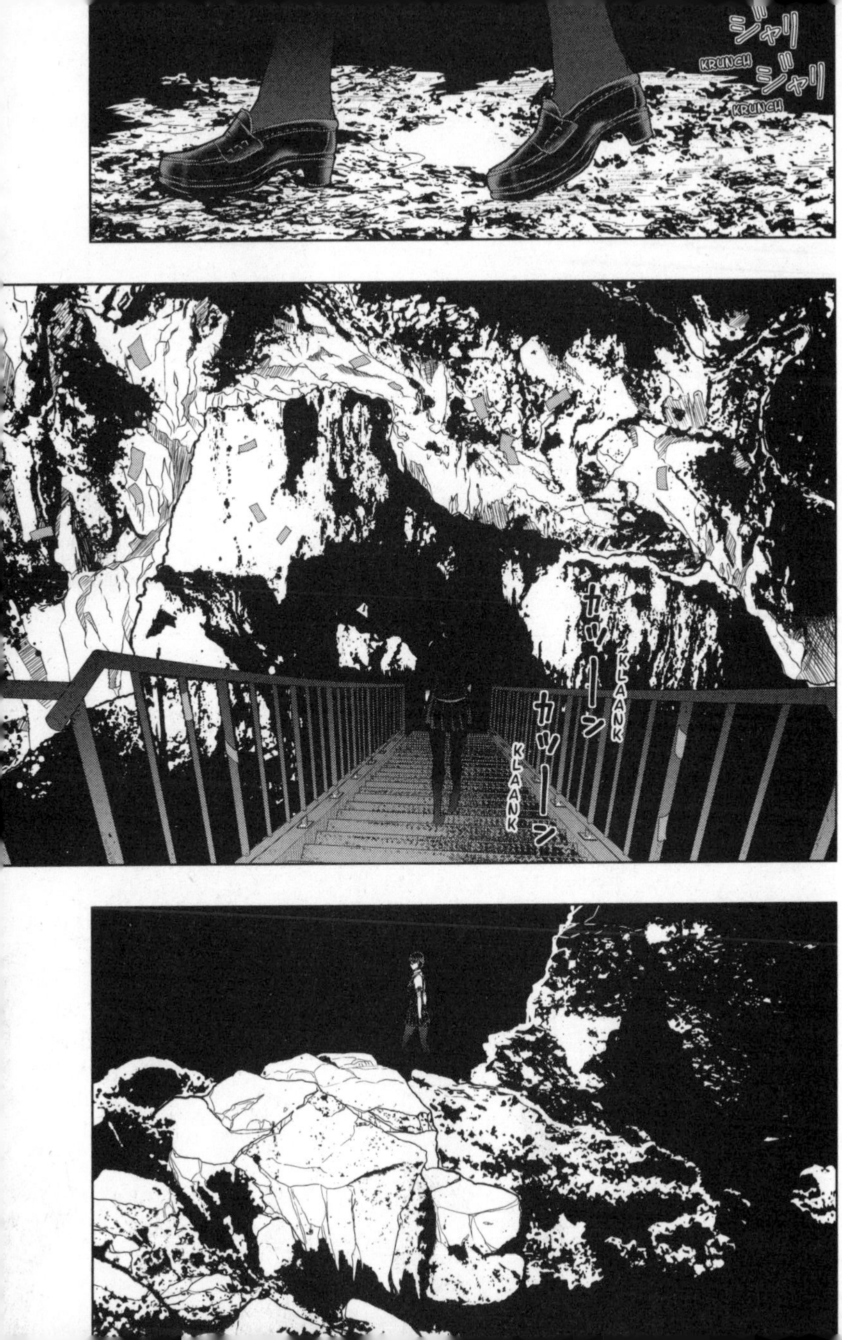
ジャリ
KRUNCH
ジャリ
KRUNCH
カツーーン
KLAANK
カツーーン
KLAANK

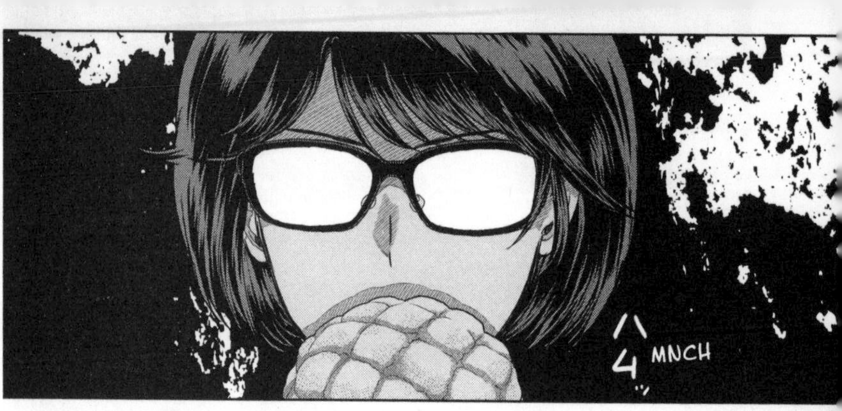
MNCH

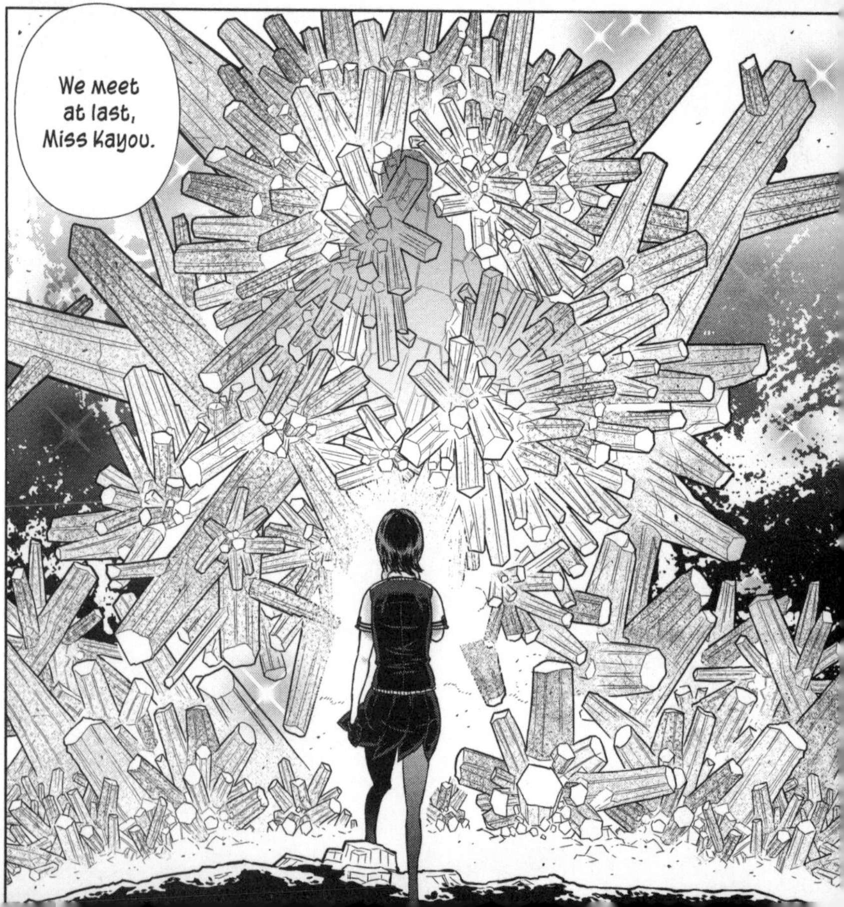
We meet at last, Miss Kayou.

CHAPTER 49 END

Witchcraft Works

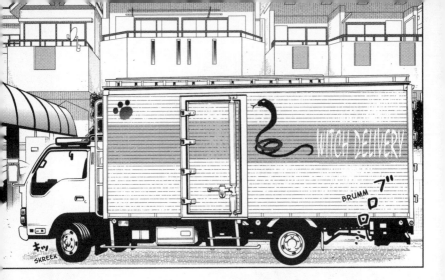

WITCH DELIVERY

BRUMM

キッ
SKREEK

HUSTLE
えっさ
ほっさ
BUSTLE

MEOW

BTAM
バタ
ム

They really did move in next door.

...

KWAAK

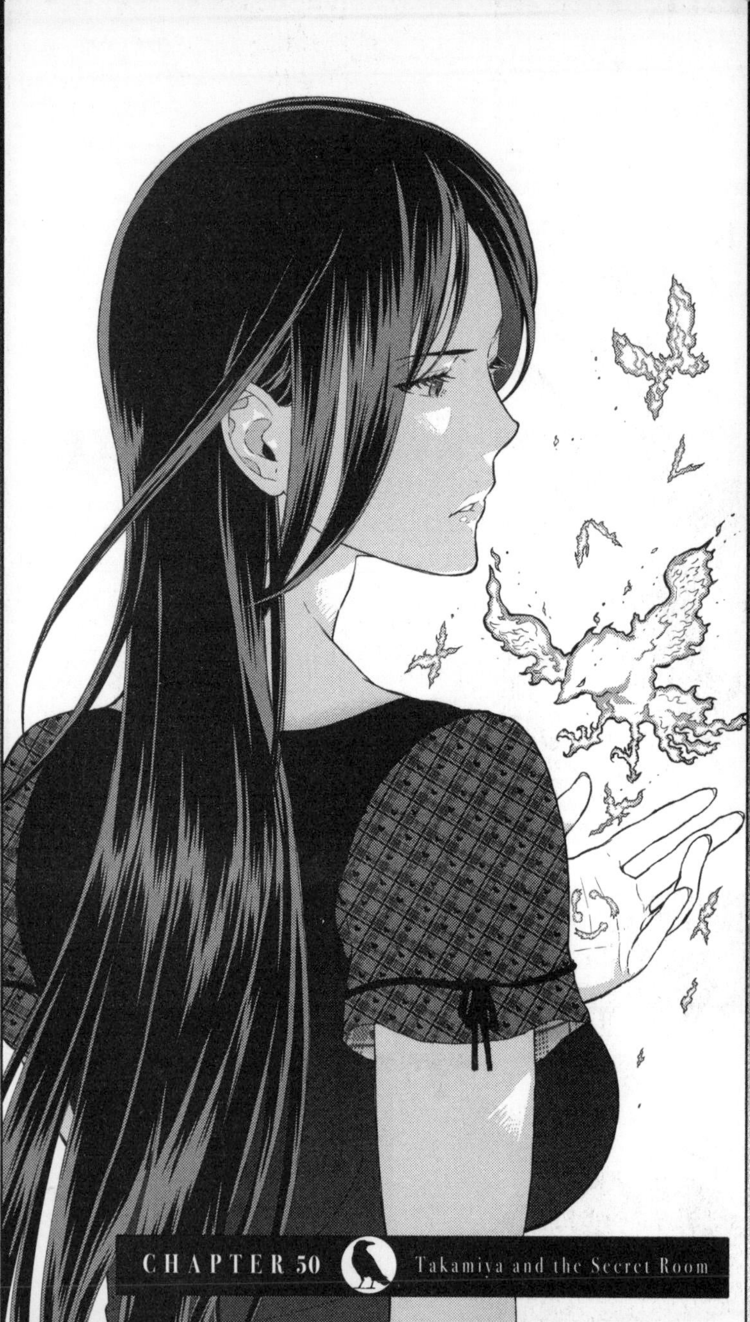
CHAPTER 50
Takamiya and the Secret Room

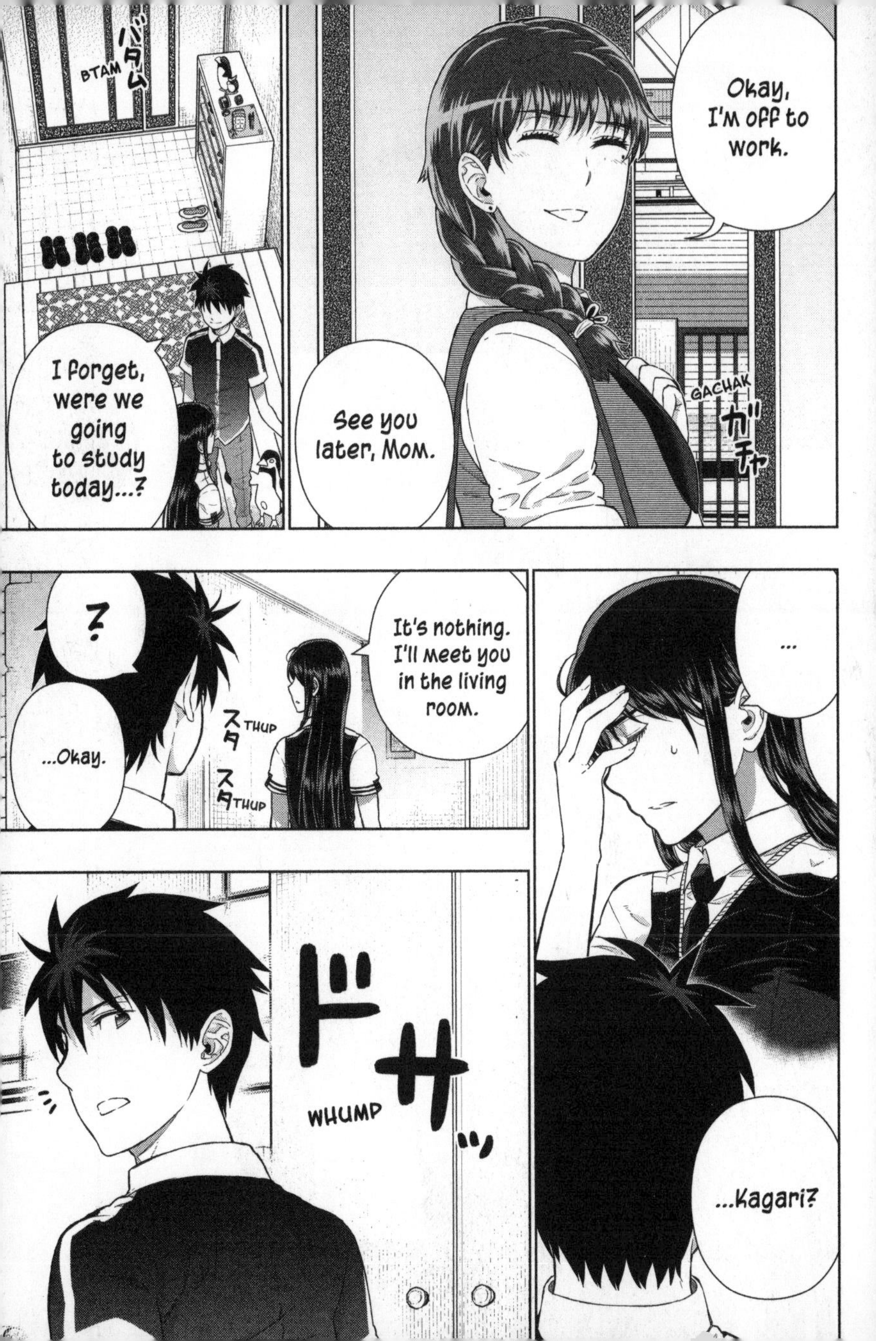
Okay, I'm off to work.
GACHAK
ガチャ
See you later, Mom.
BTAM
バタム
I forget, were we going to study today...?
...
...Kagari?
It's nothing. I'll meet you in the living room.
スタ THUP
スタ THUP
?
...Okay.
ドサッ
WHUMP

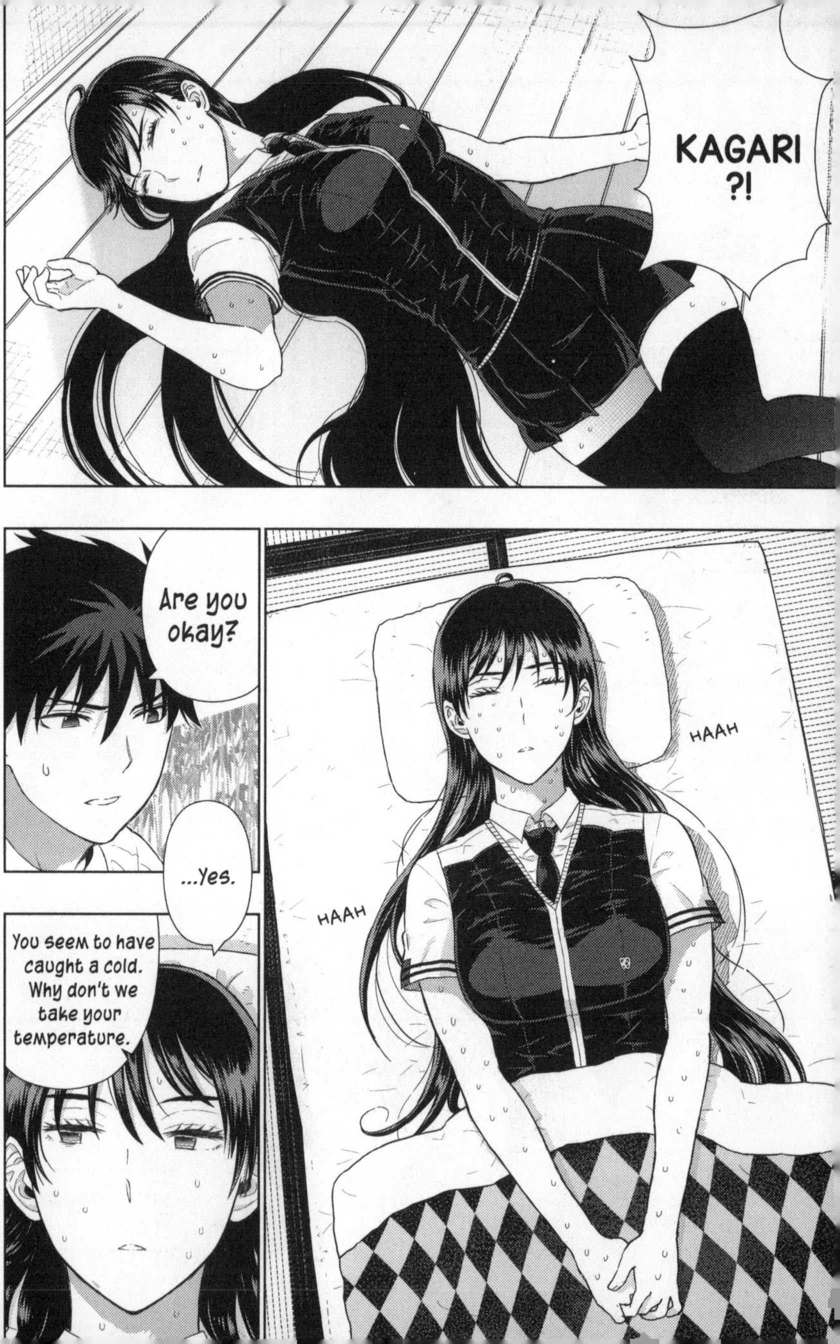
KAGARI ?!
HAAH
HAAH
Are you okay?
...Yes.
You seem to have caught a cold. Why don't we take your temperature.

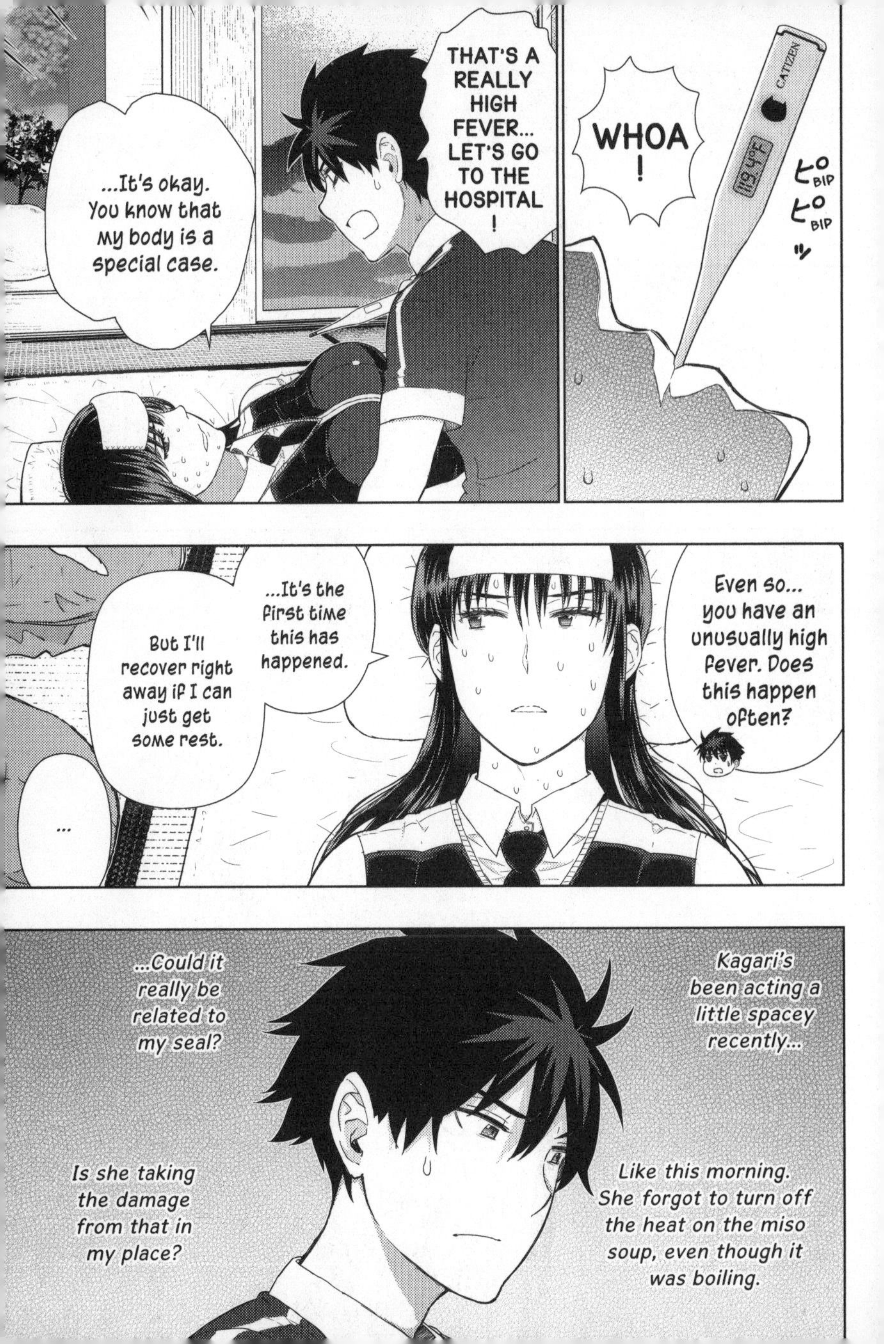
ピ BIP
ピ BIP
ッ
CATIZEN
WHOA!
THAT'S A REALLY HIGH FEVER... LET'S GO TO THE HOSPITAL!
...It's okay. You know that my body is a special case.
Even so... you have an unusually high fever. Does this happen often?
...It's the first time this has happened.
But I'll recover right away if I can just get some rest.
...
Kagari's been acting a little spacey recently...
Like this morning. She forgot to turn off the heat on the miso soup, even though it was boiling.
...Could it really be related to my seal?
Is she taking the damage from that in my place?

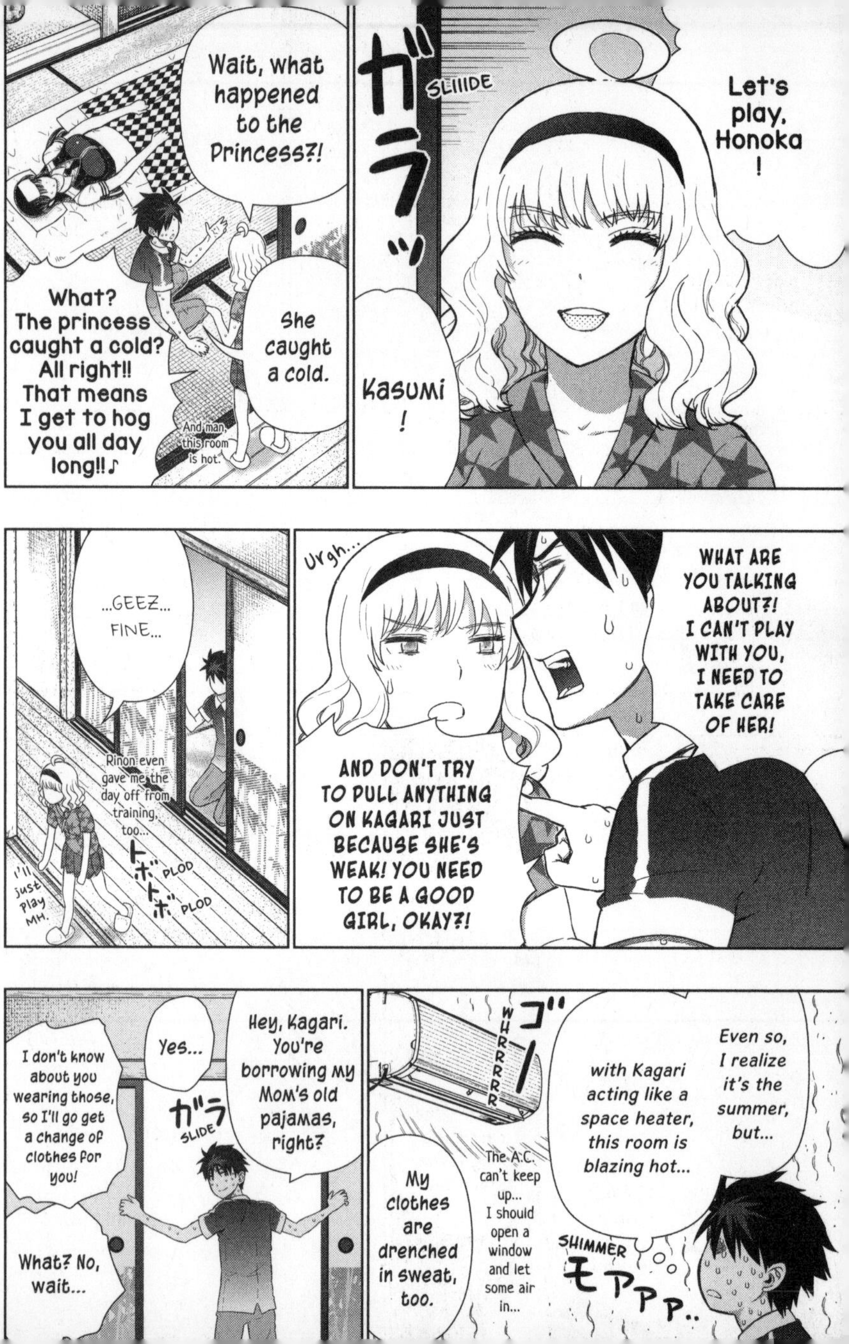

Let's play, Honoka!
ガラッ
SLIIIDE
Kasumi!
Wait, what happened to the Princess?!
She caught a cold.
What? The princess caught a cold? All right!! That means I get to hog you all day long!!♪
And man, this room is hot.
WHAT ARE YOU TALKING ABOUT?! I CAN'T PLAY WITH YOU, I NEED TO TAKE CARE OF HER!
Urgh...
AND DON'T TRY TO PULL ANYTHING ON KAGARI JUST BECAUSE SHE'S WEAK! YOU NEED TO BE A GOOD GIRL, OKAY?!
...GEEZ... FINE...
Rinon even gave me the day off from training, too...
トボトボ
PLOD PLOD
I'll just play MH.
Even so, I realize it's the summer, but...
with Kagari acting like a space heater, this room is blazing hot...
ゴー
WHRRRRRR
SHIMMER
モアアア..
The A.C. can't keep up... I should open a window and let some air in...
My clothes are drenched in sweat, too.
Hey, Kagari. You're borrowing my Mom's old pajamas, right?
Yes...
ガラ
SLIDE
I don't know about you wearing those, so I'll go get a change of clothes for you!
What? No, wait...

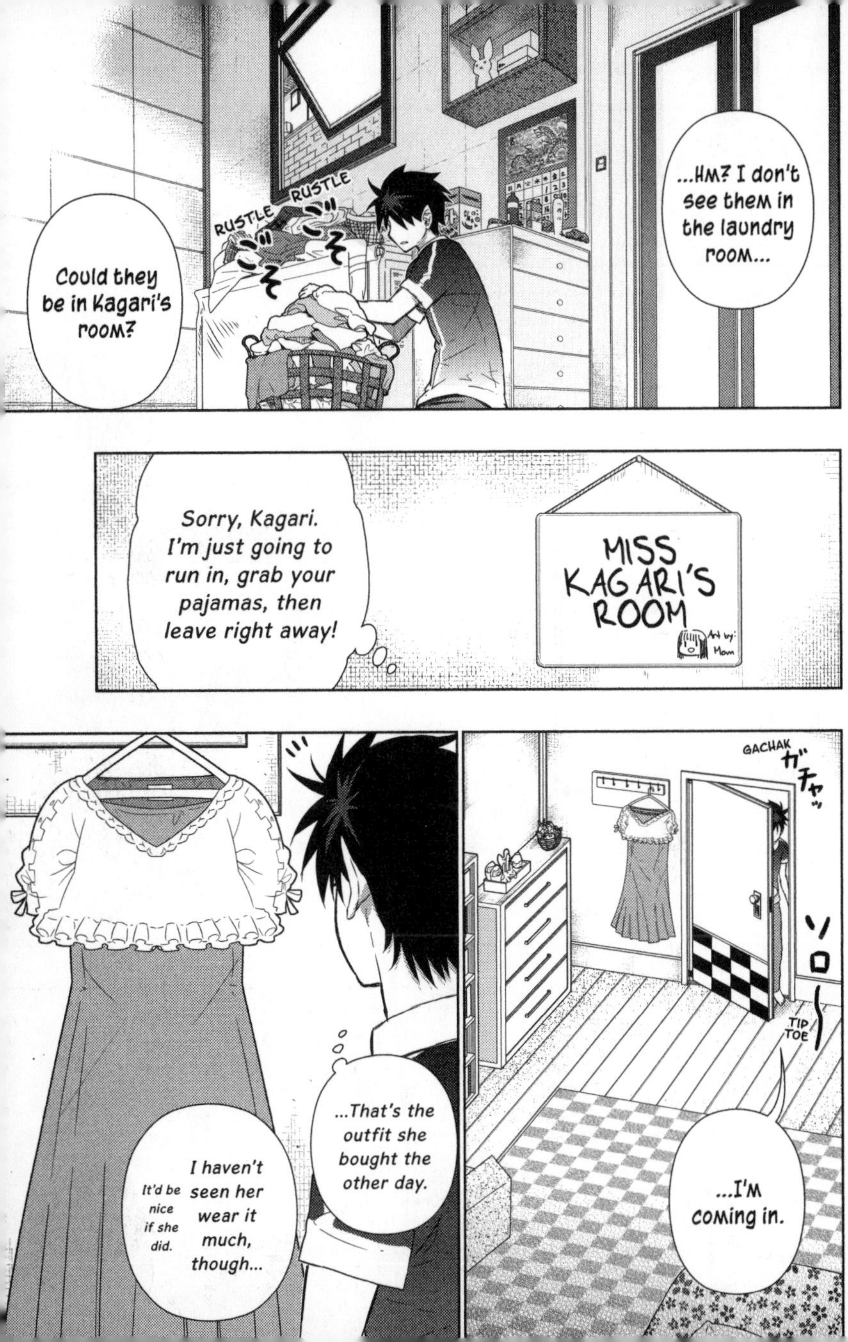
...HM? I don't see them in the laundry room...
RUSTLE
RUSTLE
Could they be in Kagari's room?
MISS KAGARI'S ROOM
Art by: Mom
Sorry, Kagari. I'm just going to run in, grab your pajamas, then leave right away!
GACHAK
ガチャッ
TIP TOE
...I'M coming in.
...That's the outfit she bought the other day.
I haven't seen her wear it much, though...
It'd be nice if she did.

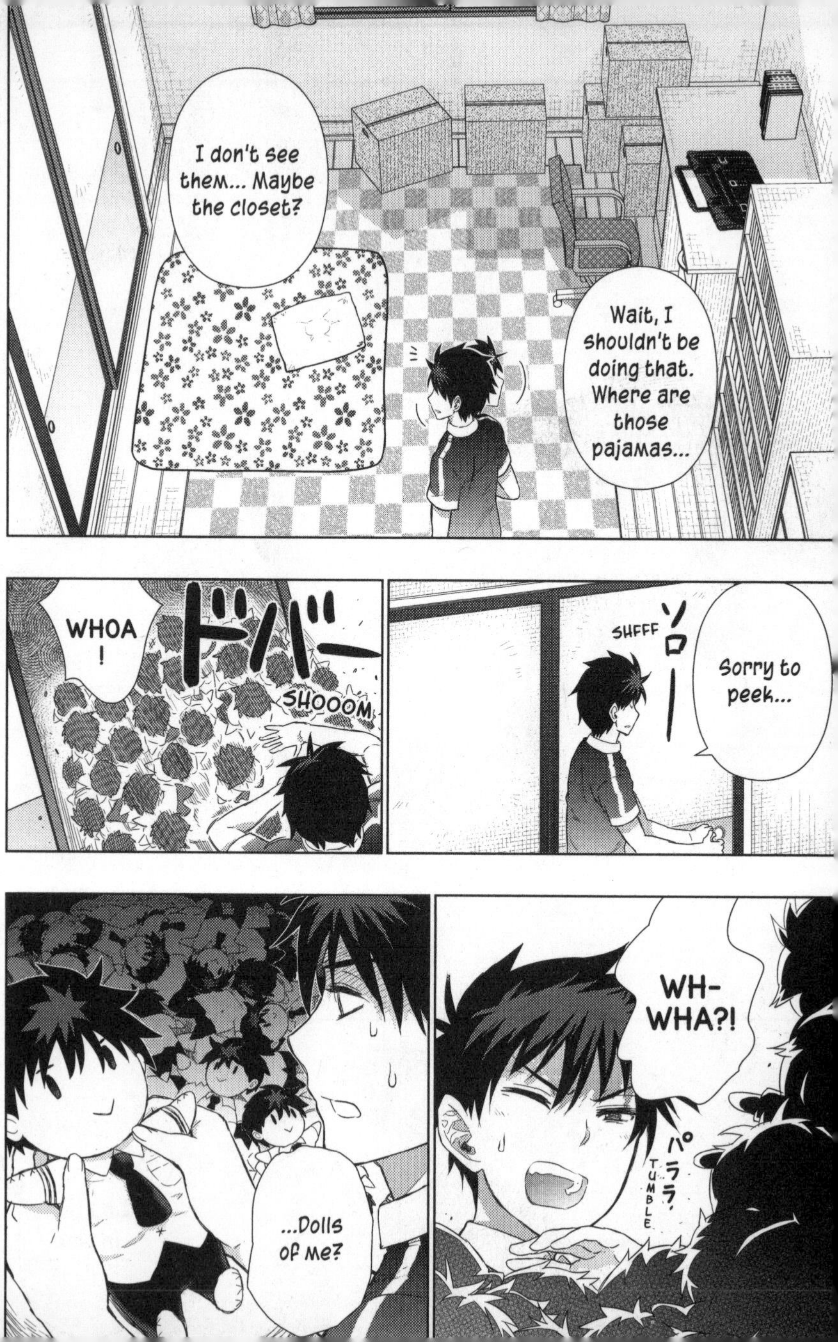
I don't see them... Maybe the closet?
Wait, I shouldn't be doing that. Where are those pajamas...
Sorry to peek...
ソロー
SHFFF
WHOA!
ドバー
SHOOOM
WH-WHA?!
パララ
TUMBLE
...Dolls of me?

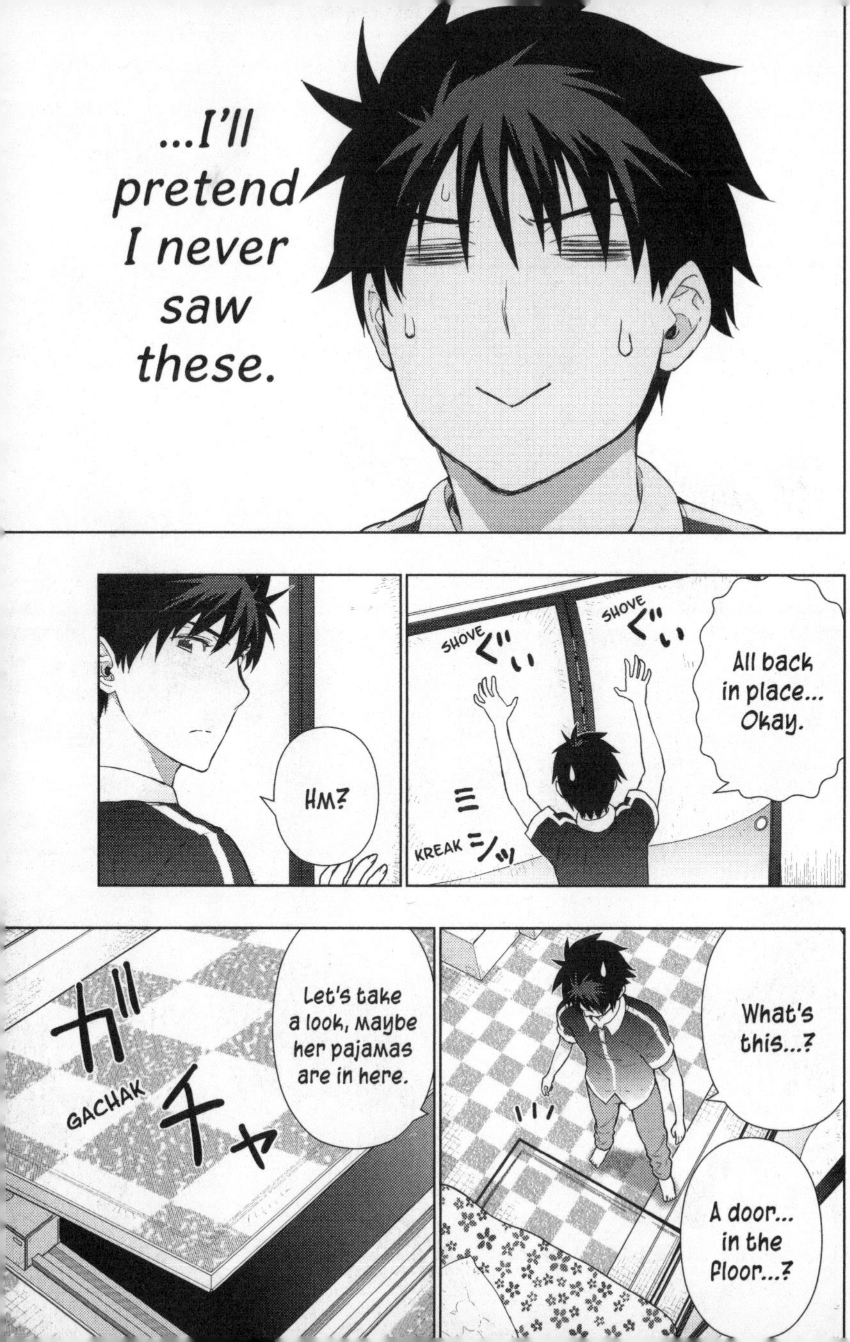
...I'll pretend I never saw these.
SHOVE ぐい
SHOVE ぐい
All back in place... Okay.
KREAK ミシッ
HM?
What's this...?
A door... in the floor...?
Let's take a look, maybe her pajamas are in here.
GACHAK ガチャ

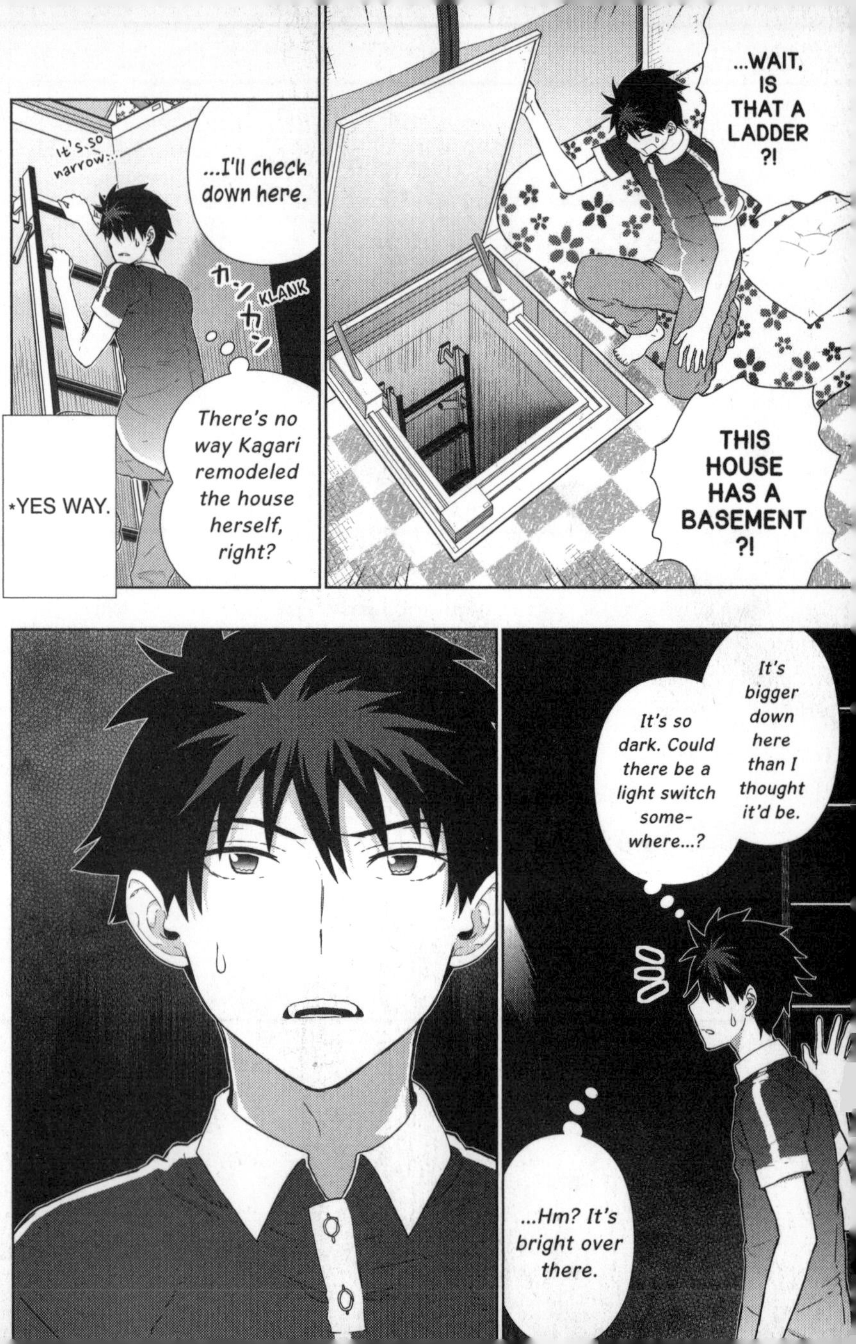
...WAIT, IS THAT A LADDER ?!
THIS HOUSE HAS A BASEMENT ?!
...I'll check down here.
It's so narrow...
KLANK
There's no way Kagari remodeled the house herself, right?
*YES WAY.
It's bigger down here than I thought it'd be.
It's so dark. Could there be a light switch some-where...?
...Hm? It's bright over there.

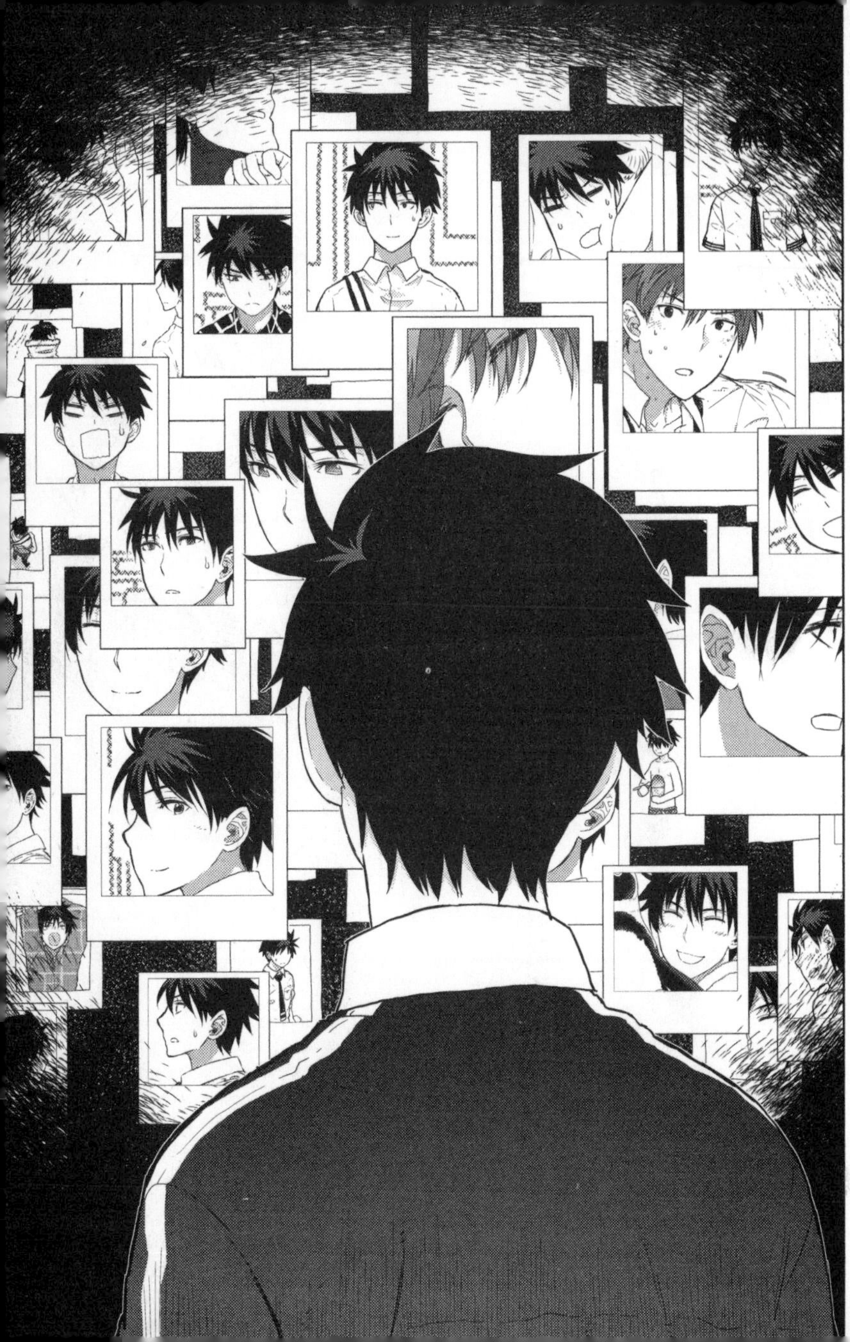

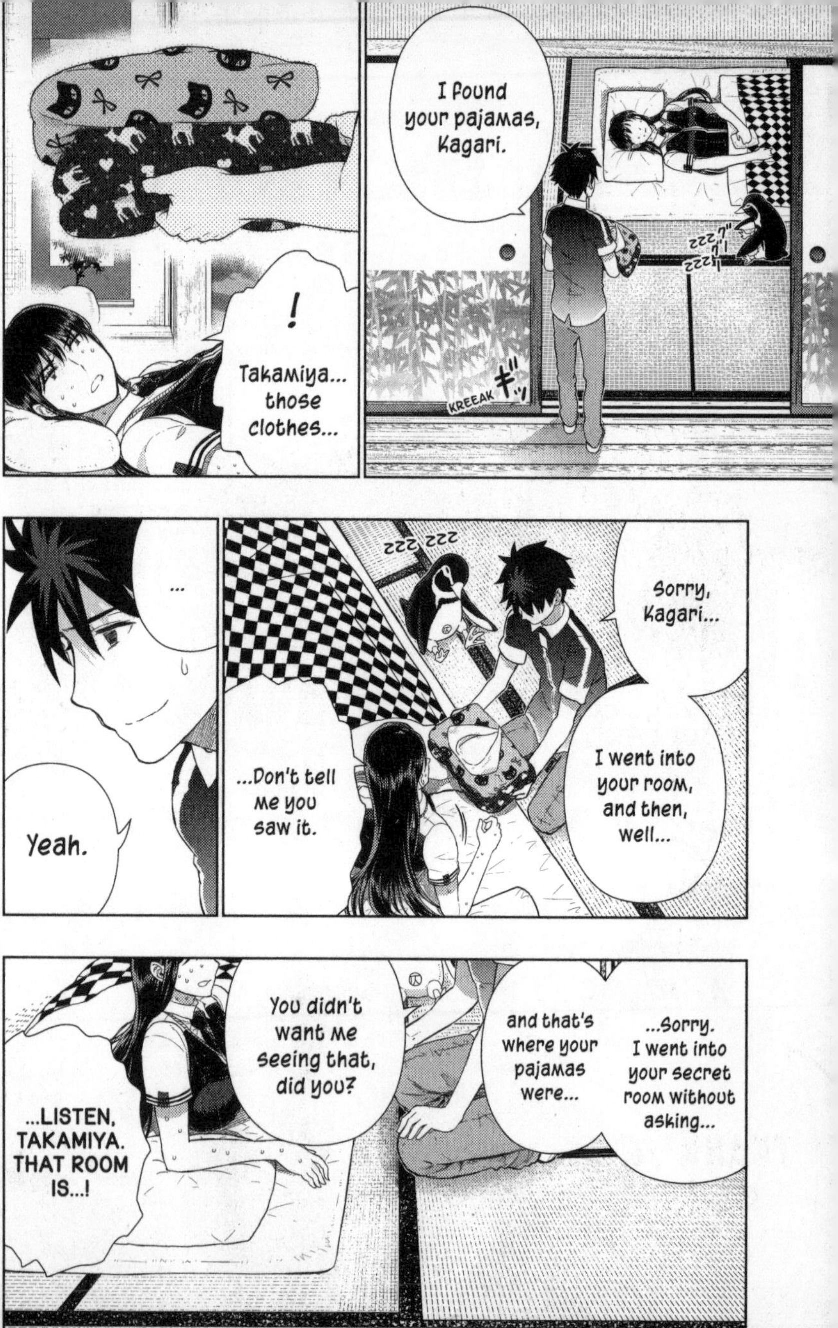
I found your pajamas, Kagari.
zzz
KREEAK
!
Takamiya... those clothes...
Sorry, Kagari...
I went into your room, and then, well...
zzz zzz
...Don't tell me you saw it.
...
Yeah.
...Sorry. I went into your secret room without asking...
and that's where your pajamas were...
You didn't want me seeing that, did you?
...LISTEN, TAKAMIYA. THAT ROOM IS...!

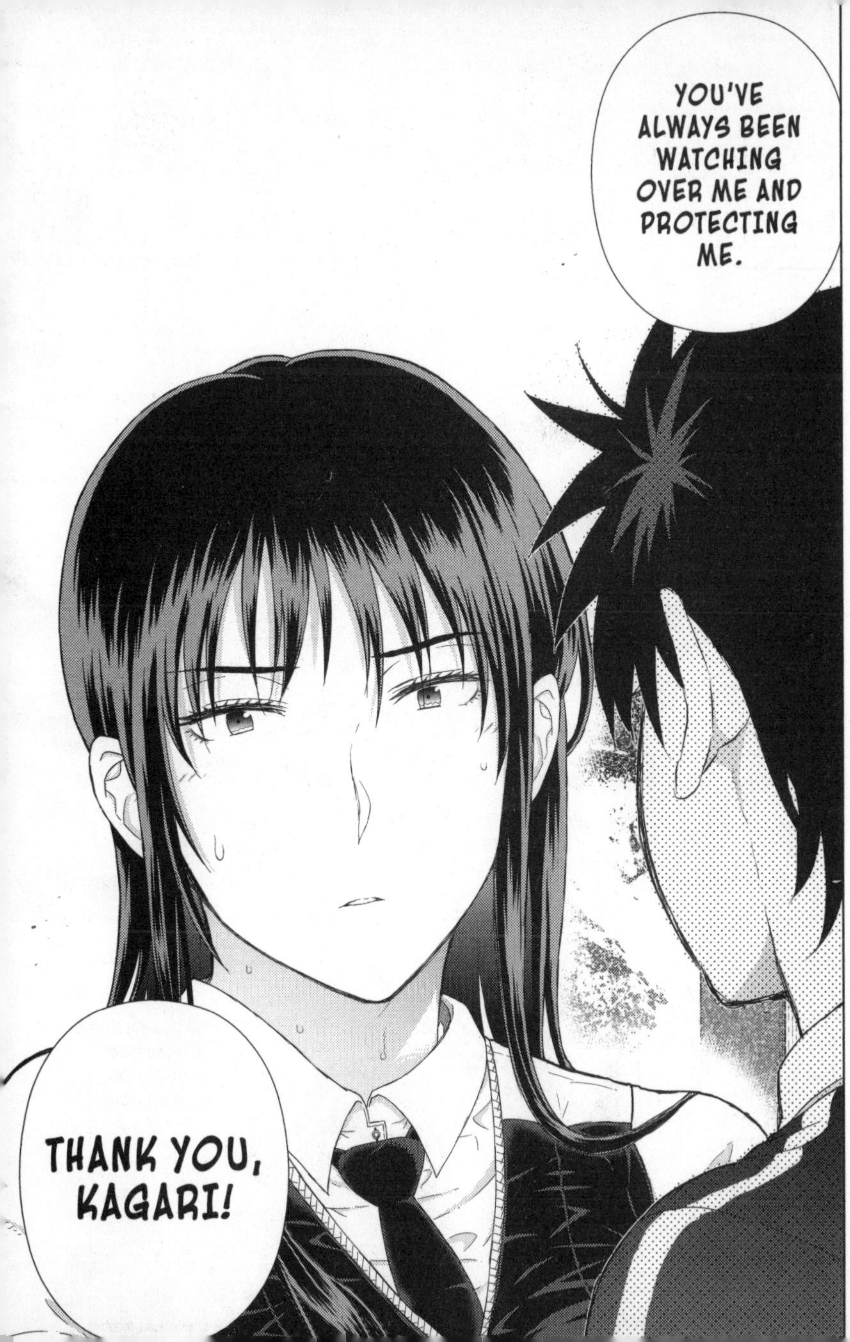
YOU'VE ALWAYS BEEN WATCHING OVER ME AND PROTECTING ME.
THANK YOU, KAGARI!

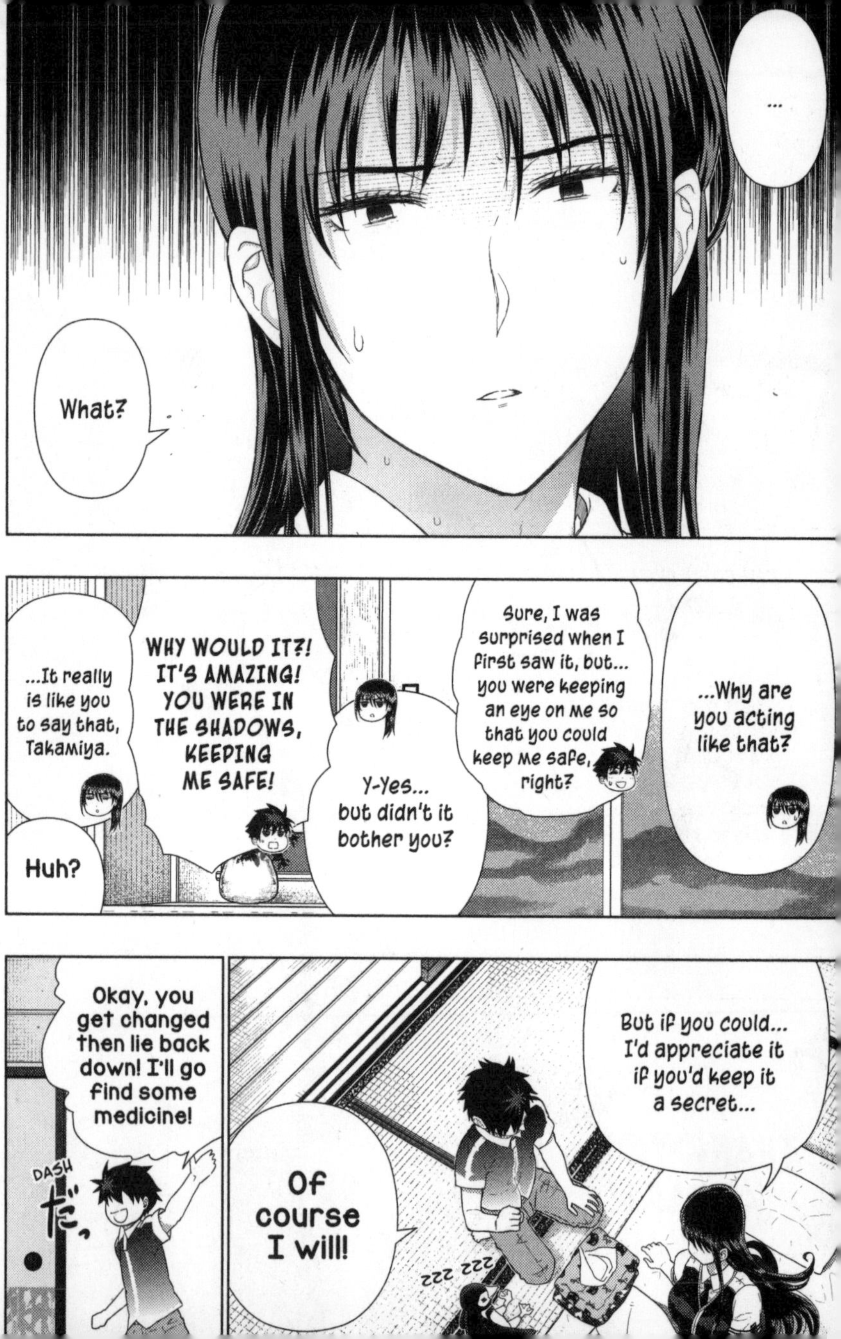
...
What?
...Why are you acting like that?
Sure, I was surprised when I first saw it, but... you were keeping an eye on me so that you could keep me safe, right?
Y-Yes... but didn't it bother you?
WHY WOULD IT?! IT'S AMAZING! YOU WERE IN THE SHADOWS, KEEPING ME SAFE!
...It really is like you to say that, Takamiya.
Huh?
But if you could... I'd appreciate it if you'd keep it a secret...
Of course I will!
zzz zzz
Okay, you get changed then lie back down! I'll go find some medicine!
DASH

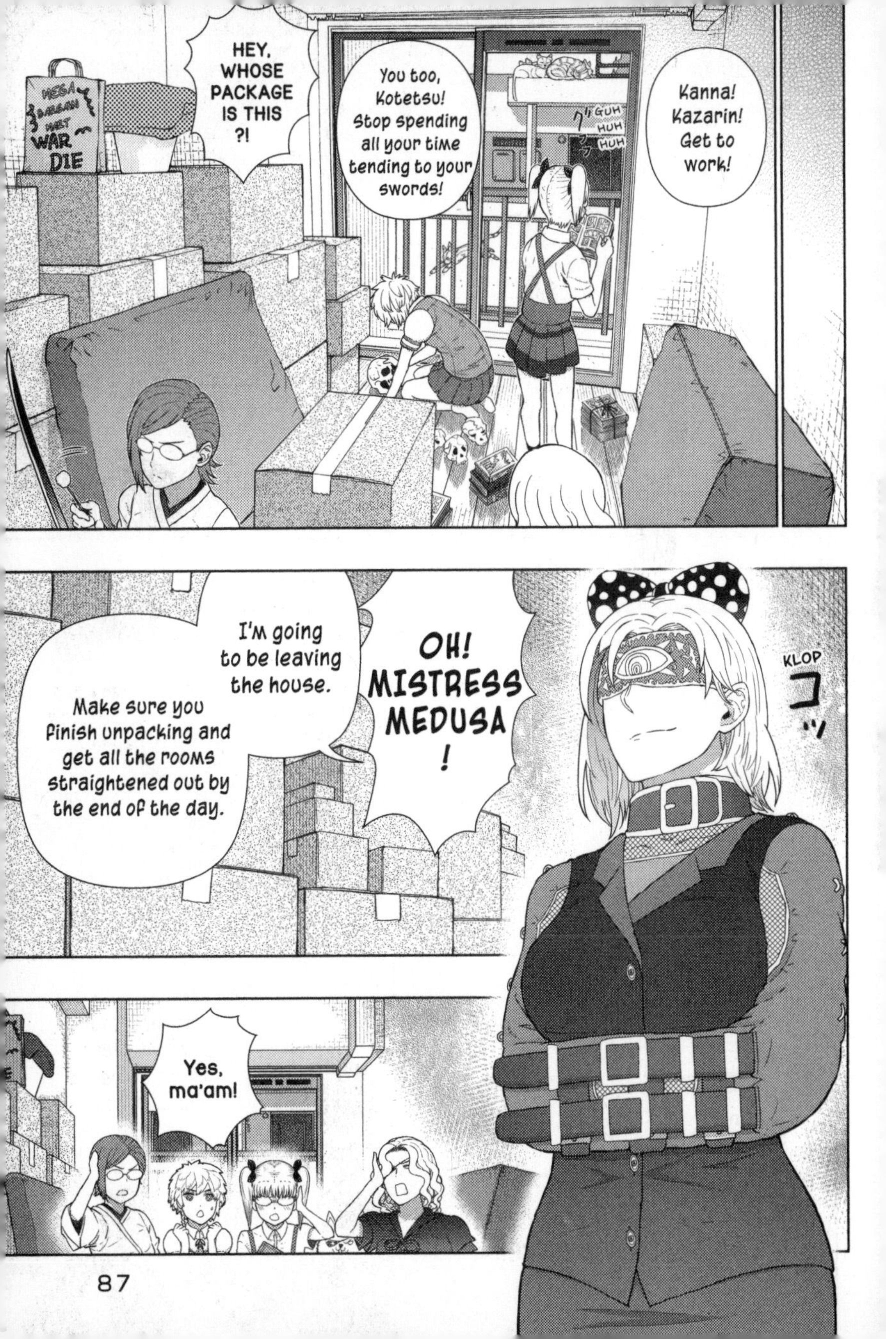
Kanna! Kazarin! Get to work!
GUH HUH HUH
You too, Kotetsu! Stop spending all your time tending to your swords!
HEY, WHOSE PACKAGE IS THIS ?!
KLOP
OH! MISTRESS MEDUSA !
I'm going to be leaving the house.
Make sure you finish unpacking and get all the rooms straightened out by the end of the day.
Yes, ma'am!

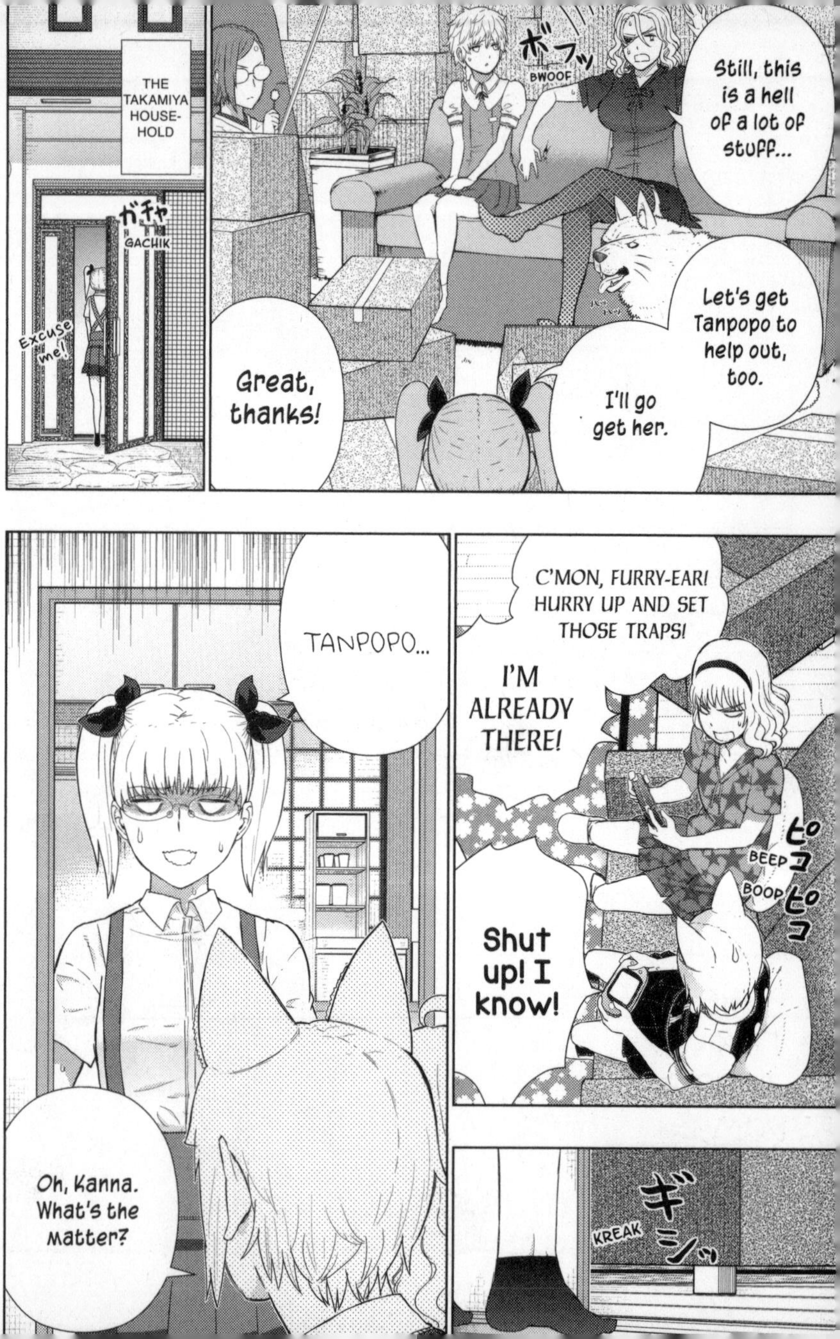

Still, this is a hell of a lot of stuff...
ボフッ
BWOOF
Let's get Tanpopo to help out, too.
I'll go get her.
Great, thanks!
THE TAKAMIYA HOUSE-HOLD
ガチャ
GACHIK
Excuse me!
C'MON, FURRY-EAR! HURRY UP AND SET THOSE TRAPS!
I'M ALREADY THERE!
ピコ
BEEP
ピコ
BOOP
Shut up! I know!
ギシッ
KREAK
TANPOPO...
Oh, Kanna. What's the matter?

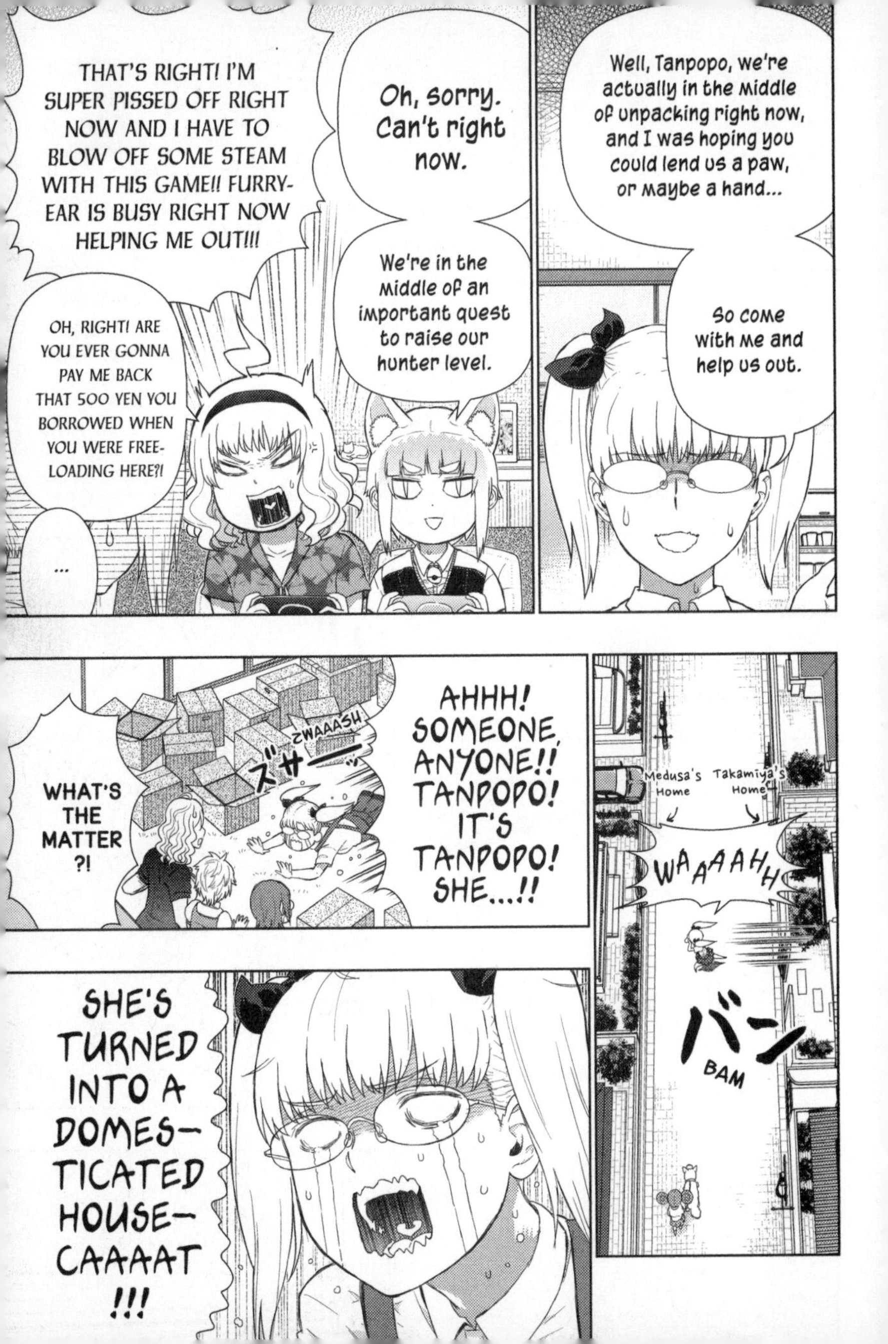
Well, Tanpopo, we're actually in the middle of unpacking right now, and I was hoping you could lend us a paw, or maybe a hand...
So come with me and help us out.
Oh, sorry. Can't right now.
We're in the middle of an important quest to raise our hunter level.
THAT'S RIGHT! I'M SUPER PISSED OFF RIGHT NOW AND I HAVE TO BLOW OFF SOME STEAM WITH THIS GAME!! FURRY-EAR IS BUSY RIGHT NOW HELPING ME OUT!!!
OH, RIGHT! ARE YOU EVER GONNA PAY ME BACK THAT 500 YEN YOU BORROWED WHEN YOU WERE FREE-LOADING HERE?!
...
Medusa's Home
Takamiya's Home
WAAAAHH
バン
BAM
AHHH! SOMEONE, ANYONE!! TANPOPO! IT'S TANPOPO! SHE...!!
ズサー
ZWAAASH
WHAT'S THE MATTER?!
SHE'S TURNED INTO A DOMES-TICATED HOUSE-CAAAAT!!!

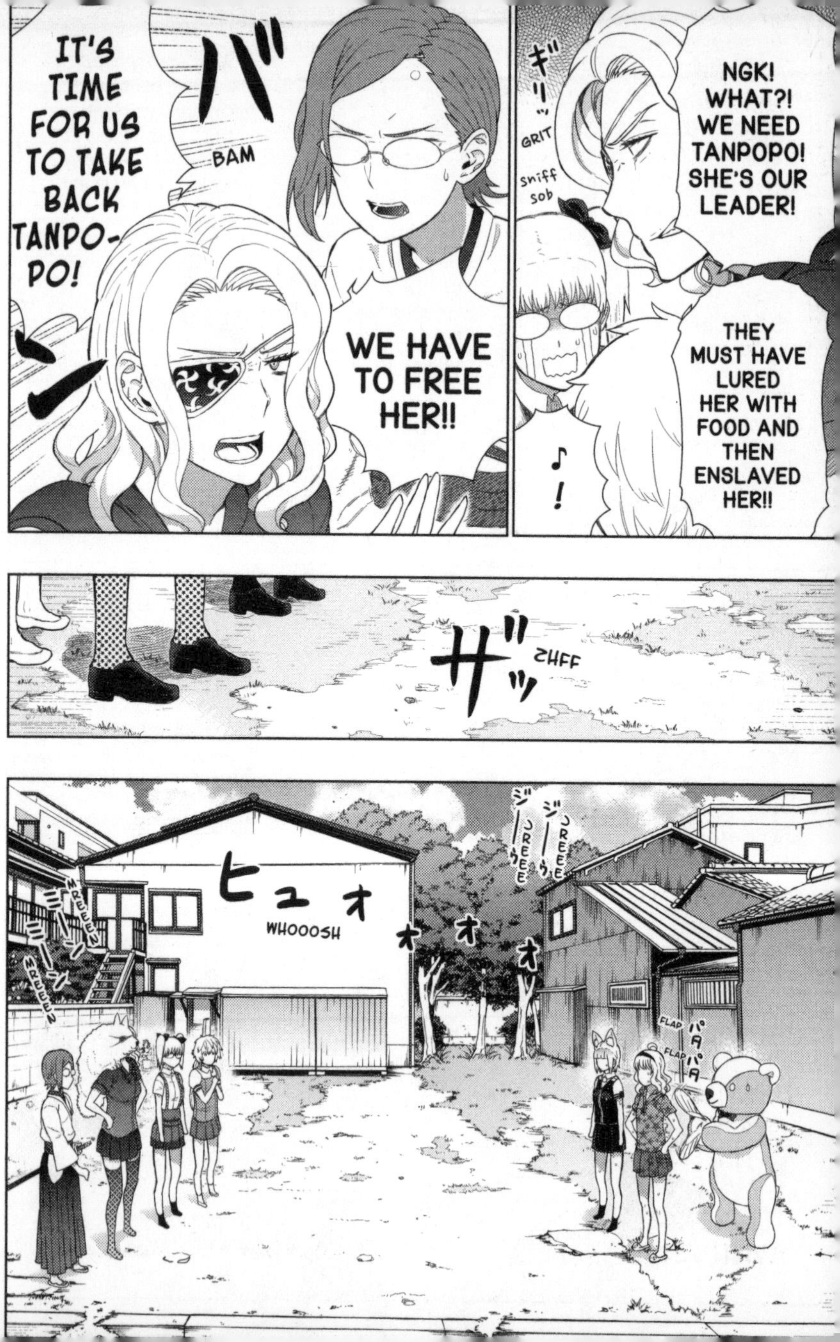
NGK! WHAT?! WE NEED TANPOPO! SHE'S OUR LEADER!
ギリッ
GRIT
sniff sob
THEY MUST HAVE LURED HER WITH FOOD AND THEN ENSLAVED HER!!
♪ !
バ
BAM
IT'S TIME FOR US TO TAKE BACK TANPO-PO!
WE HAVE TO FREE HER!!
ザッ
ZHFF
ジーーウ
JREEE
ジーーウ
JREEE
ヒュオォオオ
WHOOOSH
ミーン
MREEEN
ミーン
MREEEN
パタパタ
FLAP FLAP

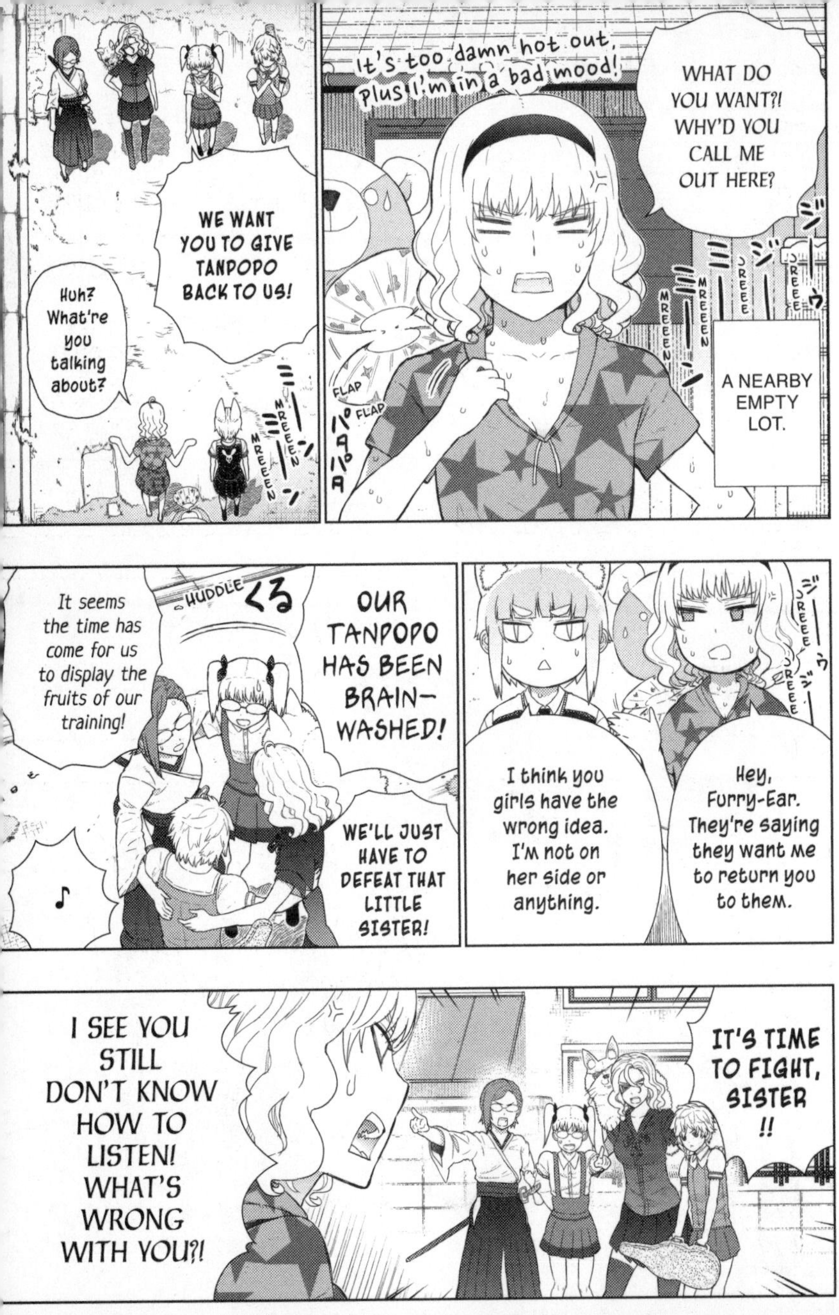
WHAT DO YOU WANT?! WHY'D YOU CALL ME OUT HERE?
It's too damn hot out, plus I'm in a bad mood!
JREEE
MREEEN
FLAP FLAP
A NEARBY EMPTY LOT.
WE WANT YOU TO GIVE TANPOPO BACK TO US!
Huh? What're you talking about?
MREEEN
Hey, Furry-Ear. They're saying they want me to return you to them.
I think you girls have the wrong idea. I'm not on her side or anything.
JREEE
OUR TANPOPO HAS BEEN BRAIN-WASHED!
WE'LL JUST HAVE TO DEFEAT THAT LITTLE SISTER!
HUDDLE
It seems the time has come for us to display the fruits of our training!
♪
IT'S TIME TO FIGHT, SISTER!!
I SEE YOU STILL DON'T KNOW HOW TO LISTEN! WHAT'S WRONG WITH YOU?!

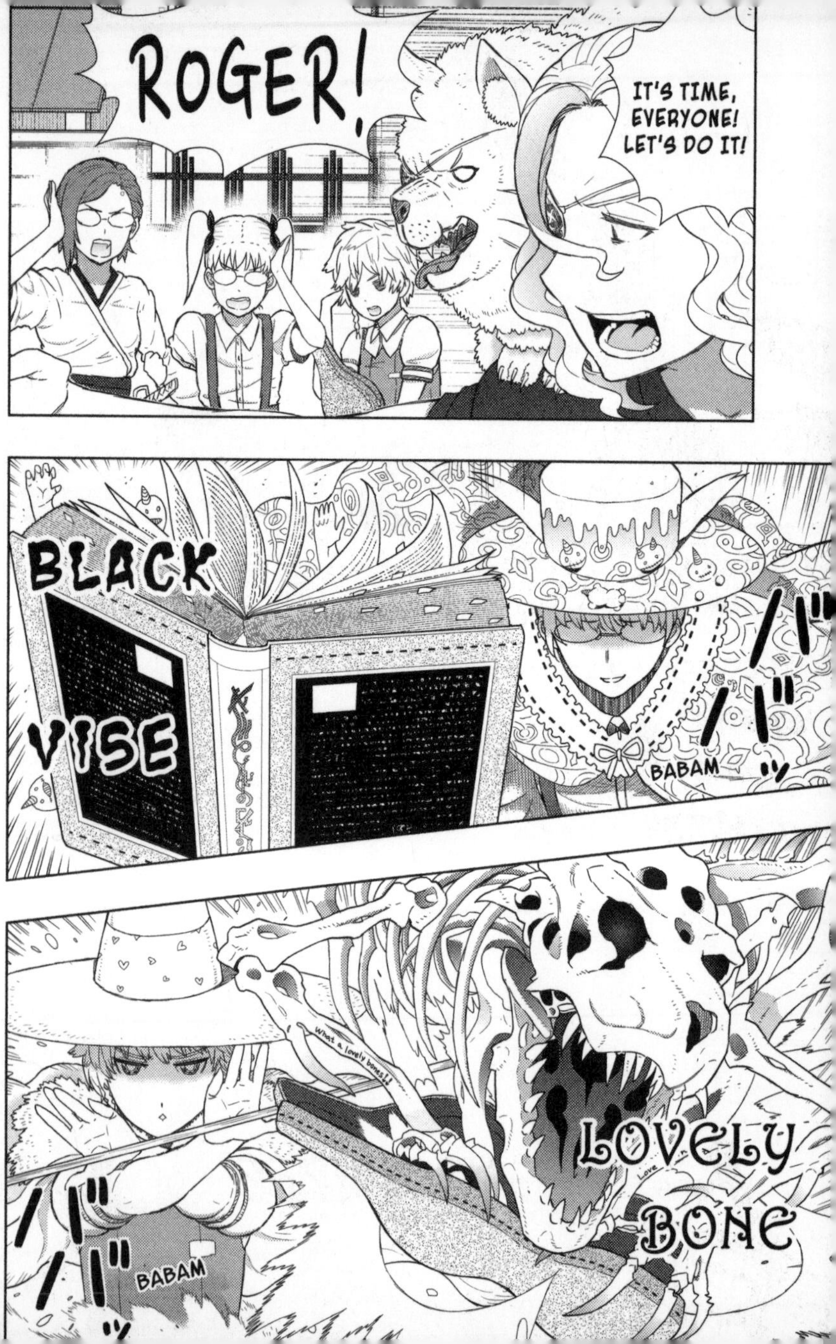
IT'S TIME, EVERYONE! LET'S DO IT!
ROGER!
BABAM
BLACK VISE
LOVELY BONE
What a lovely bones!!
BABAM

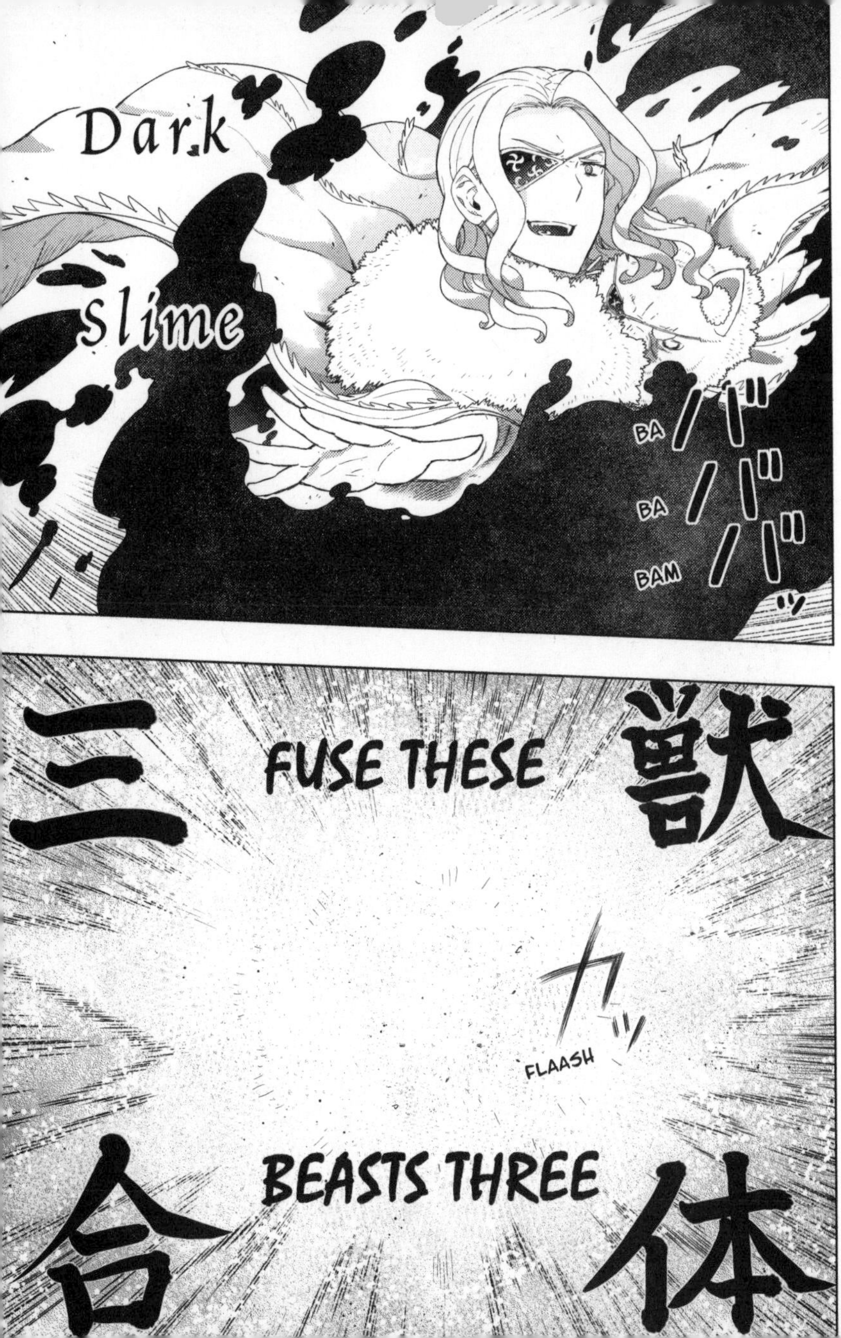
Dark slime
BA BA BAM
バババッ
獣体
三合
FUSE THESE BEASTS THREE
カッ
FLAASH

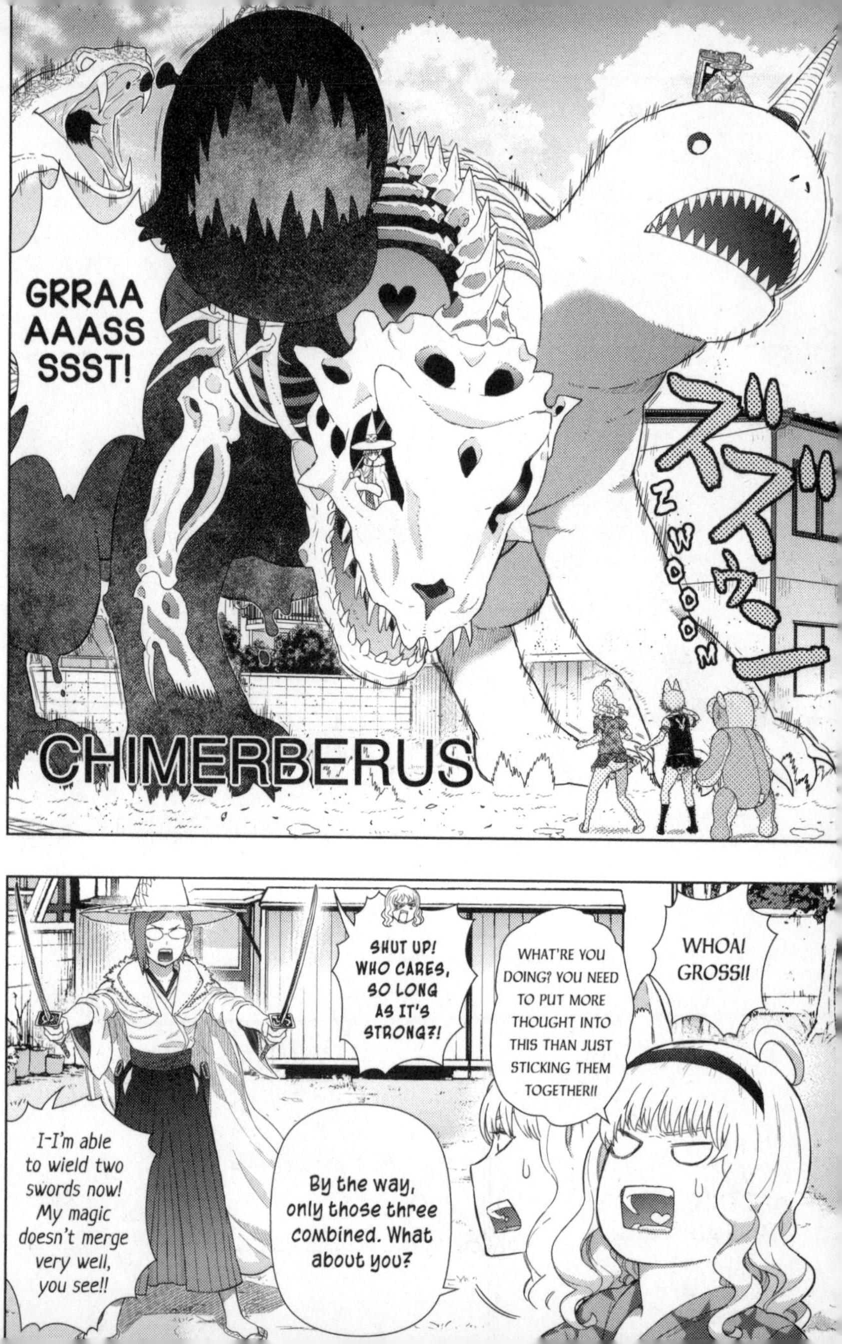
ZWOOOM
GRRAA AAASS SSST!
CHIMERBERUS
WHOA! GROSS!!
WHAT'RE YOU DOING? YOU NEED TO PUT MORE THOUGHT INTO THIS THAN JUST STICKING THEM TOGETHER!!
SHUT UP! WHO CARES, SO LONG AS IT'S STRONG?!
By the way, only those three combined. What about you?
I-I'm able to wield two swords now! My magic doesn't merge very well, you see!!

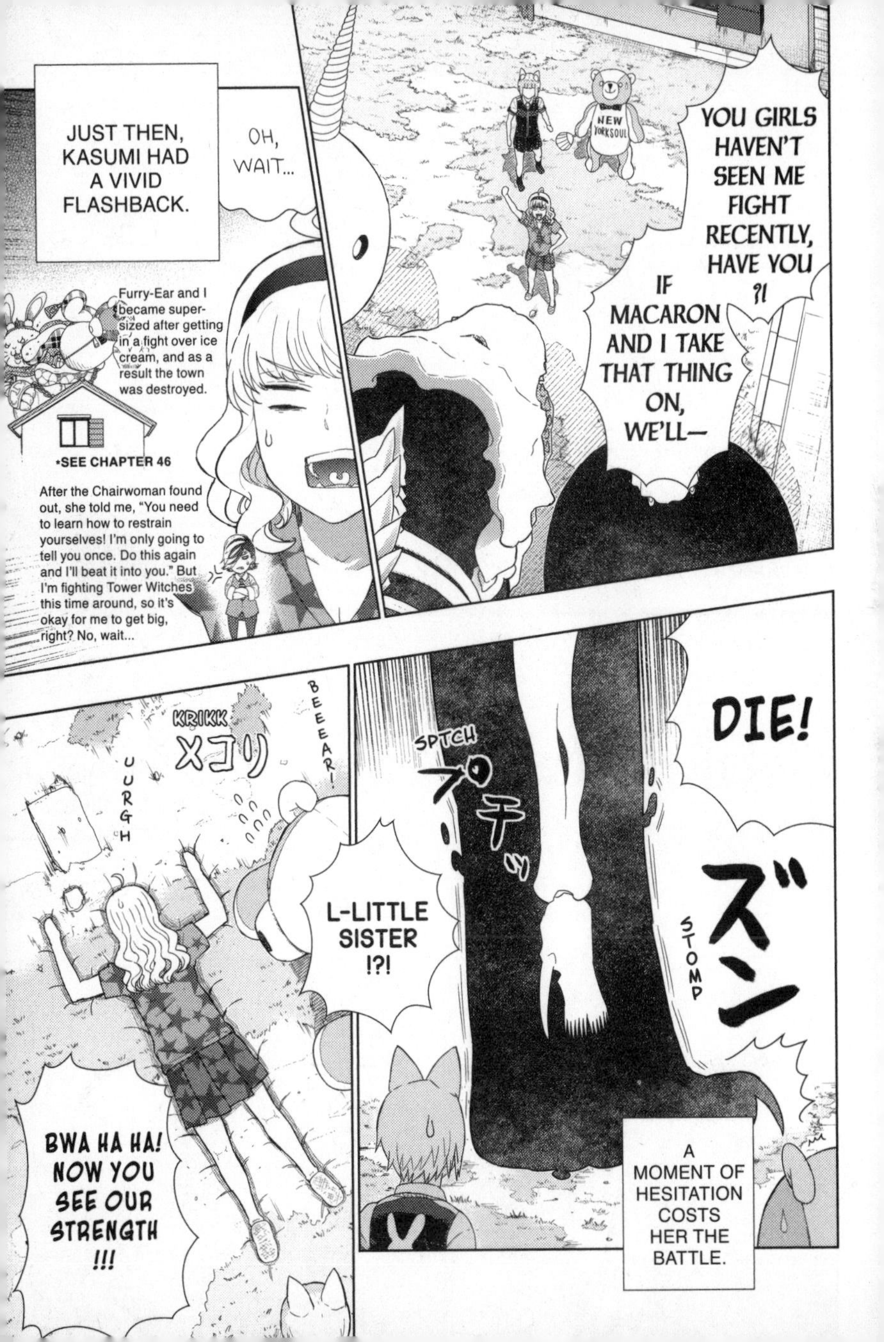

YOU GIRLS HAVEN'T SEEN ME FIGHT RECENTLY, HAVE YOU ?!
IF MACARON AND I TAKE THAT THING ON, WE'LL—
OH, WAIT...
JUST THEN, KASUMI HAD A VIVID FLASHBACK.
Furry-Ear and I became super-sized after getting in a fight over ice cream, and as a result the town was destroyed.
*SEE CHAPTER 46
After the Chairwoman found out, she told me, "You need to learn how to restrain yourselves! I'm only going to tell you once. Do this again and I'll beat it into you." But I'm fighting Tower Witches this time around, so it's okay for me to get big, right? No, wait...
DIE!
SPTCH
プチッ
ズン
STOMP
A MOMENT OF HESITATION COSTS HER THE BATTLE.
BEEEAR!
KRIKK
メコリ
UURGH
L-LITTLE SISTER !?!
BWA HA HA! NOW YOU SEE OUR STRENGTH !!!

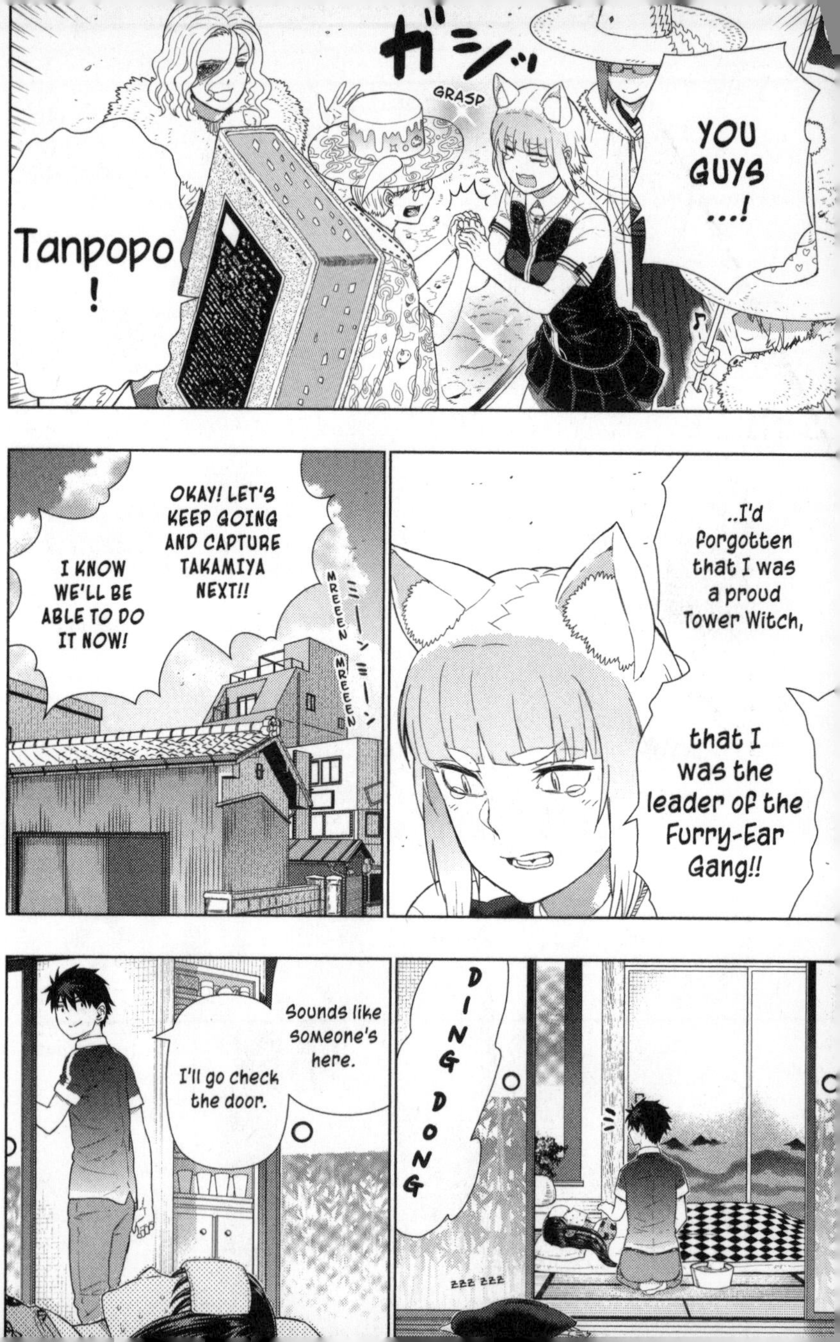
YOU GUYS ...!
ガシッ
GRASP
Tanpopo!
..I'd forgotten that I was a proud Tower Witch,
that I was the leader of the Furry-Ear Gang!!
OKAY! LET'S KEEP GOING AND CAPTURE TAKAMIYA NEXT!!
MREEEN
MREEEN
I KNOW WE'LL BE ABLE TO DO IT NOW!
DING DONG
zzz zzz
Sounds like someone's here.
I'll go check the door.

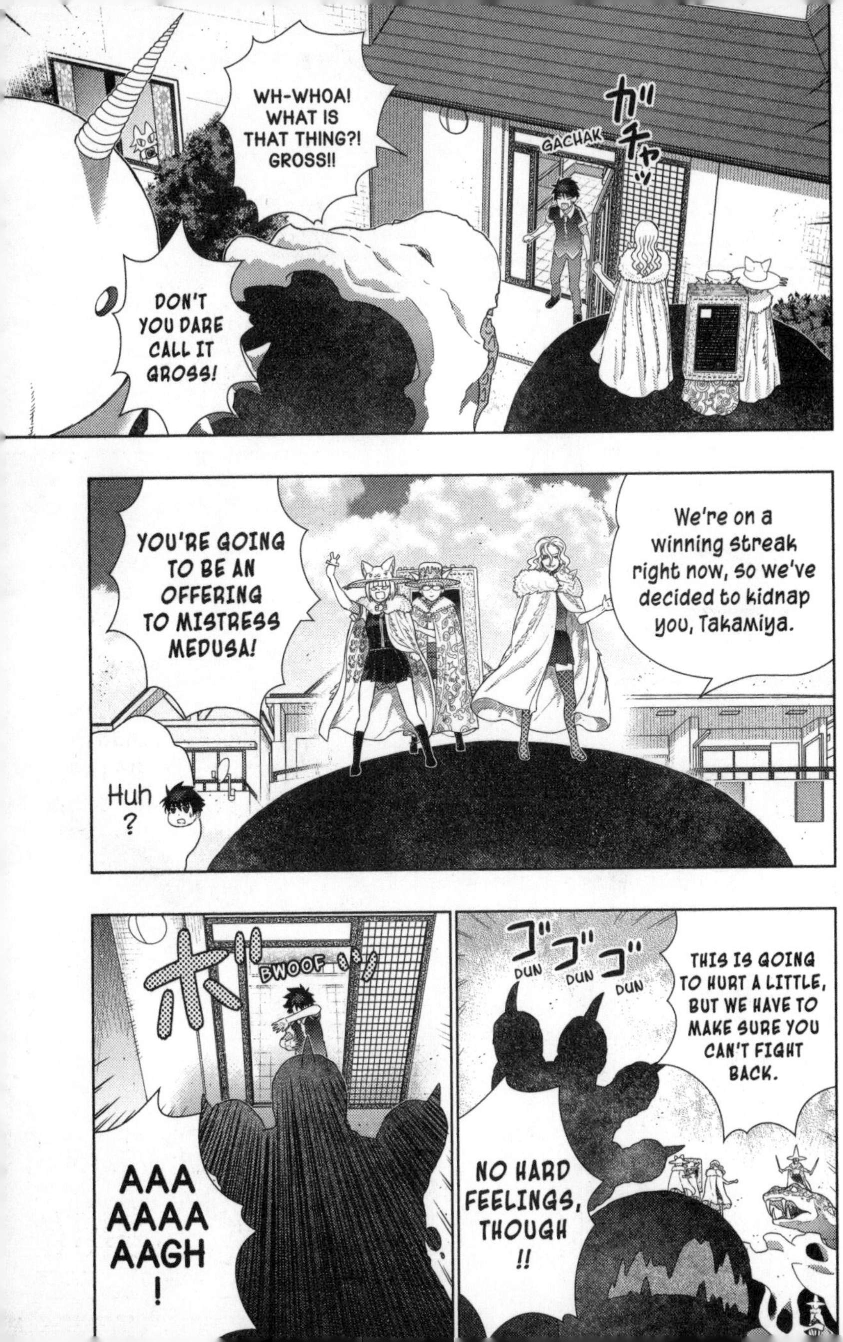
ガチャッ
GACHAK
WH-WHOA! WHAT IS THAT THING?! GROSS!!
DON'T YOU DARE CALL IT GROSS!
We're on a winning streak right now, so we've decided to kidnap you, Takamiya.
YOU'RE GOING TO BE AN OFFERING TO MISTRESS MEDUSA!
Huh?
ゴゴゴ
DUN DUN DUN
THIS IS GOING TO HURT A LITTLE, BUT WE HAVE TO MAKE SURE YOU CAN'T FIGHT BACK.
NO HARD FEELINGS, THOUGH!!
ボッ
BWOOF
AAAAAAAAAGH!

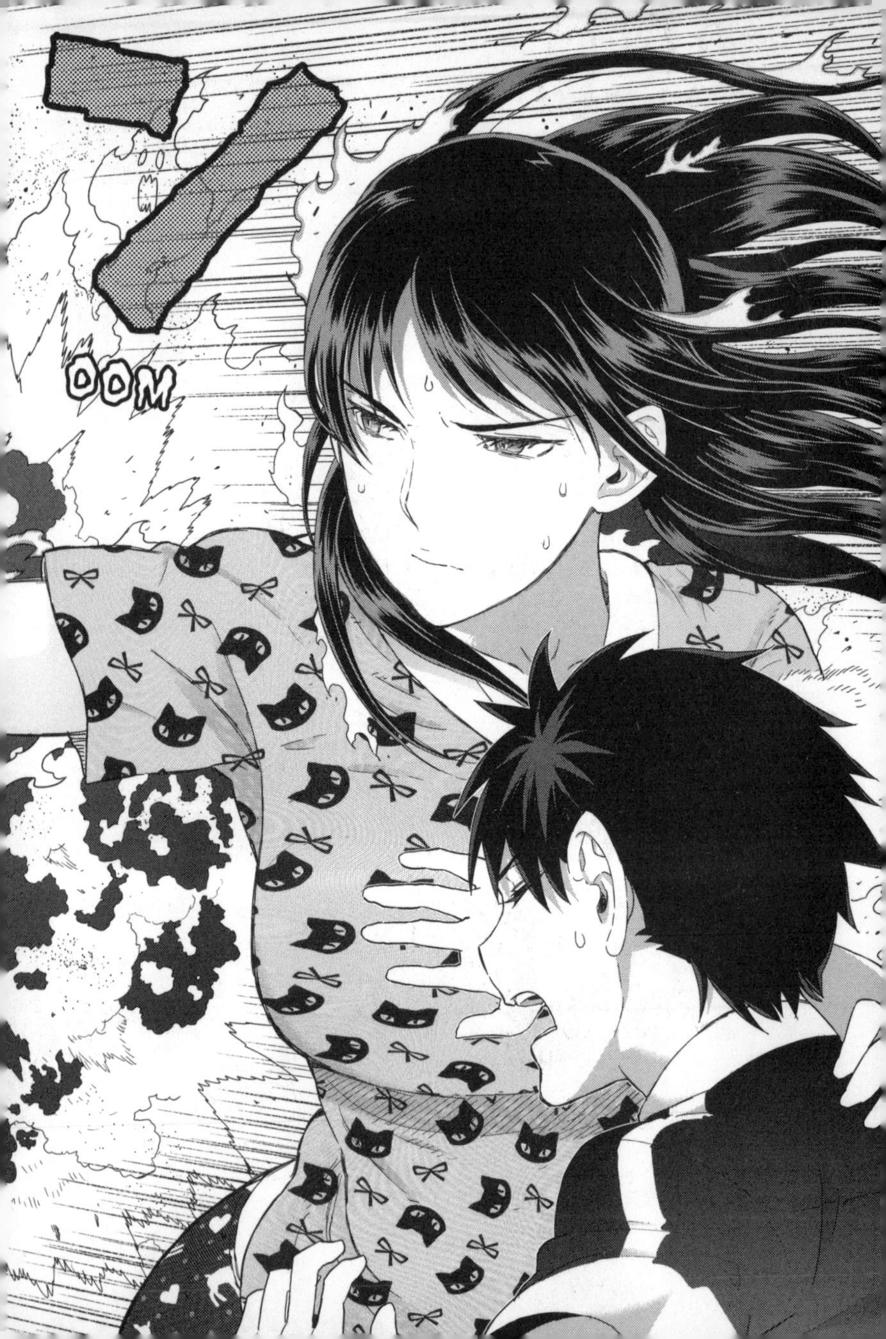
OOM

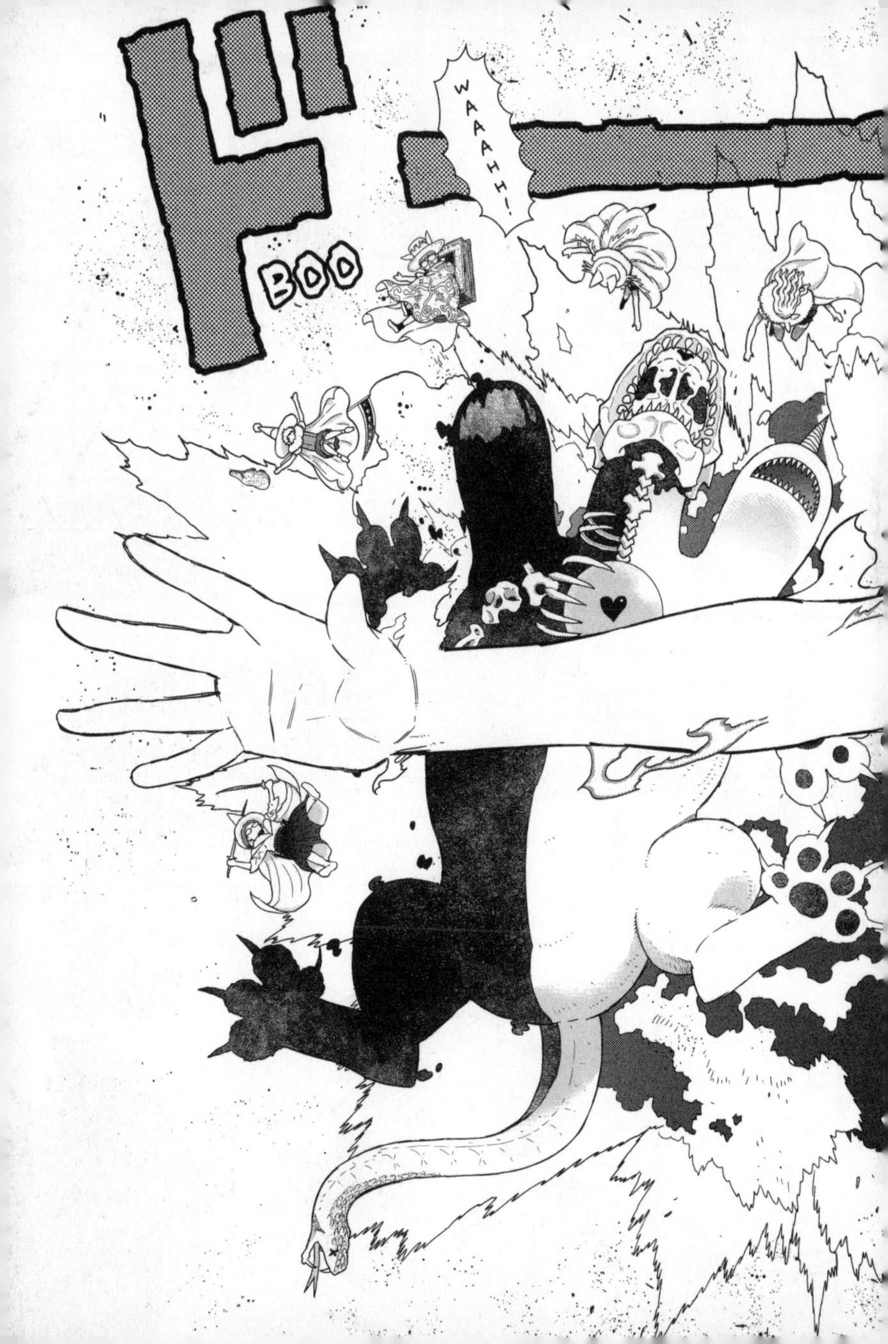
WAAAAHH!
ド
BOO

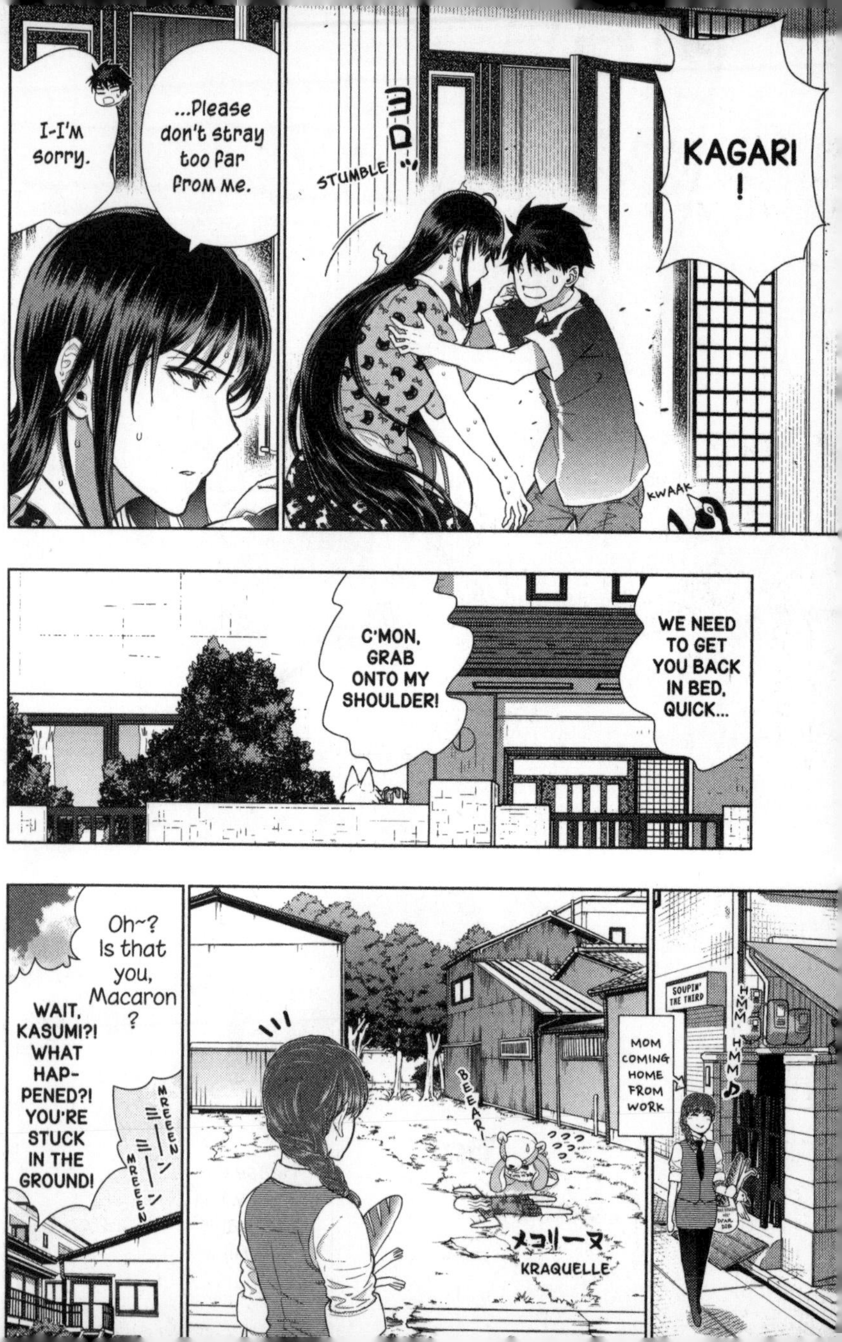
KAGARI !
ヨロ
STUMBLE
KWAAK
...Please don't stray too far from me.
I-I'm sorry.
WE NEED TO GET YOU BACK IN BED, QUICK...
C'MON, GRAB ONTO MY SHOULDER!
SOUPIN' THE THIRD
MOM COMING HOME FROM WORK
HMM HMM HMM♪
BEEARI
メコリーヌ
KRAQUELLE
Oh~? Is that you, Macaron?
WAIT, KASUMI?! WHAT HAP-PENED?! YOU'RE STUCK IN THE GROUND!
ミーン
MREEEN
ミーン
MREEEN

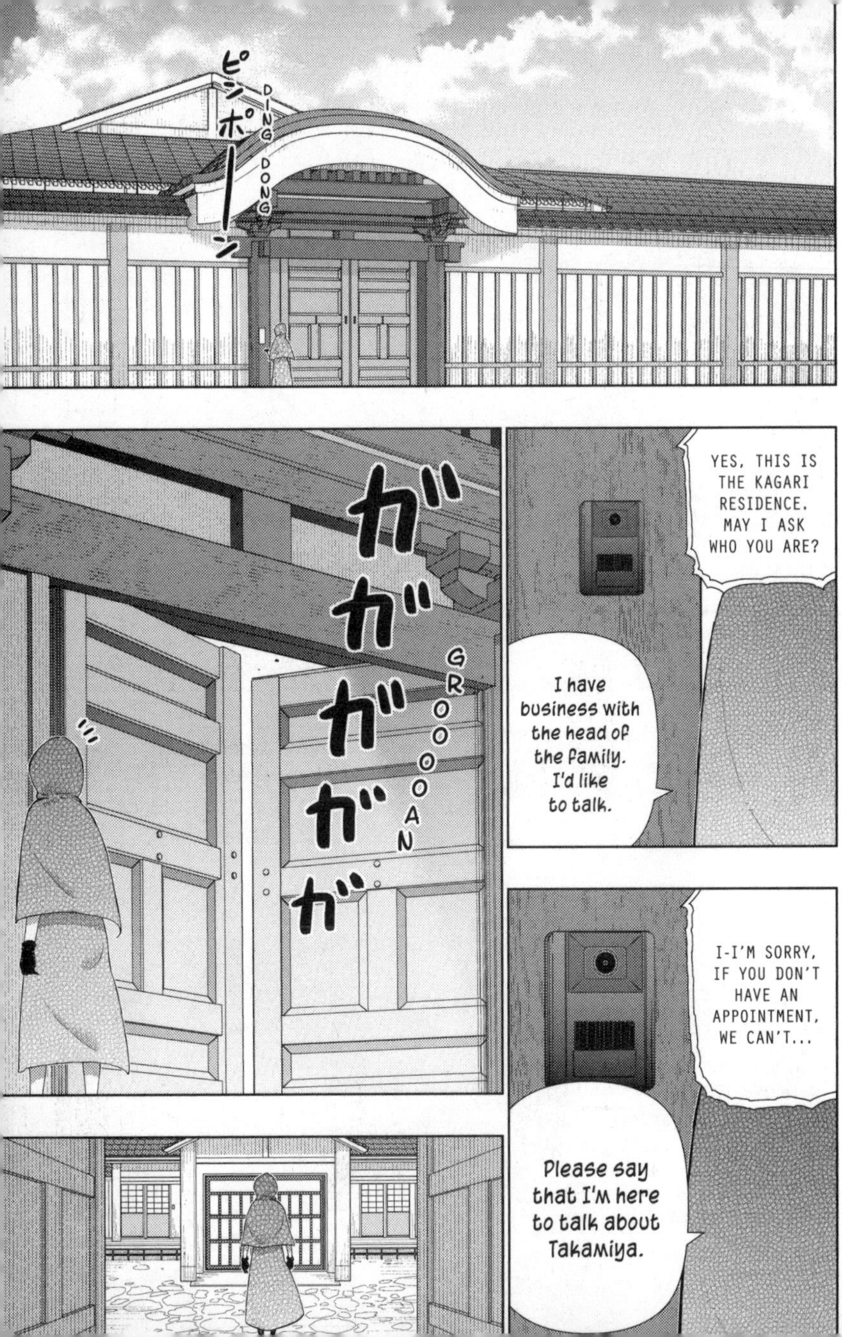
ピンポーン
DING DONG
YES, THIS IS THE KAGARI RESIDENCE. MAY I ASK WHO YOU ARE?
I have business with the head of the family. I'd like to talk.
I-I'M SORRY, IF YOU DON'T HAVE AN APPOINTMENT, WE CAN'T...
Please say that I'm here to talk about Takamiya.
ガガガガガ
GROOOOAN
...

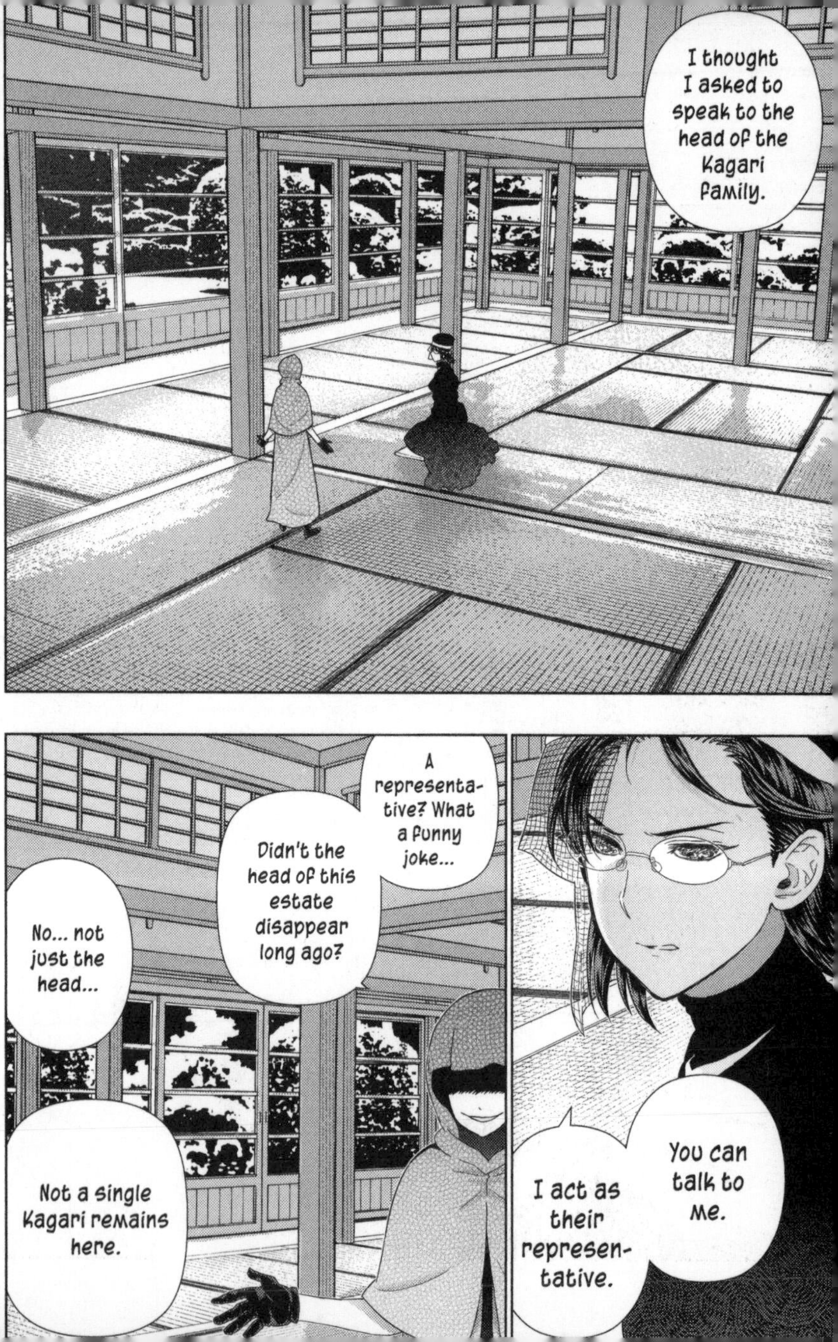
I thought I asked to speak to the head of the Kagari family.
You can talk to me.
I act as their representative.
A representative? What a funny joke...
Didn't the head of this estate disappear long ago?
No... not just the head...
Not a single Kagari remains here.

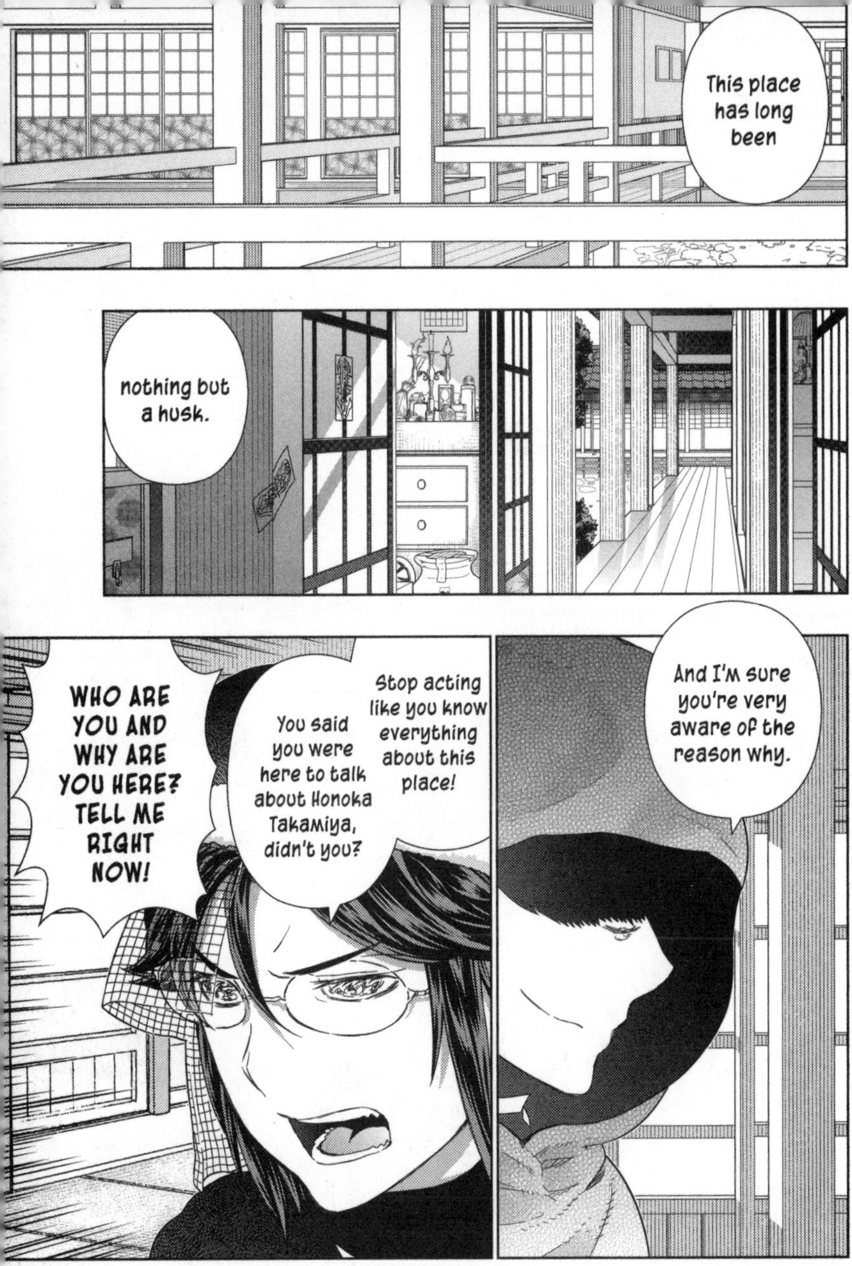

This place has long been
nothing but a husk.
And I'm sure you're very aware of the reason why.
Stop acting like you know everything about this place!
You said you were here to talk about Honoka Takamiya, didn't you?
WHO ARE YOU AND WHY ARE YOU HERE? TELL ME RIGHT NOW!

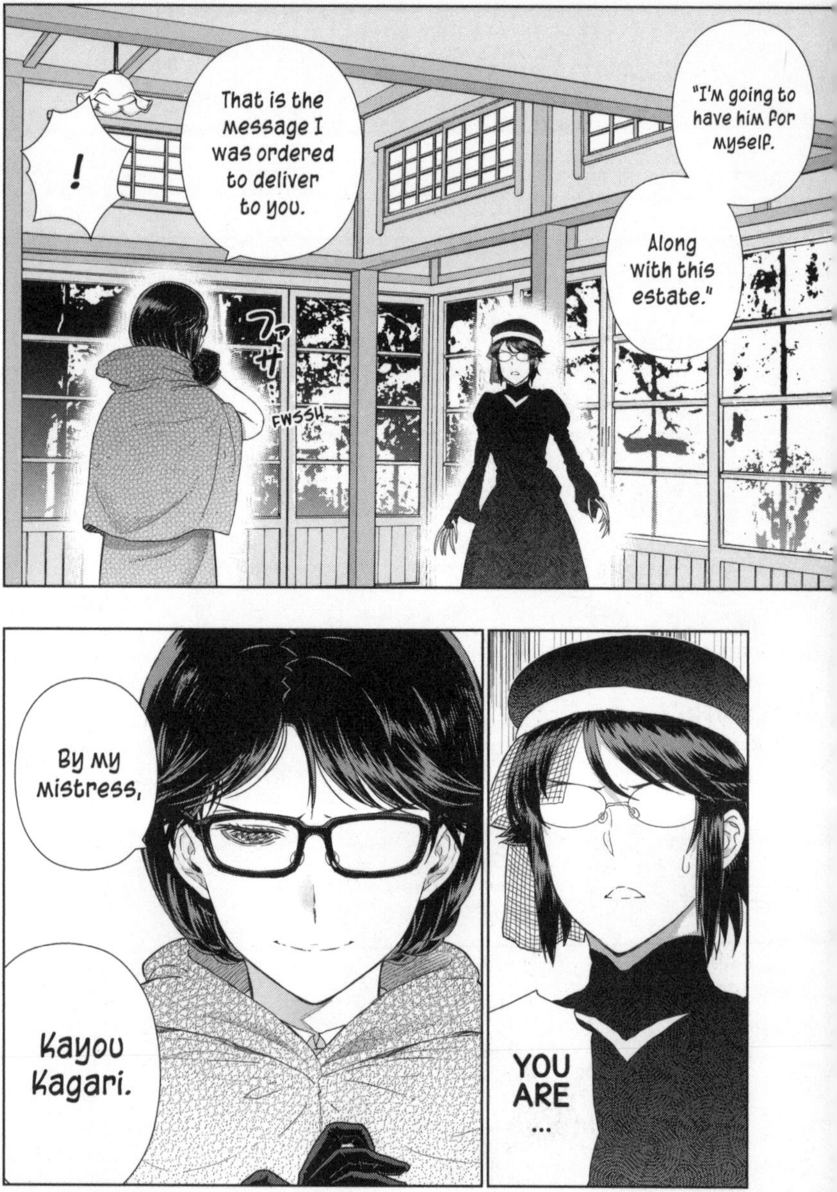
"I'm going to have him for myself.
Along with this estate."
That is the message I was ordered to deliver to you.
!
ファサ
FWSSH
YOU ARE ...
By my Mistress,
Kayou Kagari.

CHAPTER 50: *END*

Witchcraft Works

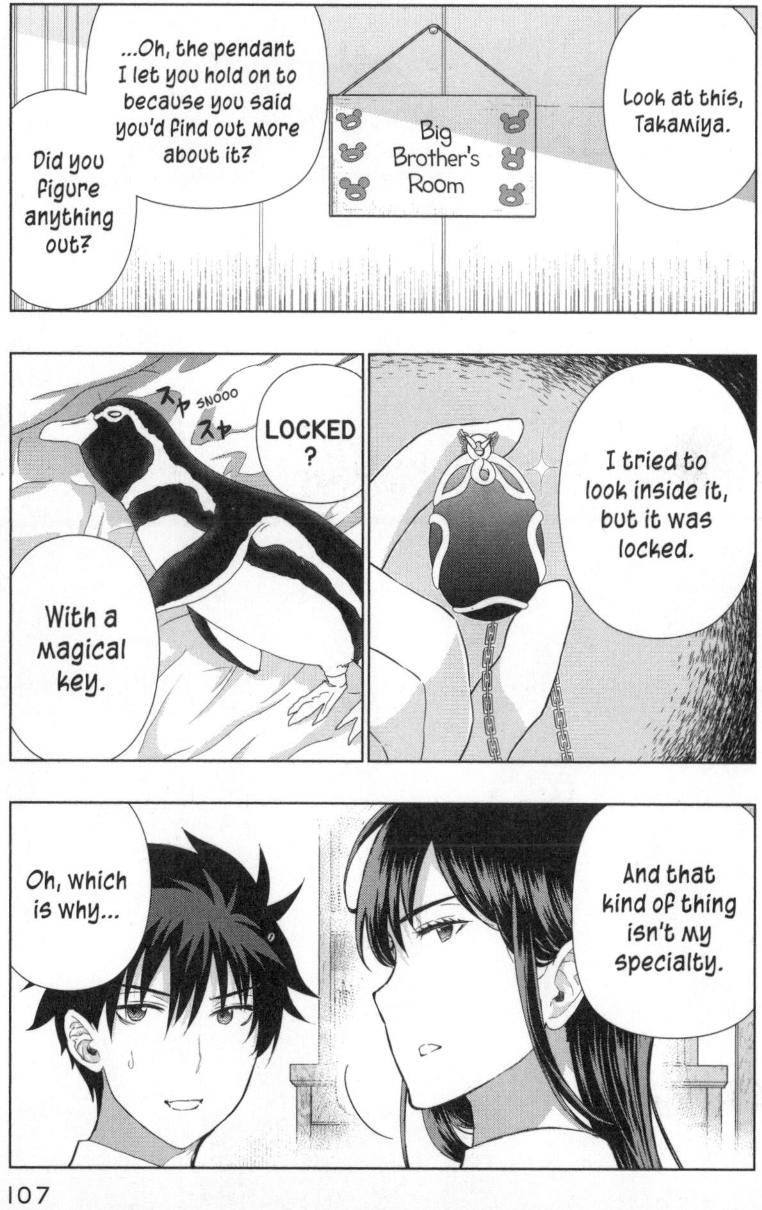
Look at this, Takamiya.
Big Brother's Room
...Oh, the pendant I let you hold on to because you said you'd find out more about it?
Did you figure anything out?
I tried to look inside it, but it was locked.
LOCKED?
スャ SNOOO スャ
With a magical key.
And that kind of thing isn't my specialty.
Oh, which is why...

CHAPTER 51 Takamiya and the Pendant's World (Part 1)

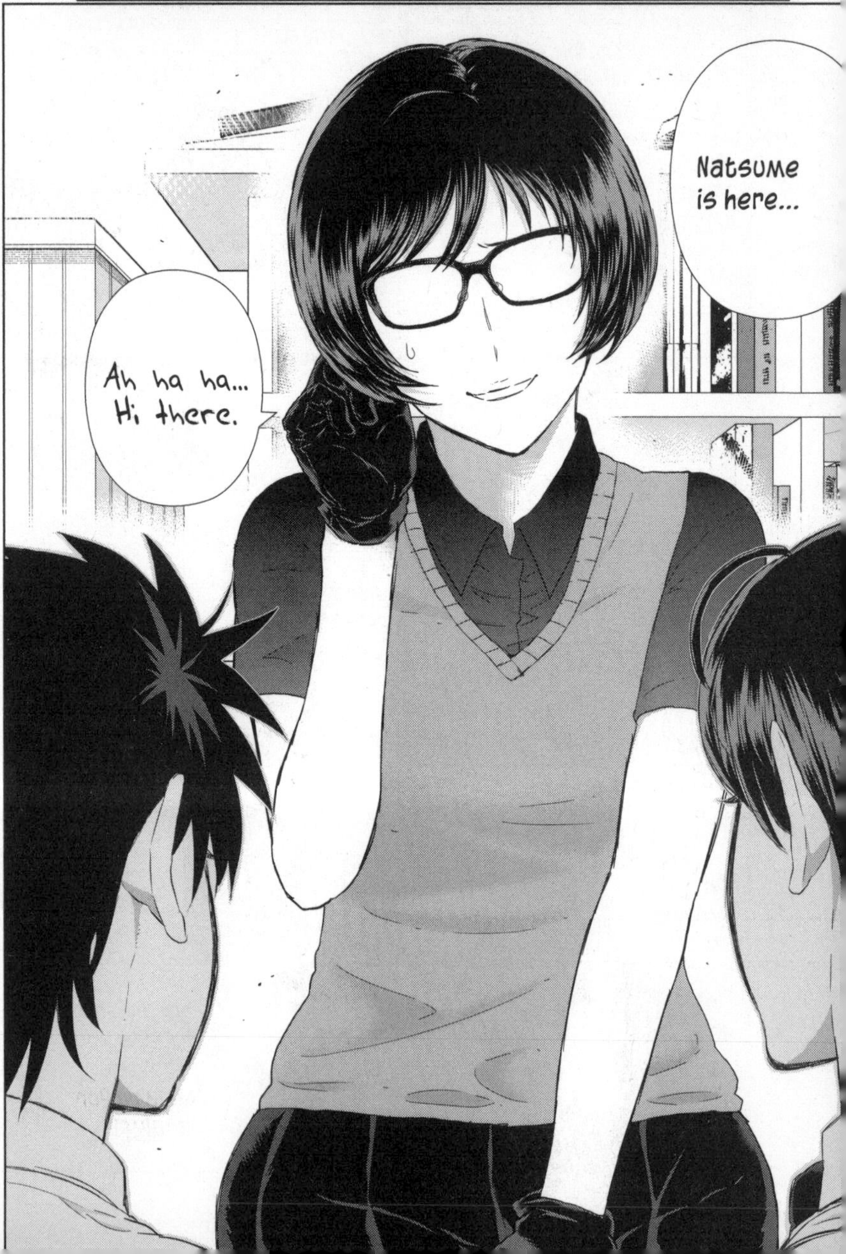
Natsume is here...
Ah ha ha... Hi there.

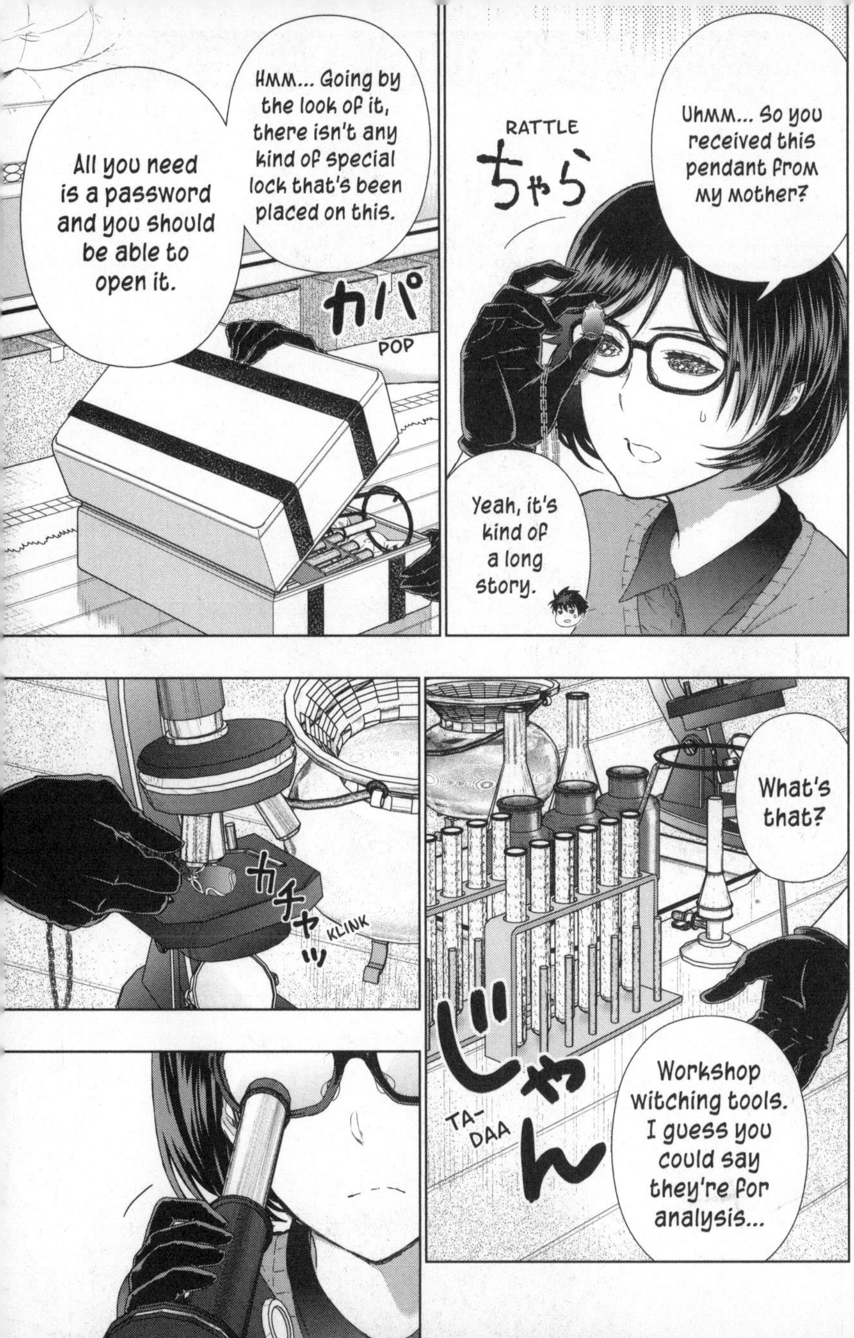
Uhmm... So you received this pendant from my mother?
ちゃら
RATTLE
Yeah, it's kind of a long story.
Hmm... Going by the look of it, there isn't any kind of special lock that's been placed on this.
All you need is a password and you should be able to open it.
カパ
POP
What's that?
じゃん
TA-DAA
Workshop witching tools. I guess you could say they're for analysis...
カチャッ
KLINK

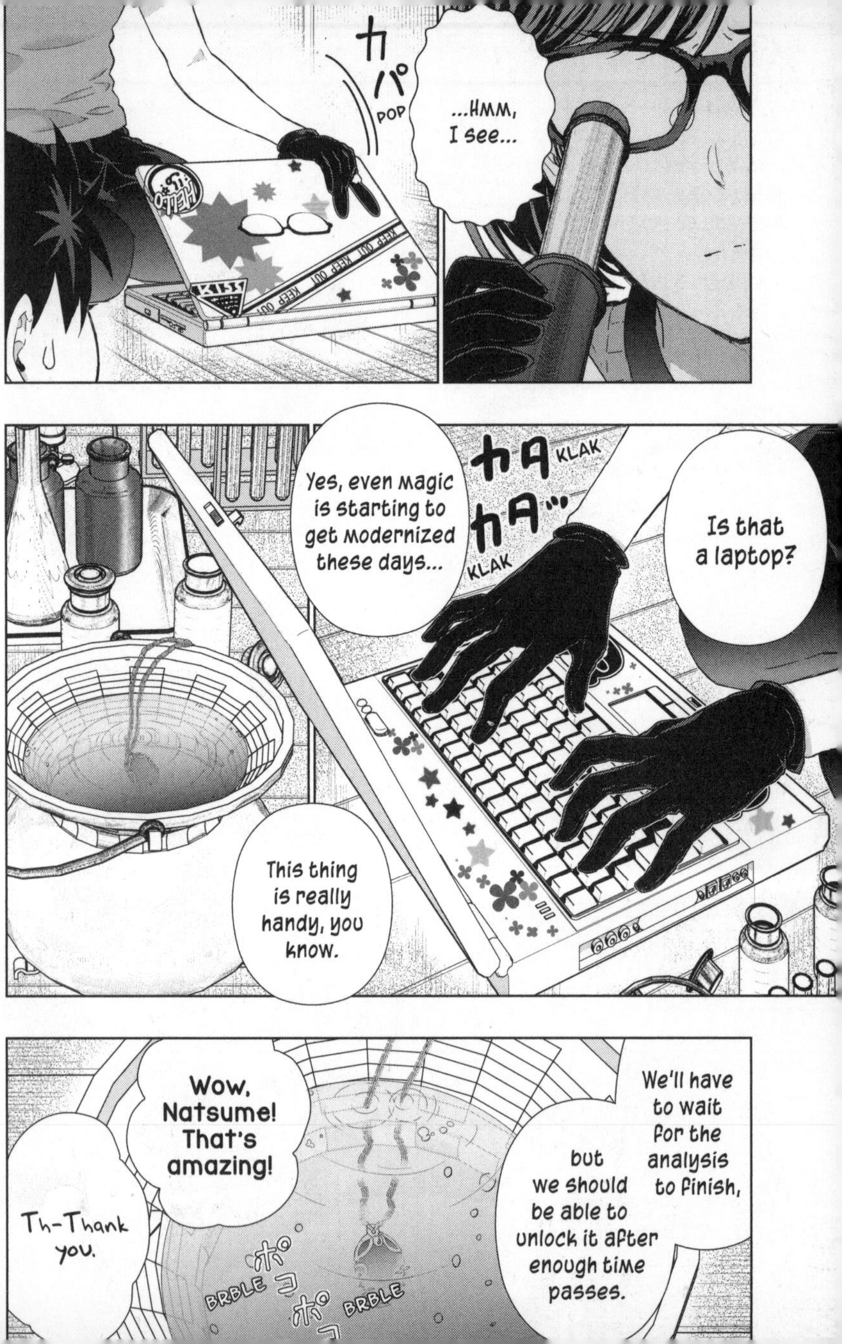
...HMM,
I see...
カパ
POP
HELLO
KISS
KEEP OUT
Is that a laptop?
カタ KLAK
カタ… KLAK
Yes, even magic is starting to get modernized these days...
This thing is really handy, you know.
We'll have to wait for the analysis to finish, but we should be able to unlock it after enough time passes.
Wow, Natsume! That's amazing!
Th-Thank you.
ポコ BRBLE
ポコ BRBLE

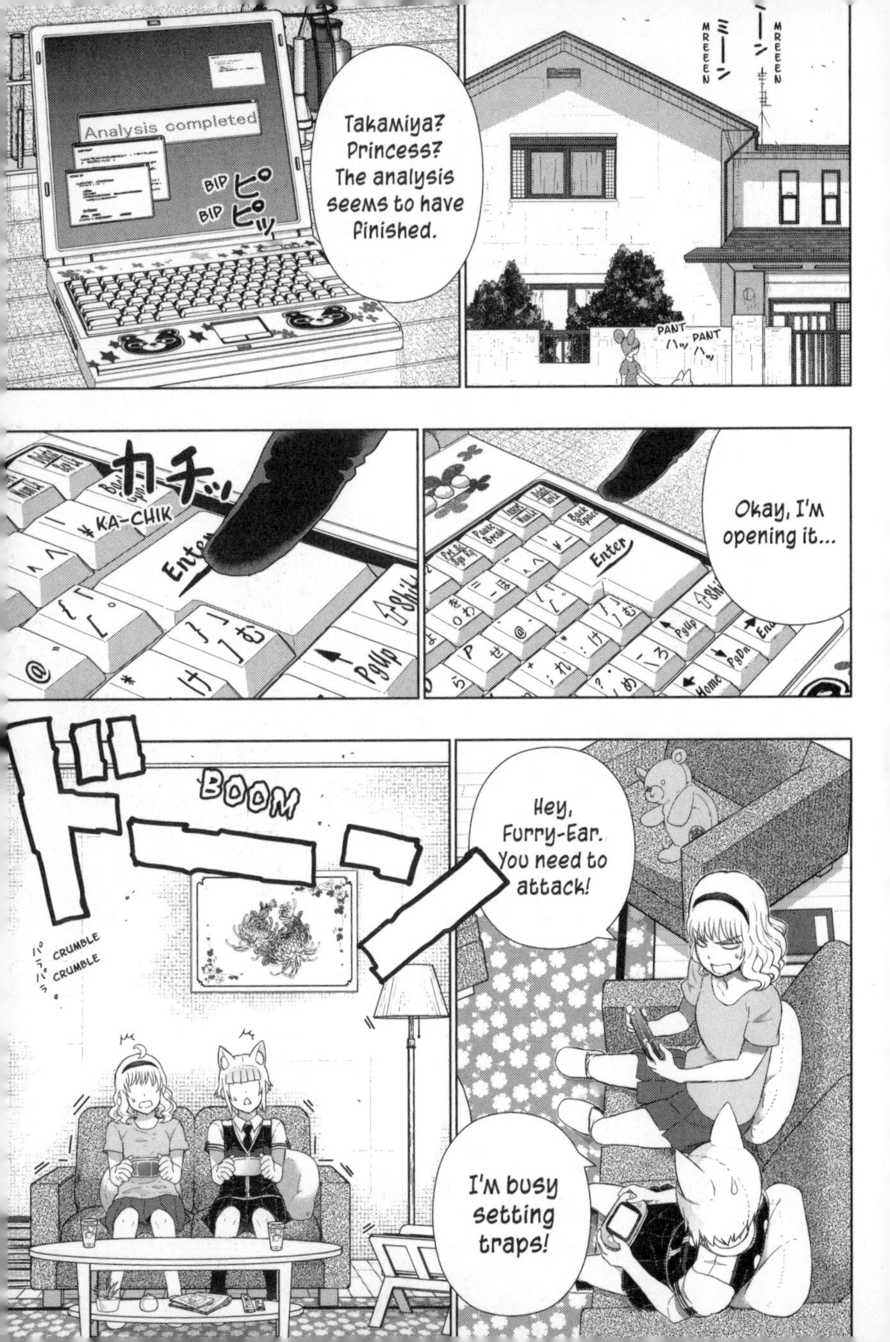

ミーン MREEEN
ミーン MREEEN
ハッ PANT
ハッ PANT
Takamiya? Princess? The analysis seems to have finished.
Analysis completed
ピッ BIP
ピッ BIP
Okay, I'm opening it...
カチッ KA-CHIK
Hey, Furry-Ear. You need to attack!
I'm busy setting traps!
ドーン BOOM
パラパラ CRUMBLE CRUMBLE

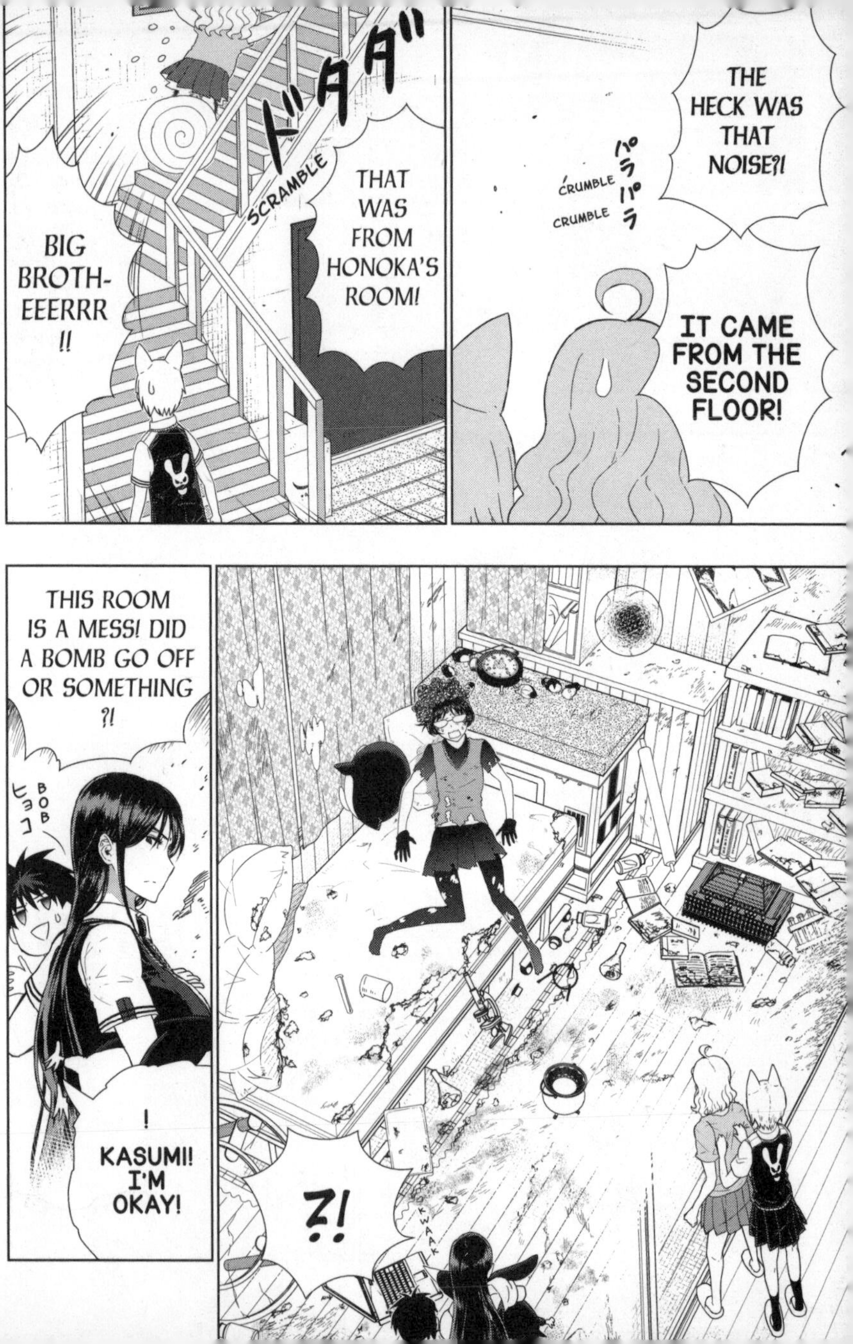
THE HECK WAS THAT NOISE?!
パラパラ
CRUMBLE CRUMBLE
IT CAME FROM THE SECOND FLOOR!
ドタダ
SCRAMBLE
THAT WAS FROM HONOKA'S ROOM!
BIG BROTH-EEERRR!!
?!
KWAAK
THIS ROOM IS A MESS! DID A BOMB GO OFF OR SOMETHING?!
ヒョコ
BOB
!
KASUMI! I'M OKAY!

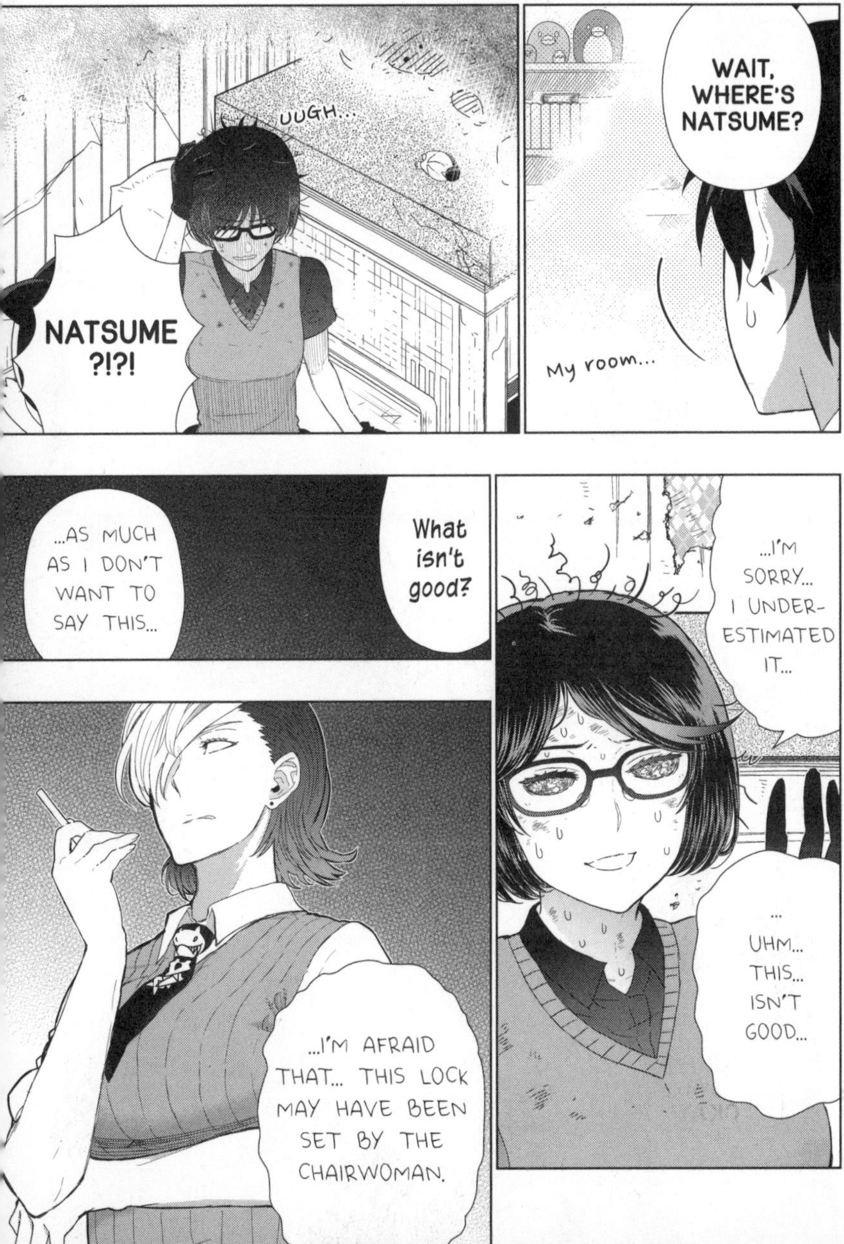
WAIT, WHERE'S NATSUME?
My room...
UUGH...
NATSUME ?!?!
...I'M SORRY... I UNDER-ESTIMATED IT...
... UHM... THIS... ISN'T GOOD...
What isn't good?
...AS MUCH AS I DON'T WANT TO SAY THIS...
...I'M AFRAID THAT... THIS LOCK MAY HAVE BEEN SET BY THE CHAIRWOMAN.

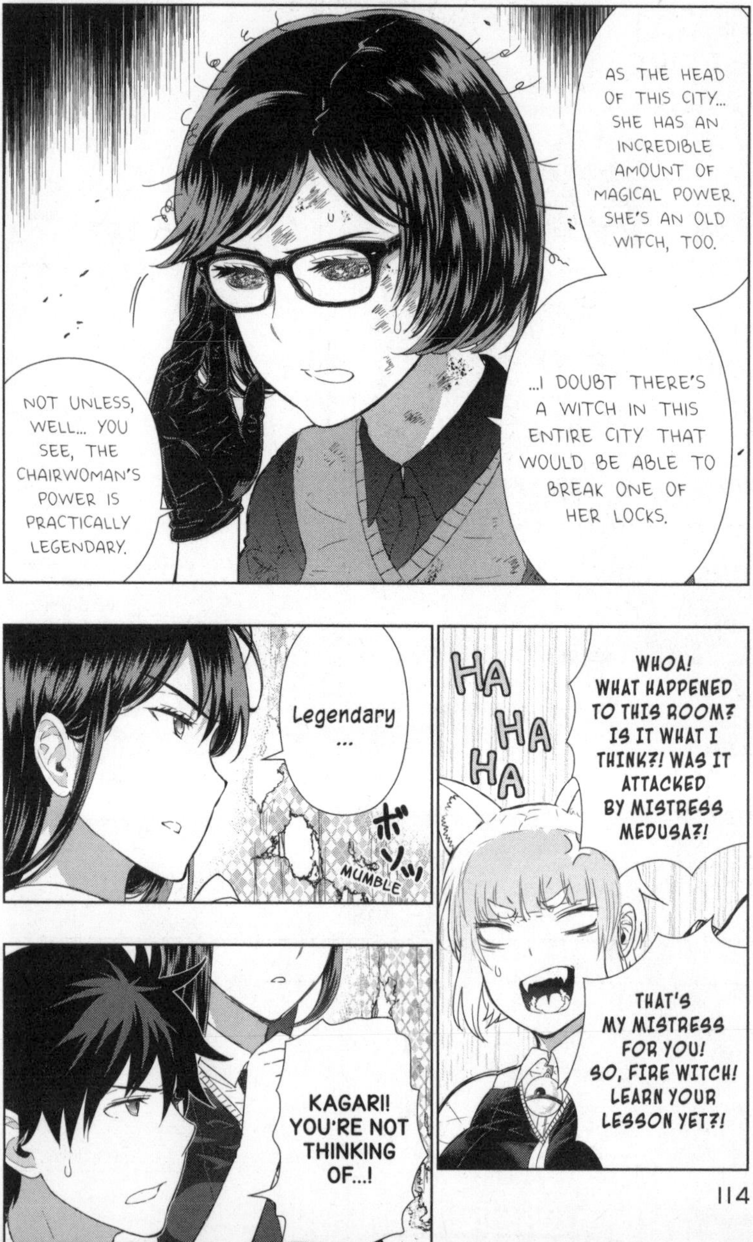
AS THE HEAD OF THIS CITY... SHE HAS AN INCREDIBLE AMOUNT OF MAGICAL POWER. SHE'S AN OLD WITCH, TOO.
...I DOUBT THERE'S A WITCH IN THIS ENTIRE CITY THAT WOULD BE ABLE TO BREAK ONE OF HER LOCKS.
NOT UNLESS, WELL... YOU SEE, THE CHAIRWOMAN'S POWER IS PRACTICALLY LEGENDARY.
WHOA! WHAT HAPPENED TO THIS ROOM? IS IT WHAT I THINK?! WAS IT ATTACKED BY MISTRESS MEDUSA?!
HA HA HA
THAT'S MY MISTRESS FOR YOU! SO, FIRE WITCH! LEARN YOUR LESSON YET?!
Legendary ...
ボソッ
MUMBLE
KAGARI! YOU'RE NOT THINKING OF...!

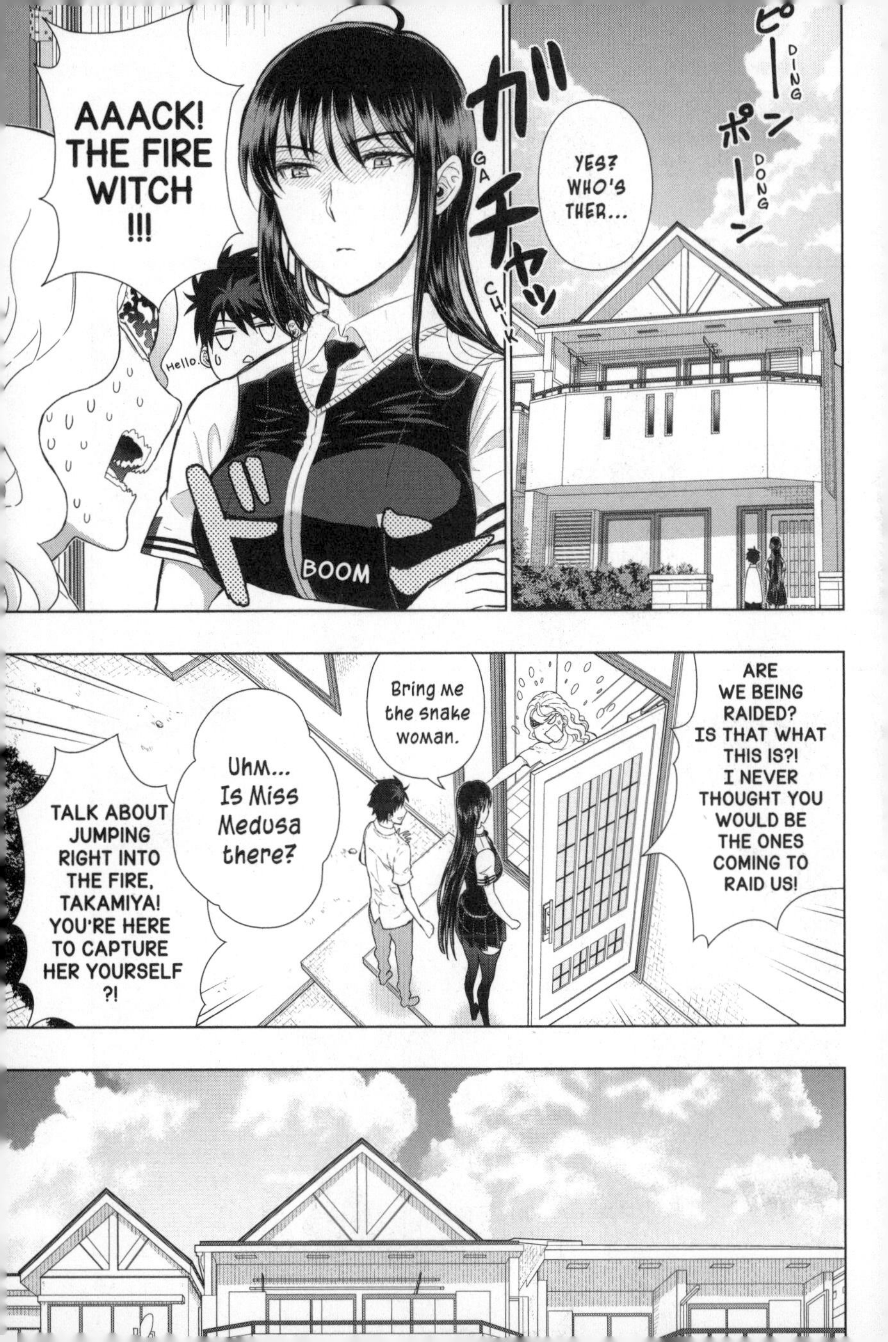
ピーンポーン
DING DONG
YES? WHO'S THER...
ガチャッ
GA CHIK
AAACK! THE FIRE WITCH !!!
Hello.
ドッ
BOOM
ARE WE BEING RAIDED? IS THAT WHAT THIS IS?! I NEVER THOUGHT YOU WOULD BE THE ONES COMING TO RAID US!
Bring me the snake woman.
Uhm... Is Miss Medusa there?
TALK ABOUT JUMPING RIGHT INTO THE FIRE, TAKAMIYA! YOU'RE HERE TO CAPTURE HER YOURSELF ?!

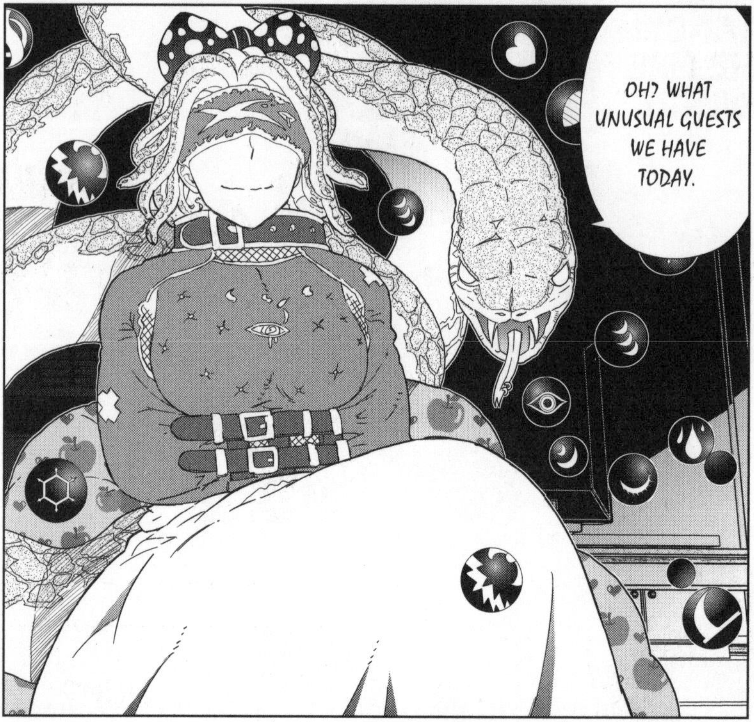
OH? WHAT UNUSUAL GUESTS WE HAVE TODAY.

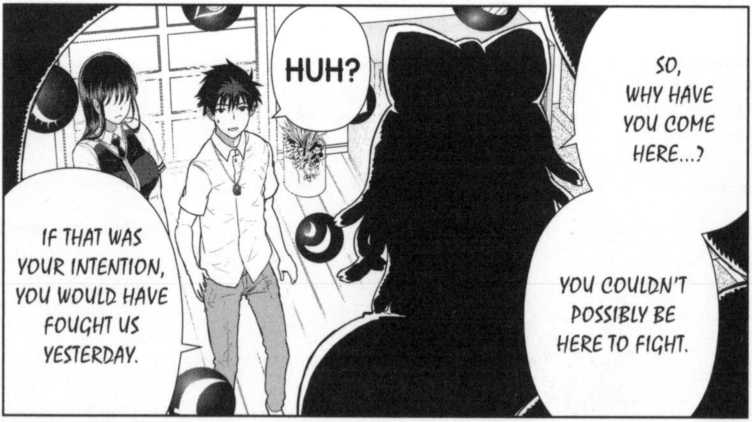
SO, WHY HAVE YOU COME HERE...?
HUH?
YOU COULDN'T POSSIBLY BE HERE TO FIGHT.
IF THAT WAS YOUR INTENTION, YOU WOULD HAVE FOUGHT US YESTERDAY.

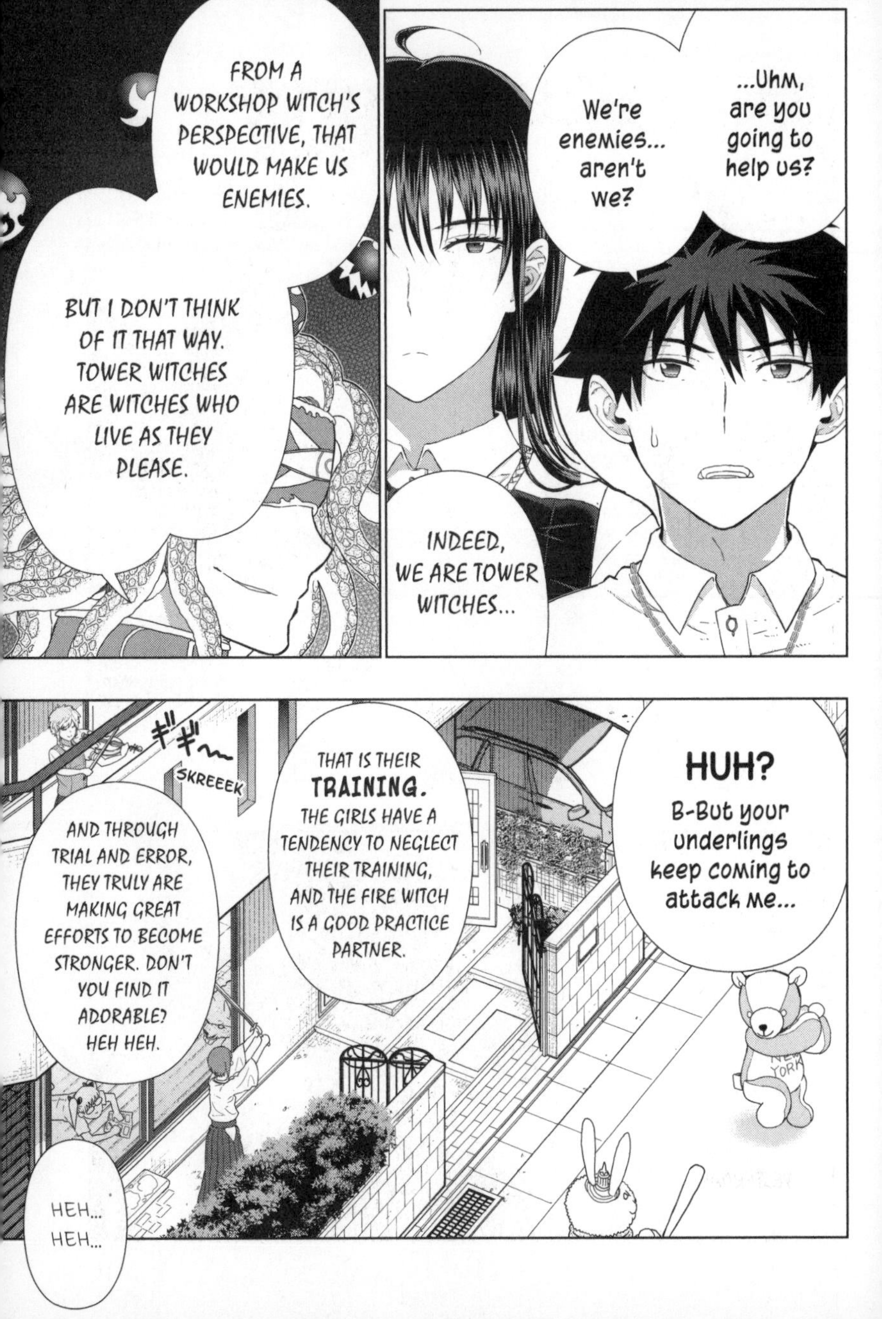
...Uhm, are you going to help us?
We're enemies... aren't we?
INDEED, WE ARE TOWER WITCHES...
FROM A WORKSHOP WITCH'S PERSPECTIVE, THAT WOULD MAKE US ENEMIES.
BUT I DON'T THINK OF IT THAT WAY. TOWER WITCHES ARE WITCHES WHO LIVE AS THEY PLEASE.
HUH?
B-But your underlings keep coming to attack me...
THAT IS THEIR **TRAINING.** THE GIRLS HAVE A TENDENCY TO NEGLECT THEIR TRAINING, AND THE FIRE WITCH IS A GOOD PRACTICE PARTNER.
ギギ~
SKREEEK
AND THROUGH TRIAL AND ERROR, THEY TRULY ARE MAKING GREAT EFFORTS TO BECOME STRONGER. DON'T YOU FIND IT ADORABLE? HEH HEH.
HEH... HEH...

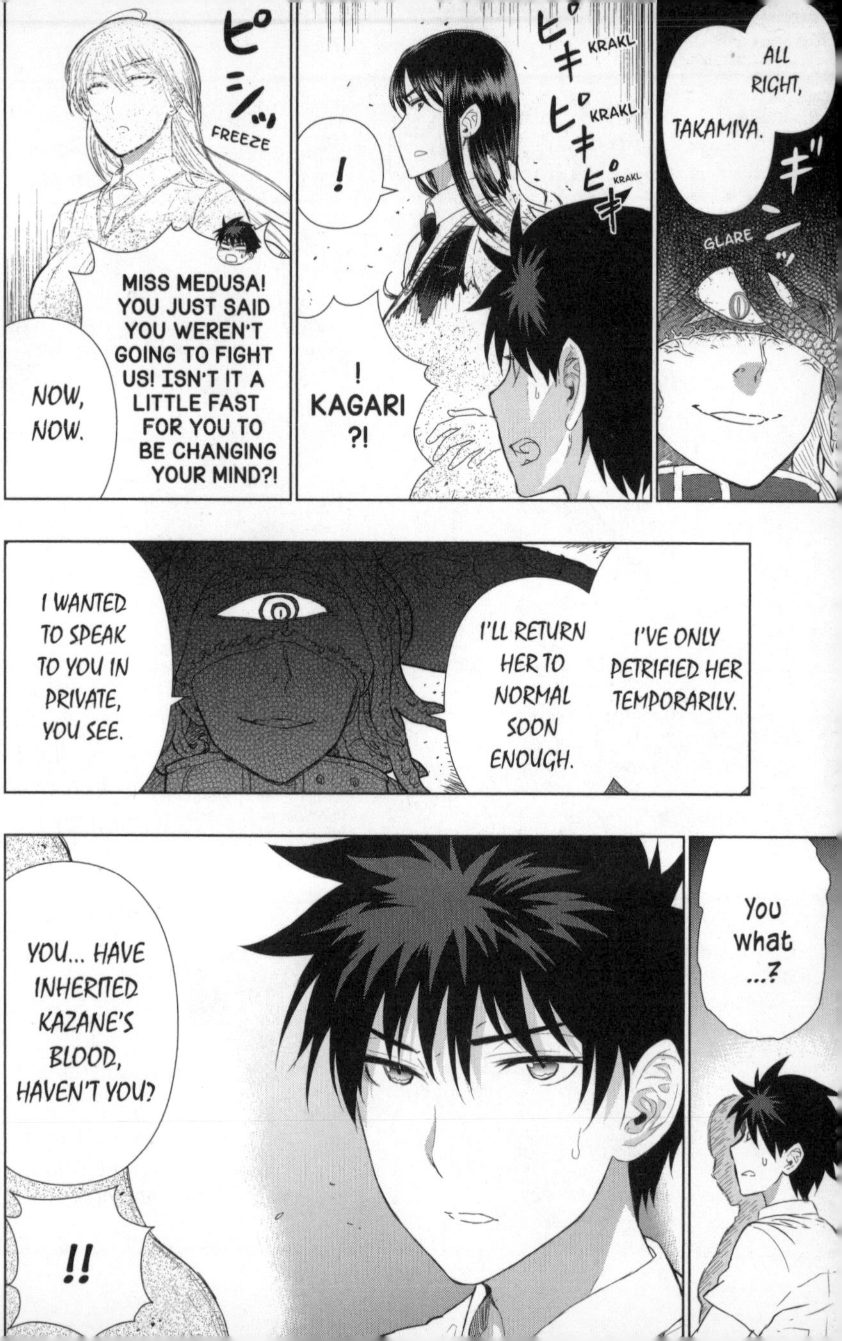
ALL RIGHT, TAKAMIYA.
ギンッ
GLARE
ピキ ピキ ピキ
KRAKL KRAKL KRAKL
!
! KAGARI ?!
ピシッ
FREEZE
MISS MEDUSA! YOU JUST SAID YOU WEREN'T GOING TO FIGHT US! ISN'T IT A LITTLE FAST FOR YOU TO BE CHANGING YOUR MIND?!
NOW, NOW.
I'VE ONLY PETRIFIED HER TEMPORARILY.
I'LL RETURN HER TO NORMAL SOON ENOUGH.
I WANTED TO SPEAK TO YOU IN PRIVATE, YOU SEE.
You what ...?
YOU... HAVE INHERITED KAZANE'S BLOOD, HAVEN'T YOU?
!!

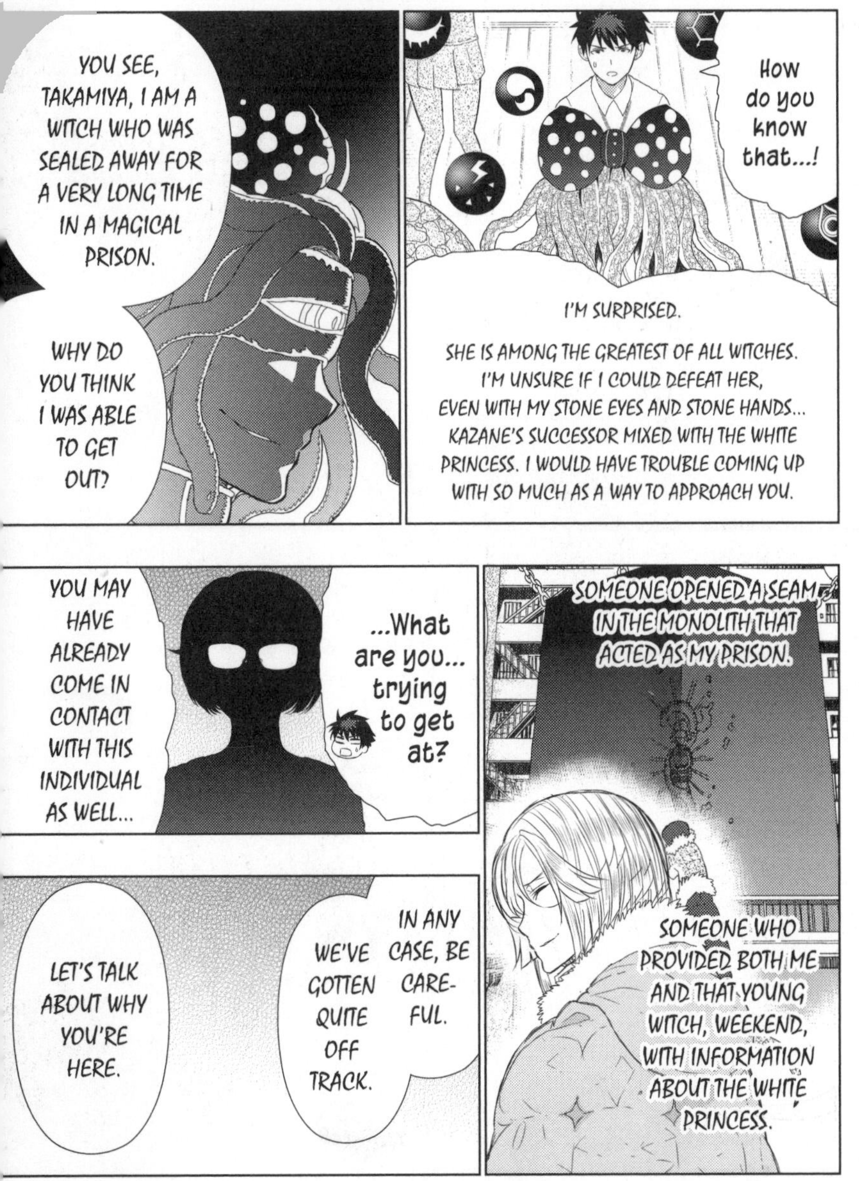
How do you know that...!
I'M SURPRISED.
SHE IS AMONG THE GREATEST OF ALL WITCHES. I'M UNSURE IF I COULD DEFEAT HER, EVEN WITH MY STONE EYES AND STONE HANDS... KAZANE'S SUCCESSOR MIXED WITH THE WHITE PRINCESS. I WOULD HAVE TROUBLE COMING UP WITH SO MUCH AS A WAY TO APPROACH YOU.
YOU SEE, TAKAMIYA, I AM A WITCH WHO WAS SEALED AWAY FOR A VERY LONG TIME IN A MAGICAL PRISON.
WHY DO YOU THINK I WAS ABLE TO GET OUT?
SOMEONE OPENED A SEAM IN THE MONOLITH THAT ACTED AS MY PRISON.
SOMEONE WHO PROVIDED BOTH ME AND THAT YOUNG WITCH, WEEKEND, WITH INFORMATION ABOUT THE WHITE PRINCESS.
...What are you... trying to get at?
YOU MAY HAVE ALREADY COME IN CONTACT WITH THIS INDIVIDUAL AS WELL...
IN ANY CASE, BE CARE-FUL.
WE'VE GOTTEN QUITE OFF TRACK.
LET'S TALK ABOUT WHY YOU'RE HERE.

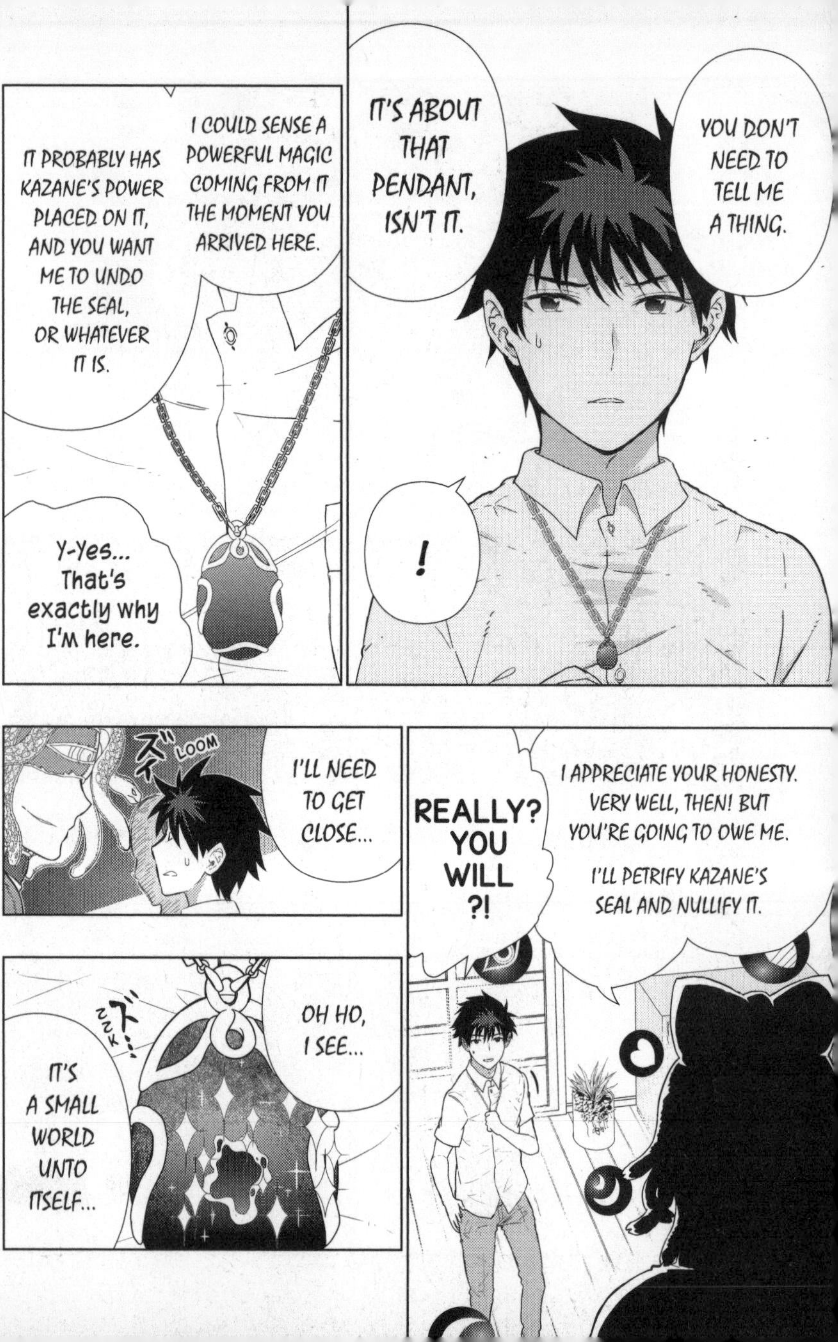

YOU DON'T NEED TO TELL ME A THING.
IT'S ABOUT THAT PENDANT, ISN'T IT.
!
I COULD SENSE A POWERFUL MAGIC COMING FROM IT THE MOMENT YOU ARRIVED HERE.
IT PROBABLY HAS KAZANE'S POWER PLACED ON IT, AND YOU WANT ME TO UNDO THE SEAL, OR WHATEVER IT IS.
Y-Yes... That's exactly why I'm here.
I APPRECIATE YOUR HONESTY. VERY WELL, THEN! BUT YOU'RE GOING TO OWE ME.
I'LL PETRIFY KAZANE'S SEAL AND NULLIFY IT.
REALLY? YOU WILL ?!
ズイ
LOOM
I'LL NEED TO GET CLOSE...
OH HO, I SEE...
ズ...
ZZK
IT'S A SMALL WORLD UNTO ITSELF...

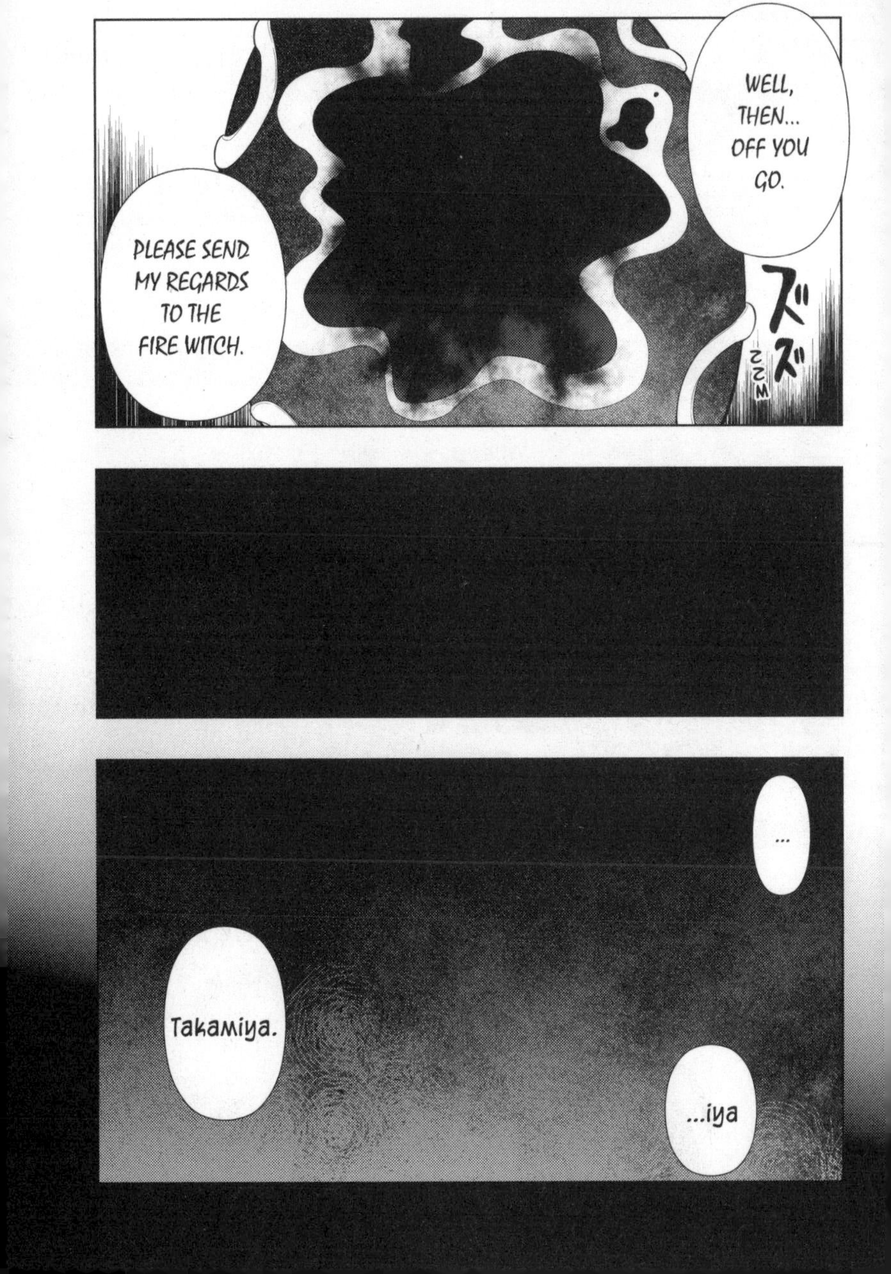
WELL, THEN... OFF YOU GO.
ズズ
ZZM
PLEASE SEND MY REGARDS TO THE FIRE WITCH.
...
Takamiya.
...iya

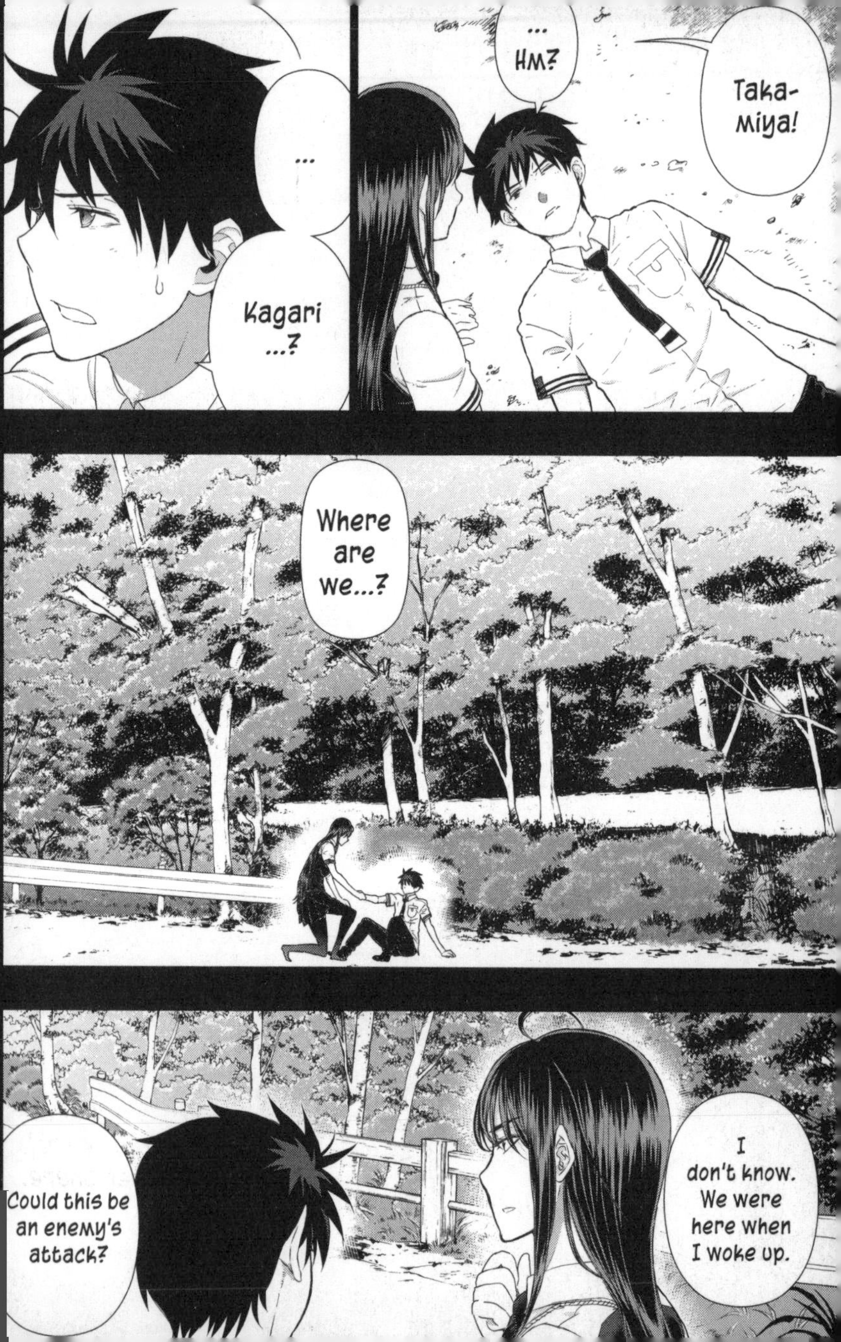
Taka-miya!
... Hm?
...
Kagari ...?
Where are we...?
I don't know. We were here when I woke up.
Could this be an enemy's attack?

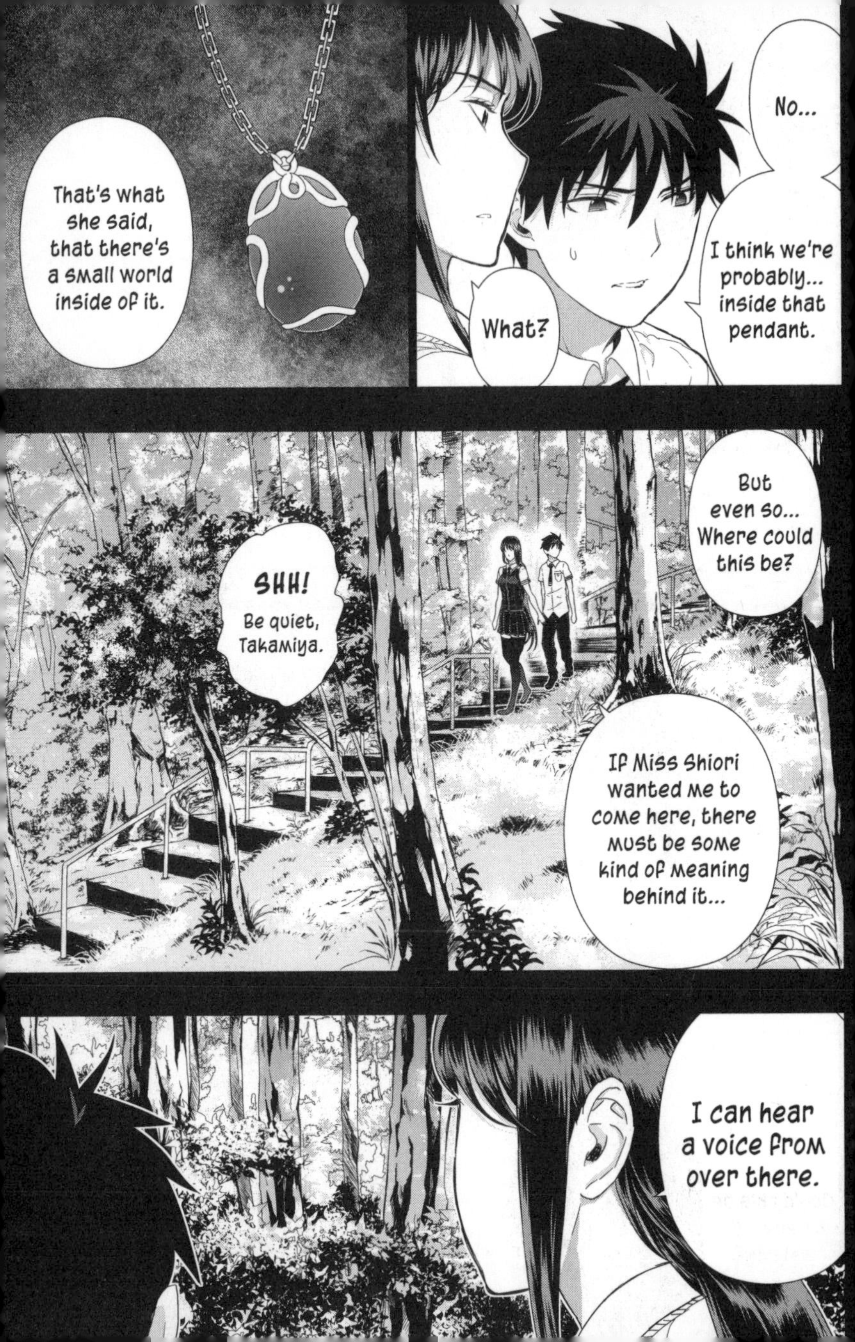
No...
I think we're probably... inside that pendant.
What?
That's what she said, that there's a small world inside of it.
But even so... Where could this be?
If Miss Shiori wanted me to come here, there must be some kind of meaning behind it...
SHH! Be quiet, Takamiya.
I can hear a voice from over there.

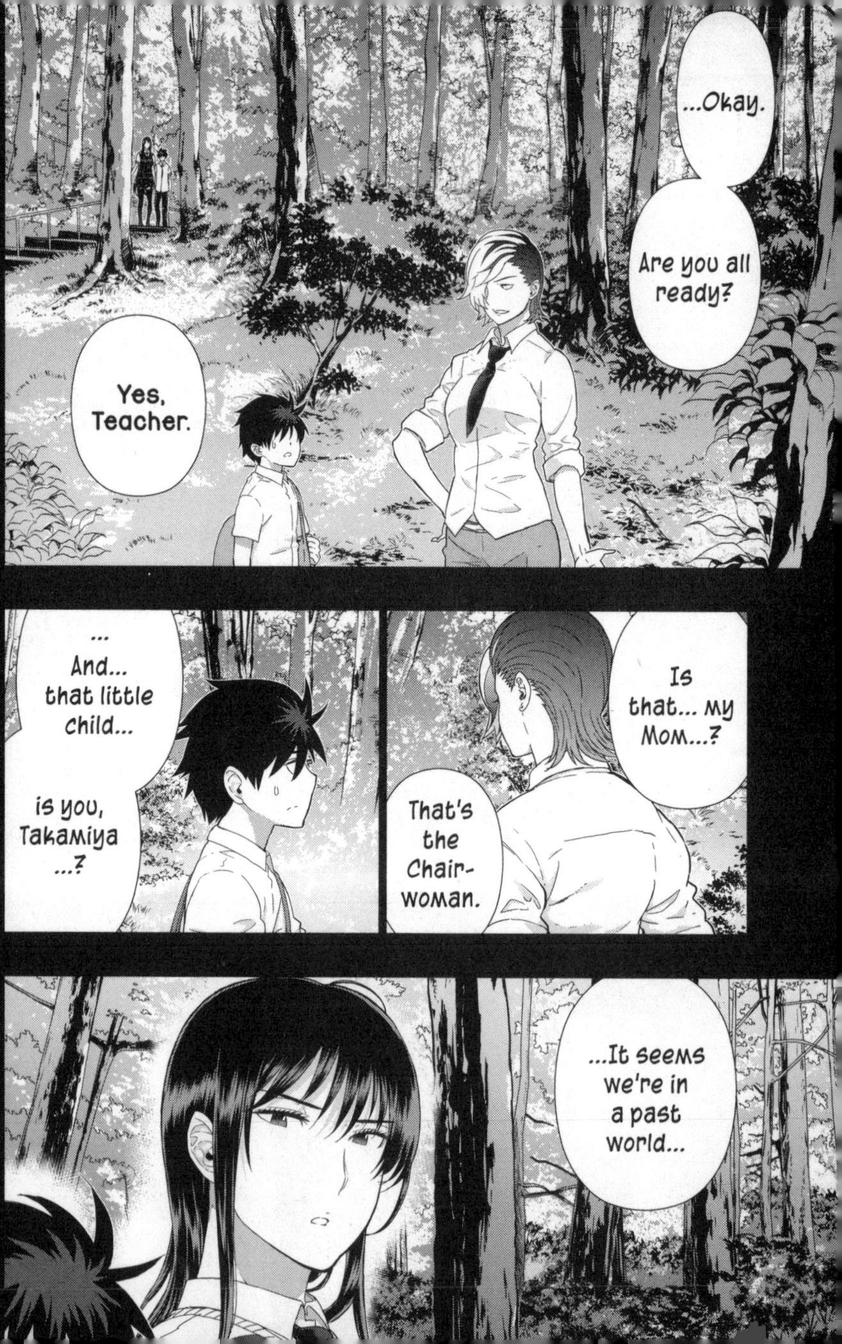
...Okay.
Are you all ready?
Yes, Teacher.
Is that... my Mom...?
That's the Chair-woman.
... And... that little child...
is you, Takamiya ...?
...It seems we're in a past world...

CHAPTER 51 END

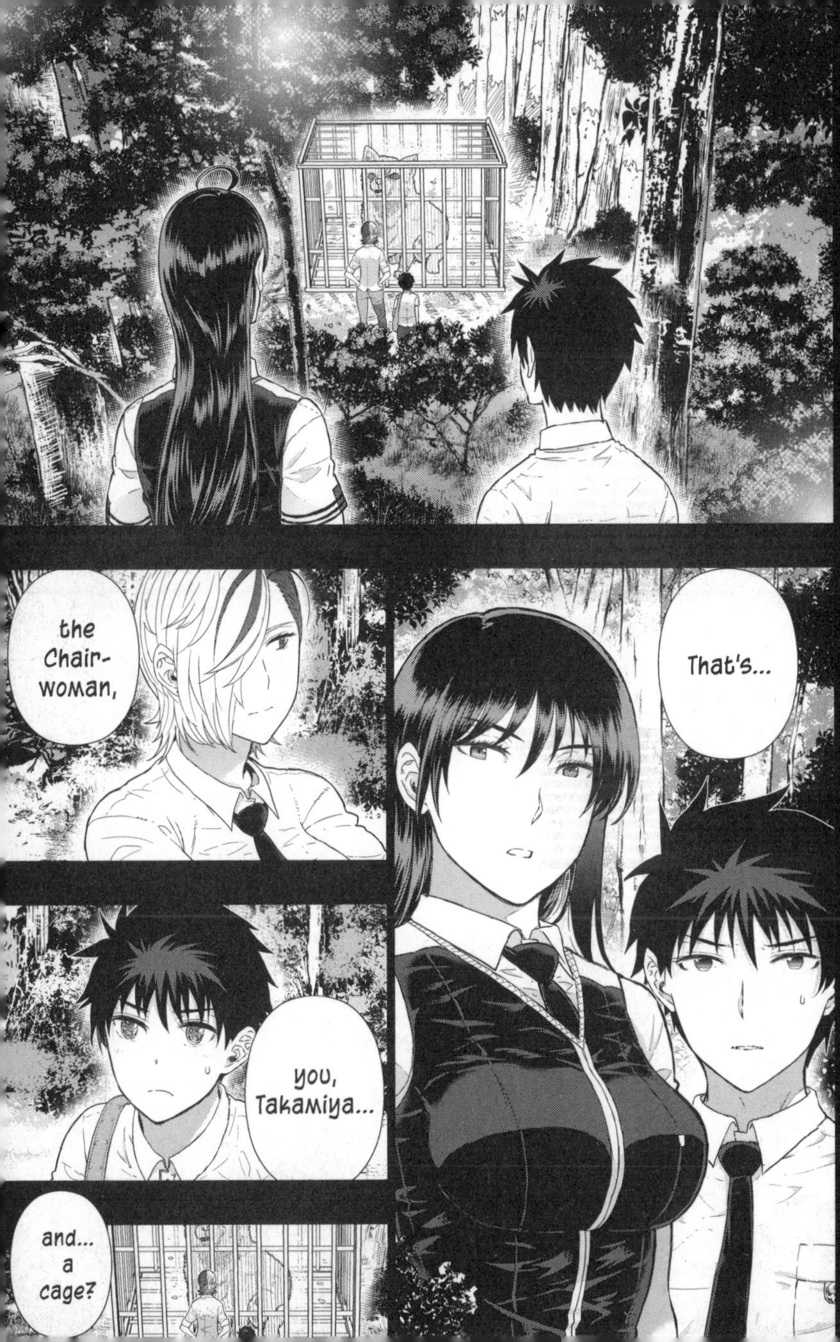
That's...
the Chair-woman,
you, Takamiya...
and... a cage?

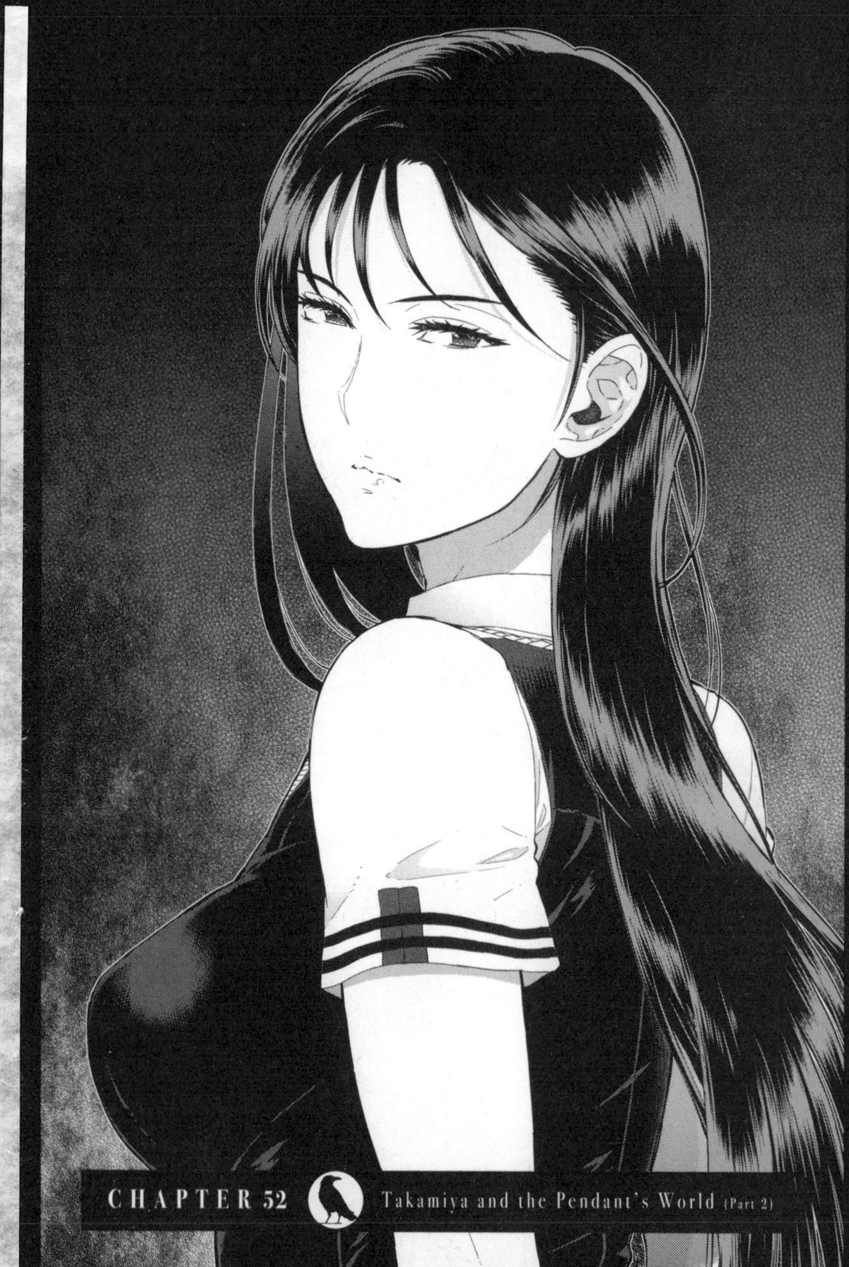

CHAPTER 52 Takamiya and the Pendant's World (Part 2)

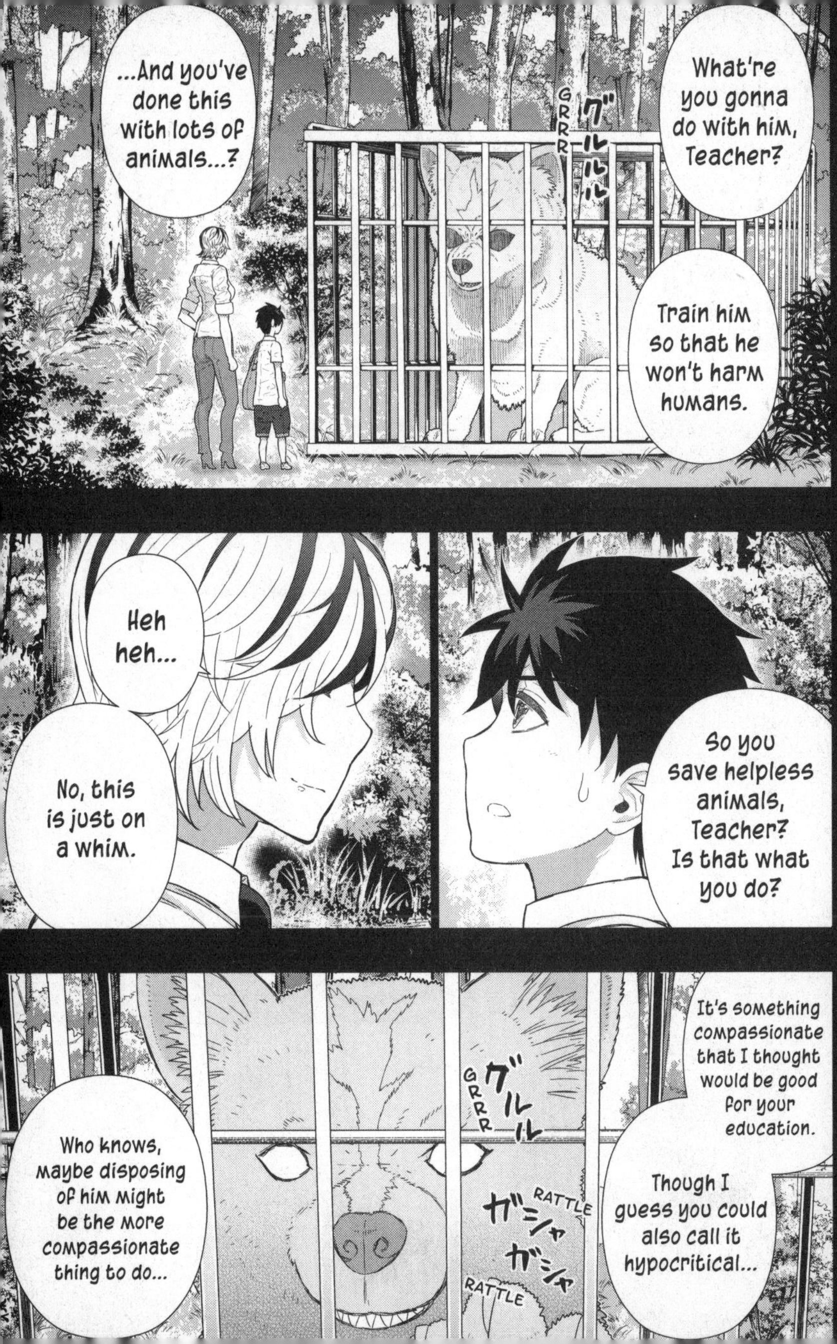
What're you gonna do with him, Teacher?
GRRR グルルル
Train him so that he won't harm humans.
...And you've done this with lots of animals...?
So you save helpless animals, Teacher? Is that what you do?
Heh heh...
No, this is just on a whim.
It's something compassionate that I thought would be good for your education.
Though I guess you could also call it hypocritical...
GRRR グルル
RATTLE ガシャ
RATTLE ガシャ
Who knows, maybe disposing of him might be the more compassionate thing to do...

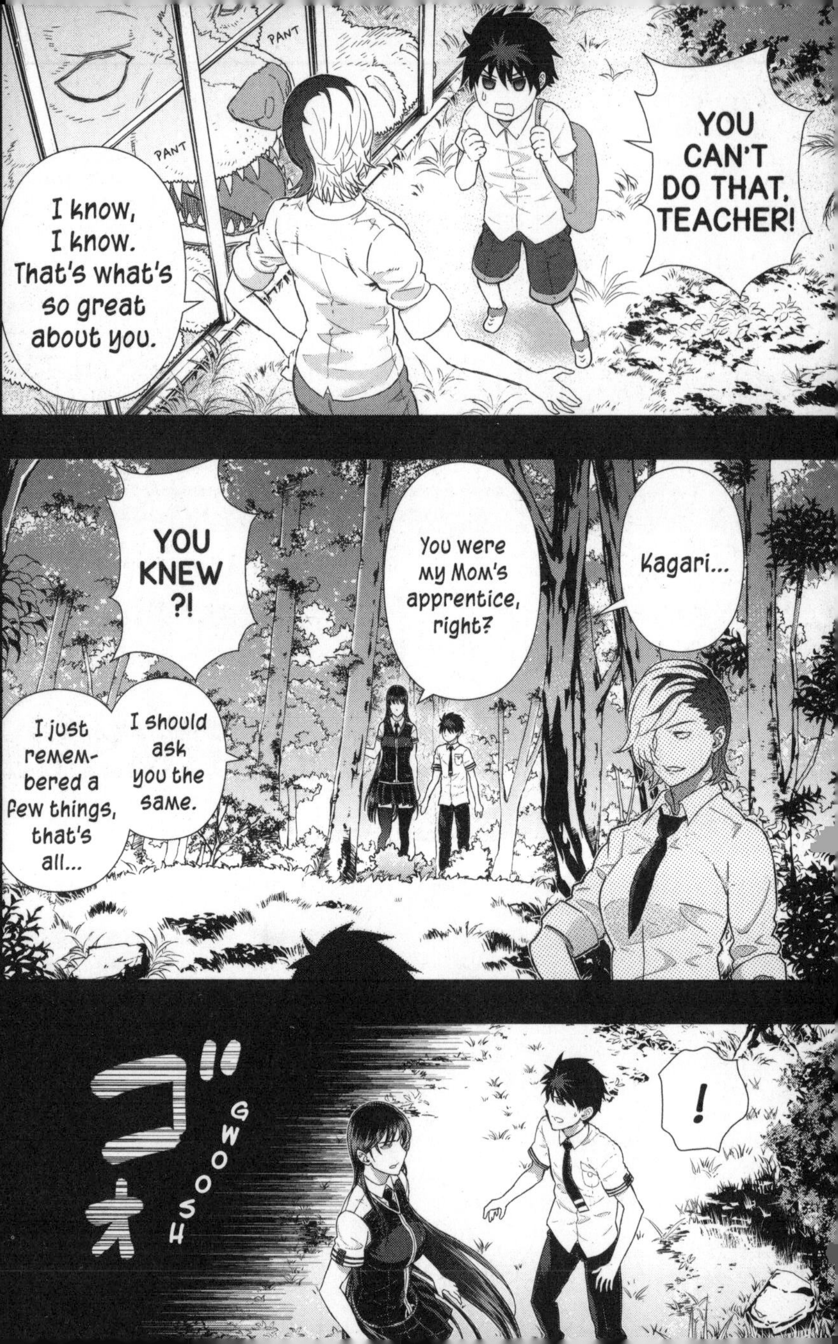
PANT
YOU CAN'T DO THAT, TEACHER!
PANT
I know, I know. That's what's so great about you.
Kagari...
You were my Mom's apprentice, right?
YOU KNEW ?!
I should ask you the same.
I just remem-bered a few things, that's all...
!
GWOOSH

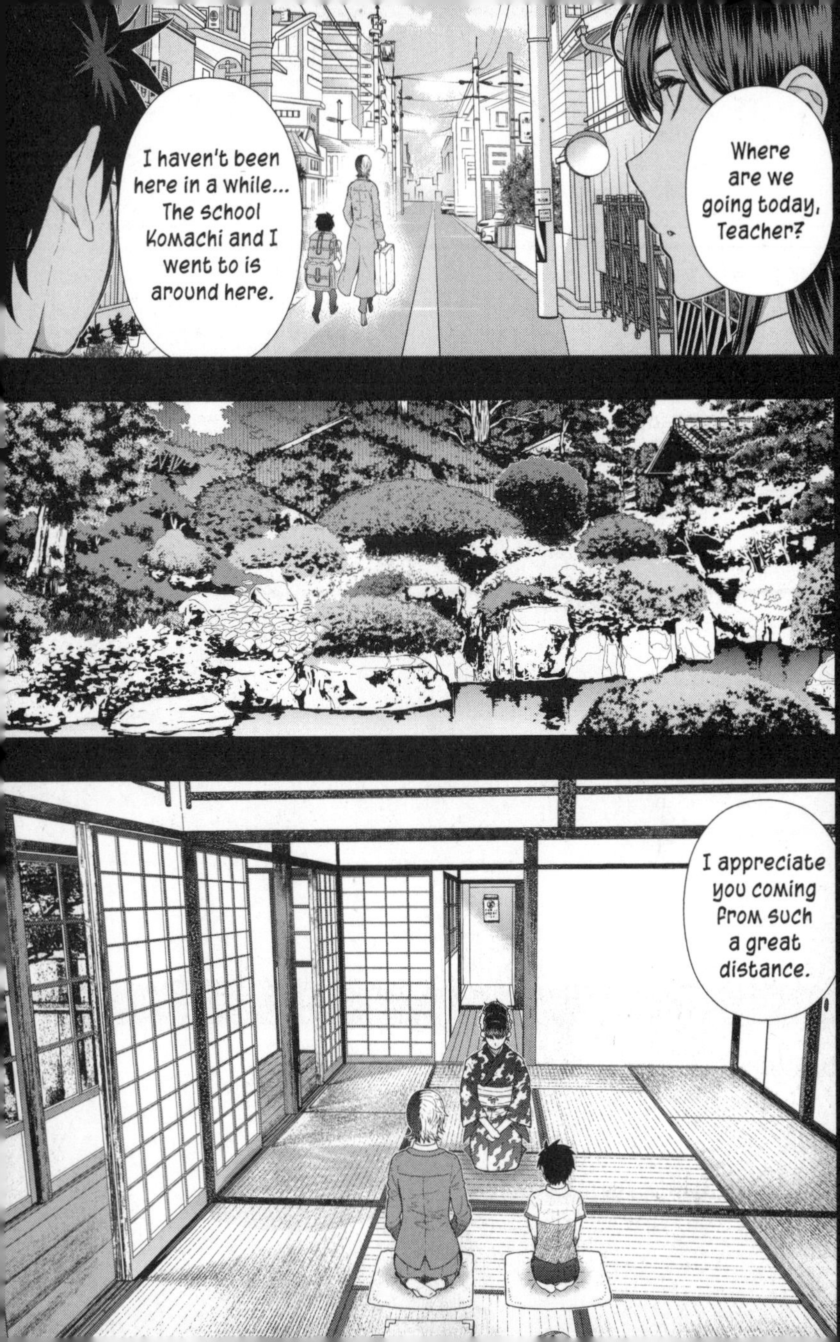
Where are we going today, Teacher?
I haven't been here in a while... The school Komachi and I went to is around here.
I appreciate you coming from such a great distance.

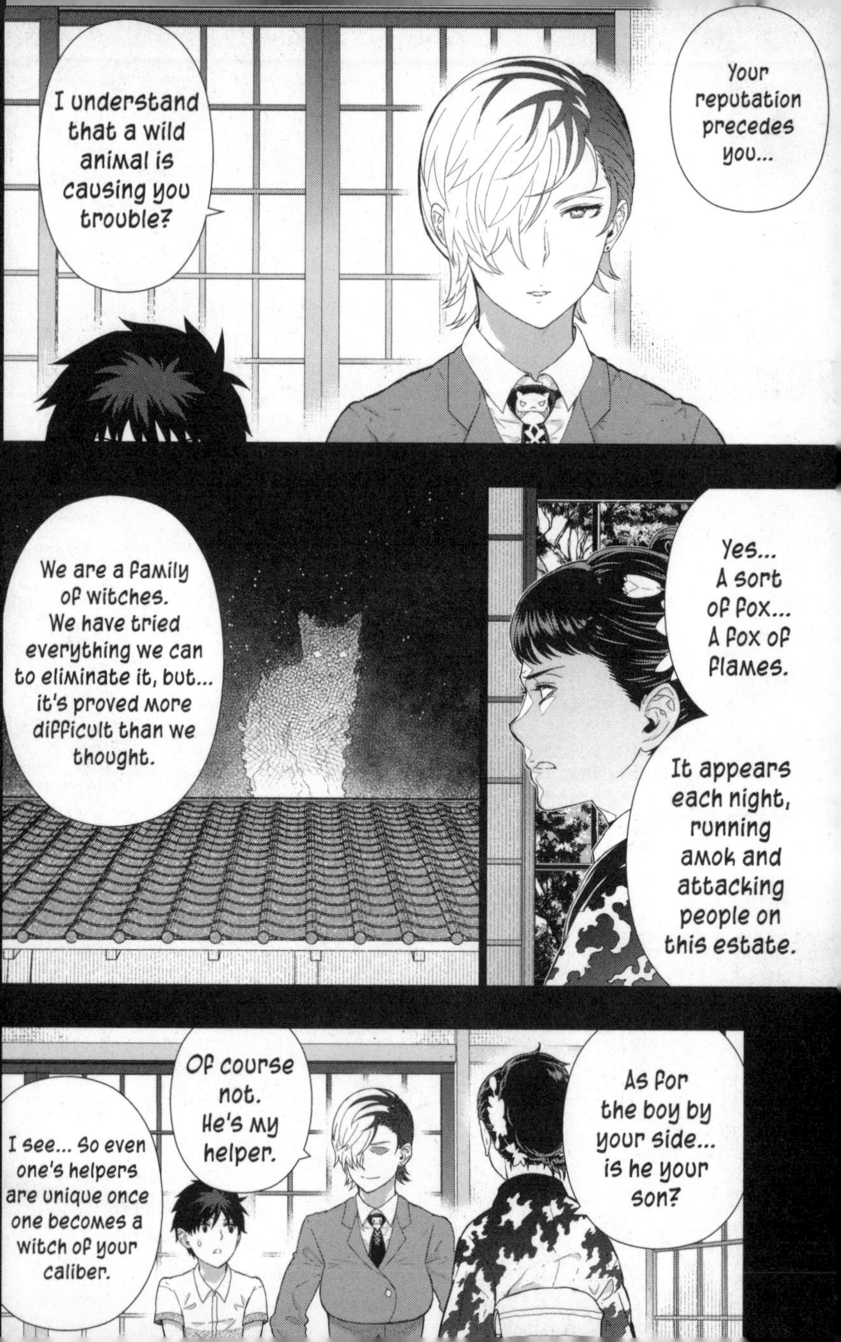
Your reputation precedes you...
I understand that a wild animal is causing you trouble?
Yes... A sort of fox... A fox of flames.
It appears each night, running amok and attacking people on this estate.
We are a family of witches. We have tried everything we can to eliminate it, but... it's proved more difficult than we thought.
As for the boy by your side... is he your son?
Of course not. He's my helper.
I see... So even one's helpers are unique once one becomes a witch of your caliber.

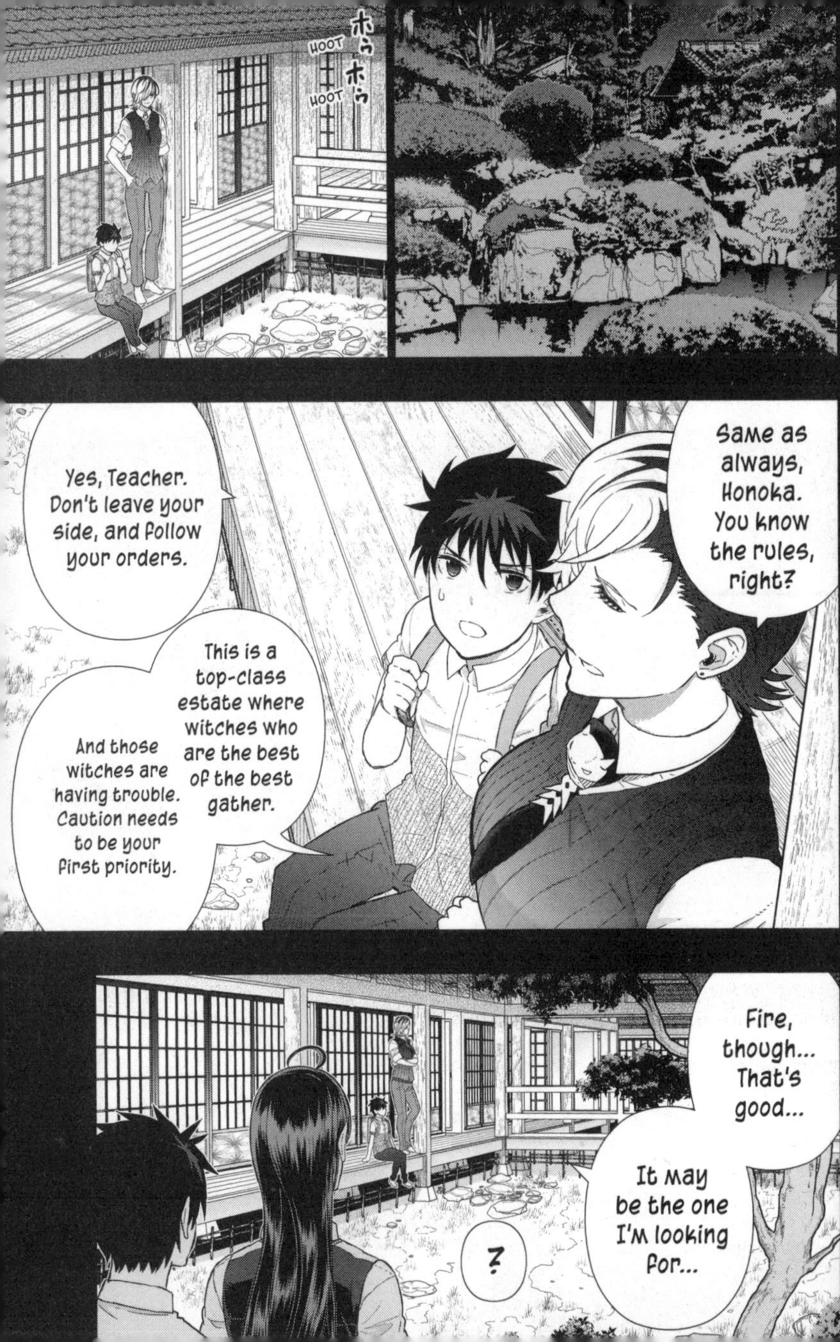
ホゥ
HOOT
ホゥ
HOOT
Same as always, Honoka. You know the rules, right?
Yes, Teacher. Don't leave your side, and follow your orders.
This is a top-class estate where witches who are the best of the best gather.
And those witches are having trouble. Caution needs to be your first priority.
Fire, though... That's good...
It may be the one I'm looking for...
?

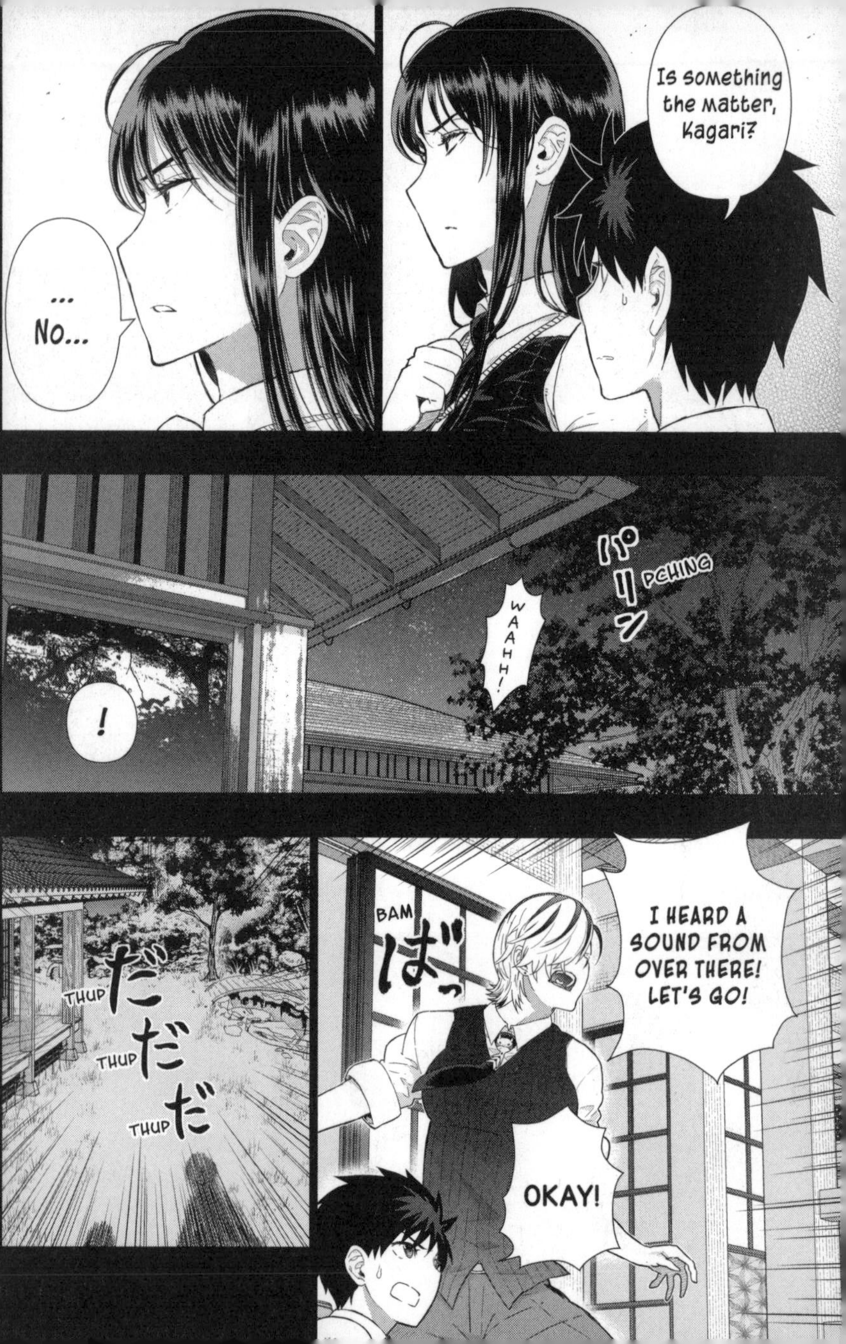
Is something the matter, Kagari?
... No...
パリン
PCHING
WAAHH!
!
BAM
ばっ
I HEARD A SOUND FROM OVER THERE! LET'S GO!
OKAY!
THUP
だ
THUP
だ
THUP
だ

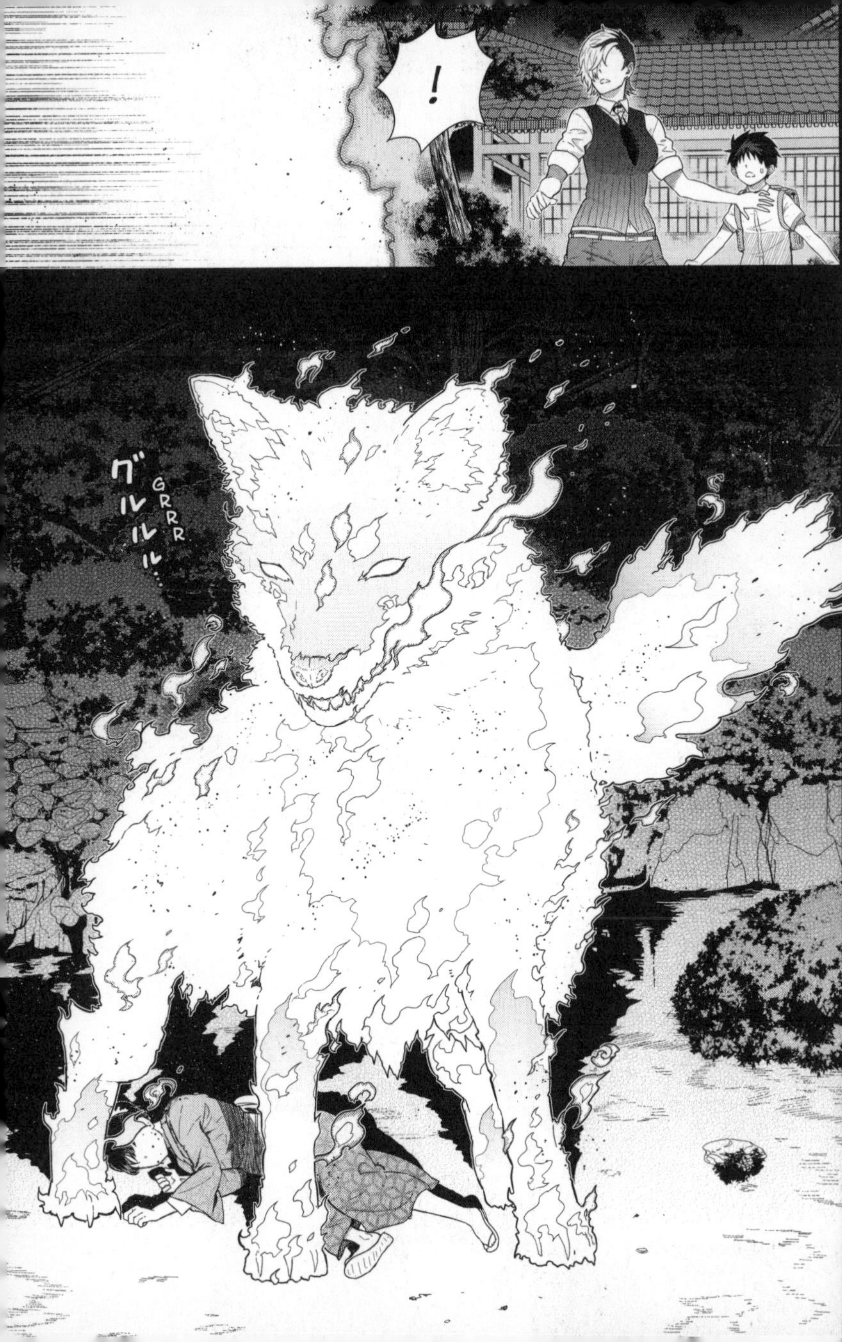
!
グルルル…
GRRR

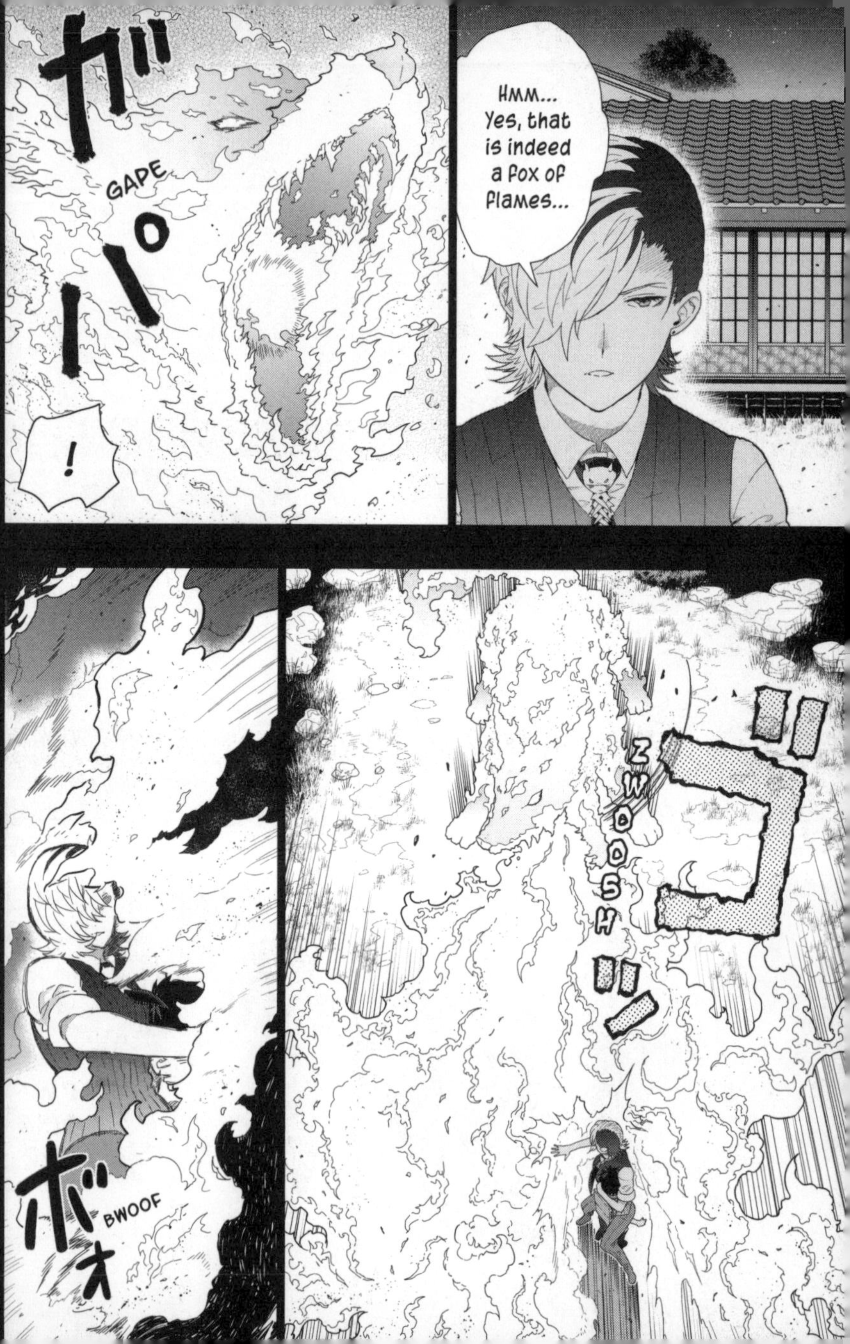
Hmm... Yes, that is indeed a fox of flames...
ガパ
GAPE
!
ゴッ
ZWOOSH
ボオ
BWOOF

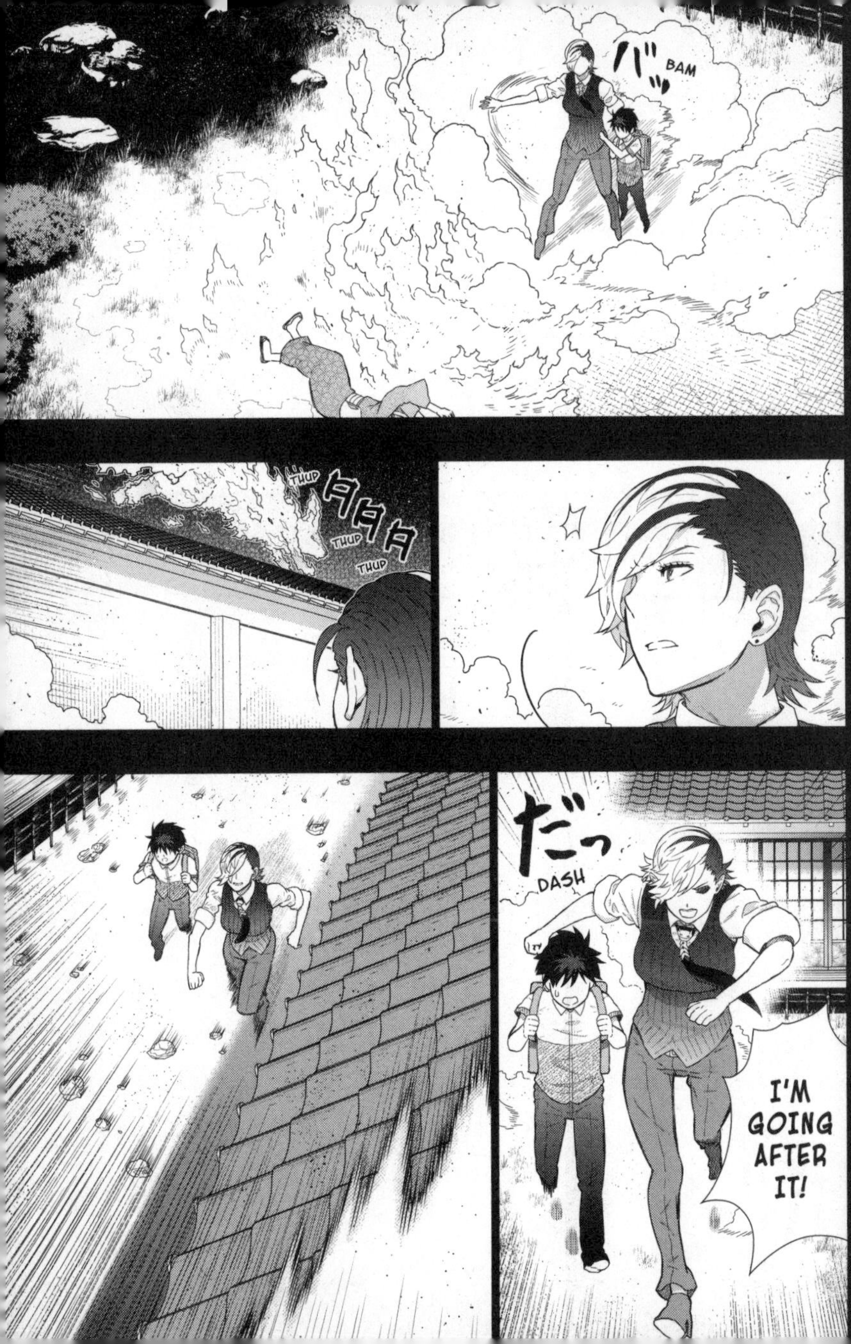
バッ
BAM
タタタ
THUP
THUP
THUP
だっ
DASH
I'M GOING AFTER IT!

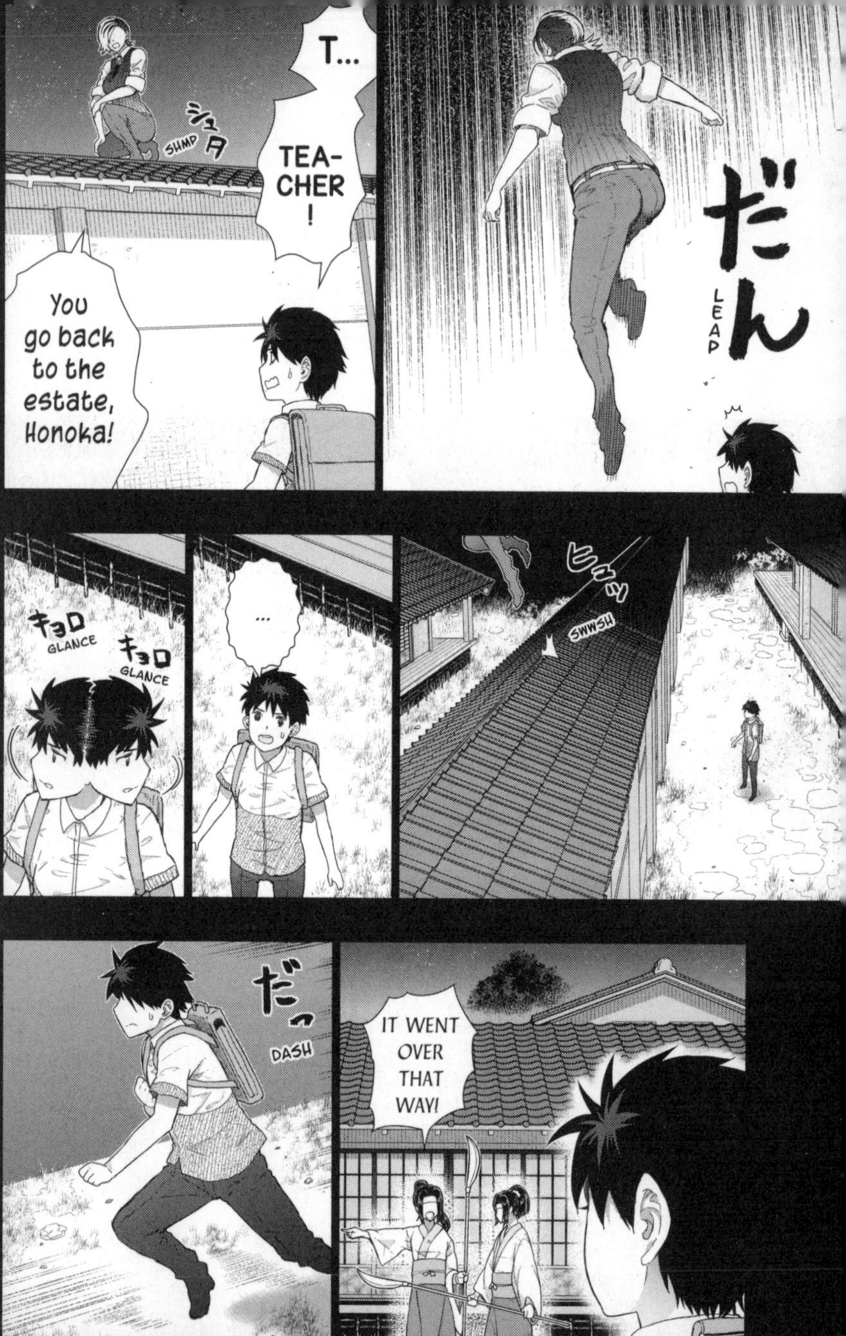
だん
LEAP
T...
TEA-CHER!
シュタ
SHMP
You go back to the estate, Honoka!
ヒュッ
SWWSH
...
キョロ
GLANCE
キョロ
GLANCE
IT WENT OVER THAT WAY!
だっ
DASH

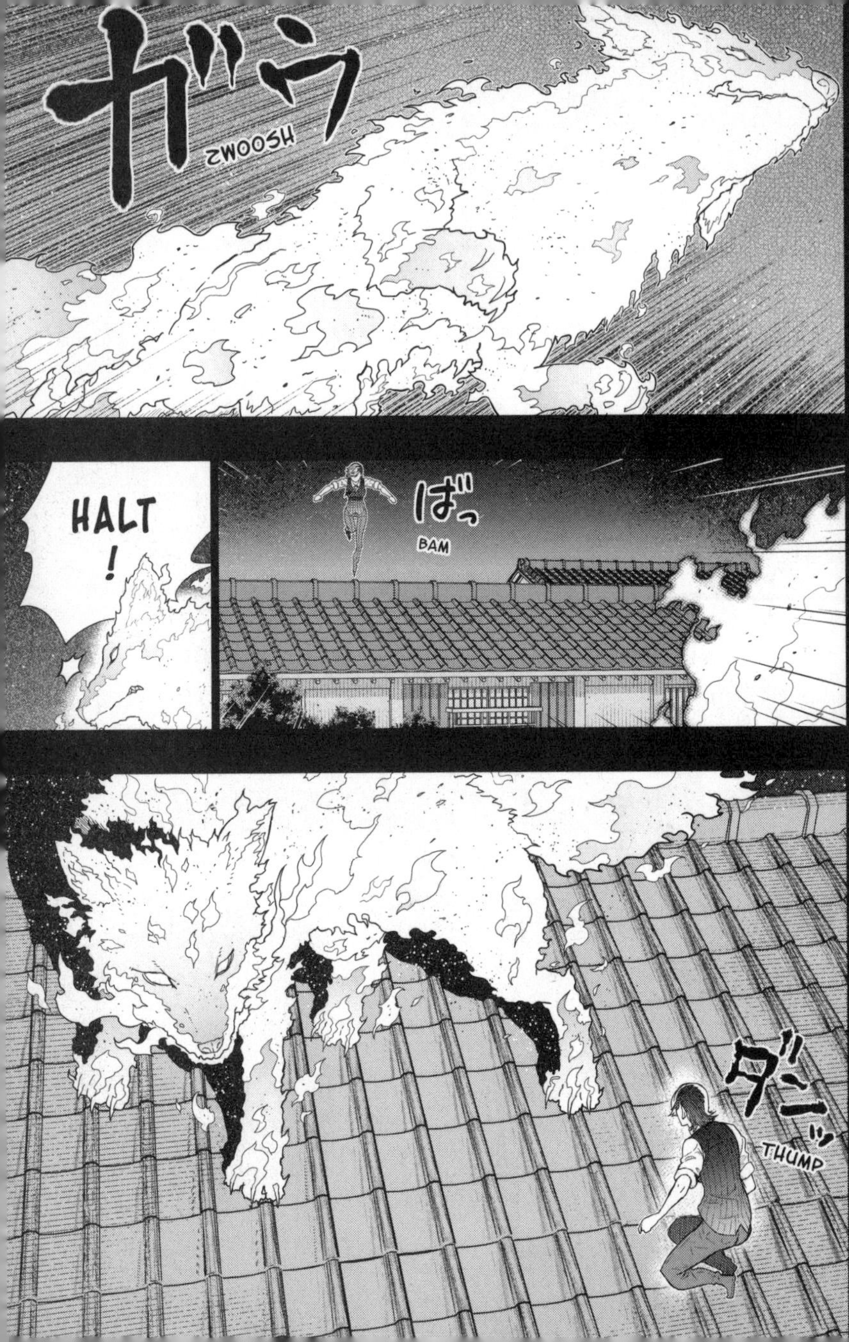
ガウ
ZWOOSH
ばっ
BAM
HALT!
ダンッ
THUMP

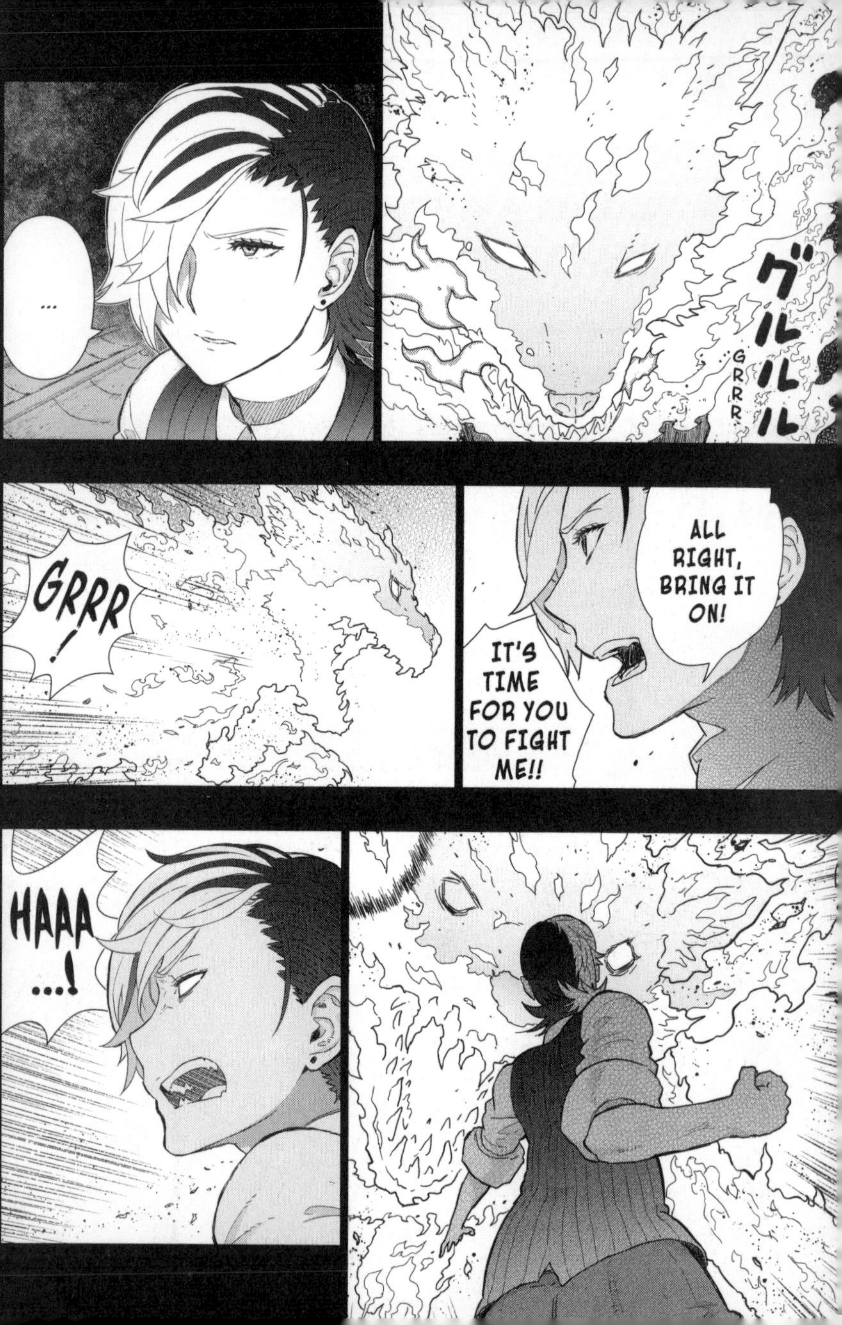
グルルル
GRRR
...
ALL RIGHT, BRING IT ON!
IT'S TIME FOR YOU TO FIGHT ME!!
GRRR!
HAAA ...!

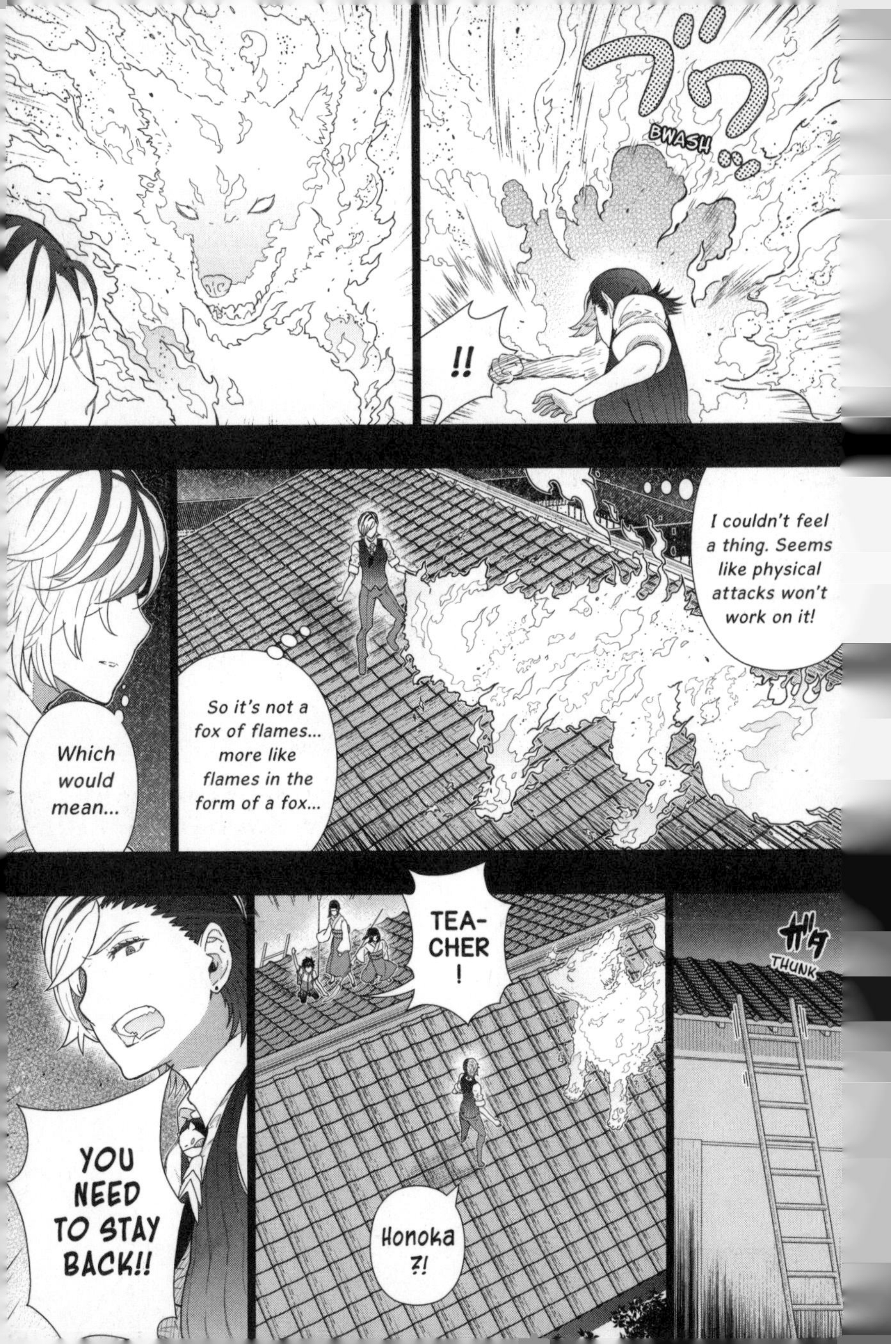
BWASH
!!
I couldn't feel a thing. Seems like physical attacks won't work on it!
So it's not a fox of flames... more like flames in the form of a fox...
Which would mean...
THUNK
TEA-CHER!
Honoka?!
YOU NEED TO STAY BACK!!

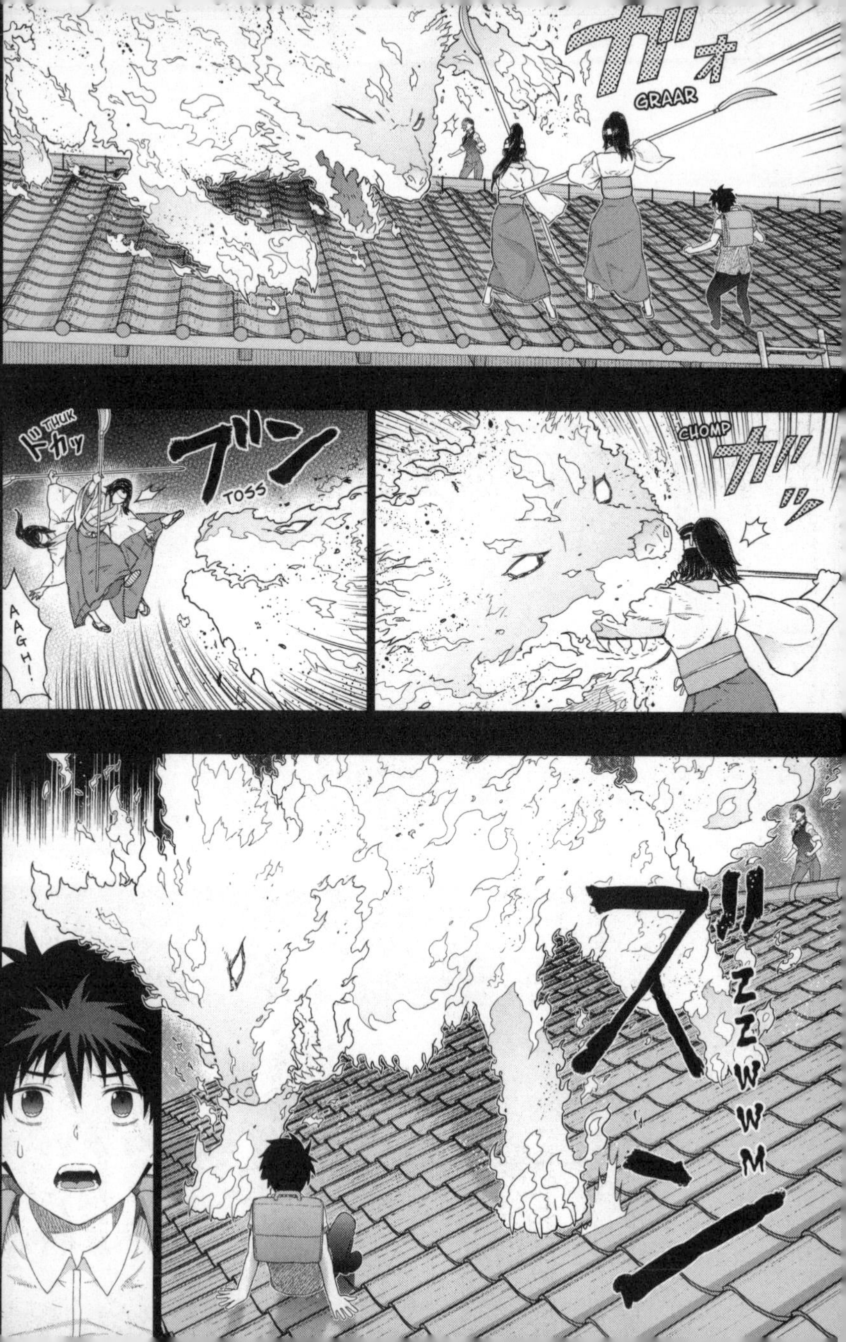
ガォ
GRAAR
ガッ
CHOMP
ブン
TOSS
ドカッ
THUK
AAGH!
ZZWWM

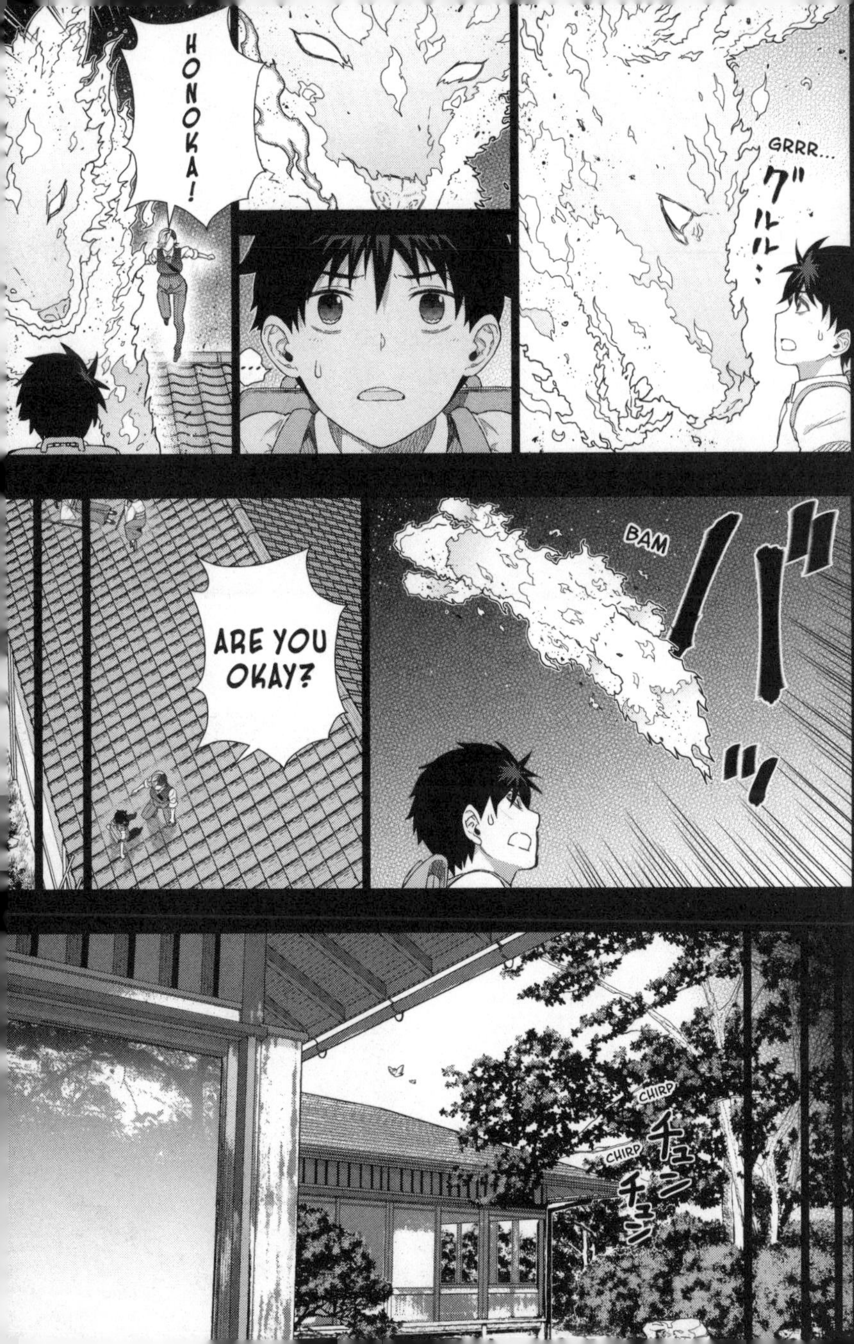
GRRR...
グルル…
HONOKA!
BAM
バッ
ARE YOU OKAY?
CHIRP
チュン
CHIRP
チュン

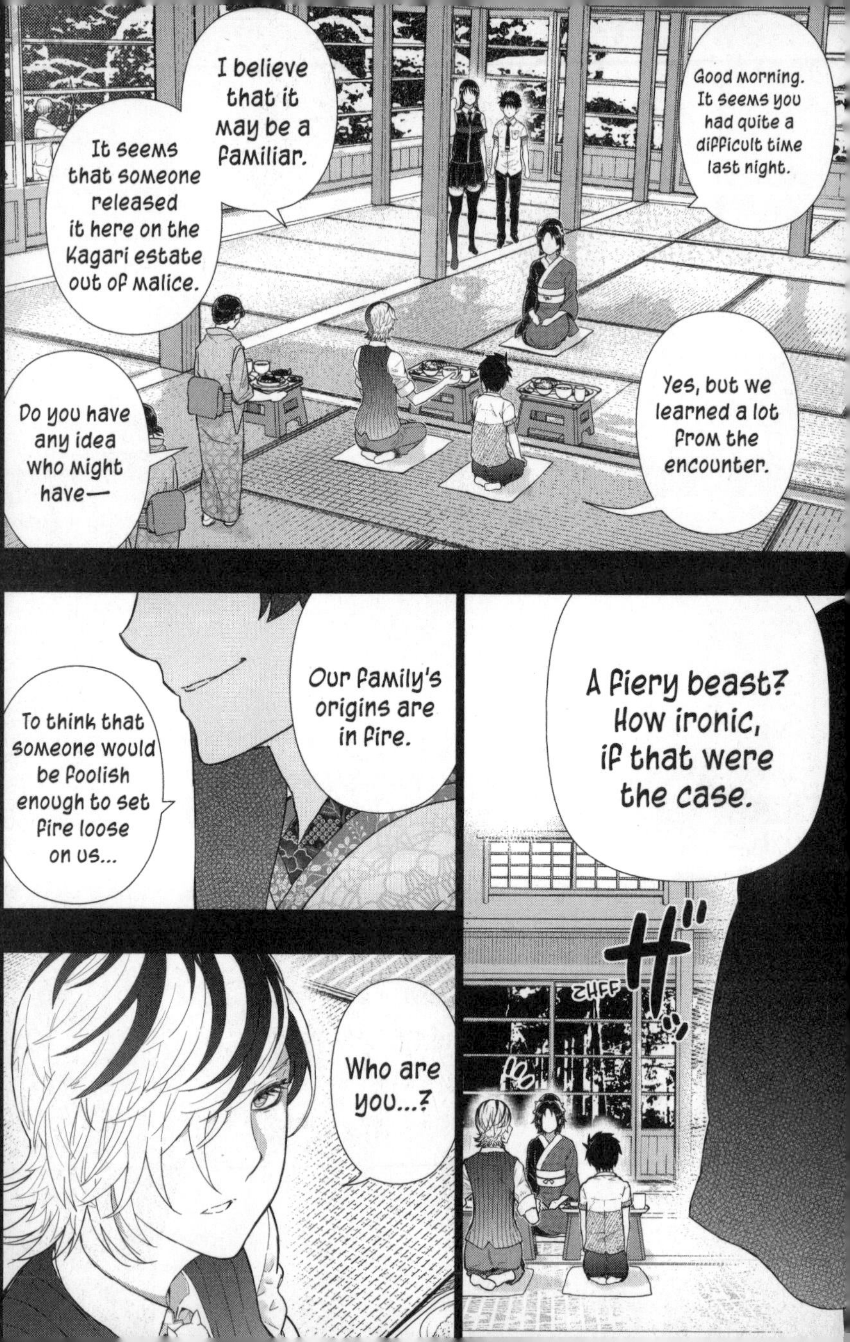

Good morning. It seems you had quite a difficult time last night.
Yes, but we learned a lot from the encounter.
I believe that it may be a familiar.
It seems that someone released it here on the Kagari estate out of malice.
Do you have any idea who might have—
A fiery beast? How ironic, if that were the case.
ZHFF
Our family's origins are in fire.
To think that someone would be foolish enough to set fire loose on us...
Who are you...?

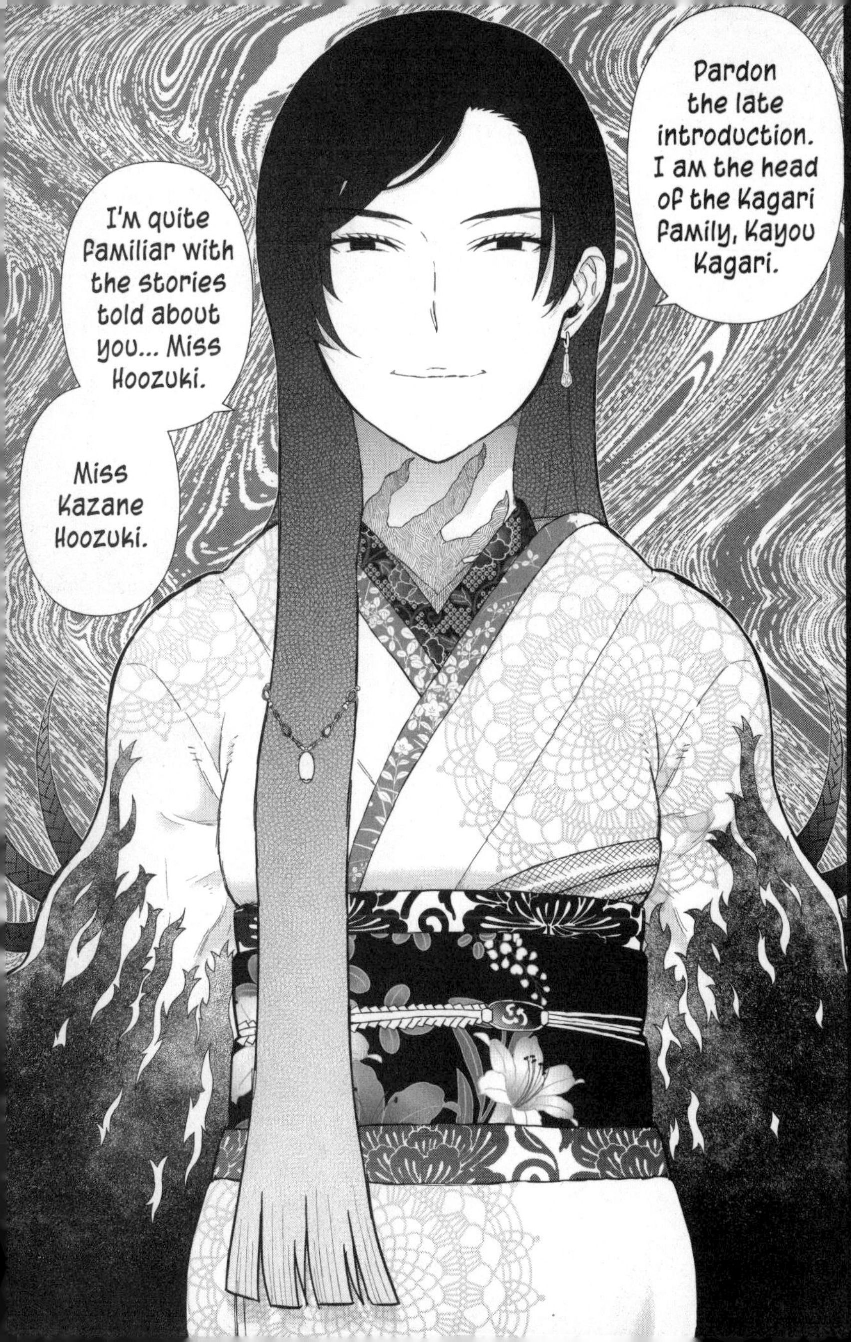
Pardon the late introduction. I am the head of the Kagari family, Kayou Kagari.
I'm quite familiar with the stories told about you... Miss Hoozuki.
Miss Kazane Hoozuki.

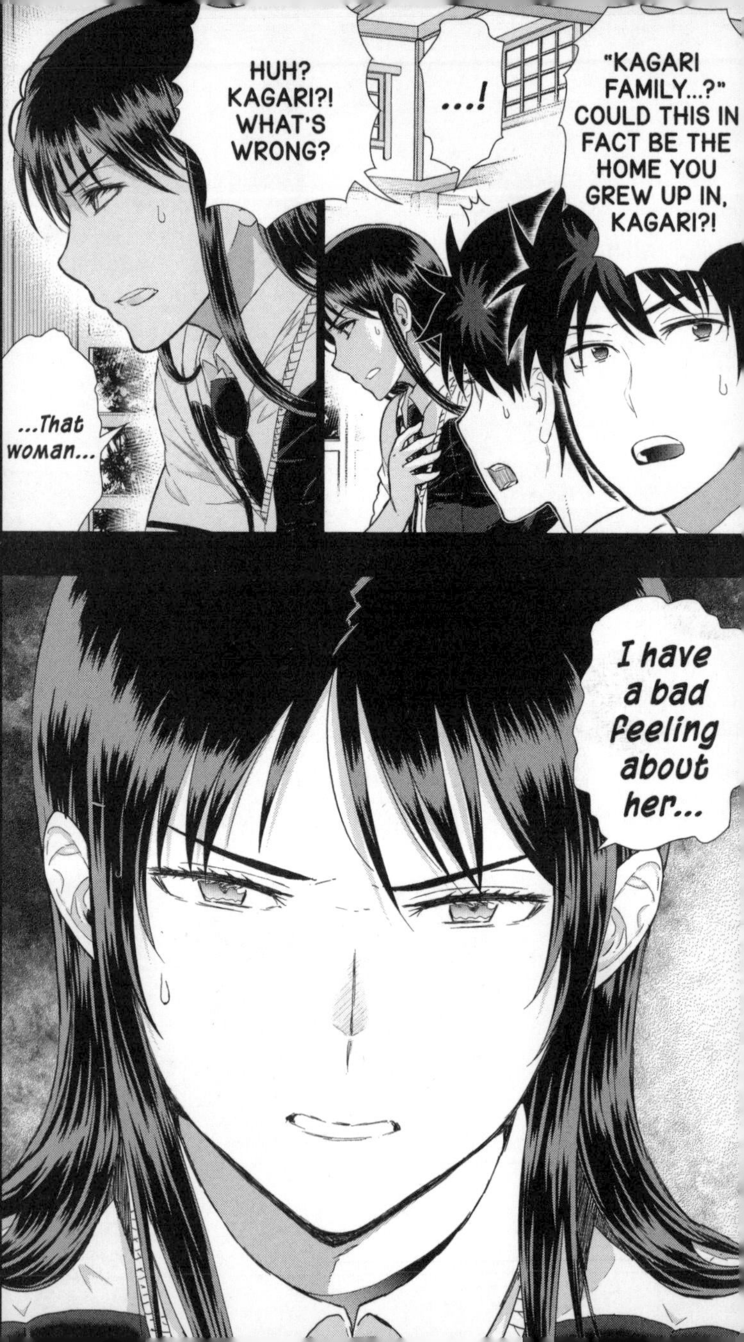
"KAGARI FAMILY...?" COULD THIS IN FACT BE THE HOME YOU GREW UP IN, KAGARI?!
...!
HUH? KAGARI?! WHAT'S WRONG?
...That woman...
I have a bad feeling about her...

CHAPTER 52 END

Witchcraft Works

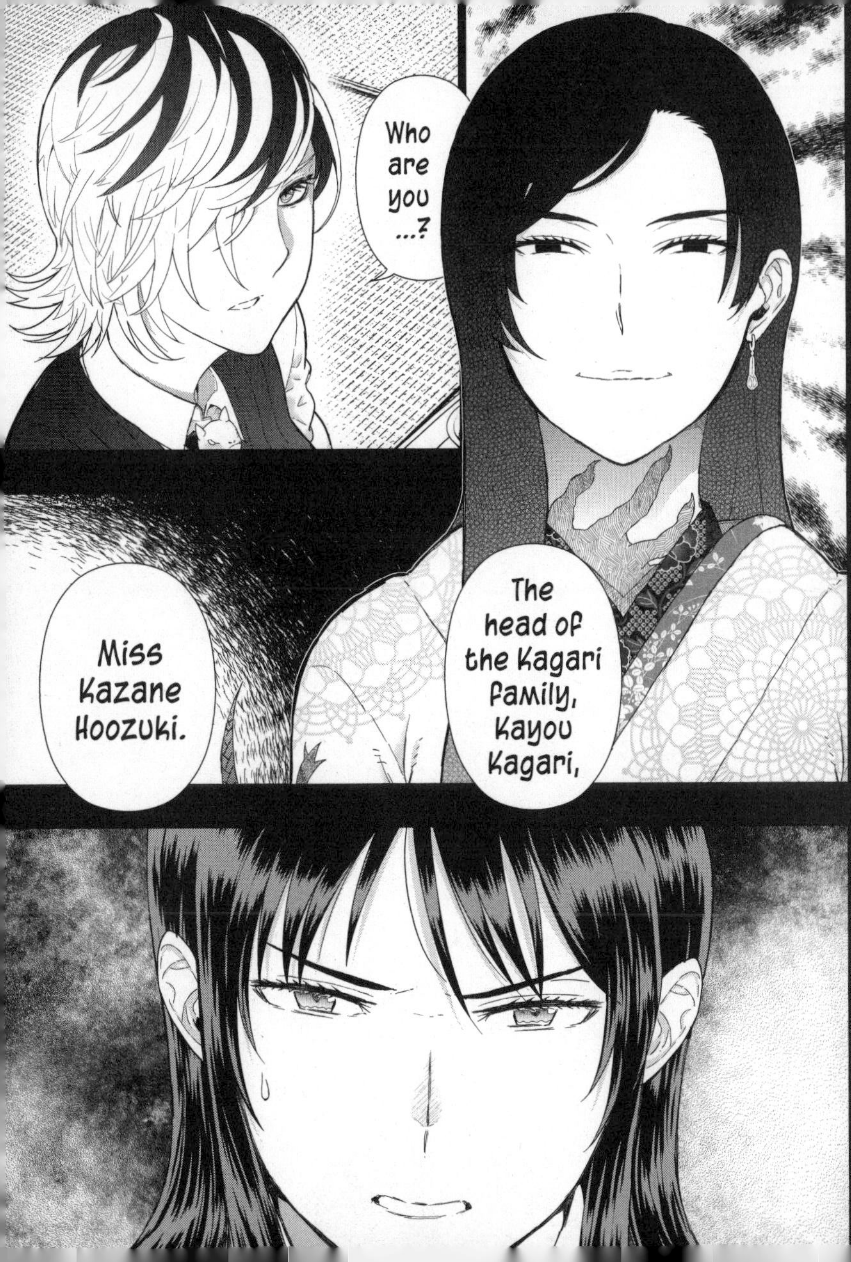
Who are you ...?
The head of the Kagari family, Kayou Kagari,
Miss Kazane Hoozuki.

CHAPTER 53 Takamiya and the Pendant's World (Part 3)

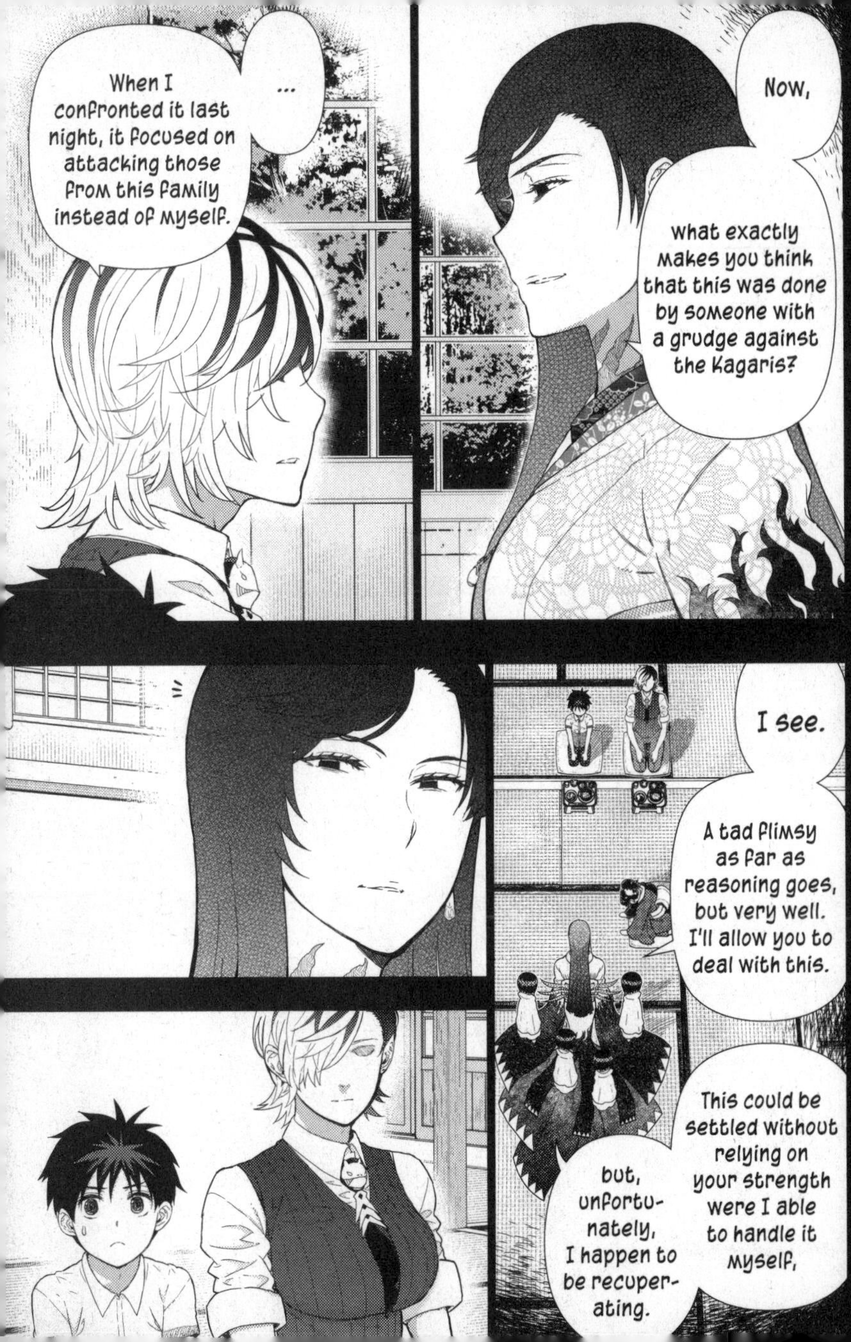
Now,
what exactly makes you think that this was done by someone with a grudge against the Kagaris?
...
When I confronted it last night, it focused on attacking those from this family instead of myself.
I see.
A tad flimsy as far as reasoning goes, but very well. I'll allow you to deal with this.
This could be settled without relying on your strength were I able to handle it myself,
but, unfortu-nately, I happen to be recuper-ating.

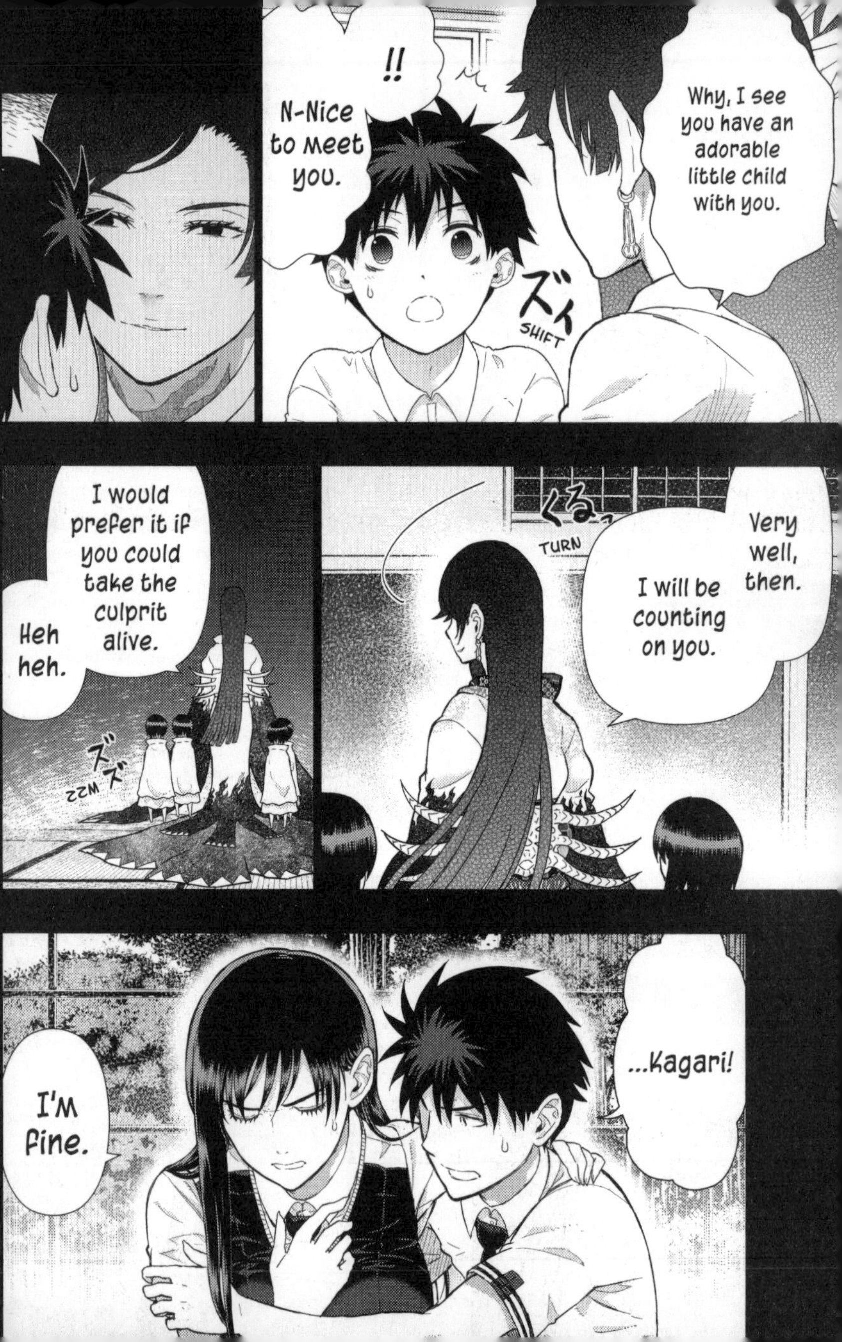

Why, I see you have an adorable little child with you.
!!
N-Nice to meet you.
ズイ
SHIFT
Very well, then.
I will be counting on you.
くるっ
TURN
I would prefer it if you could take the culprit alive.
Heh heh.
ズズ
...Kagari!
I'M fine.

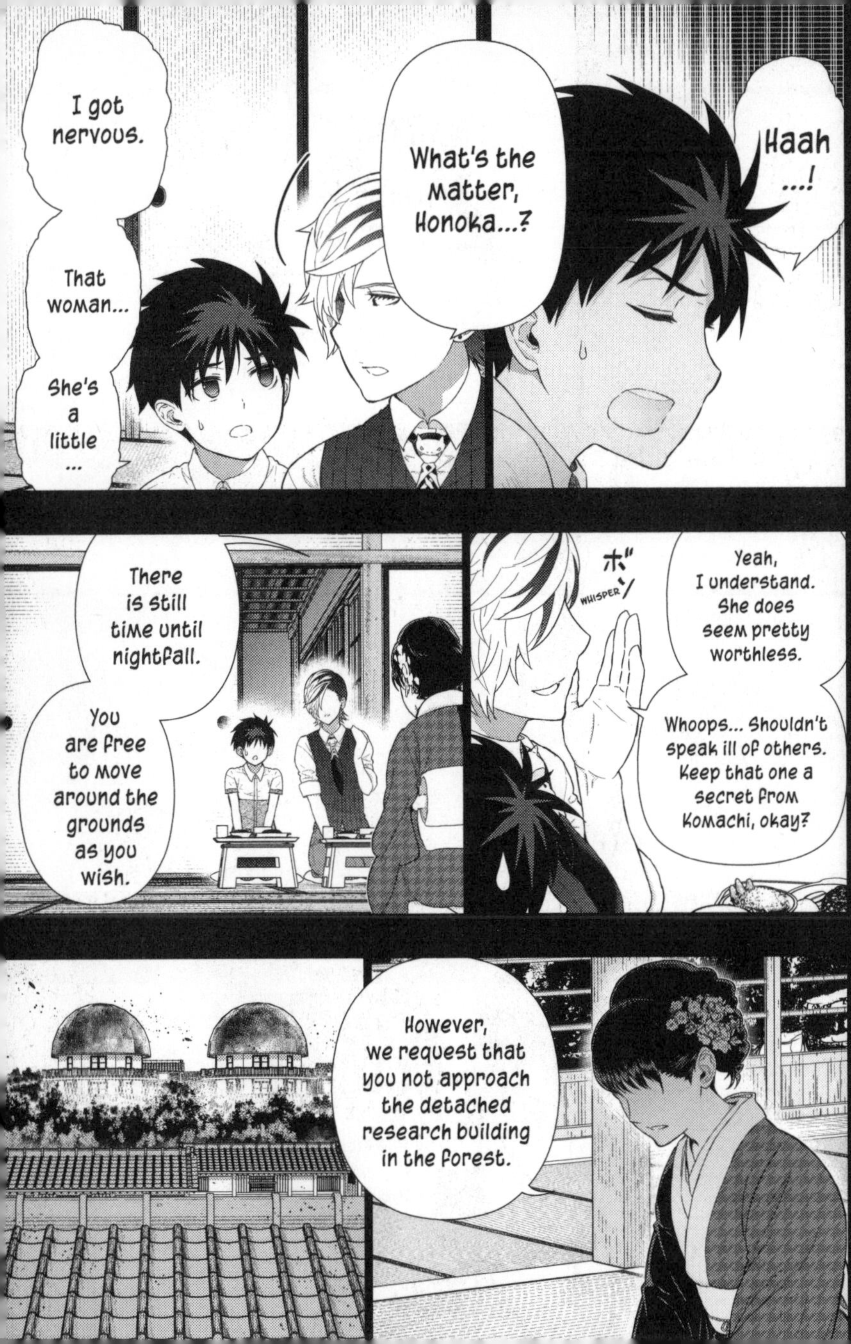
Haah ...!
What's the matter, Honoka...?
I got nervous.
That woman...
She's a little ...
ボソ
WHISPER
Yeah, I understand. She does seem pretty worthless.
Whoops... Shouldn't speak ill of others. Keep that one a secret from Komachi, okay?
There is still time until nightfall.
You are free to move around the grounds as you wish.
However, we request that you not approach the detached research building in the forest.

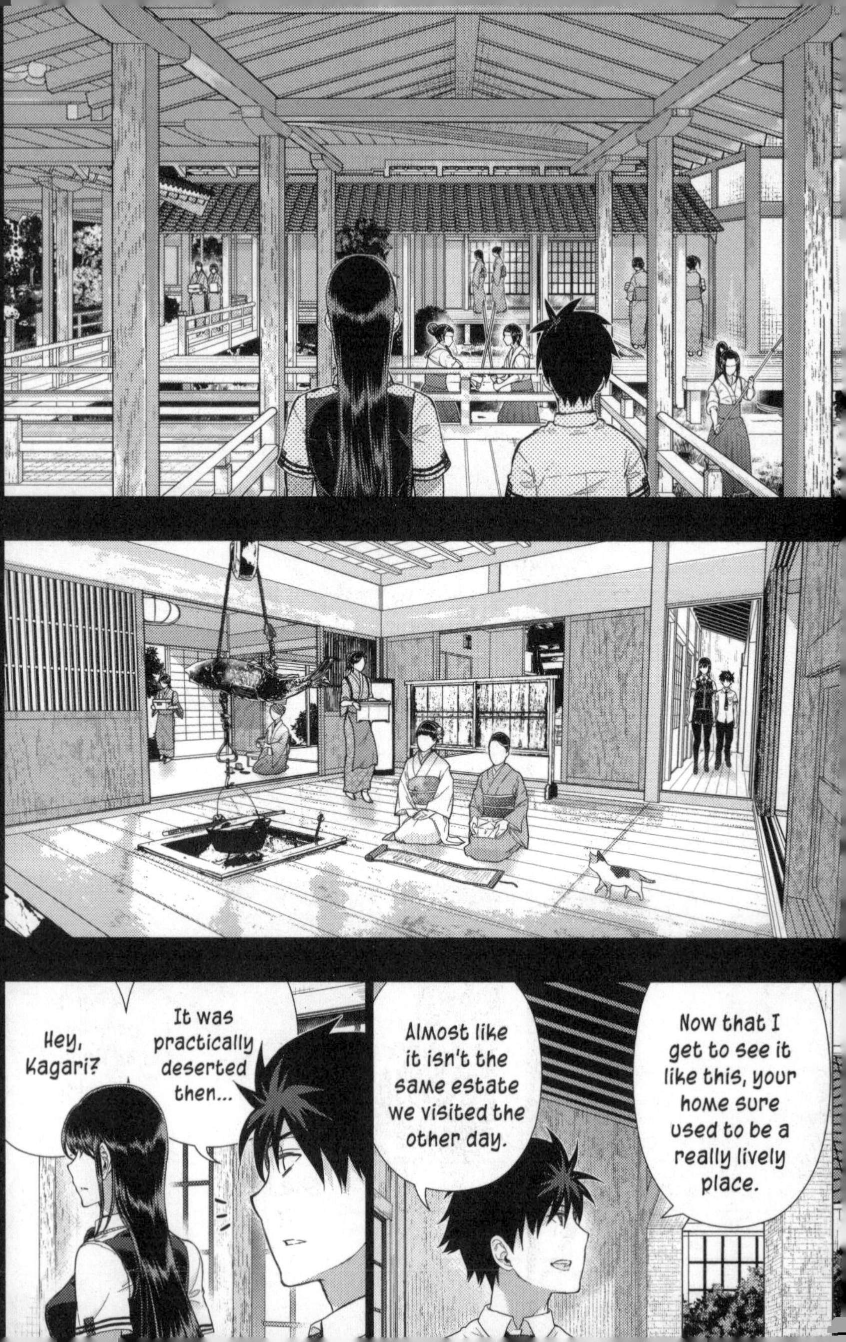
Now that I get to see it like this, your home sure used to be a really lively place.
Almost like it isn't the same estate we visited the other day.
It was practically deserted then...
Hey, Kagari?

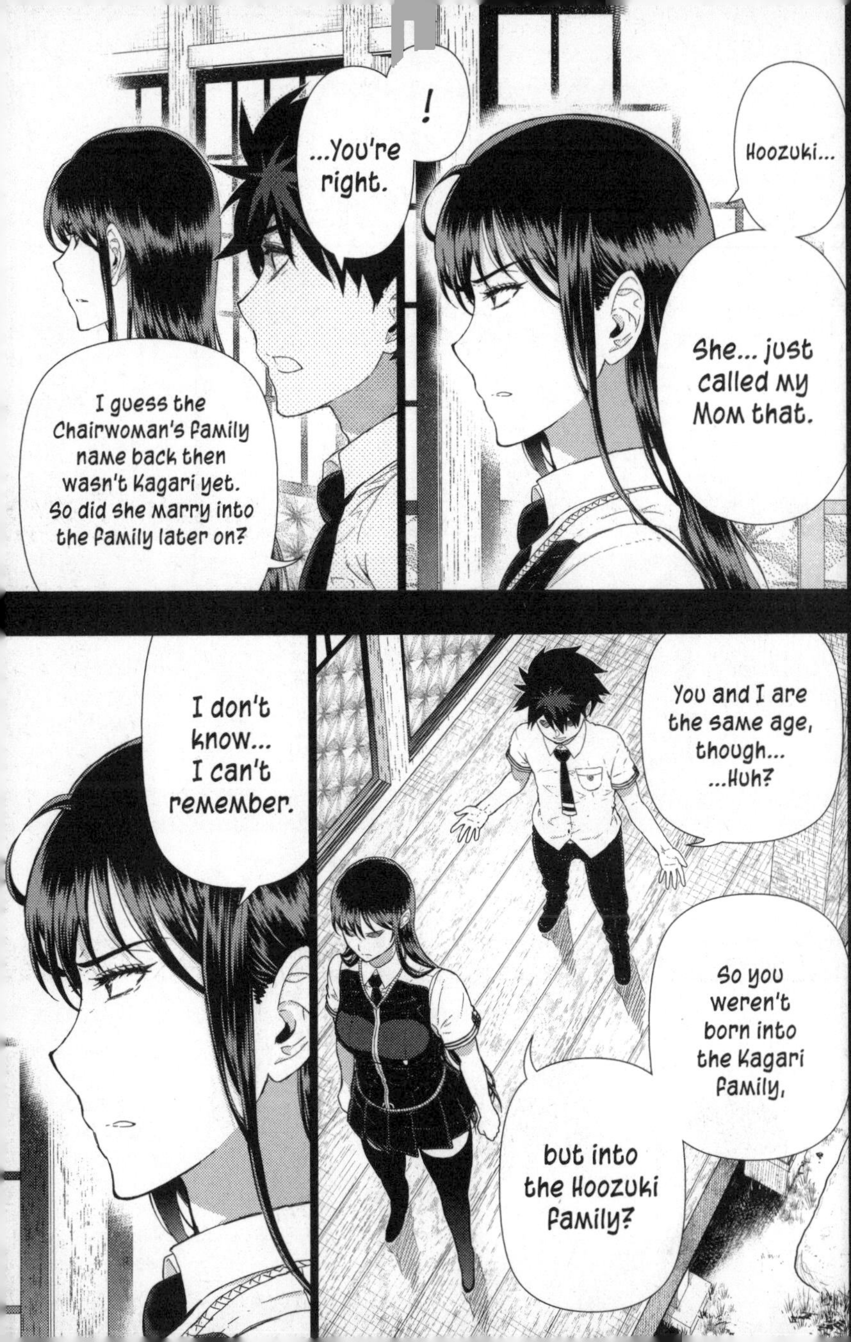
Hoozuki...
She... just called my Mom that.
! ...You're right.
I guess the Chairwoman's family name back then wasn't Kagari yet. So did she marry into the family later on?
You and I are the same age, though... ...Huh?
So you weren't born into the Kagari family,
but into the Hoozuki family?
I don't know... I can't remember.

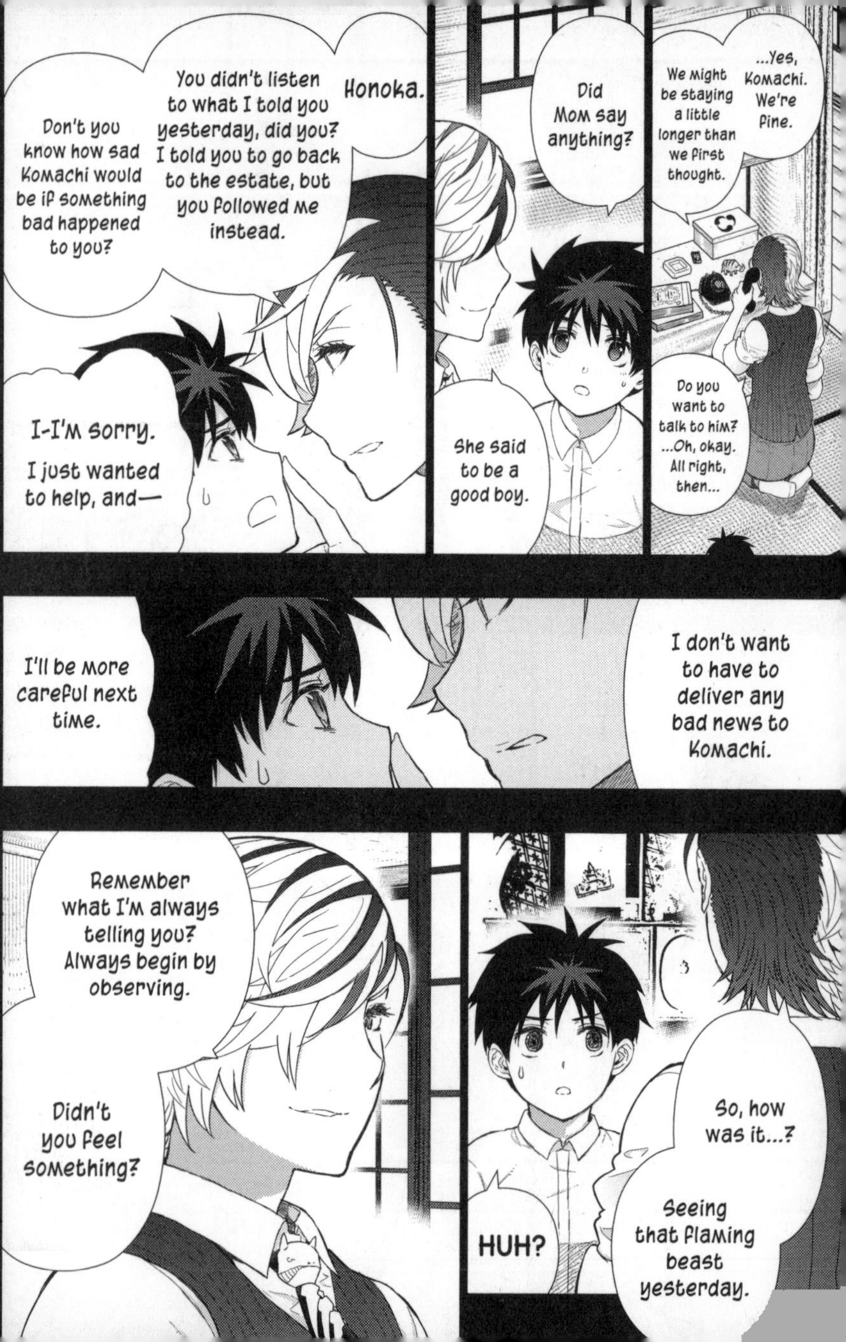
...Yes, Komachi. We're fine.
We might be staying a little longer than we first thought.
Do you want to talk to him? ...Oh, okay. All right, then...
Did Mom say anything?
She said to be a good boy.
Honoka.
You didn't listen to what I told you yesterday, did you? I told you to go back to the estate, but you followed me instead.
Don't you know how sad Komachi would be if something bad happened to you?
I-I'm sorry.
I just wanted to help, and—
I don't want to have to deliver any bad news to Komachi.
I'll be more careful next time.
So, how was it...?
Seeing that flaming beast yesterday.
HUH?
Remember what I'm always telling you? Always begin by observing.
Didn't you feel something?

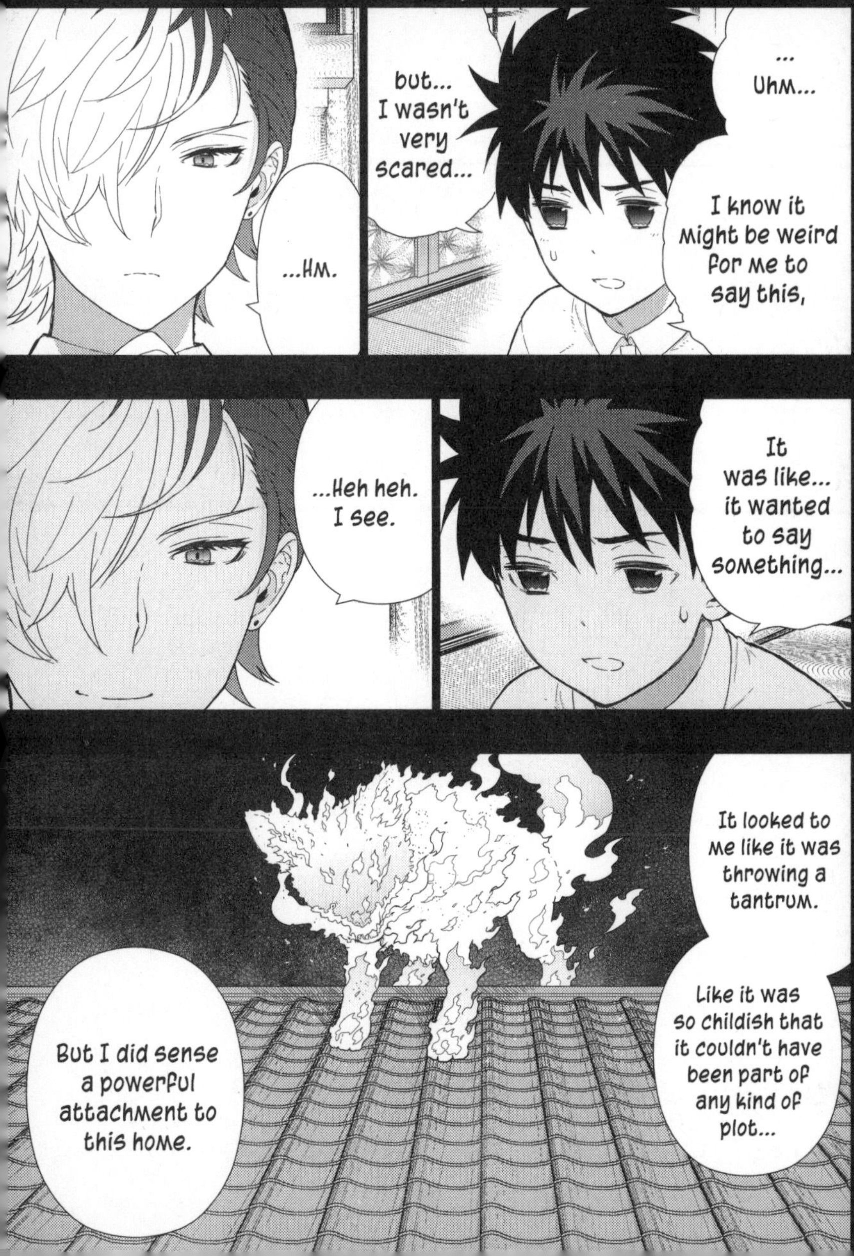
... Uhm...
I know it might be weird for me to say this,
but... I wasn't very scared...
...Hm.
It was like... it wanted to say something...
...Heh heh. I see.
It looked to me like it was throwing a tantrum.
Like it was so childish that it couldn't have been part of any kind of plot...
But I did sense a powerful attachment to this home.

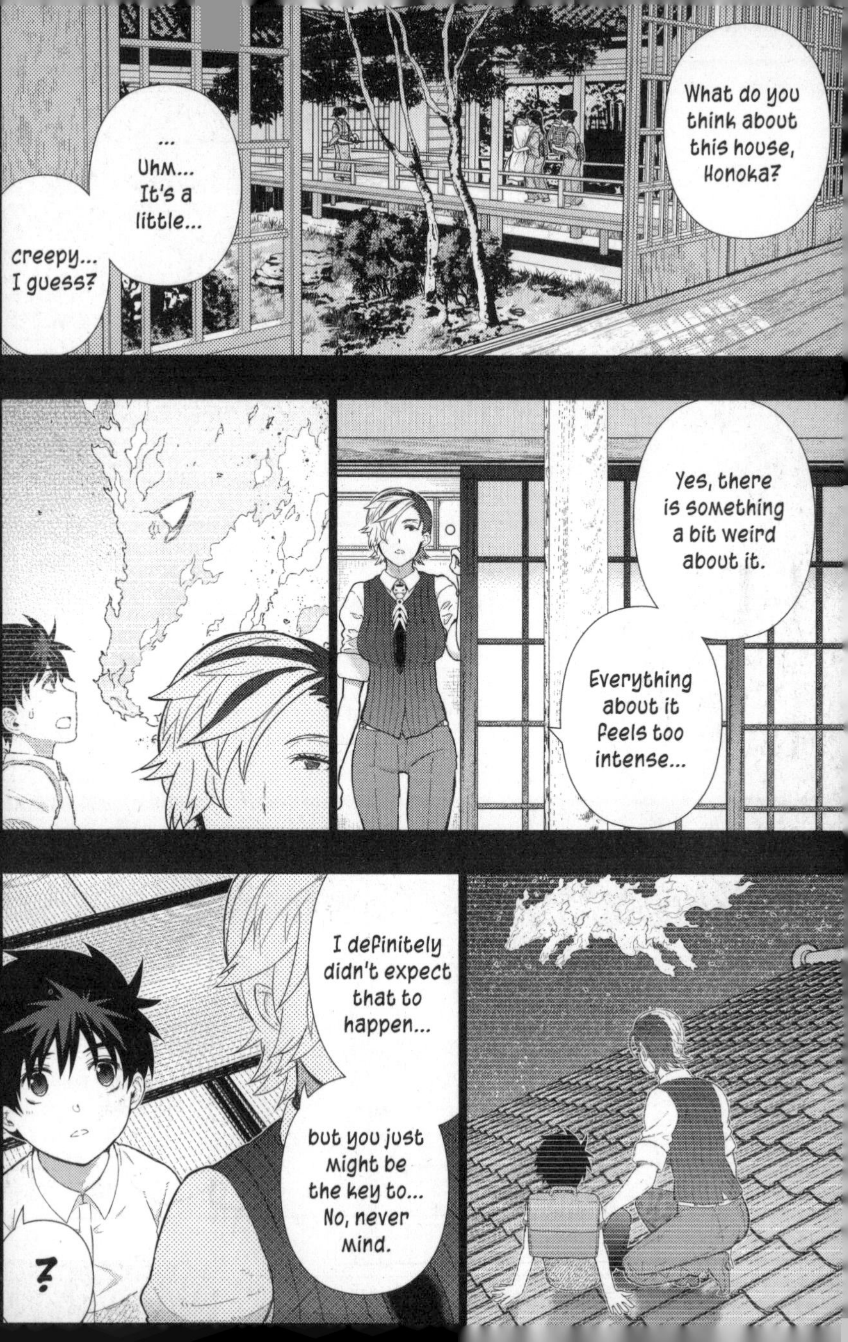
What do you think about this house, Honoka?
... Uhm... It's a little...
creepy... I guess?
Yes, there is something a bit weird about it.
Everything about it feels too intense...
I definitely didn't expect that to happen...
but you just might be the key to... No, never mind.
?

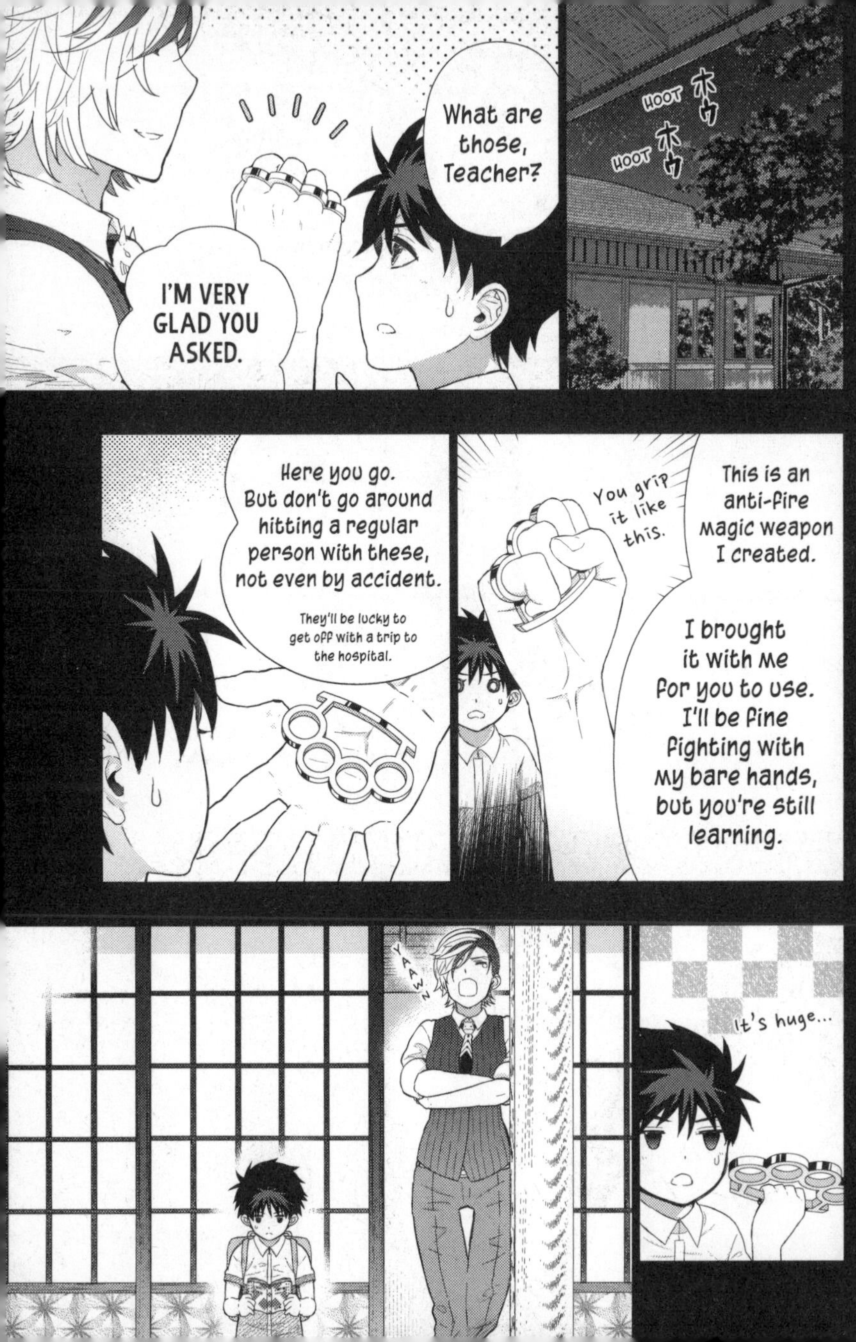
HOOT ホウ
HOOT ホウ
What are those, Teacher?
I'M VERY GLAD YOU ASKED.
This is an anti-fire magic weapon I created.
You grip it like this.
I brought it with me for you to use. I'll be fine fighting with my bare hands, but you're still learning.
Here you go. But don't go around hitting a regular person with these, not even by accident.
They'll be lucky to get off with a trip to the hospital.
It's huge...
YAAWN

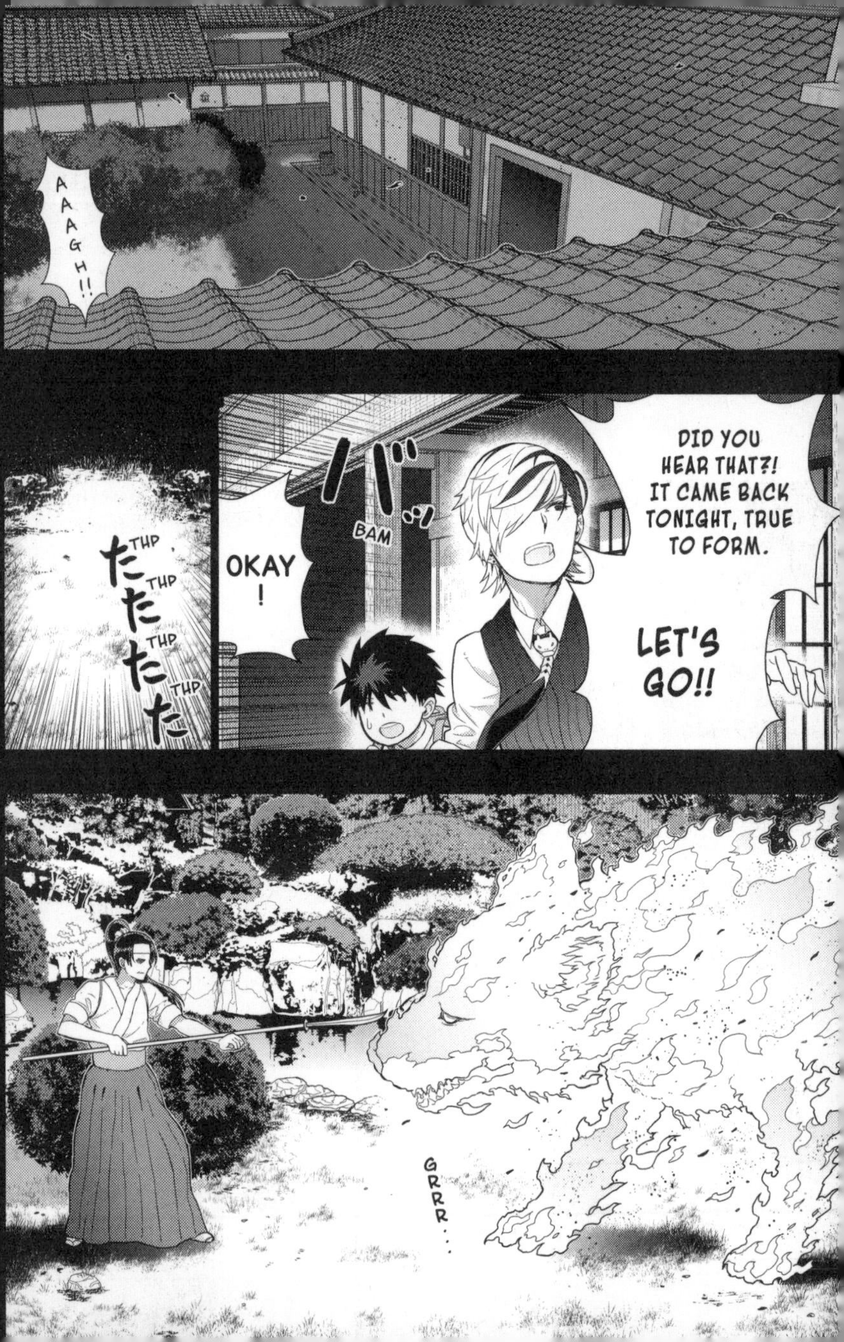
AAAGH!!
DID YOU HEAR THAT?! IT CAME BACK TONIGHT, TRUE TO FORM.
LET'S GO!!
BAM
OKAY!
THP THP THP THP
GRRR...

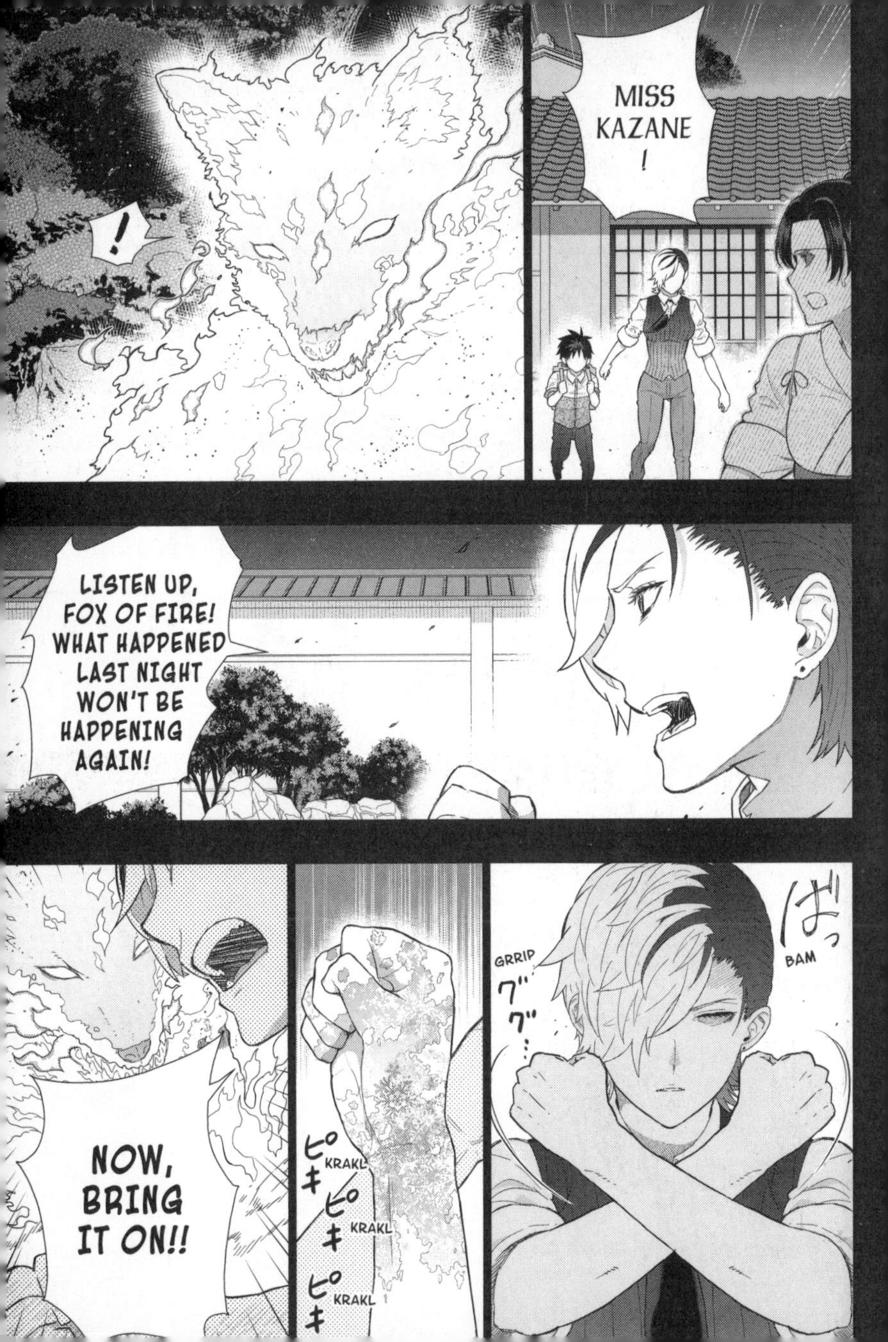
MISS KAZANE !
!
LISTEN UP, FOX OF FIRE! WHAT HAPPENED LAST NIGHT WON'T BE HAPPENING AGAIN!
ぱっ
BAM
GRRIP
グ グ
ピキ
KRAKL
ピキ
KRAKL
ピキ
KRAKL
NOW, BRING IT ON!!

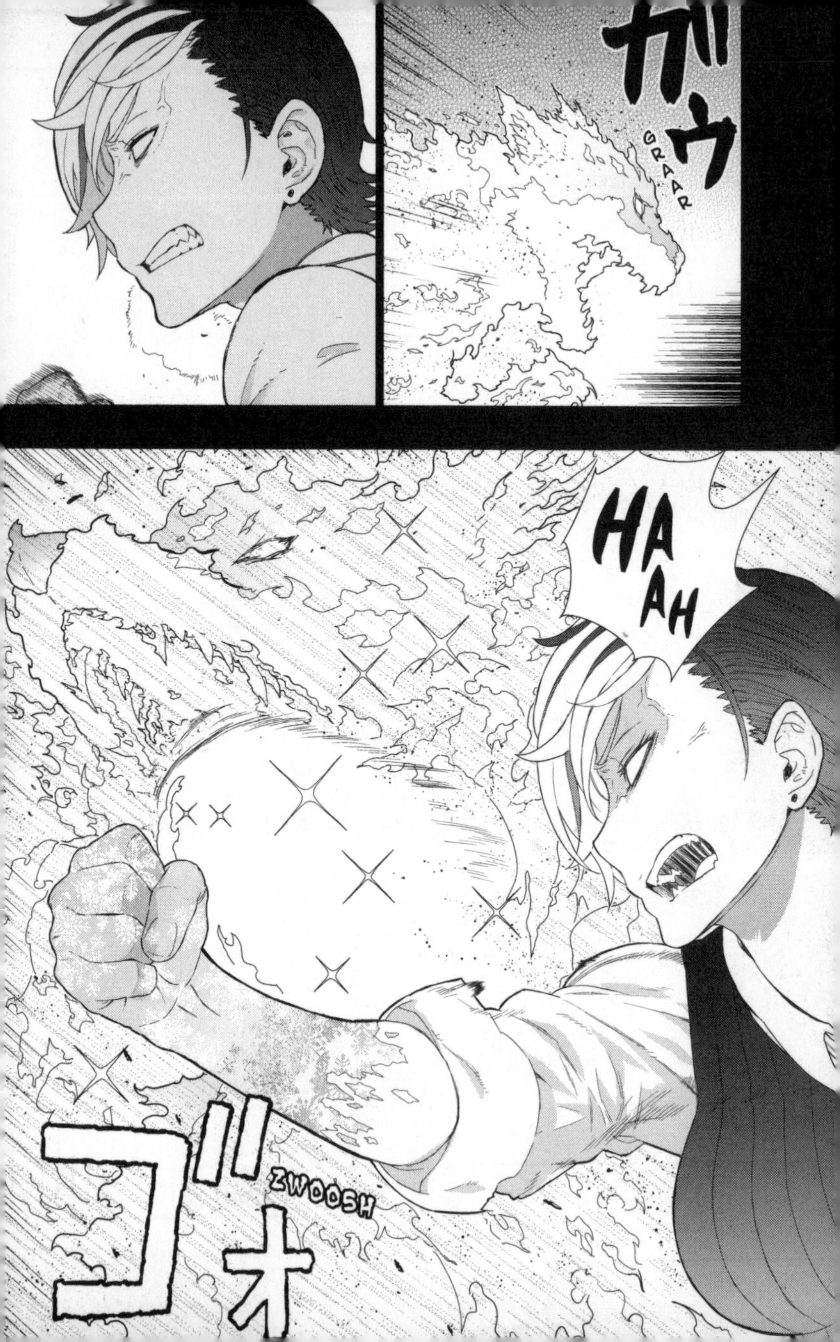
ガウ
GRAAAR
HAAAH
ゴオ
ZWOOSH

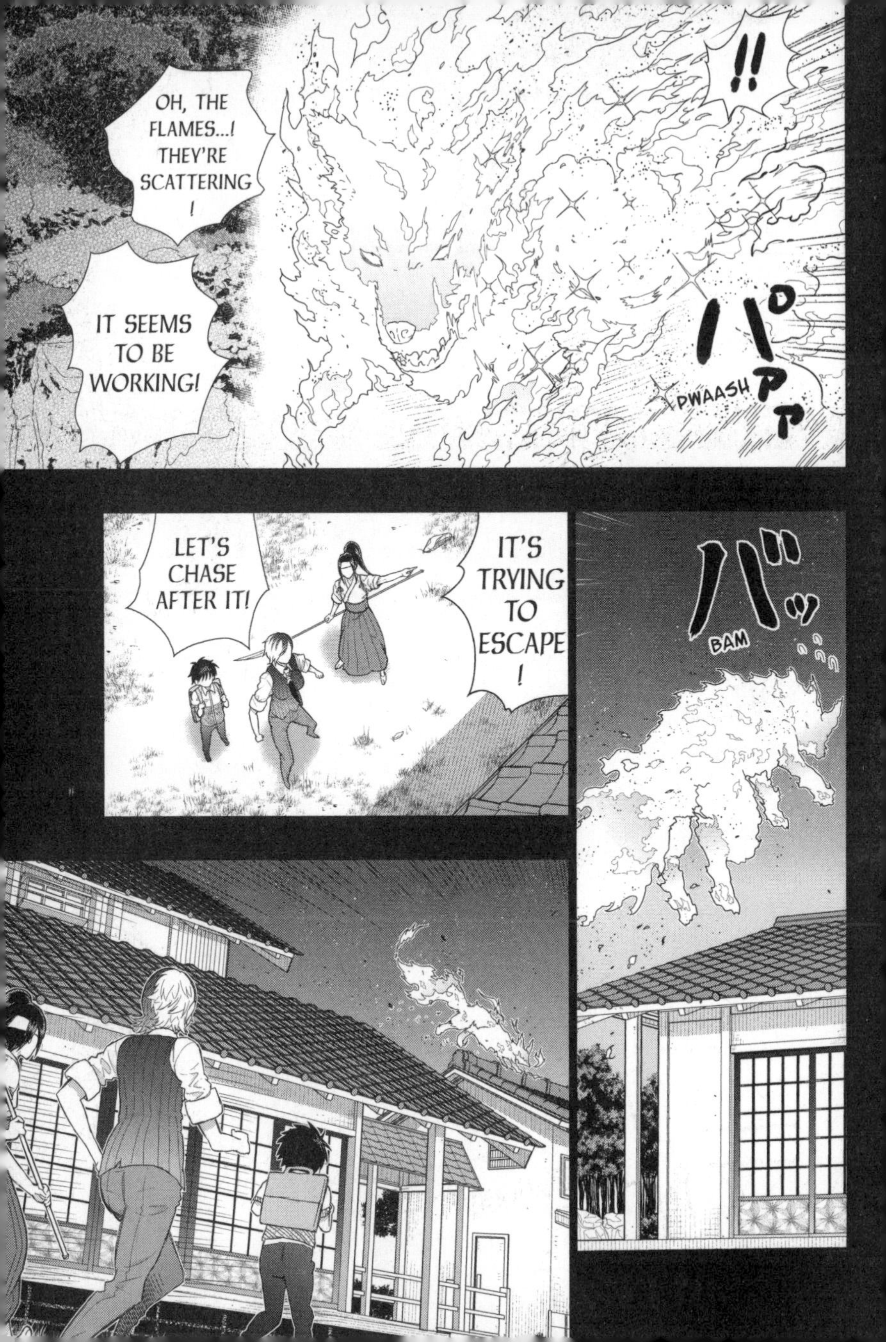
!!
OH, THE FLAMES...! THEY'RE SCATTERING!
パァァ
PWAASH
IT SEEMS TO BE WORKING!
バッ
BAM
IT'S TRYING TO ESCAPE!
LET'S CHASE AFTER IT!

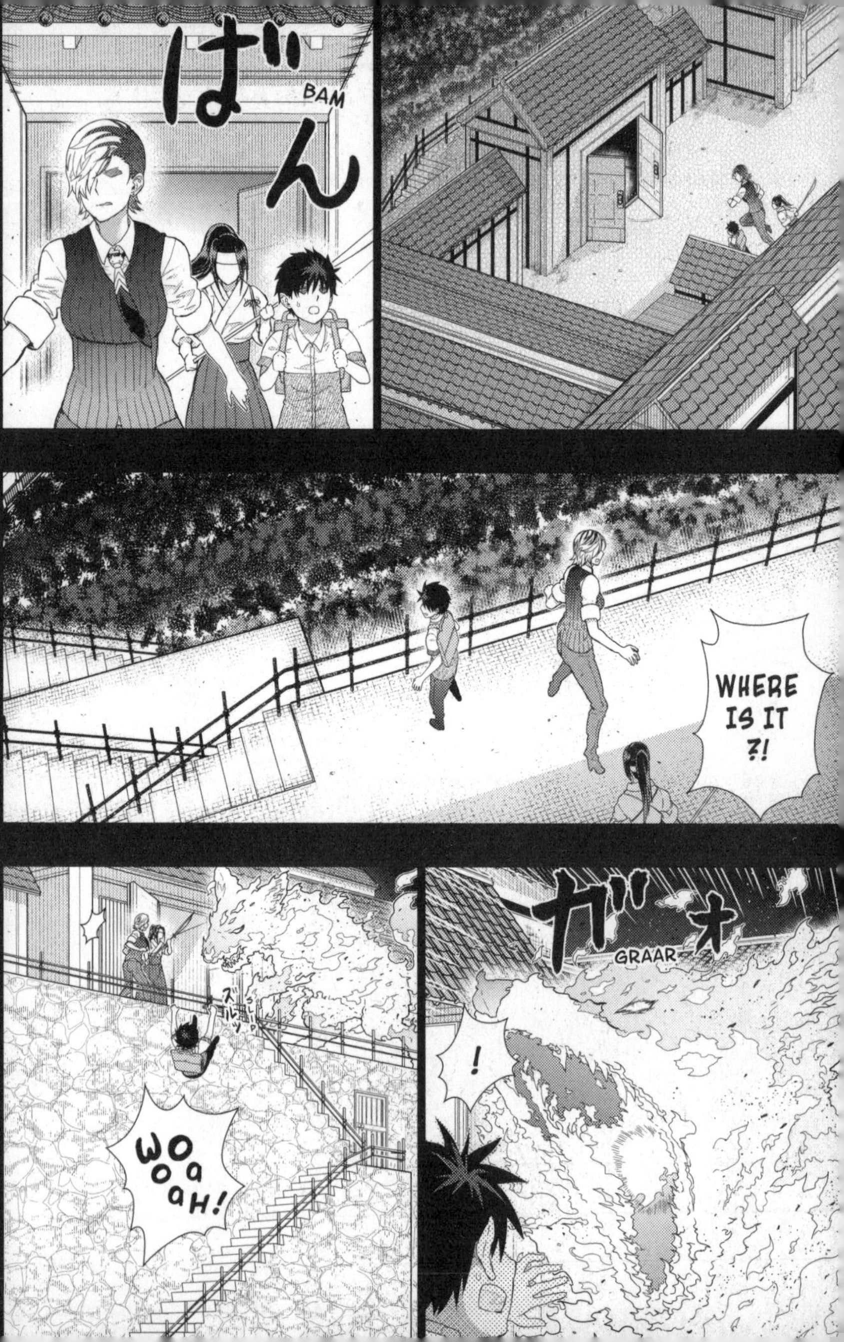
ばん
BAM
WHERE IS IT ?!
ガオ
GRAAR
!
ズルッ
SLIP
WOaH WOaH!

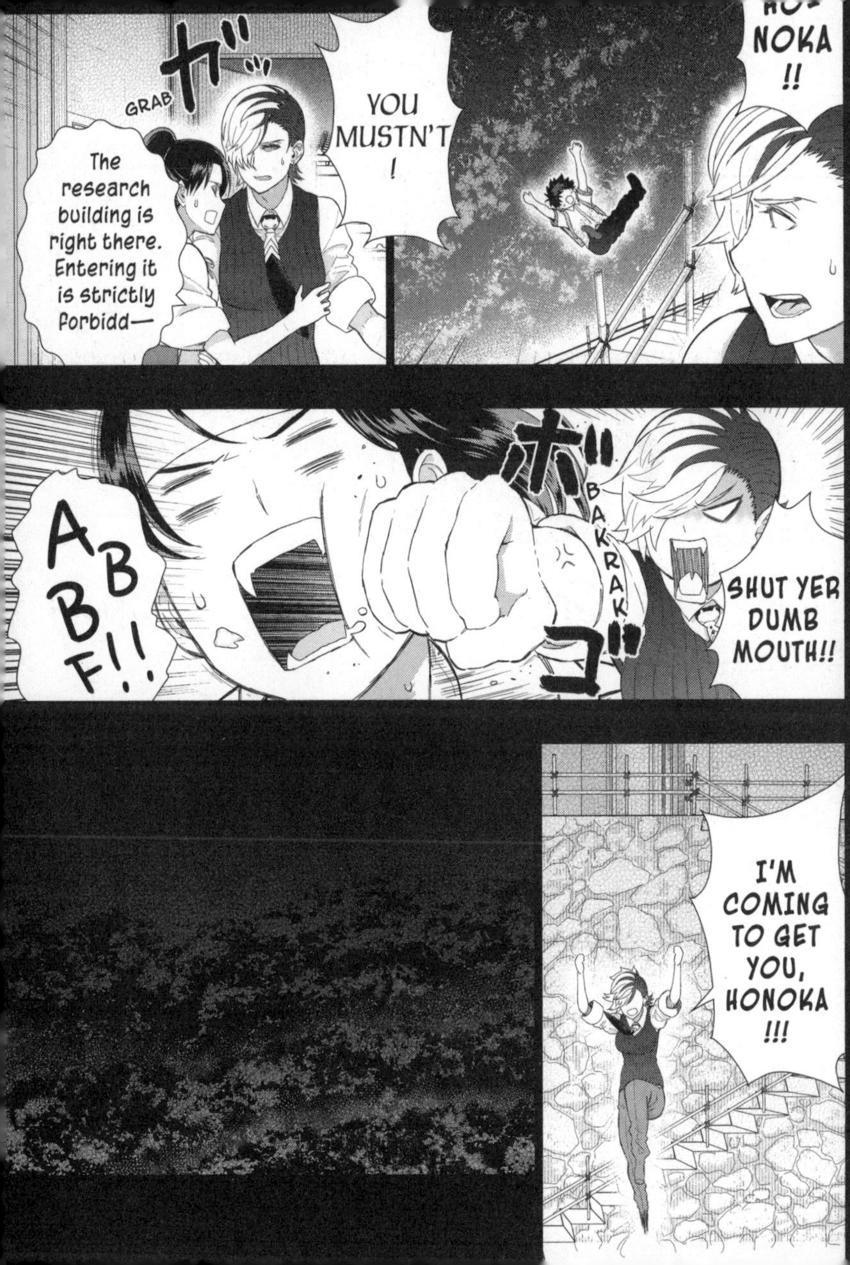
NOKA!!
YOU MUSTN'T!
GRAB
The research building is right there. Entering it is strictly forbidd—
SHUT YER DUMB MOUTH!!
BAKRAK
ABBF!!
I'M COMING TO GET YOU, HONOKA!!!

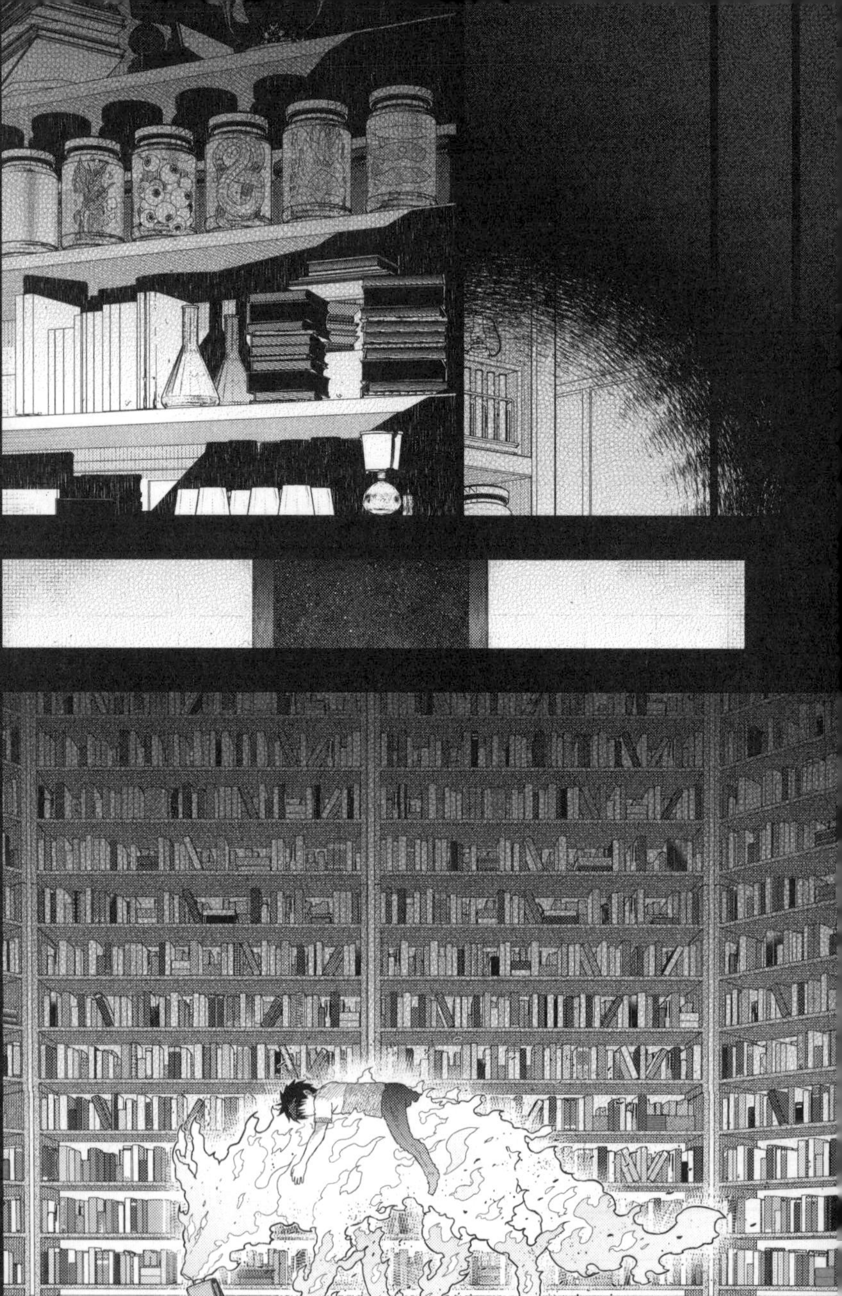

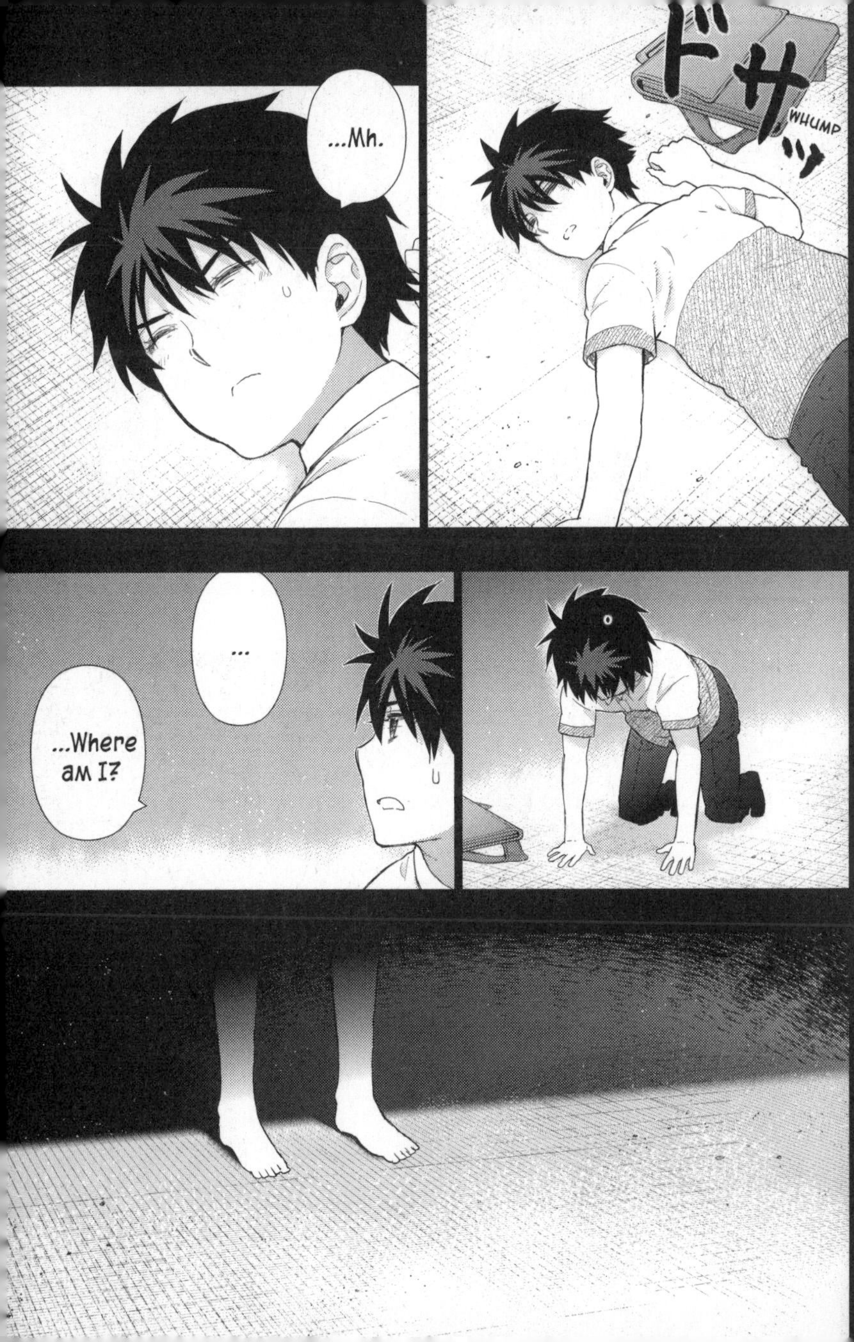
ドサッ
WHUMP
...Mh.
...
...Where am I?

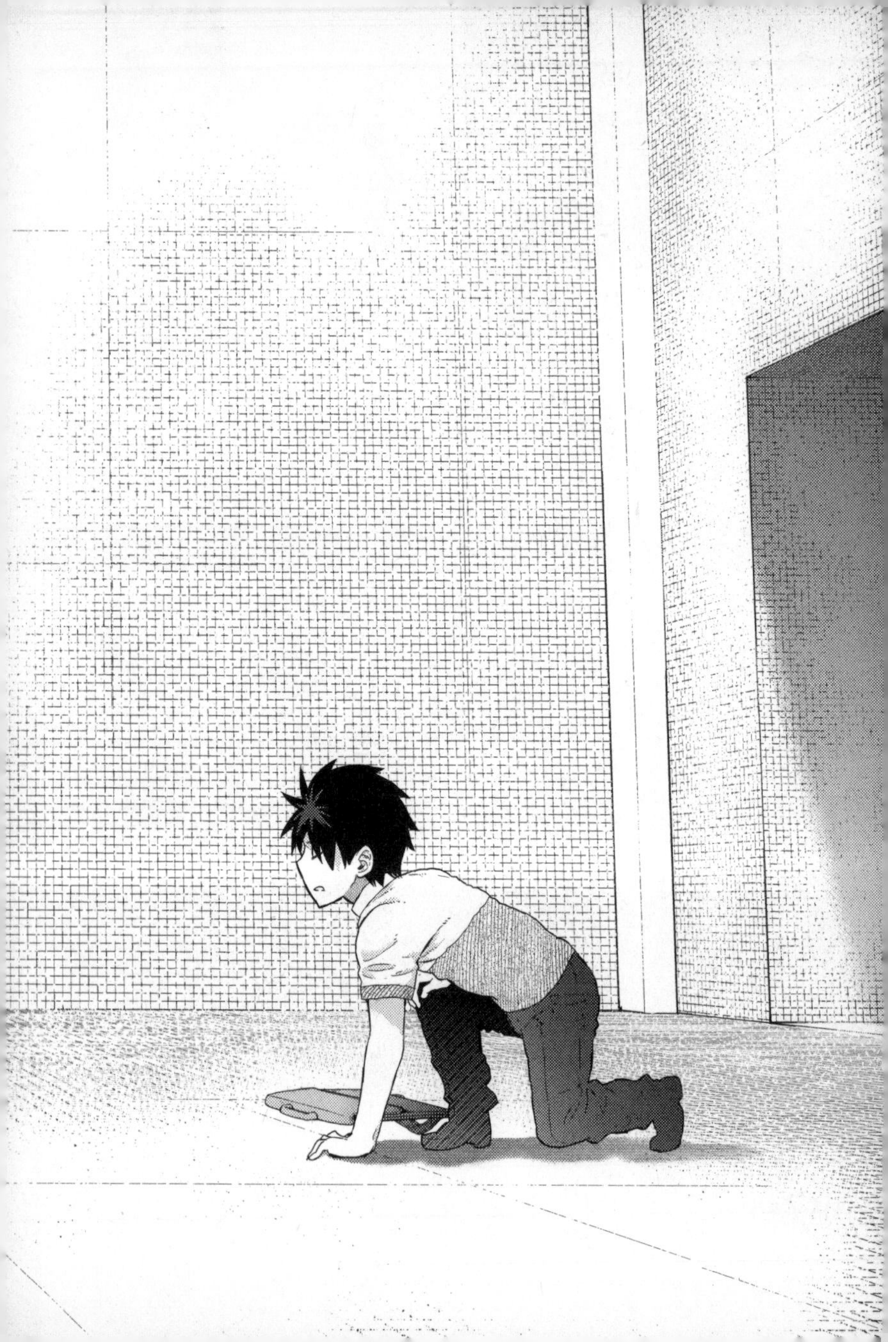

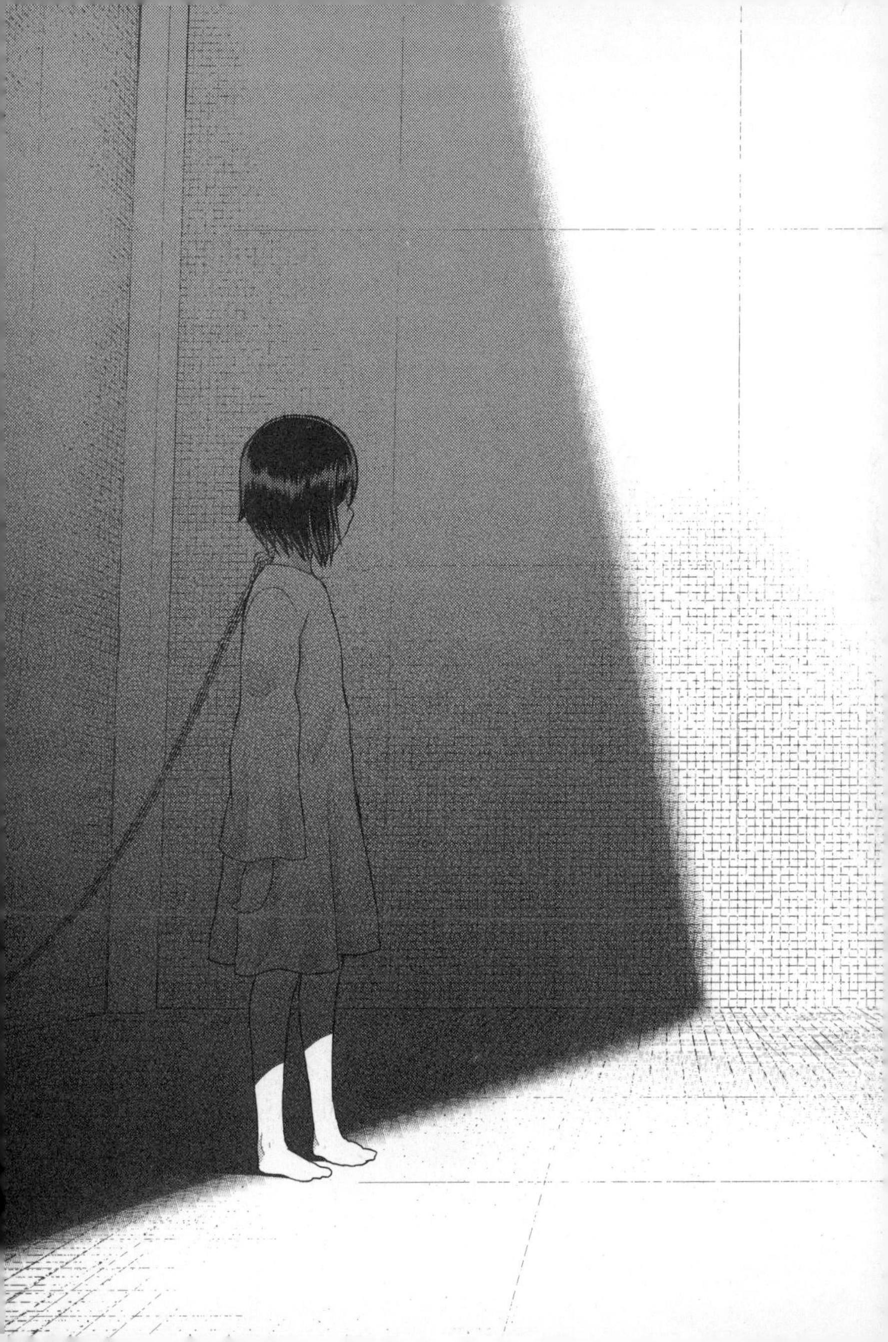

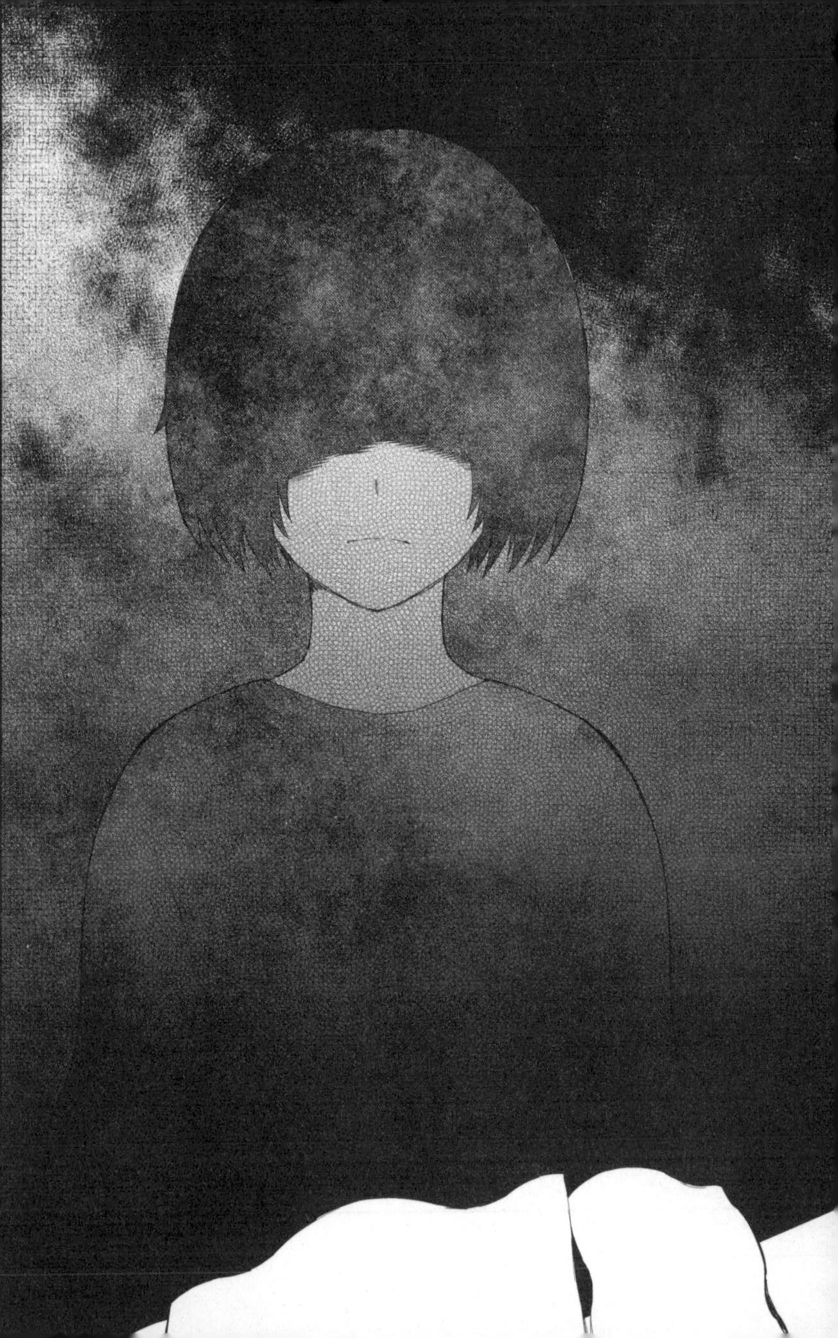

CHAPTER 53 END

Witchcraft Works

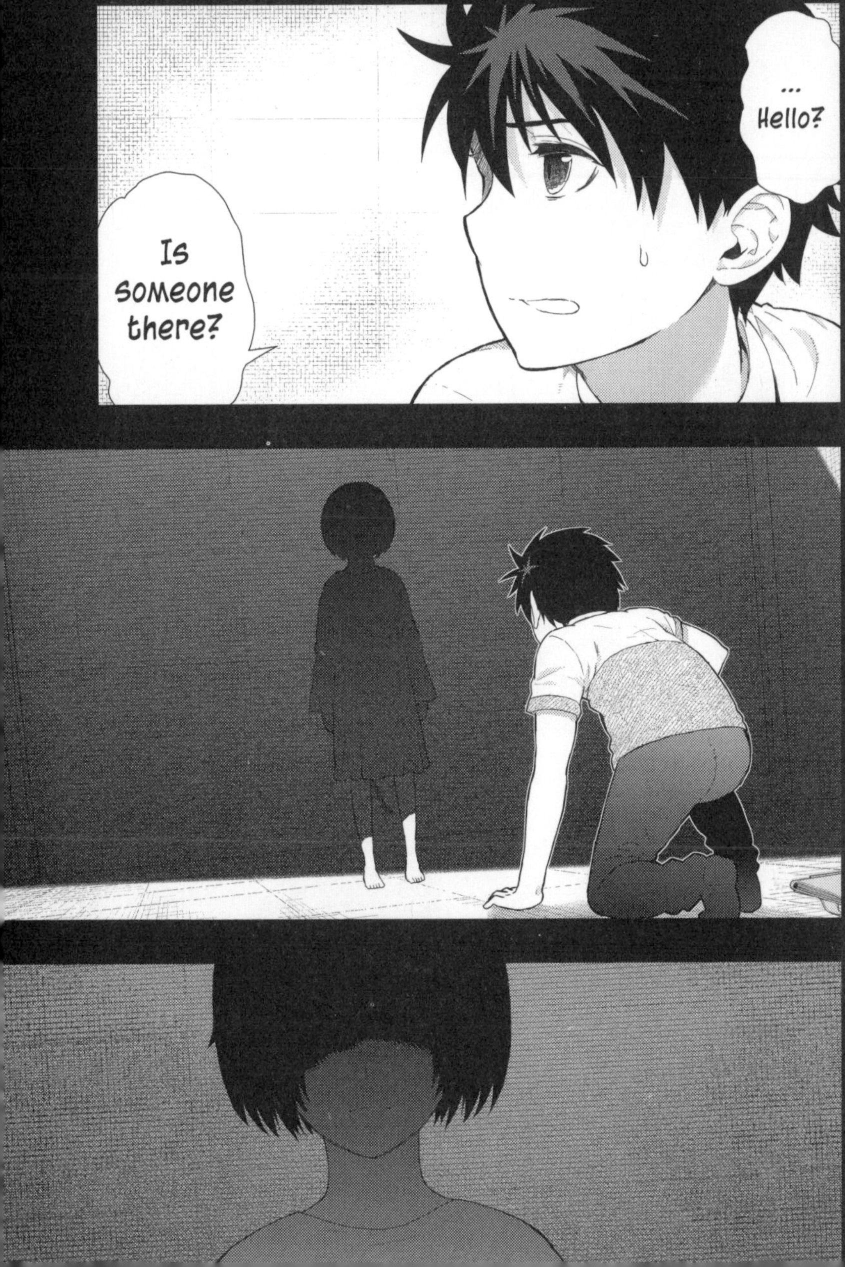
... Hello?
Is someone there?

CHAPTER 54 Takamiya and the Pendant's World (Part 1)

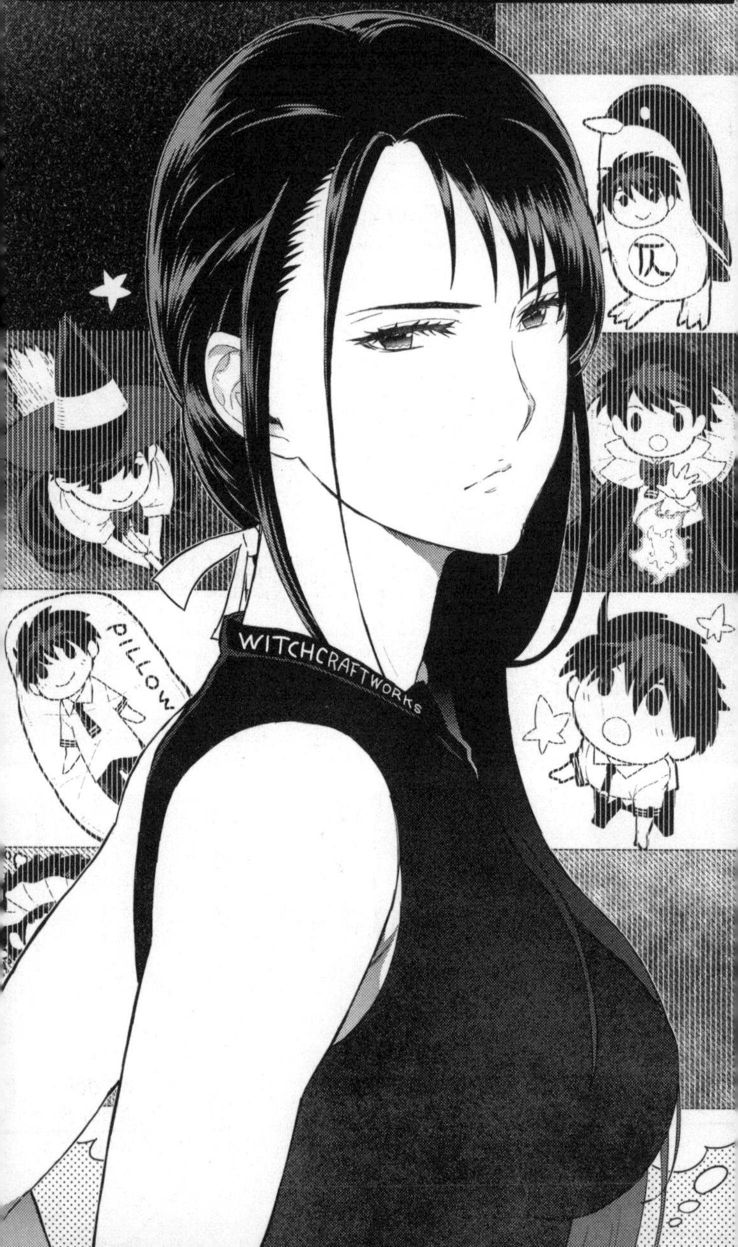
PILLOW
WITCHCRAFTWORKS

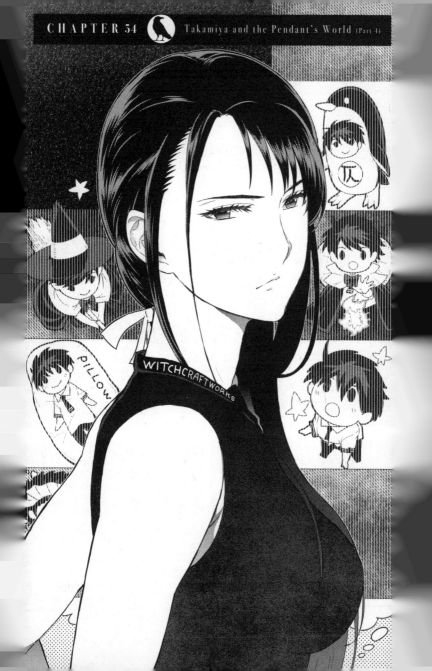

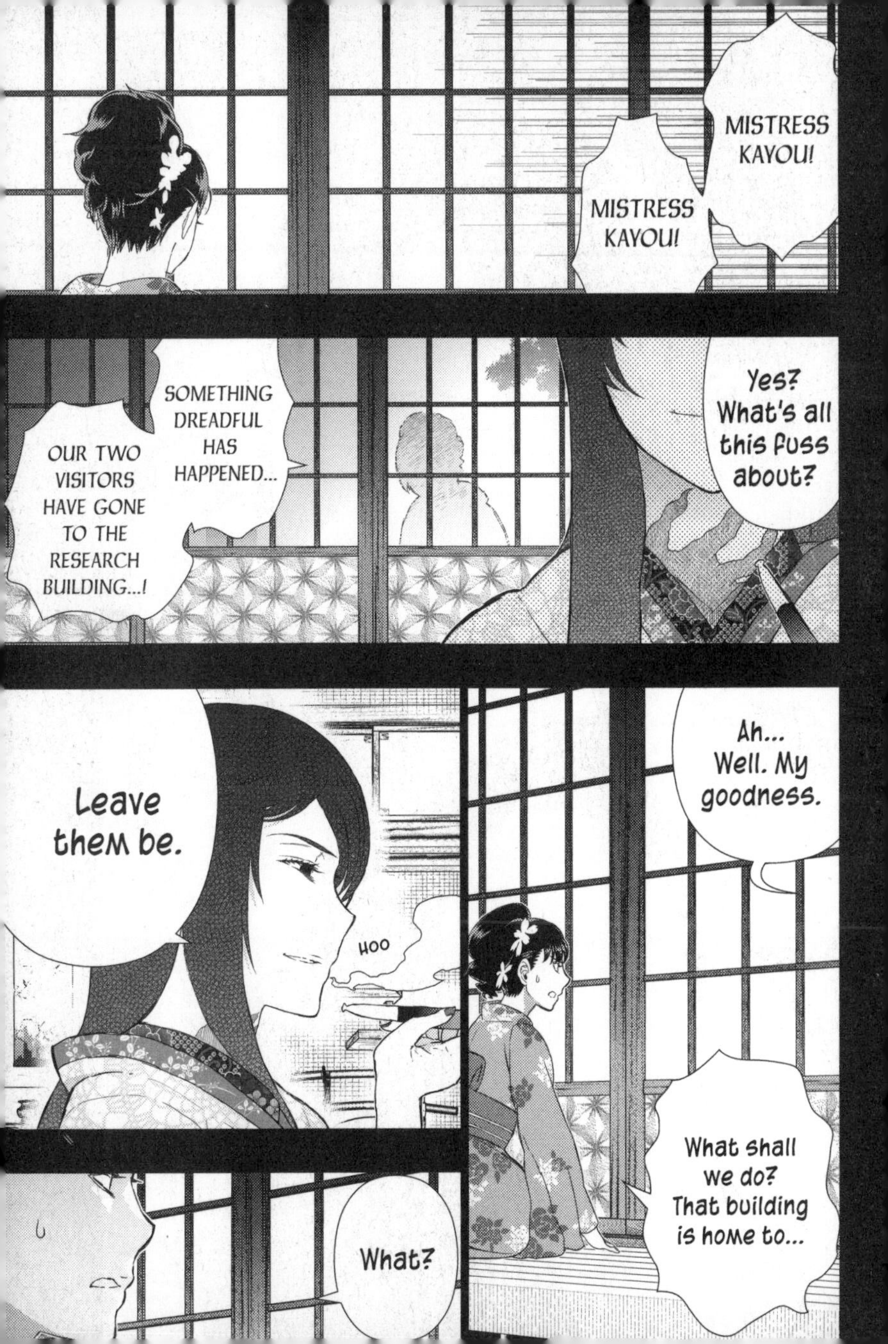
MISTRESS KAYOU!
MISTRESS KAYOU!
Yes? What's all this fuss about?
SOMETHING DREADFUL HAS HAPPENED...
OUR TWO VISITORS HAVE GONE TO THE RESEARCH BUILDING...!
Ah... Well. My goodness.
What shall we do? That building is home to...
Leave them be.
HOO
What?

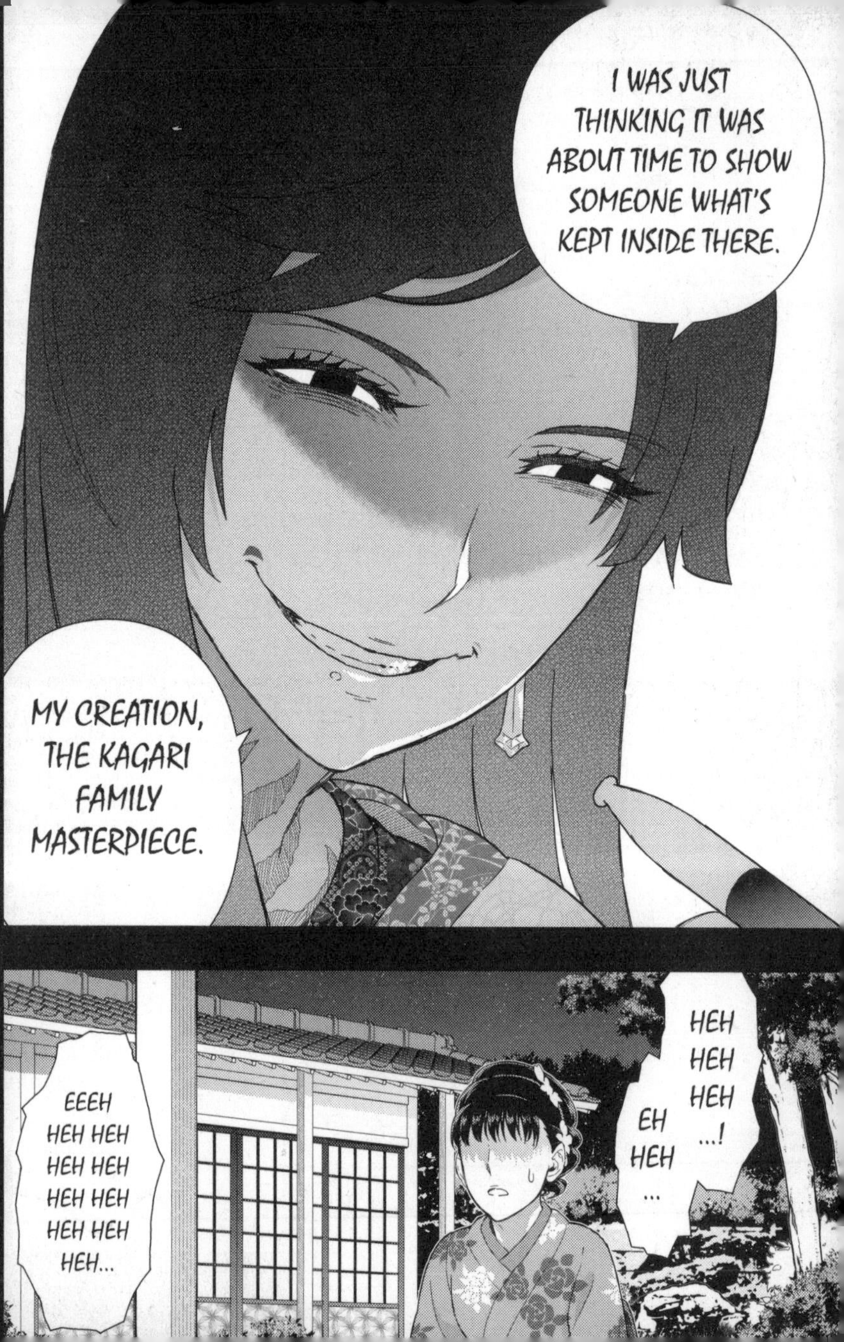
I WAS JUST THINKING IT WAS ABOUT TIME TO SHOW SOMEONE WHAT'S KEPT INSIDE THERE.
MY CREATION, THE KAGARI FAMILY MASTERPIECE.
HEH HEH HEH ...!
EH HEH ...
EEEH HEH HEH HEH HEH HEH HEH HEH HEH HEH...

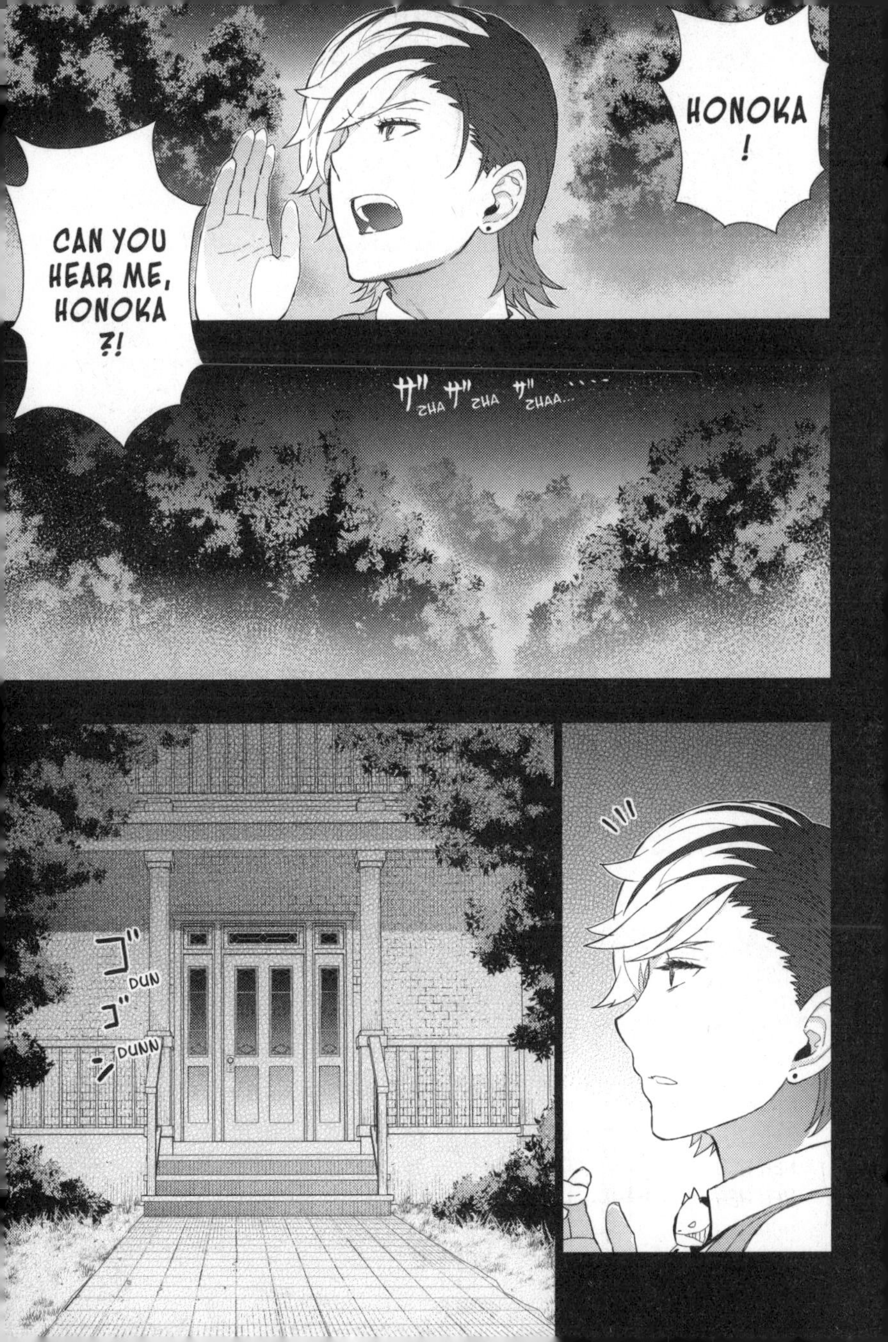
HONOKA!
CAN YOU HEAR ME, HONOKA?!
ザ ZHA ザ ZHA ザ ZHAA...
ゴ DUN ゴ DUNN ン

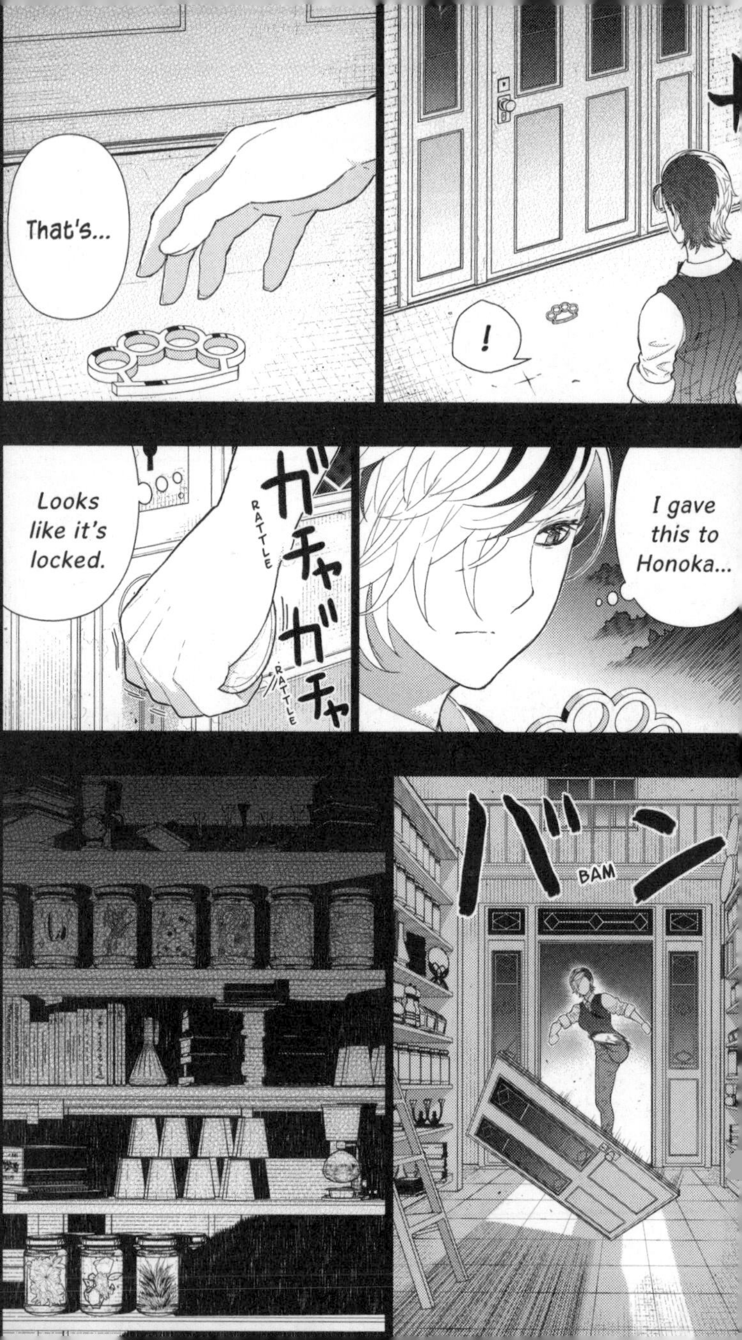
!
That's...
I gave this to Honoka...
Looks like it's locked.
ガチャガチャ
RATTLE RATTLE
バーン
BAM

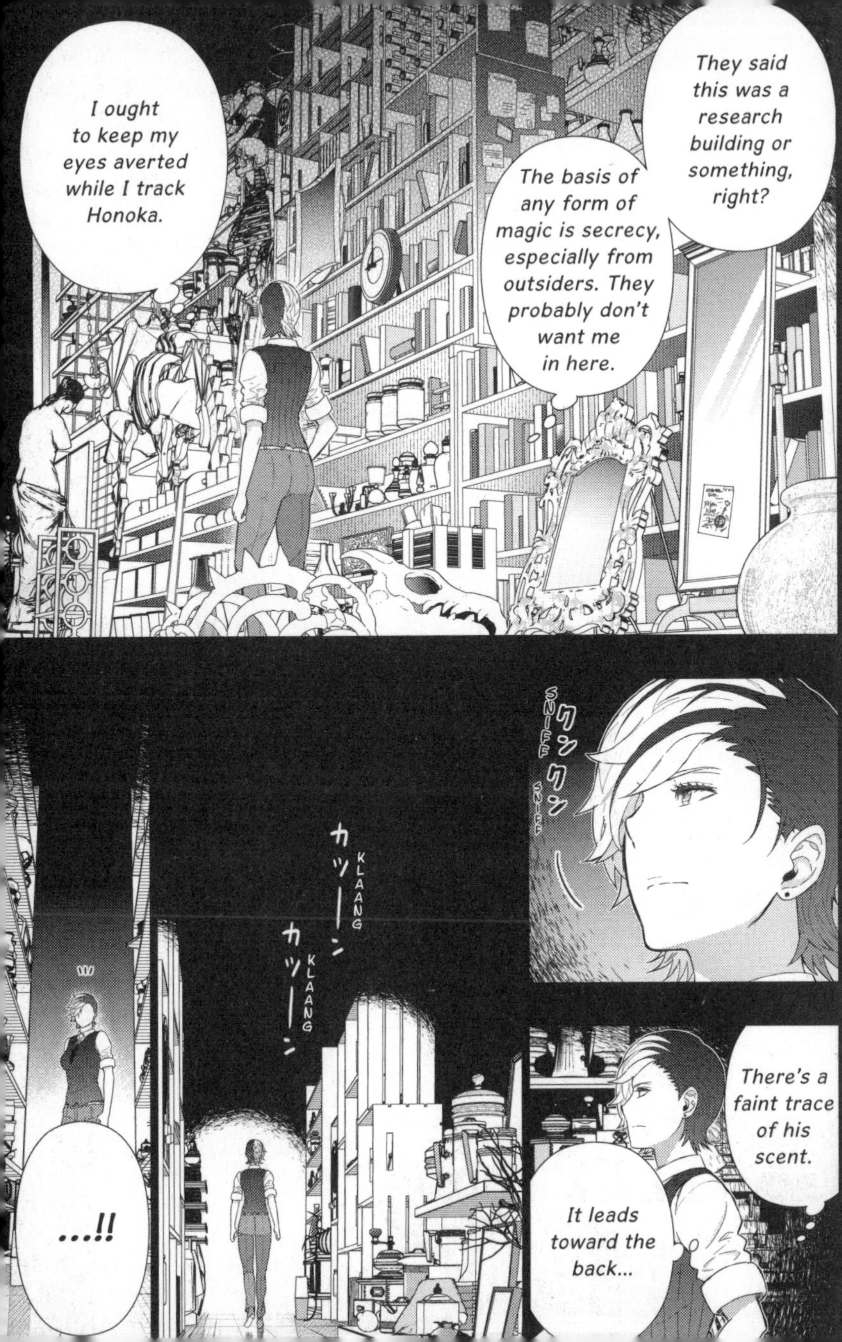
They said this was a research building or something, right?
The basis of any form of magic is secrecy, especially from outsiders. They probably don't want me in here.
I ought to keep my eyes averted while I track Honoka.
クン SNIFF
クン SNIFF
There's a faint trace of his scent.
It leads toward the back...
カッーン KLAANG
カッーン KLAANG
...!!

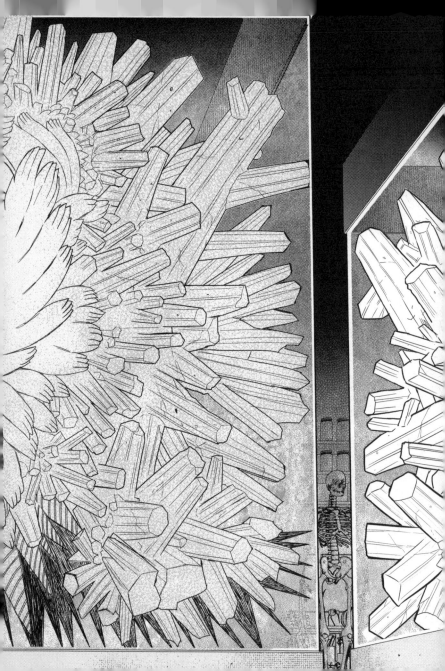

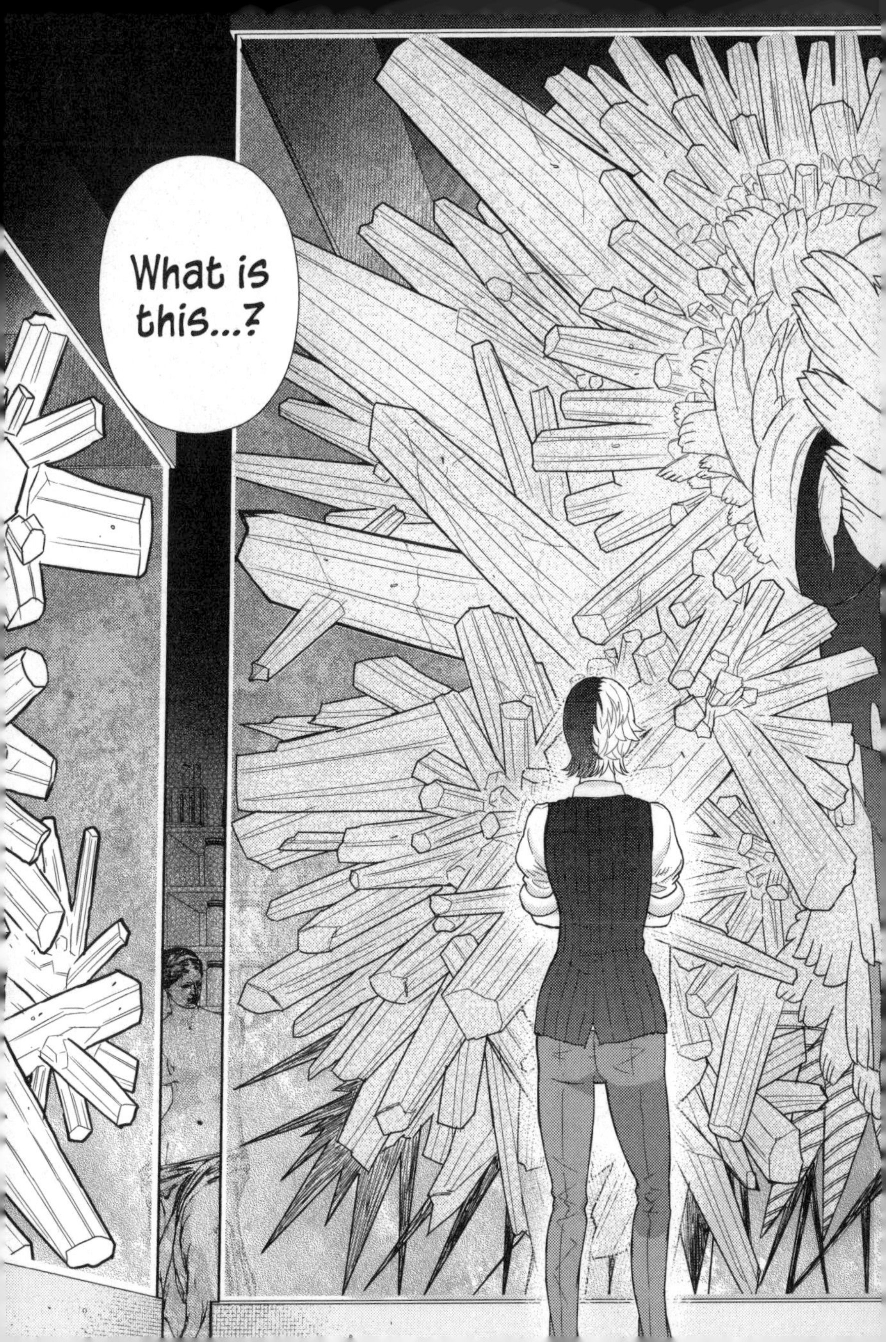
What is this...?

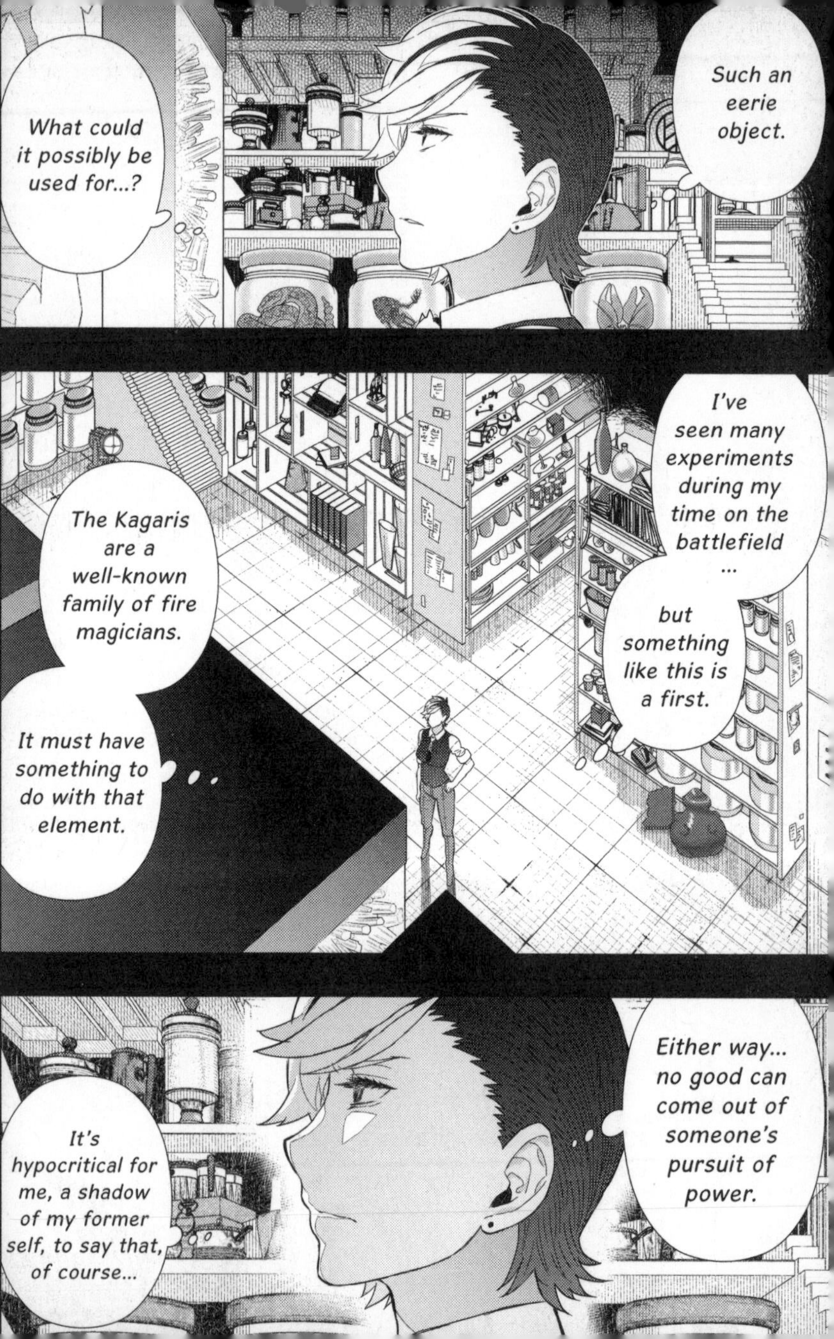
Such an eerie object.
What could it possibly be used for...?
I've seen many experiments during my time on the battlefield ...
but something like this is a first.
The Kagaris are a well-known family of fire magicians.
It must have something to do with that element.
Either way... no good can come out of someone's pursuit of power.
It's hypocritical for me, a shadow of my former self, to say that, of course...

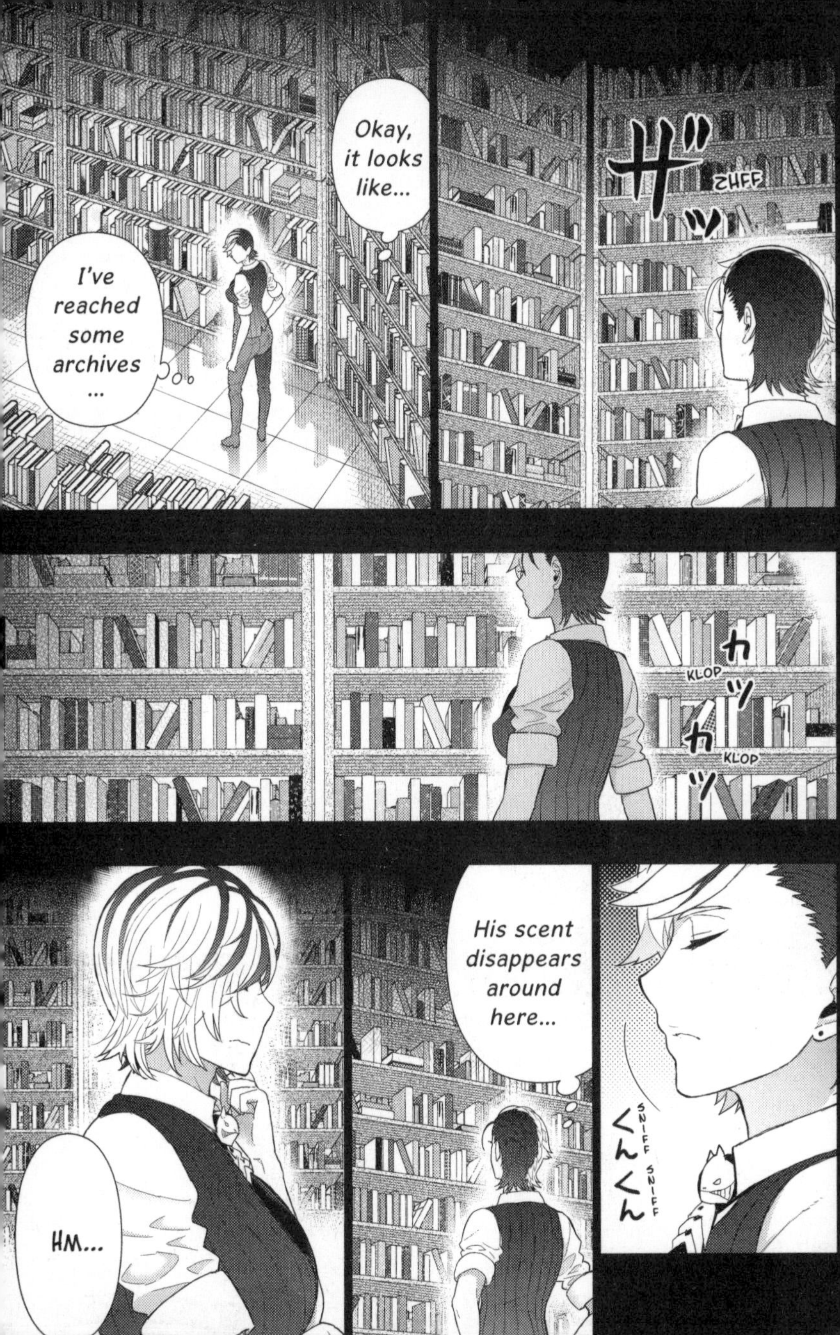
ザッ
ZHFF
Okay, it looks like...
I've reached some archives...
カッ
KLOP
カッ
KLOP
くんくん
SNIFF SNIFF
His scent disappears around here...
HM...

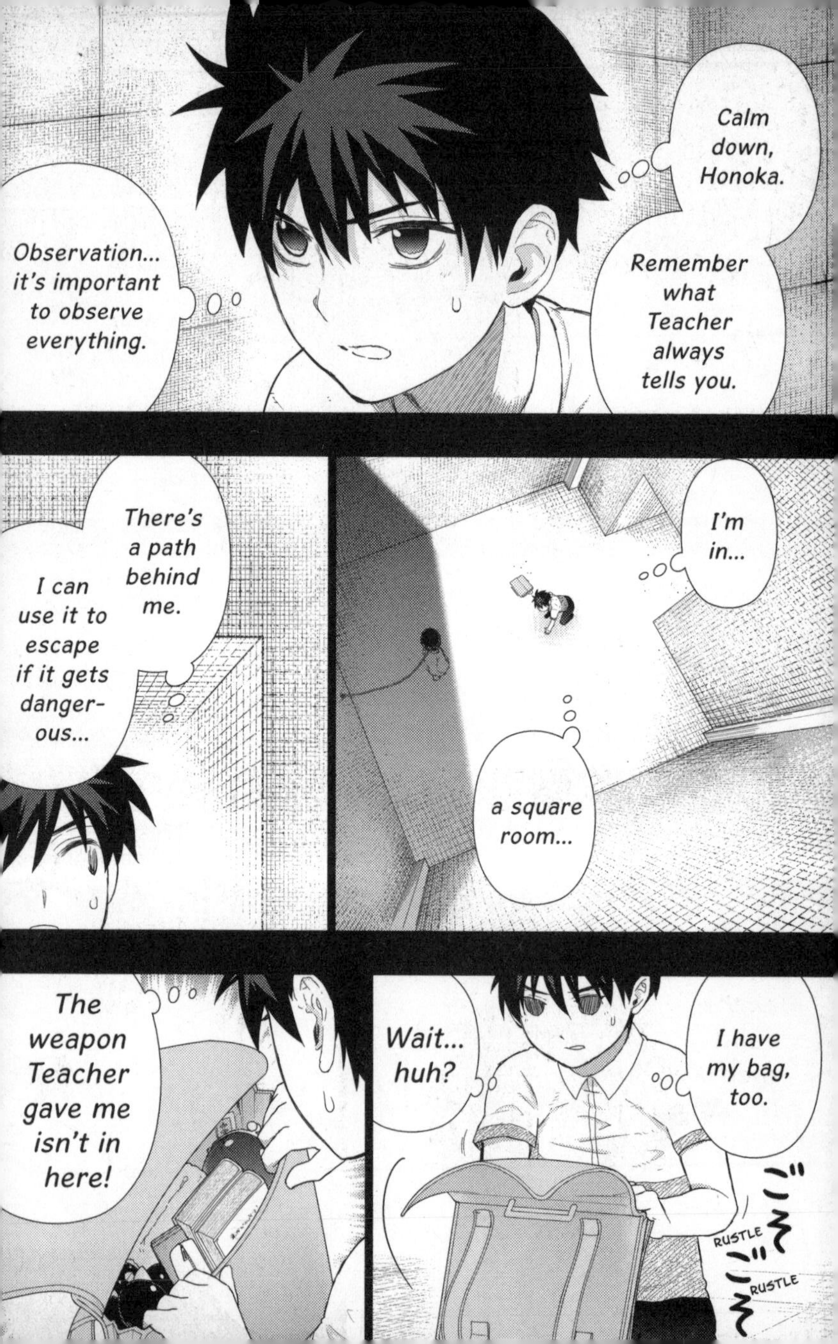
Calm down, Honoka.
Remember what Teacher always tells you.
Observation... it's important to observe everything.
I'm in...
a square room...
There's a path behind me.
I can use it to escape if it gets danger-ous...
I have my bag, too.
RUSTLE
RUSTLE
Wait... huh?
The weapon Teacher gave me isn't in here!

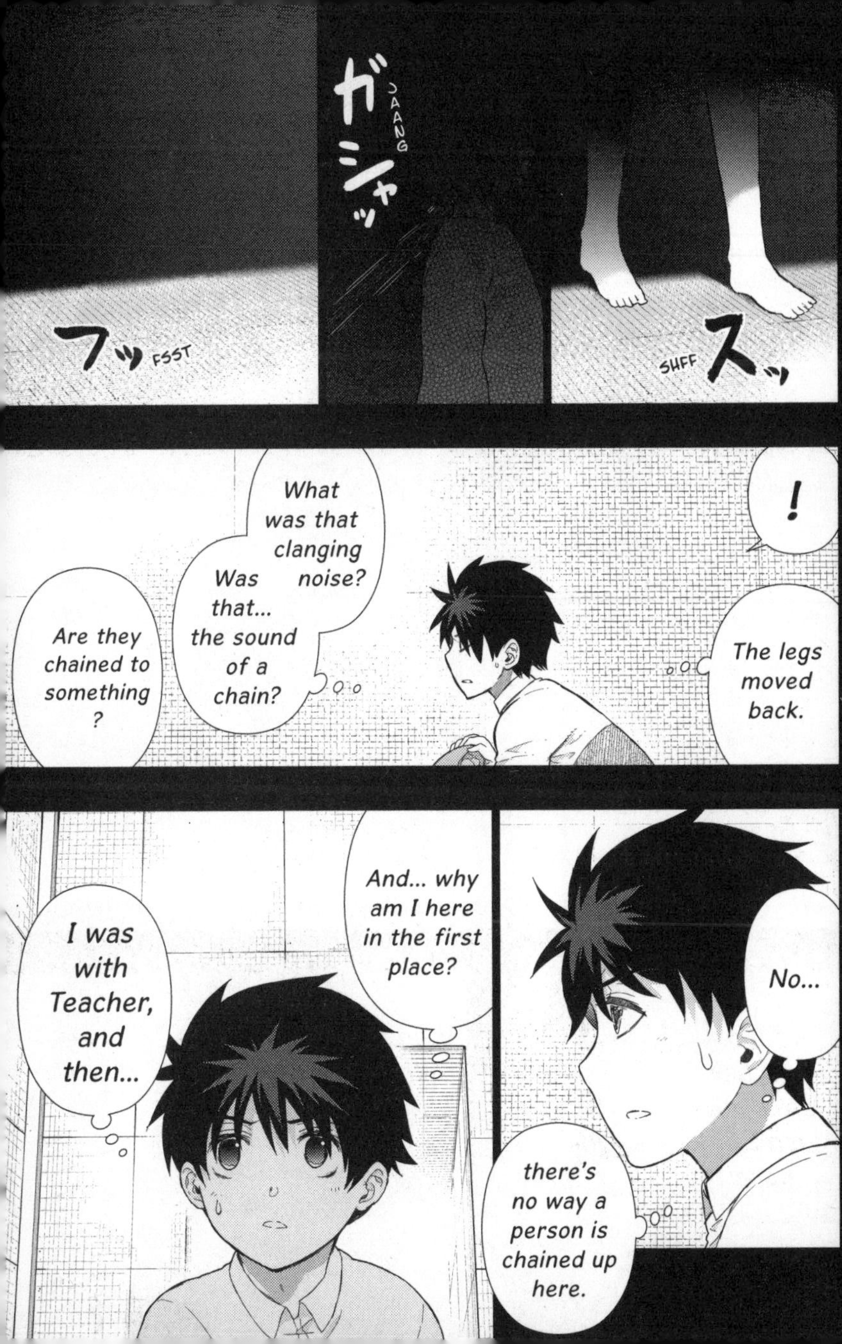
スッ SHUFF
ガシャッ JAAANG
フッ FSST
!
The legs moved back.
What was that clanging noise?
Was that... the sound of a chain?
Are they chained to something?
No...
there's no way a person is chained up here.
And... why am I here in the first place?
I was with Teacher, and then...

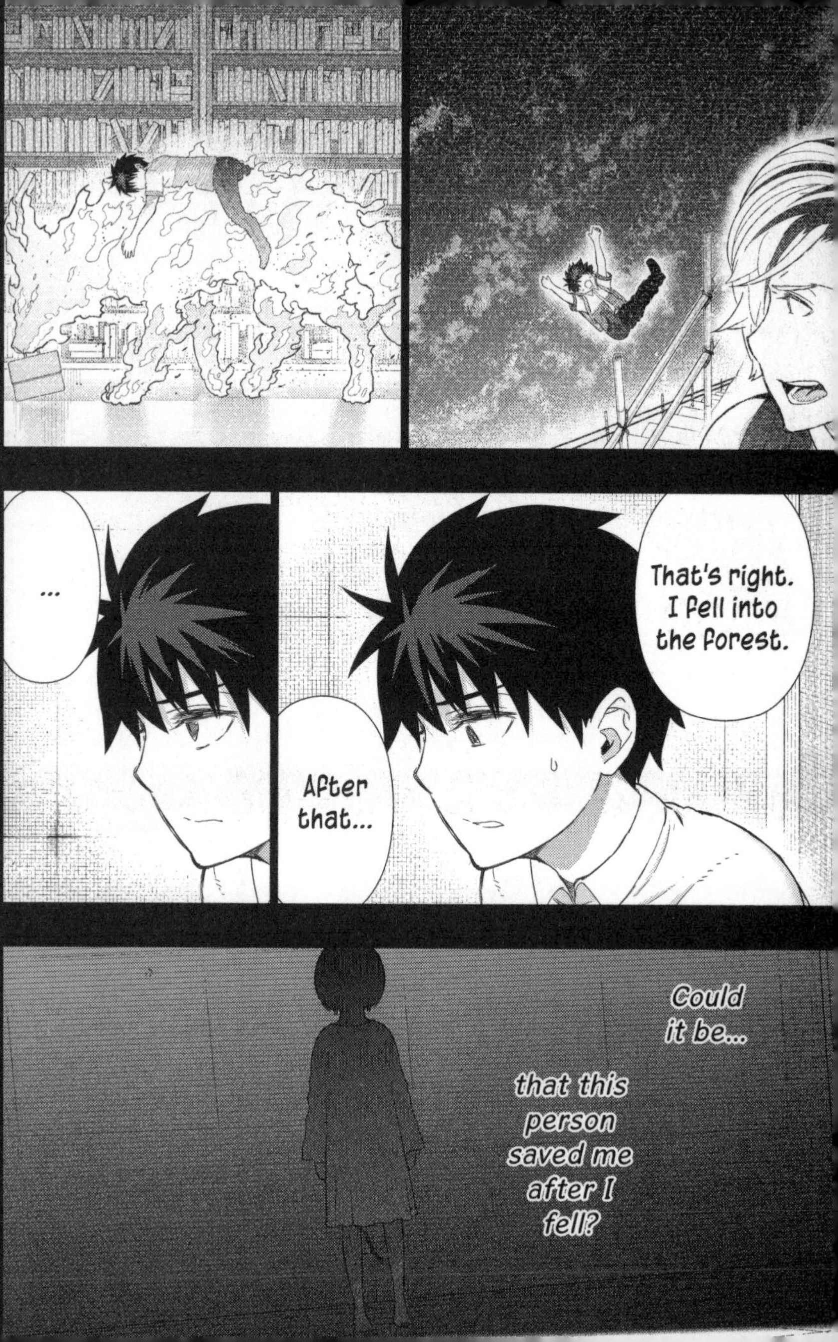
That's right. I fell into the forest.
After that...
...
Could it be...
that this person saved me after I fell?

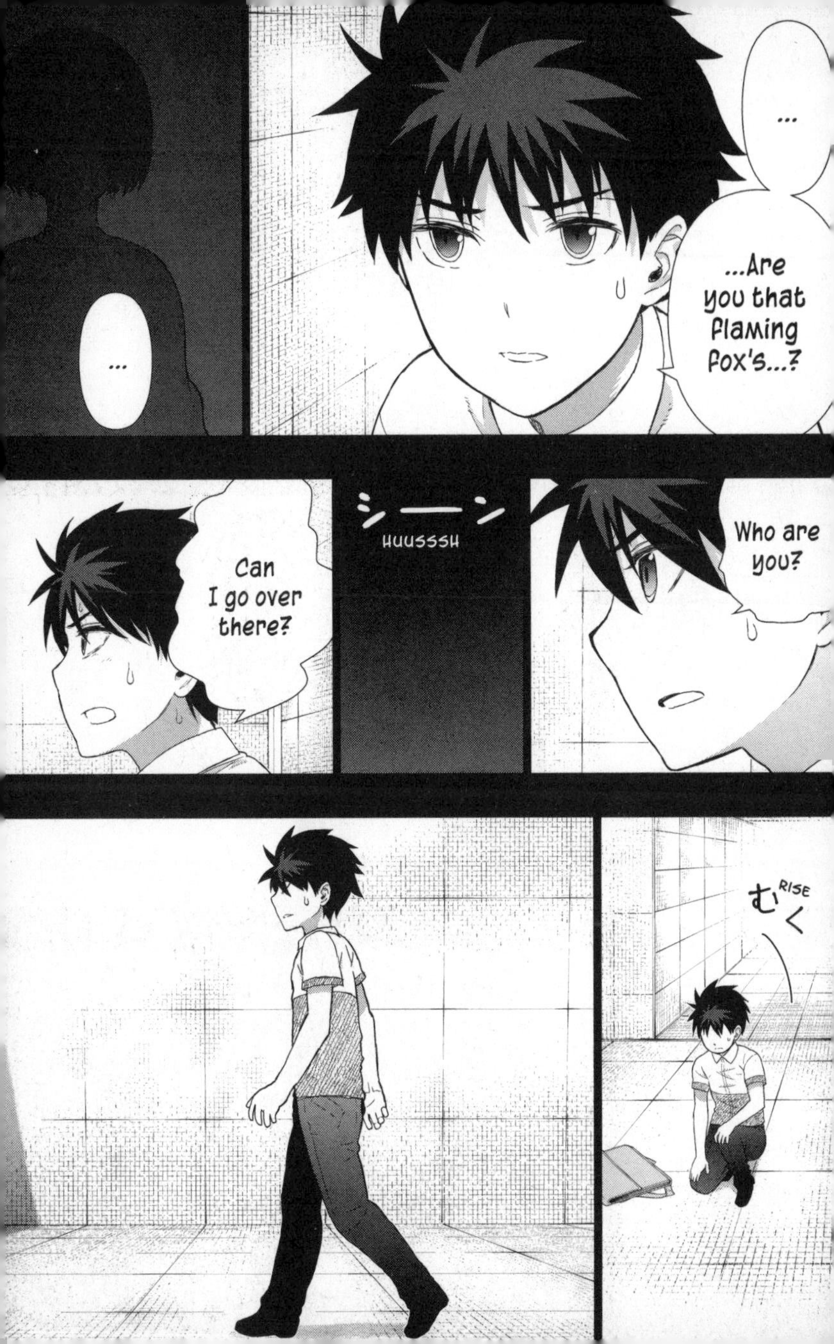

...
...Are you that flaming fox's...?
...
Who are you?
シーーン
HUUSSSH
Can I go over there?
むく
RISE

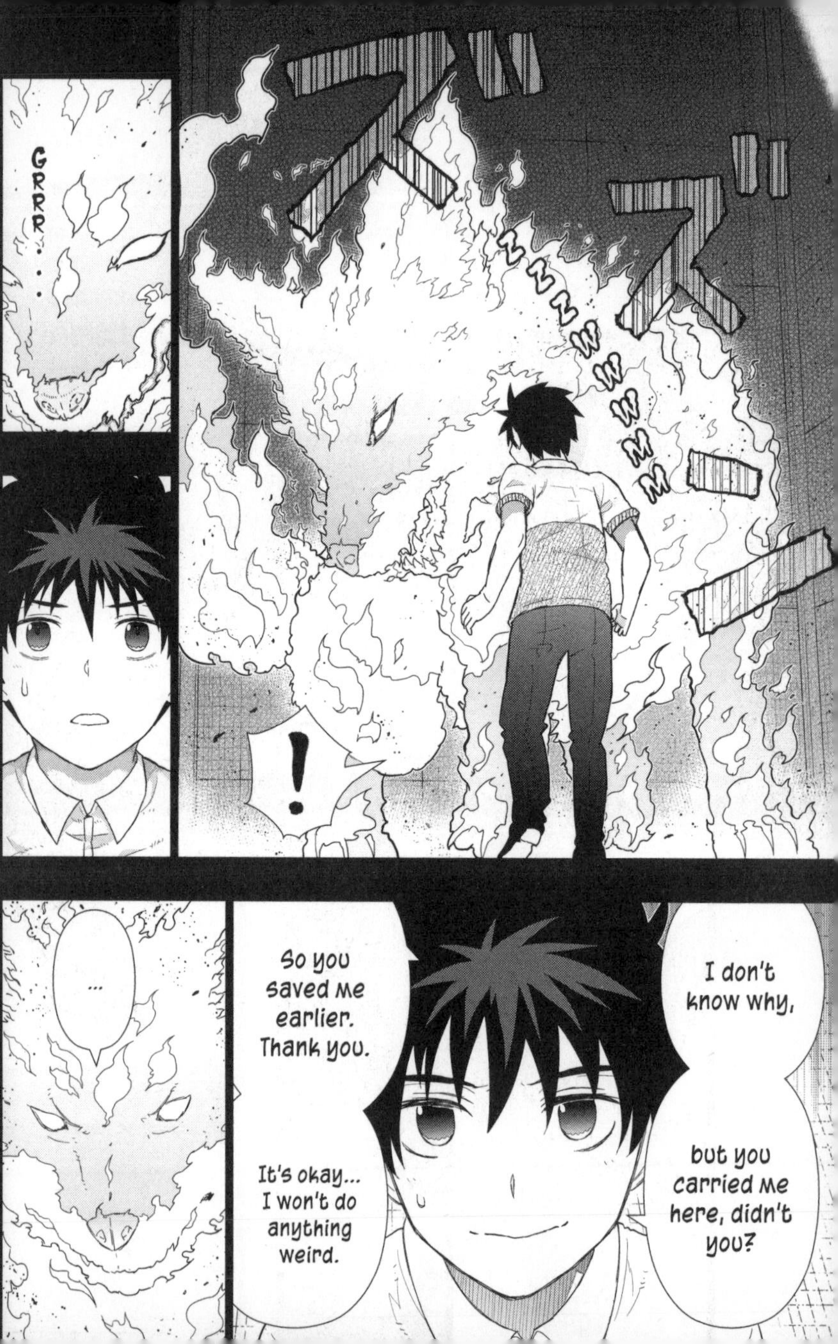
ズズ
ZZZWWWMMM
!
GRRR...
I don't know why,
but you carried me here, didn't you?
So you saved me earlier. Thank you.
It's okay... I won't do anything weird.
...

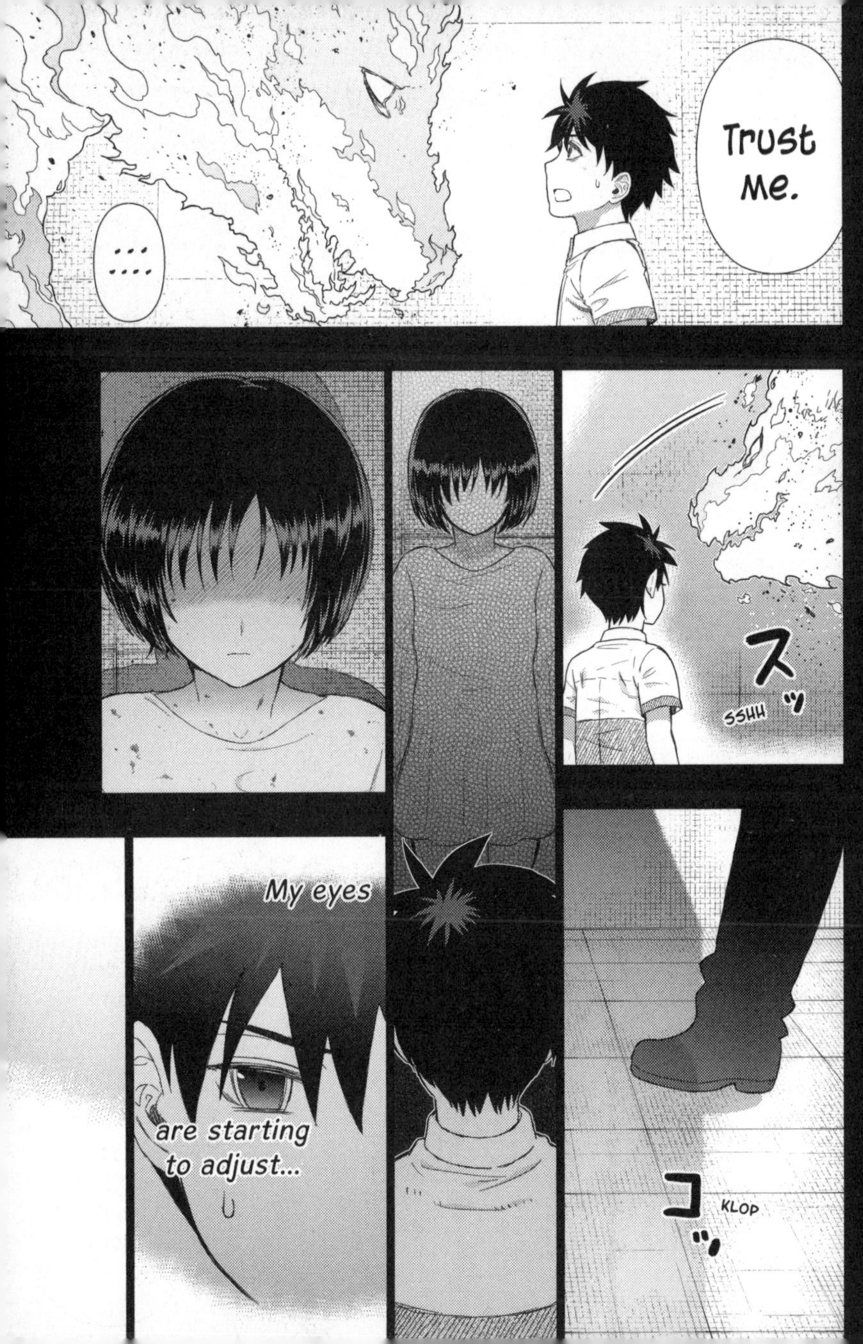
Trust me.
......
ス ッ
SSHH
コ ッ
KLOP
My eyes
are starting to adjust...

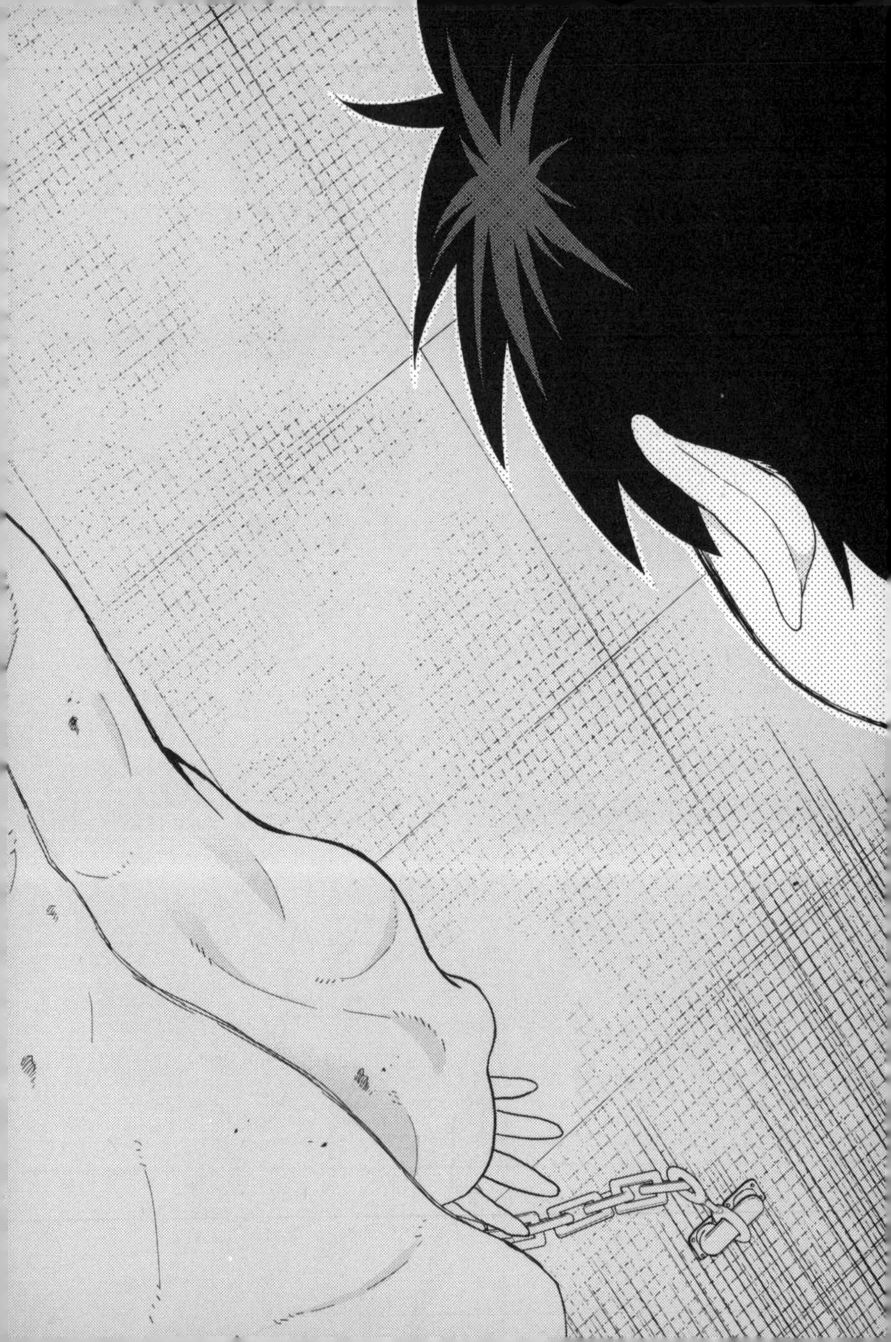

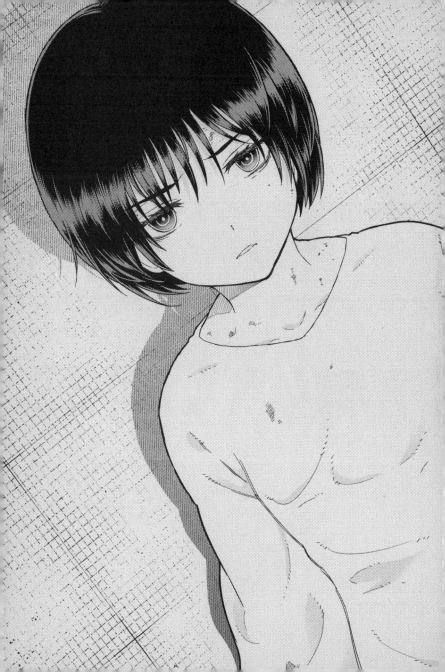

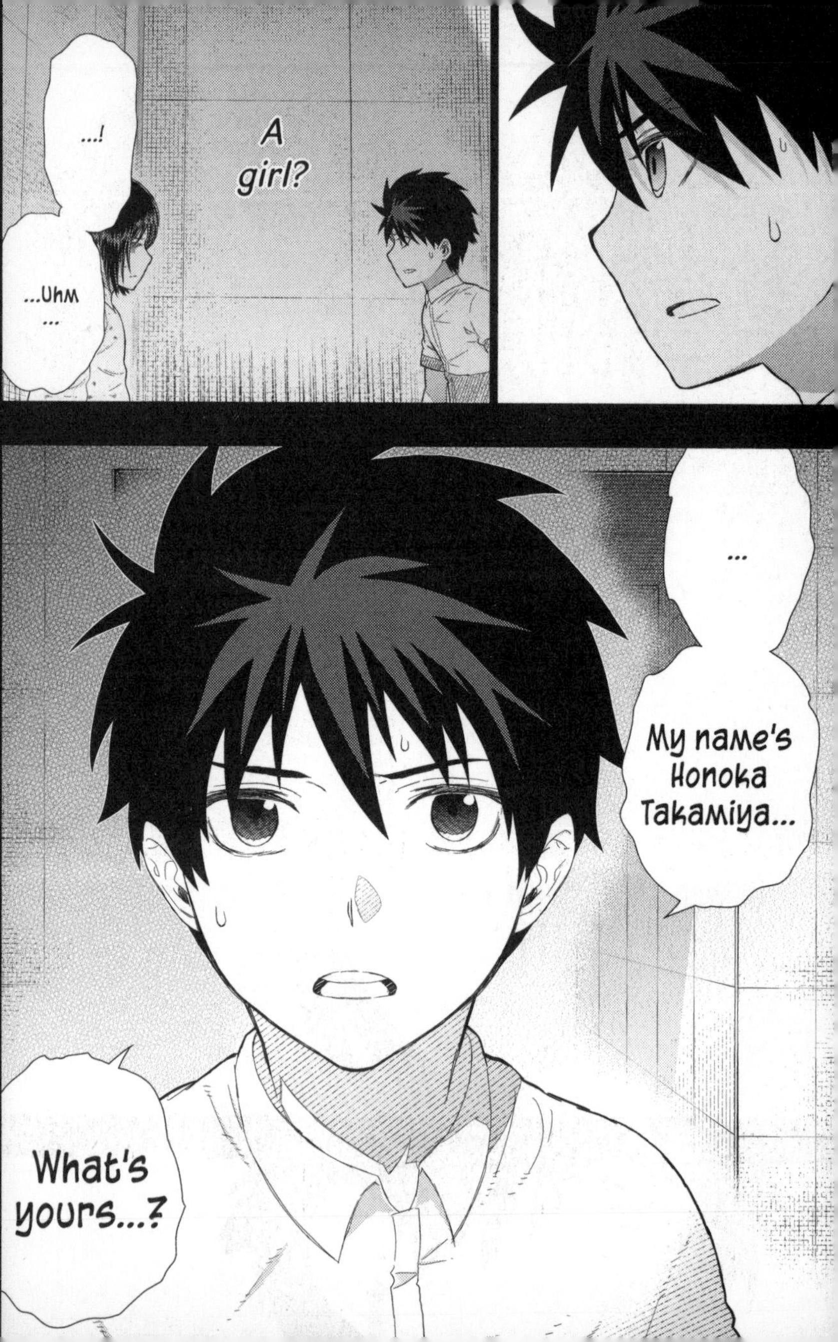
A girl?
...!
...Uhm ...
...
My name's Honoka Takamiya...
What's yours...?

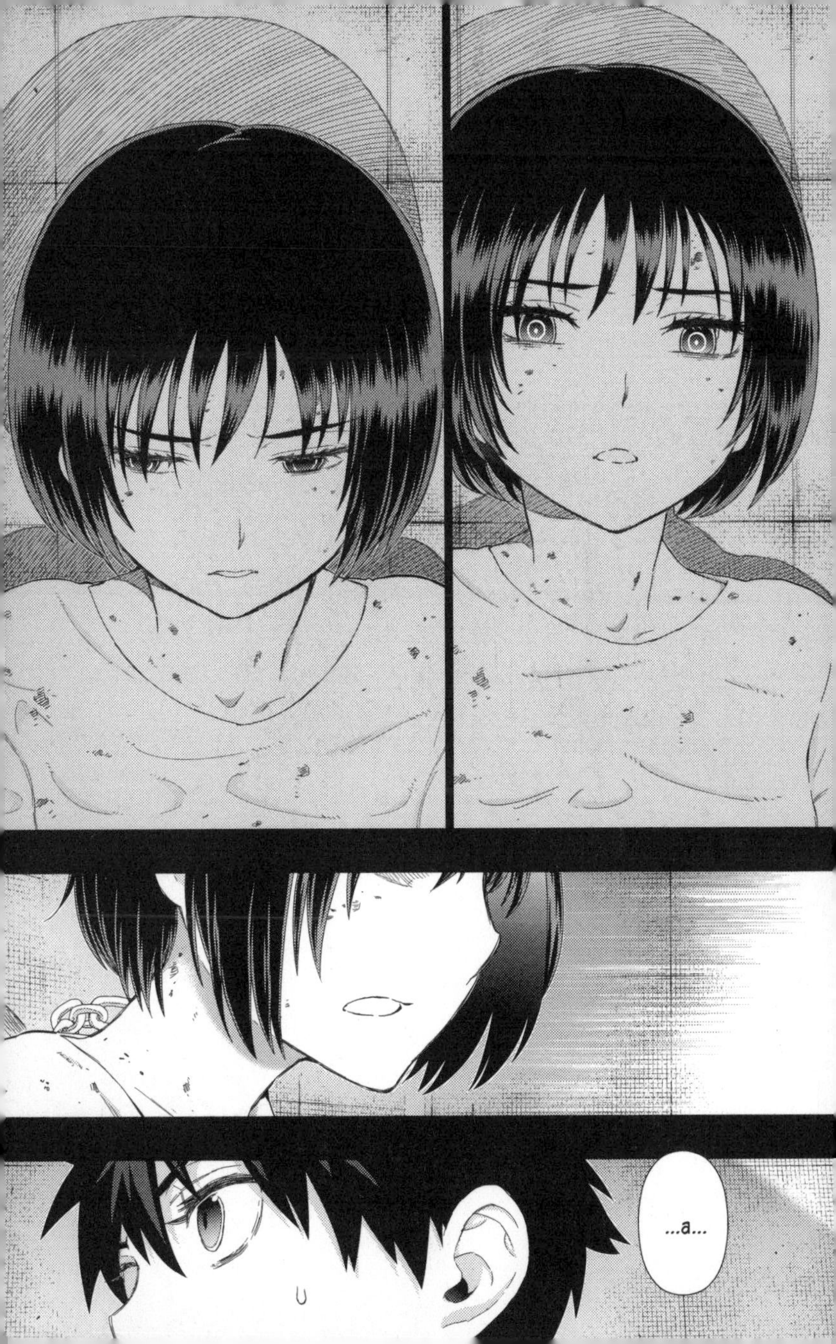
...a...

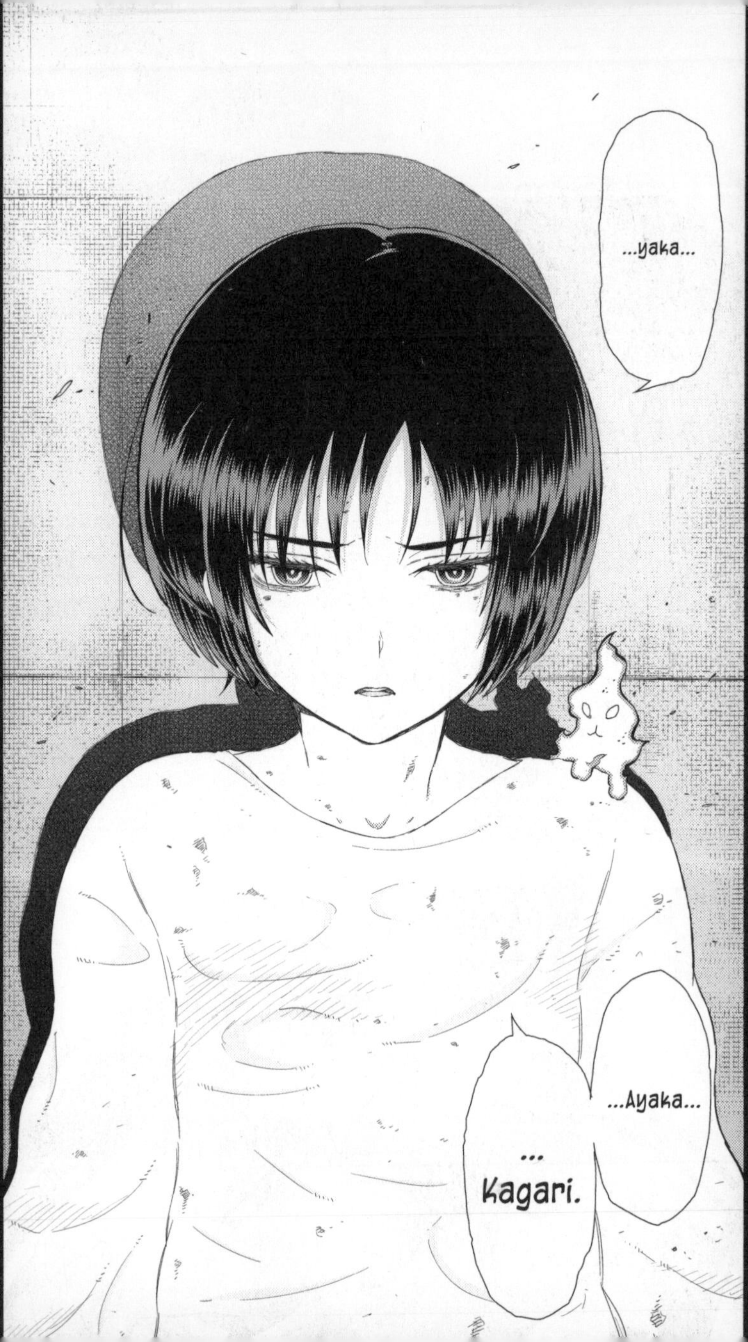
...yaka...
...Ayaka...
... Kagari.

WITCHCRAFT WORKS 10 END

Afterword

Hello, this is Mizunagi. Did you enjoy volume 10 of Witchcraft Works?

Now that we're ten volumes in, it looks like Kasumi and Furry-Ear have gotten pretty friendly. I imagine their relationship is starting to put a smile on your face, too. They should be getting even closer in volume 11. Please look forward to it.

As a bonus, I think Takamiya and Kagari will also be growing closer.

Ryu Mizunagi

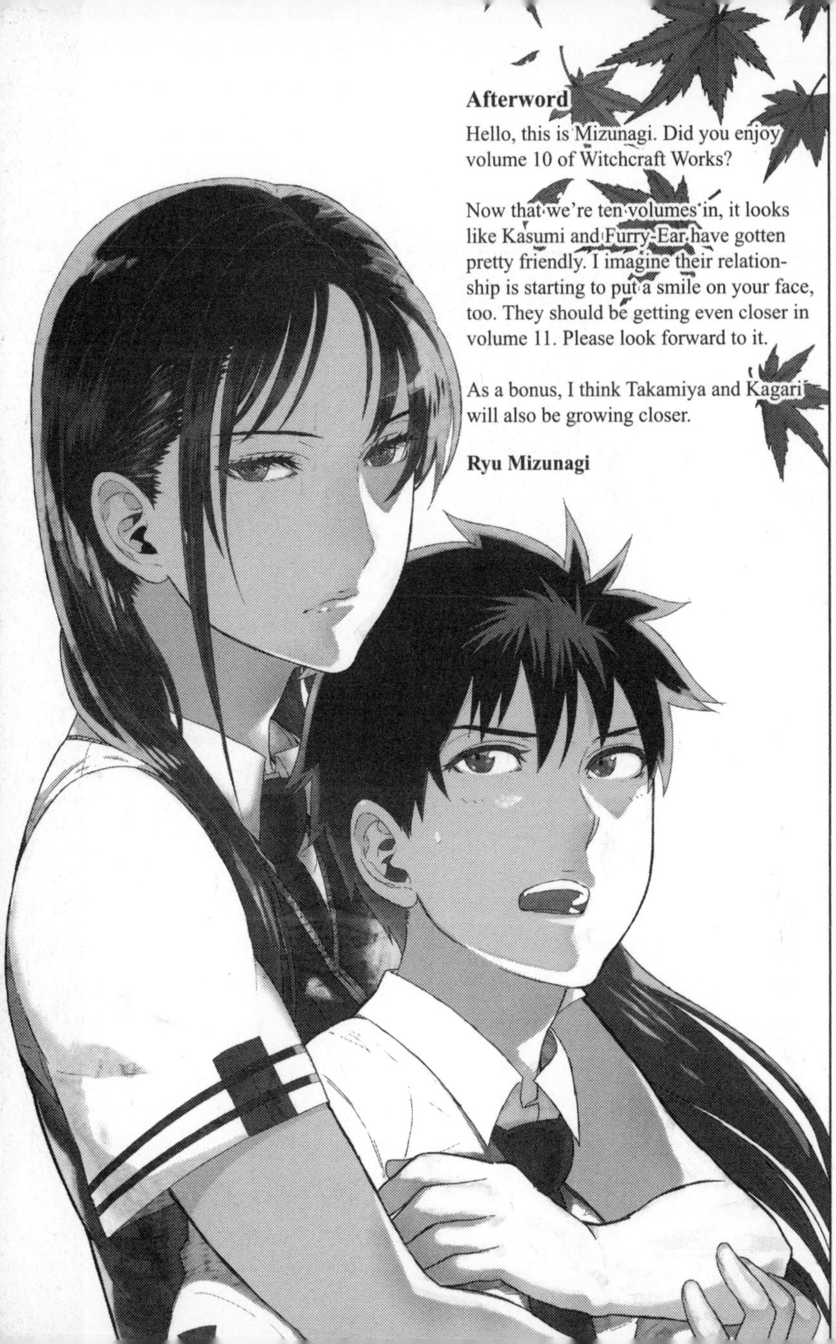

Witchcraft Works

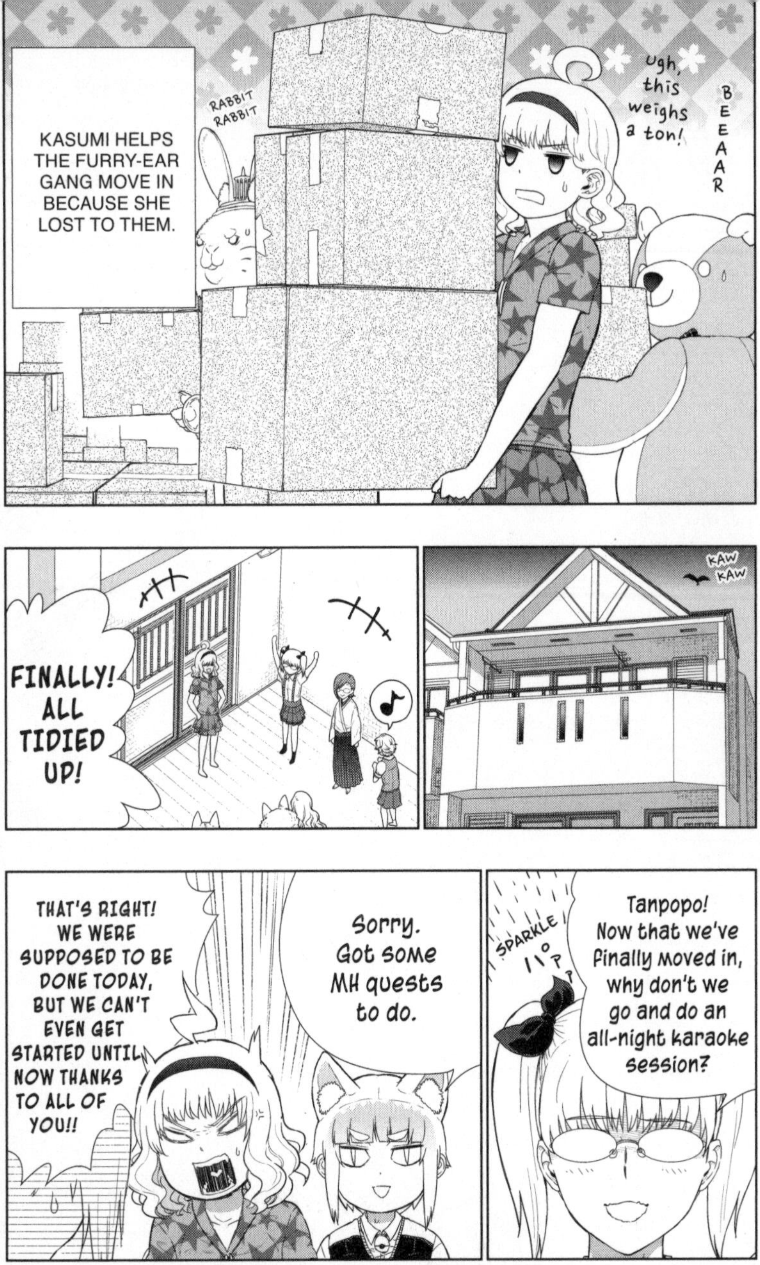
Ugh, this weighs a ton!
BEEAAR
RABBIT RABBIT
KASUMI HELPS THE FURRY-EAR GANG MOVE IN BECAUSE SHE LOST TO THEM.
KAW KAW
FINALLY! ALL TIDIED UP!
Tanpopo! Now that we've finally moved in, why don't we go and do an all-night karaoke session?
SPARKLE
Sorry. Got some MH quests to do.
THAT'S RIGHT! WE WERE SUPPOSED TO BE DONE TODAY, BUT WE CAN'T EVEN GET STARTED UNTIL NOW THANKS TO ALL OF YOU!!

HER FERAL NATURE, LOST AND FORGOTTEN.

Witchcraft Works | SETTING + SECRETS

This page is a collection of behind-the-scenes character and story elements that probably won't affect or appear in the main story, as well as comments by the author. If you finish reading the story and think, "I want to know more!" then we hope you enjoy the information here.

Chapter 47

A story of two quibbling witches trying to work together.

Weekend ends up searching for Kazane's enemy after striking a deal with her. Kazane then called up Chronoire since she didn't have anything else planned (she was sleeping) and asked her to help (and observe) Weekend. Chronoire agreed, saying, "It does sound like an interesting excursion."

★ Smartphones
Weekend has a tendency to go out of her way and adopt whatever items are modern at the time. She seems to hate the old mindset that magic and science don't mix, just as she hates old witches. Of course, you could also say she's nothing more than a sucker for trends...

In contrast, Chronoire doesn't like how unprincipled this makes her look.

By the way, the smartphone is rigged so that it can be blown up at any time.

• Takamiya + Kagari
Studying. Kasumi and Tanpopo are lazing around nearby.

Chapter 48

• Atori
Atori now lives in the ceiling above Takamiya's room, which she remodeled

in secret, just like Kagari's basement. She's friends with Natsume and spends all her days off hanging out in her room, enjoying anime, manga, and games. If she has any complaint about Natsume, it's that all her media has middle-aged guys as protagonists, for whatever reason. Atori is also aware of the gigantic Kyoichiro Mikage tapestry hanging in Natsume's room that she hides whenever someone comes in, but she's kept silent about it. In fact, she knows about all the different Kyoichiro merchandise Natsume has, but again, she hasn't said a word.

• Shiori
Natsume's mother. Gave the pendant to Takamiya.

• Kagari
She seems to know exactly where Takamiya is.

Chapter 49

The reconstruction of Kazane's home.

• Kazane
We see in this chapter how Kazane lives after her home was blown away, caus-ing her to lose her fortune. She is forced to rebuild her house after being chased out of the chairperson's office that she had been making private use of and losing the housemaid she had made out of the former student council president. You can see Kazane's unique inability to plan ahead by her decision to use all her remaining funds to rebuild her home's gate for whatever reason. She's searching for a way to rebuild a towering home so that she can live high in the sky, but who knows when that will happen. Kazane has many animals she can count on that she used to take care of in her giant yard. They went feral after the house was destroyed, but Atori and Touko have been climbing the mountains now and then to feed them. The log cabin they build apparently started to slant after a few days.

• Komachi
When Komachi has time on her days off, she can often be found in the gym, making sure that her body can look good in a dress at any given moment. This can only be chalked up to love. She also has a tuxedo prepared for Kazane, but it has so far gone unused.

• Medusa and Co.
Medusa and her underlings have rented the house across the street and moved

in. It doesn't seem like Medusa is interested in fighting for the moment, though... While the other members have an emotional reunion with Furry-Ear, they are forced to face the cruel reality that she has become domesticated. Now that the Furry-Ear Gang has lost their leader (even their name is in danger), will they ever be able to regain their former glory?

• Kasumi and Furry-Ear
While neither one shows much emotion to the other, the two always seem to end up hanging out regardless. It isn't rare for them to take baths together, either. The one thing that Kasumi doesn't like about Furry-Ear is that she eats potato chips on her bed and leaves a mess. The two have been sleeping in the same bed since she noticed this, leading to annoyance when she gets slept on top of or kicked out of bed.

Chapter 50

Kagari gets a fever.

• Takamiya
When Takamiya, while caring for the feverish Kagari, goes into her room to search for pajamas, he discovers a huge number of dolls of himself, as well as photos of himself in a basement room. Now that Kagari knows he isn't bothered by these things, what will she do next?

• Furry-Ear Gang
Kanna visits Takamiya's home to ask for Furry-Ear's help as they move in. But once more, the girls find themselves turned into fools by the tragic reality we saw in the previous chapter: Furry-Ear has actually been domesticated. And by a Workshop witch at that, someone the Furry-Ear Gang should consider an arch-rival. The Gang challenges Kasumi to a fight in order to get her back, and they're ready with new magic... They end up beating Kasumi through a stroke of luck, but then they get cocky as always and challenge Kagari to a fight. As always, they suffer defeat in the end.

Chapter 51-53

The pendant is analyzed and its memories are read.

• Takamiya and Kagari

The two use Medusa's power to move their consciousness into the world of memories held inside the pendant. They find a young Takamiya there, and the Chairwoman is by his side.

• Kazane and Honoka
The two head to a house being plagued by a flaming beast. At the time, the estate was occupied by the Kagari family. Unlike now, it was bustling and full of people.

Though her name has been mentioned many times in the past, Kayou Kagari makes her first appearance here. We learn that Kazane had yet to have the family name of Kagari when Kayou calls her Hoozuki. Given the way that Kagari talks about Kayou, could they have some sort of history with one another?

Honoka falls into the forest and is taken somewhere by the flaming beast. Kazane follows after him.

Chapter 54

The pendant is analyzed and its memories are read.

• Kayou Kagari
Kayou is unbothered by the fact that the two have gone into the research building they had been forbidden to enter. She seems to be planning something.

• Kazane
There's something beast-like about the way she chases after Takamiya, or maybe it's just Kazane-like.

• Honoka
Honoka meets a girl chained up in a jail-like room. She says her name is Ayaka Kagari.

Prepare to be Bewitched!

Makoto Kowata, a novice witch, packs up her belongings
(including a black cat familiar) and moves in with her distant
cousins in rural Aomori to complete her training and become
a full-fledged witch.

"*Flying Witch* emphasizes that while actual magic is nice, there
is ultimately magic in everything." —*Anime News Network*

The Basis for the Hit Anime from Sentai Filmworks!

Volumes 1-4 Available Now!

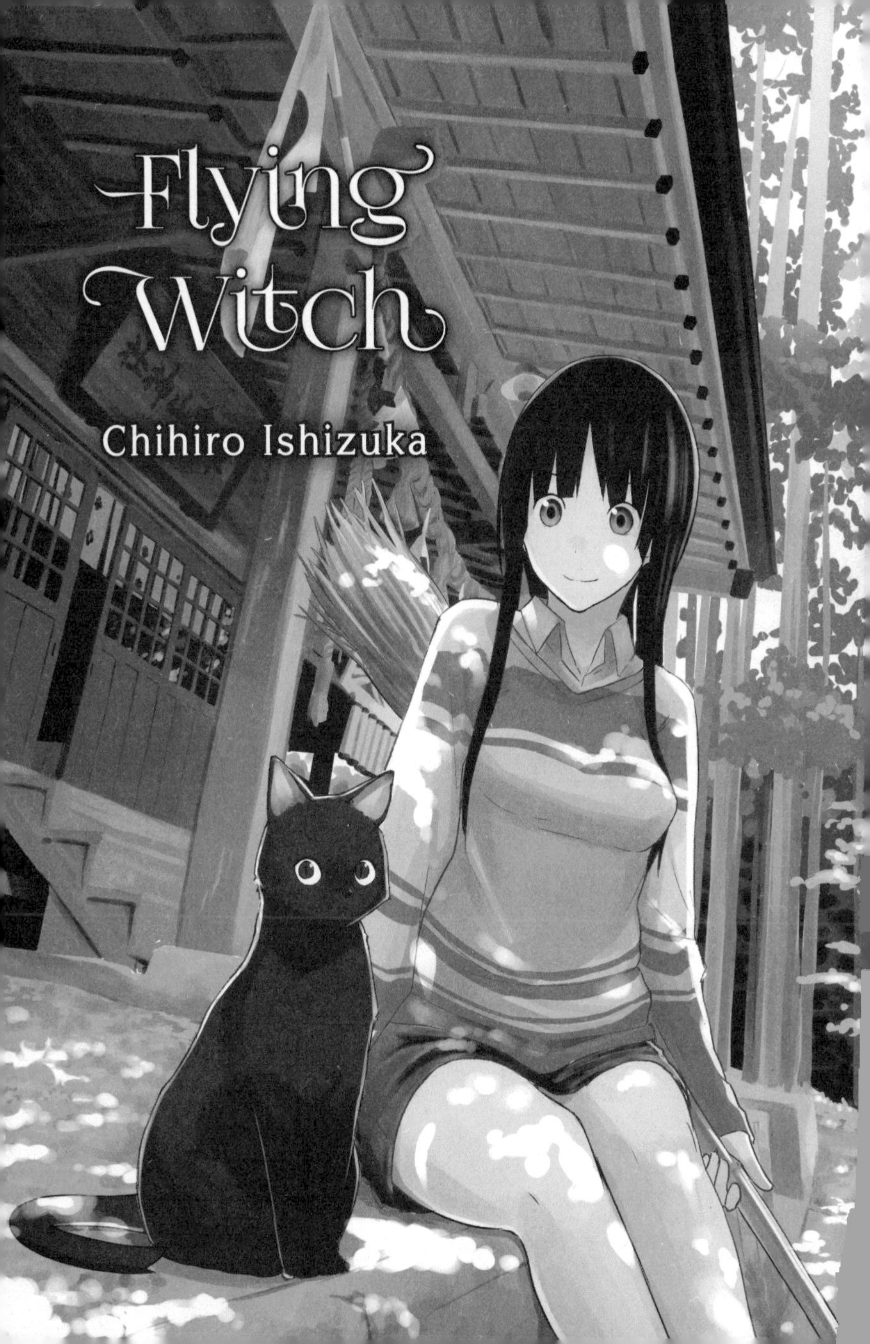
Flying Witch
Chihiro Ishizuka

Witchcraft Works, volume 10

A Vertical Comics Edition

Translation: Ko Ransom
Production: Risa Cho
Melissa DeJesus

First published in Japan in 2016 by Kodansha, Ltd., Tokyo
Publication rights for this English edition arranged through Kodansha, Ltd., Tokyo
English language version produced by Vertical, Inc., New York

Translation provided by Vertical Comics, 2017
Published by Vertical, Inc., New York

Originally published in Japanese as *Uicchi Kurafuto Waakusu 10* by Kodansha, Ltd., 2016
Uicchi Kurafuto Waakusu first serialized in *good! Afternoon*, Kodansha, Ltd., 2010-

ISBN: 978-1-942993-92-6

Manufactured in Canada

First Edition

Vertical, Inc.
451 Park Avenue South
7th Floor
New York, NY 10016
www.vertical-comics.com

Vertical books are distributed through Penguin-Random House Publisher Services.